BEYOND DOGMA AND DESPAIR

Beyond Dogma
and Despair

*Toward a Critical Phenomenology
of Politics*

FRED R. DALLMAYR

UNIVERSITY OF NOTRE DAME PRESS
NOTRE DAME   LONDON

Library of Congress Cataloging in Publication Data

Dallmayr, Fred R., 1928–
  Beyond dogma and despair.

  Includes bibliographical references and index.
  1. Political science. 2. Frankfurt school of sociology. 3. Hermeneutics. 4. Phenomenology. I. Title.
JA76.D23   320'.01'1   80-53179
ISBN 0-268-00661-X   AACR2

Contents

For My Father

In memoria aeterna erit iustus,
ab auditione mala non timebit

Preface

THE PRESENT VOLUME IS an outgrowth of, and meant as a contribution to, the "post-behavioral" reorientation of the study of politics, a reorientation which has been going on now for over a decade. The term "post-behavioral" signals only a contrast to the past, not a substantive direction. Broadly speaking, the common denominator of the reorientation consists in dissatisfaction with the earlier "behavioral" consensus, which aimed to transform political inquiry into a strictly empirical discipline modeled after the methodological canons of the natural sciences. Regarding the future shape of the discipline, however, proposals and direction signals vary widely. The majority of professional students of politics have turned to pragmatic problem-solving, that is, to the attempt to alleviate social and political ills through concrete "policy analysis." A smaller group of practitioners have sought to reshape or revitalize the discipline through resort to broader intellectual vistas. In addition to efforts to recover or restore classical and premodern teachings, professional attention has also been directed to contemporary philosophical and social-theoretical literature. Thus, while some theorists have found in the writings of Michael Polanyi an antidote to behavioral methodology, others have turned to Wittgenstein and ordinary language analysis in search of a more viable framework of inquiry. Recently, in his *The Crisis of Political Understanding*, my friend Hwa Yol Jung has invoked the insights of the phenomenological movement inaugurated by Husserl. This volume is similar in aspiration, while differing in approach; it tries to delineate a perspective labeled *critical phenomenology*, whose intellectual parentage and focal areas of concern are outlined in the Introduction.

The essays collected here were first published in the decade between 1968 and 1978 (given the delays of publication this means they were written between the mid-sixties and mid-seventies), when ferment in the discipline was at its height. Assembling essays for publication in a new format involves an encounter with one's own past. I have tried to act as little as possible as *raconteur* or narrator of that past, preferring instead to let the materials speak for themselves. Changes from the original texts were made in only a few instances, and mainly with an eye toward eliminating needless duplication or repetition. The only new addition is the Introduction; but even in that case I have incorporated passages from an essay published in 1976. The assembly of the various materials, I might add, is not simply an afterthought: they are all animated by a similar outlook or concern, and it is the character of this concern which has dictated the sequence or ordering of topics in this study.

A renewed reading of the essays has impressed on me one aspect which was not as clear to me at the time of their writing: namely, their Kantian overtones or affinities. The title "Beyond Dogma and Despair" evokes the basic thrust of Kant's philosophical enterprise: his endeavor to steer a course between the Scylla of a skeptical empiricism and the Charybdis of a dogmatic-metaphysical rationalism. The philosophical anthropology or conception of the "human condition" presented in this volume displays the same overtones, by harking back to Kant's view of man as a "crooked timber" and his portrayal of intersubjective relations in terms of an "unsociable sociability." To be sure, critical phenomenology modifies the Kantian legacy in important respects, especially by connecting human consciousness much more intimately with perceived "phenomena" and the social fabric—but without erasing the noted affinities.

The primary sources of inspiration on which these essays draw are the writings of Jürgen Habermas and the early works of Merleau-Ponty. In the case of Habermas, his sociological training and his affiliation with critical Marxism entail an effort to correlate critical reflection with the domain of human interaction and the experiences of social-political constraints. In Merleau-Ponty's outlook, the stress on "embodiment" and the "primacy of perception" results in a close liaison of consciousness and world and an interpenetration of "immanence" and "transcendence." To a considerable extent, the arguments of both writers encourage a replacement of Kant's "noumenal" subjectivity by concretely situated but not externally predetermined subjects capable, at least in principle, of marshalling environmental resources and shaping the course of social-political events.

Apart from these two primary mentors, I am indebted to numerous people, not all of whom can be mentioned or credited here. In the course of writing these essays I have benefited at many points from discussions with such colleagues (in political science and adjacent disciplines) as Hwa Yol Jung, Herbert Reid, William Connolly, David

Kettler, William T. Bluhm, John O'Neill, and Richard Bernstein. Since most of the essays were written while I was teaching at Purdue University I want to single out a small circle of people whose weekly or biweekly luncheon meetings helped me in sorting out my thoughts: Calvin Schrag, Richard Grabau, William McBride, and also Karl-Otto Apel (during the time he served as a visiting professor). A few of the essays were written during a two-year stay at the University of Georgia; from that time I want to recall especially the comments offered by Eugene Miller and Bernard Dauenhauer. In both settings I learned much from students in graduate seminars, especially from their perceptive grasp of intellectual linkages and contrasts and from their unwillingness to settle for easy answers. Needless to say, the usual disclaimer holds: mentors, colleagues, and friends are entirely blameless for the faults of this volume.

Gratitude, of course, is not restricted to these professional confines. None of these essays would have been written without the constant encouragement and selfless support provided by my wife, Ilse (who also typed the original versions), and without the patience of my children, Dominique and Philip, who arrived on the scene while the essays were being written. The volume is dedicated to the memory of my father who died when the volume was nearing completion.

Acknowledgments

The author and publisher are grateful to the following for permission to reprint:

American Political Science Review, 70 (1976), for portions of "Beyond Dogma and Despair: Toward a Critical Theory of Politics";

Journal of General Education, 19 (1968), for "Political Science and the Two Cultures";

Polity, 2 (1970), for "Empirical Political Theory and the Image of Man";

Inquiry, 17 (1974), and Universitetsforlaget, Oslo-Bergen-Tromsø, for "Plessner's Philosophical Anthropology: Implications for Role Theory and Politics";

Martinus Nijhoff Publishers B. V., The Hague, The Netherlands, for "Phenomenology and Social Science: An Overview and Appraisal," published in Edward S. Casey and David Carr, eds., *Explorations in Phenomenology*, 1974;

Journal of Politics, 31 (1969), and 36 (1974), for "Hobbes and Existentialism: Some Affinities" and for "Toward a Critical Reconstruction of Ethics and Politics" respectively;

The Review of Politics, 39 (1977), for "Hermeneutics and Historicism: Reflections on Winch, Apel and Vico";

John Wiley & Sons, Inc. Publishers, New York, for "Phenomenology and Marxism: A Salute to Enzo Paci," published in George Psathas, ed., *Phenomenological Society*, 1973;

Politics and Society, 1 (1970), for "History and Class Consciousness: Lukacs' Theory of Social Change";

Man and World, 5 (1972), for "Reason and Emancipation: Notes on Habermas"; and

Philosophy of the Social Sciences, 2 (1972), for "Critical Theory Criticized."

Introduction: Critical Phenomenology and the Study of Politics

THAT POLITICAL THOUGHT HAS FALLEN on bad days is a commonplace among diagnosticians of our age. Although distressing, the circumstance is perhaps not surprising, given the general political malaise prevalent in Western societies today. Obviously, the infirmity of political thought signifies neither an end of politics nor necessarily a cessation of philosophical reflection as such. Our century has not been marked by a lack of political drama or ideological commitment; politics—conceived both as spontaneous activity and as the more systematic planning and implementation of social panaceas—has left its indelible imprint on the physiognomy of our age. At the same time, intellectual endeavors have netted remarkable advances in terms of analytical rigor and methodological refinement; academic philosophers have made great strides in clarifying the logical and conceptual arsenal of inquiry. What is at issue is not so much the analytical sagacity of our time but the fate of political philosophy and, more broadly, the relationship between thought and everyday practice. By and large, contemporary philosophers have been reluctant to venture beyond academic boundary lines; discouraged by the inhospitable character of the political arena, they have been insufficiently concerned about the lot of their fellow-men to exchange the ivory tower for the hazards of the marketplace. To this extent, the dearth of political theory illustrates and corroborates a basic symptom of the crisis of our period: the disintegration of public deliberation and discourse among members of the political community.

The present volume seeks to contribute, however modestly, to a resurgence or "revival" of political theory, a resurgence attentive both to modern and contemporary philosophical developments and to the political agonies of our time.[1] To make some headway along these lines

1

the volume delineates a perspective which can be broadly described as a *critical phenomenology of politics.* The perspective draws its inspiration primarily from two major currents in twentieth-century philosophy and social thought: one is phenomenology and particularly the French version of "existential phenomenology"; the other is critical (or nonorthodox) Marxism, especially as articulated by members of the so-called "Frankfurt School." To be sure, the two currents are not entirely congruent; in fact, if Marxism is identified with a metaphysical materialism or determinism and phenomenology with the intuitions of "subjective consciousness," their concerns appear diametrically opposed. Yet, it seems to me there is sufficient common ground between the two currents to support the suggested linkage.[2] Their affinity, or at least reconcilability, is particularly manifest in the domain of practice or practical thought: both existential phenomenology and critical Marxism have been enmeshed or embroiled in the concerns of the social-political "marketplace," the former by hewing always as closely as possible to concrete human experience and the latter by focusing on the fissures created in social life by the effects of exploitation and domination.

To provide some background, a few general comments on the two currents are in order. Critical Marxism, as the term is used in this volume, derives important impulses from the writings of the young Marx which clearly reveal his debt to, and involvement in, the legacy of German (particularly Hegelian) philosophical discourse. In equal measure, critical Marxist thinkers have been influenced by Georg Lukács' early studies, especially by his plea—formulated in *History and Class Consciousness*—that Marxism be treated, not as a series of fixed assertions, but as a critical method of inquiry intent on interpreting particular phenomena in the light of the broader fabric of social-political experience. Relying on these and similar precedents, the Frankfurt Institute of Social Research during the interbellum period developed a program of "critical theory" in order to unravel the intellectual and practical dilemmas of bourgeois society. As outlined by its initial protagonists, it is true, the Frankfurt program was not entirely free of doctrinaire beliefs: in the writings of the young Horkheimer, for example, the effort of comprehensive assessment was marred at crucial points by a precipitous fusion of theoretical insight and practical advice, of concrete observation and political commitment.[3] In all these respects, Frankfurt theorists in their recent investigations have tried to overcome ideological preconceptions by applying the standards of critical inquiry to such diverse fields as epistemology, ethics, and the theory of language. The leading protagonist of these efforts is the philosopher-sociologist Jürgen Habermas; he has been seconded and sometimes undergirded by Karl-Otto Apel, a philosopher broadly conversant with the major theoretical trends of our time and generally sympathetic to the Frankfurt program.[4]

Phenomenology from its inception has never claimed to be a finished system of propositions. Edmund Husserl's celebrated call "to the things themselves" (*zu den Sachen*) was an exhortation to abandon preconceived doctrines in favor of fresh observation and interpretation; rather than vouchsafing simple introspection, the procedure of *"epoché"*—involving the "bracketing" or suspension of naive assumptions about reality in favor of reflection—encouraged open-ended inquiry and the sustained scrutiny of knowledge claims. While stressing the embeddedness of "existence" and all human endeavors in an ongoing and pre-reflective life-world, Martin Heidegger's (early) hermeneutical perspective implied the purge or "destruction" of routine conceptions in an effort to permit renewed investigation and exegesis. Combining and reconciling Husserlian and Heideggerian themes, Maurice Merleau-Ponty's life-work delineated the contours of an existential phenomenology which was "critical" both by offering criticisms of social conditions and in being self-critical about its own premises. His inaugural lecture at the Collège de France, entitled *In Praise of Philosophy*, was mainly a eulogy of the Socratic method or mode of life. As he tried to show, philosophy is not a set of ready-made doctrines but an endeavor which links "inseparably the taste for evidence and the feeling for ambiguity," without lapsing into equivocation. "Even those," he noted, "who have desired to work out a completely positive philosophy have been philosophers only to the extent that, at the same time, they have refused the right to install themselves in absolute knowledge." Following in the footsteps of his Greek mentor, the Socratic thinker is equally far removed from haughty detachment—the pretense of esoteric insight—and a spurious complicity in immediate practical schemes. Seen from Merleau-Ponty's vantage point, philosophy emerged as a precarious or "limping" enterprise: "It dwells in history and in life, but it wishes to dwell at their center, at the point where they come into being with the birth of meaning."[5]

Drawing on both existential phenomenology and critical Marxism, *critical phenomenology* as sketched in this volume aims to combine their strengths or merits while avoiding their shortcomings. In line with the main tradition of phenomenology, a "critical-phenomenological" outlook is wedded to the exploration of the implicit and sometimes obscure "logos" of "phenomena," that is, to the decoding of the "meaning" or "sense" of all kinds of human experiences. As it is practiced by some members of the phenomenological movement, especially adepts of a sociological phenomenology, however, such exploration sometimes leans in the direction of a purely descriptive exercise and one that is both normatively and politically "neutral," thus shading over into quasi-positivism. In order to avoid these pitfalls it is important, in my view, to marshal the resources of critical reflection and judgment, an arsenal which has been furnished and cultivated by the founders of philosophical phenomenology and—with particular reference to normative and political questions—by the proponents of critical Marxism or a critical theory of society. Yet, while supplying an antidote to empiricist or descriptivist neutrality, critical reflection cannot or should not be viewed as self-sufficient, for that would conjure up the peril of a "critical criticism" or of a narrowly rationalistic "apriorism." To gain its own bearings and to avoid self-enclosure, critical thought must hark back to the lessons of "phenomena" and of concrete experience, remaining alert also to the prereflective underpinnings of reflection, or the linkage of thought and non-thought. In this manner, critical judgment and the study of phenomena are related in a precarious balance, neither side being able to claim primacy or to provide a secure primordial starting point.

Critical phenomenology maintains a balanced tension also in another sense. Faithful to the Socratic model, the perspective militates against both disdain for truth and doctrinaire rigidity and thus points beyond the pales of both dogma and despair. Philosophical doubt and self-criticism are not equivalent to skeptical indifference or agnosticism—just as growth in insight and understanding offers no shield against further scrutiny. It is a balanced tension of this kind that Paul Ricoeur seemed to envisage when he spoke of "a rational feeling that is regulative and purificative both of skepticism and fanaticism: skepticism which refuses to look for meaning and fanaticism which declares it prematurely." In a similar vein, Merleau-Ponty described philosophy as lodged at the interstices of knowledge and ignorance, of agnosticism and dogmatic belief. Pledged to the quest for truth and the good life, philosophical inquiry in his view involved necessarily a reverent or devoted attitude or disposition; despite its theoretical fecundity, skepsis could be "only the beginning of an attention, a seriousness, an experience on the basis of which it must be judged." By the same token, precisely in order to continue its search, inquiry had to remain aware of its shortcomings, including the temptations of doctrinaire prejudice and arrogance. Drawing the practical-social implications of this perspective, the conclusion of *In Praise of Philosophy* linked the philosopher with the "common man," whose latent thought he expresses, arguing that both are aligned against "the important one who thinks by principles and against the roué who lives without truth."[6]

The presentation of critical phenomenology in this volume is marked by two features—one intrinsic, the other more contingent. First of all, given the open-ended character of critical-phenomenological inquiry, the volume cannot aim to offer a full-fledged doctrine or "system" of thought but can only sketch the ramifications of this perspective for selected areas of discourse. The result is a lattice-work of essays and themes, all animated by a similar intellectual outlook but not reducible to a set of inductively or deductively arrayed propositions. The second feature has to do with the volume's special focus—the intent not to offer a general philosophical treatise but to probe the implications of critical phenomenology for politics or the study of politics in its theoretical, empirical, and normative-practical dimensions. Broadly speaking, this means that politics is viewed both as a world of phenomena endowed with manifest or latent (occasionally camouflaged and repressed) meanings, and as a domain of human initiative and possibly of critically reflective human agency. As a result of the peculiar correlation of world and initiative, a critical phenomenology of politics inevitably takes a stand against a number of competing postures: primarily against an empiricist or physicalist objectivism or reductionism, but also against a purely subjective or speculative idealism. In some fashion, the perspective suggests, the study of human intentions and purposes has to be linked with the investigation of non-intentional (or no longer fully intelligible) social structures and constraints, as well as with the critical scrutiny of cognitive and normative standards or claims.

Despite the absence of a strictly inductive or deductive scheme, the material presented here has been arranged in a particular sequence. For purposes of exposition and in line with its intellectual parentage, critical phenomenology accords a relative priority to "philosophical anthropology," the reflective exploration of the "human condition" or man's place in the world. The first part of the volume deals with this broad thematic area and its repercussions on the study of politics. At this point, a few general comments on the theme may be appropriate to illustrate and corroborate the suggested affinity between phenomenology and critical Marxism. Within the confines of the phenomenological movement, elucidation of human nature or (more aptly) the "human condition" has always been a central concern.

From the beginning, spokesmen of the movement opposed conceptions identifying man either with a reactive mechanism transforming stimuli into behavioral responses, or else with a set of mental, psychic, or genetic endowments. In introducing and developing the notion of "intentionality," Husserl sought to overcome the gulf customarily erected between internal psychic capacities and physical or behavioral processes, or (in Cartesian terms) between matter and thinking substance. With the stress on the intentional direction of thought and experience, man emerged as an inquiring creature capable of questioning both his environment and himself. Once man was seen in this light, the traditional compactness of human nature was bound to disintegrate. For, how can any substantive delimitation be definitive, given man's intentional self-awareness—the ability to view himself as his own alter ego? Clearly, any proposed delimitation opens itself up to critical scrutiny and self-reflection—a reflection which inevitably adds a new dimension to the postulated model and thus pushes man beyond his delimited alter ego or *doppelgänger*.

The implications of this view of man were subsequently delineated in more detail by Heidegger and existential phenomenologists. Heidegger's notion of *Dasein* pictures man as a unique "being-in-the-world," a creature intimately involved in the fabric of social and cultural practices; yet, although thrust into this web, man is not simply a reactive apparatus or a blind victim of external causes and processes. Overcome by "eeriness" (*Unheimlichkeit*), man discovers the dilemma of being involved but not properly at home in the objective universe; moved by "care" (*Sorge*), he becomes concerned and inquires about his condition and about the point of his involvement in the world. *Dasein* in this light is at best an incongruous and precarious enterprise, a relationship rather than a fixed substance. In the words of one observer: "Man is the gap which separates and at the same time unites subject and object"; instead of fitting into a compact scheme of things he discloses "a rift within Being."[7] Man's incongruous condition, however, does not sanction mental self-enclosure; the need to inquire about the significance of his condition offers no warrant for a retreat into private speculation. As Heidegger is wont to insist (especially in his later writings), genuine questioning presupposes openness toward a dimension of reality which, though immune from reification, lies beyond subjective fancy. In raising questions, the *Introduction to Metaphysics* states, "We seem to belong entirely to ourselves. Yet it is this questioning that moves us into the open, provided that in questioning it transform itself (which all true questioning does), and cast a new space over everything and into everything."[8]

Heidegger's conception was seconded and in some respects amplified in Merleau-Ponty's writings. The characterization of the human condition as "*être-au-monde*" was meant to accentuate man's precarious and incongruous status in the world. Elaborating on Hegelian insights, Merleau-Ponty argued that man, "as opposed to the pebble which is what it is," should be defined "as a place of unrest (*Unruhe*), a constant effort to get back to himself, and consequently by his refusal to limit himself to one or another of his determinations." Arguing against both empiricist and idealist premises, he stressed that man is neither an object nor a "constituting consciousness" but a special "intentional" creature: "oriented toward all things" but "not residing in any." Together with Heidegger, he rejected the label "humanist" for his outlook—"if one understands by 'man' an explanatory principle which ought to be substituted for the others." As he noted in his address at the Collège de France: "One explains nothing by man, since he is not a force but a weakness at the heart of being, a cosmological factor, but also the place where all cosmological factors, by a mutation which is never finished, change in sense and become history."[9] As in Heidegger's case, the stress on intentionality was not an endorsement of private whim. Following Gabriel Marcel, Merleau-Ponty focused attention on human "embodiment"—a term referring both to man's bodily constitution (governed by the laws of the physical universe) and to the body's function as key in an intersubjective search for meaning. In his later writings he expanded phenomenological inquiry progressively to the levels of preconscious and unconscious experience, an endeavor which, in the words of one observer, transformed his philosophy into an "archaeology which does nothing but excavate the meaning of the world which is already before us to be discovered."[10]

To a considerable extent, phenomenological and existentialist arguments find a parallel in critical Marxism. In his *Theses on Feuerbach* Marx himself rejected a naturalistic brand of humanism that reduces man to a fixed substance among other empirical factors. In a similar vein, Lukács in *History and Class Consciousness* commented that the treatment of man as the measure of things was plausible only if this measure as open-ended horizon was applied to man himself in his concrete or substantive manifestations.[11] Among critical Marxist thinkers probably no one has been more persistently concerned with the dilemmas of the human condition than Ernst Bloch. The cornerstone of Bloch's thinking has always been the incongruity and dark tension implicit in the lived moment, a tension pushing man beyond the immediate presence toward the "not-yet" of a future whose contours can at best be dimly anticipated or divined. Intentionality, in Bloch's view, means a relentless striving beyond present confinements toward a world free of despair and oppression. "The desiderium, the single honorable quality of men," he wrote in the *Principle of Hope*, "has not been investigated. The not-yet-conscious, the not-yet-become, although it fulfills the mind of every man and the horizon of all being, has not even broken through as a word, let alone as a concept." Because of the rift between present circumstances and aspirations, man's condition is basically characterized by incompleteness and deficiency: subject to detours and reversals, the human "venture is not yet successful" and in fact "no man yet really lives." In his actual state, according to Bloch, man should be described not so much as a substance but as a lack— as a hidden creature or *homo absconditus* searching for self-realization. This search is not simply an idiosyncratic exercise but is supported by a latent proclivity in nature: the proclivity toward a "humanization of nature" corresponding to man's reconciliation with his habitat.[12]

Frankfurt theorists have long been preoccupied with similar issues, although early formulations (by Horkheimer and Marcuse) tended to alternate unevenly between the stress on human freedom or indeterminacy and the notion of a predictive teleology. Later statements reflect a more circumspect approach. In an essay on "philosophical anthropology," Habermas in 1958 argued that man should be viewed simultaneously as a creature of nature and of culture and that his condition should be examined both in terms of biological evidence and cultural significance: "To speak, act and produce means not only to make use of certain bodily organs but to disclose a meaning." As he noted, the dual aspect was distantly related to Kant's distinction between a "physiological" and a "pragmatic" anthropology—the former dealing with "what nature made of man" and the latter with what man makes of himself. In Herder's terminology, man had to be seen as "the first emancipated creature of nature"; however, this does not imply a complete indeterminacy. In comparison with animals, man is marked by instinctual diffuseness and disorientation—a deficiency which is compensated by, and one of the chief impulses for, the establishment of cultural institutions and norms. "Human existence," Habermas commented, "denotes a peculiar combination of environmental confinement and purposive openness. By itself, the one or the other aspect would be applicable to animals or angels; but man is placed between both."

As he added, the attempt to transform man either into a compact creature (with a fixed environment) or into a pure spirit is bound to lead
to a substantive definition—with hazardous political consequences:
"When clinging to a substantive (ontological) procedure by focusing
on the unchanging or permanent features of human life, anthropology
becomes uncritical and encourages in the end even a dogmatism
with political implications (the more dangerous because presumably
scientific)."[13]

In developing his argument, Habermas relied in large measure on
the insights of one of the pioneers of "philosophical anthropology" in
our century, Helmuth Plessner, whose work seems at least broadly compatible with the Frankfurt perspective. The first part of this volume
contains an essay examining Plessner's central teachings, focusing on
his conception of "human nature" and its relation to the matrix of social roles, and differentiating these teachings from competing conceptions of the human condition (especially the perspective championed
by Arnold Gehlen). Part One also investigates the import of philosophical anthropology for the study of politics, both with reference to the
historical development of the discipline and with regard to prevalent
contemporary approaches to political analysis. The essay entitled "Political Science and the Two Cultures" seeks to trace the historical evolution of political inquiry and to locate the place of that inquiry in the
arbor scientiae or the broader framework of types of human knowledge.
The chapter on "Empirical Political Theory and the Image of Man"
attempts to distil the various "images of man" and of the human condition implicit in a number of recent "empirical" models of political
analysis, evaluating these images or "character masks" against the
yardsticks of philosophical anthropology.

To facilitate access to these discussions, a few preliminary remarks
may again be desirable here on the general status of social and political
inquiry as seen from a critical-phenomenological vantage point. The
review of historical evolution in the "Two Cultures" essay culminates
in the sketch of an "anthropology of knowledge" linking cognitive endeavors with basic human orientations or proclivities. Relying strongly
on arguments advanced by Habermas and Apel regarding the nexus
between "knowledge" or epistemology and "human interests," the
sketch distinguishes empirical-analytical political analysis from
practical-hermeneutical exegesis, and both from critically reflective
political inquiry. The linkage between cognition and interest or between the "context of discovery" and the "context of validation" proposed by critical theory finds ample precedents or parallels in phenomenological literature.

The issue of the connection of knowledge and experience was one
of Husserl's persistent preoccupations; throughout his life he strove to
uncover and elucidate the vital infrastructure or experiential underpinnings of cognitive endeavors. In his early writings, it is true, "subjectivity" or "consciousness" tended to be portrayed as the cornerstone
of epistemology and as the transparent receptacle of objective reality:
once purified through "bracketing," the observer's mind was supposed
to have access not only to surface appearances but to the "essence" or
inner core of phenomena. In the long run, however, the program of a
rigorously analytical or "scientific" philosophy proved less satisfactory
or manageable than initially expected. For, assuming as end goal the
correspondence and coincidence of mind and essential reality, how
could philosophy be maintained as a perpetual beginning and renewal?
In his later writings, Husserl turned his attention steadily to the human
"life-world" as the prereflective dimension underlying conscious investigations. Instead of denoting a collective psychology or a mere reservoir of heuristic guesses, the life-world, in his view, gave direction to
inquiry, and cognitive findings acquired meaning against its background. Perhaps the most balanced statement of Husserl's epistemological approach can be found in his *Experience and Judgment*—a posthumously published work which, according to its translators, is dedicated to the thesis "that, even at its most abstract, logic demands an
underlying theory of experience" and which traces the "genealogy of
logic" from pre-predicative conditions over structures of predicative
judgment to the level of conceptual thought and valid knowledge.[14]

The dimension of the life-world and pre-predicative "existence"
became the focus of exploration in Heidegger's interpretive or hermeneutical phenomenology. As he forcefully argued in *Being and Time*,
human consciousness and cognition presuppose the "facticity" of man's
being-in-the-world, his involvement in a prereflective matrix of experience. As a living context, "world" in Heidegger's usage referred neither
to an external-empirical environment nor to a subjective construction,
but to an intersubjective fabric of relationships (*Bewandtnisganzheit*)
pregnant with latent meanings and connotations. Even prior to investigation, man encounters objects and events as significant in a dimly
perceived sense and thus as implicitly interpreted and understood.
Conscious thought raises such pre-understanding to the level of an
explicit and articulate interpretation; in doing so, thinking or cognition
moves in the so-called "hermeneutical circle" in the sense that every
exegesis draws upon (without being rigidly confined by) the implicit
pre-understanding of the life-world. In delineating the basic experiential categories of the human condition, Heidegger's *Being and Time*

sketched a "triad of care" which comprises different modes of man's involvement in the life-world and which could serve as launching pad for diverse cognitive orientations: concern for workday things and pragmatic instruments and designs; solicitude for other human beings; and care for the "self" in its quest to be free from deception and unintelligible constraints. In the context of the early phenomenological movement, the cognitive implications of philosophical anthropology were elaborated in detail especially by Max Scheler. In a study antedating *Being and Time* by a couple of years, Scheler outlined a triad of types of human knowledge—namely, workday or empirical-instrumental knowledge (*Leistungswissen*), humanistic understanding (*Bildungswissen*), and reflective-speculative insight (*Erlösungswissen*)—correlating these types explicitly with different dimensions of human existence and experience.[15]

While not adhering to the same vocabulary, French phenomenology in later years developed and explored similar themes. Merleau-Ponty in particular paid close attention to the infrastructure of human knowledge, especially to the prereflective, perceptual nexus between man and the world. As he tried to show in the *Phenomenology of Perception,* "the perceived world is the always presupposed foundation of all rationality, all value and all existence." The relationship between thought and experience, he insisted, was not one between a detached intellect or thinking substance and an opaque environment but rather one between a primary web of latent meanings and a derivative effort of clarification. Scientific rationality, in particular, was not a self-contained universe of propositions; rather science was "built upon the world as directly experienced" and any effort to grasp its presuppositions must begin "by reawakening the basic experience of the world of which science is the second-order expression." The chief task of phenomenology, from this perspective, was to promote such reawakening: "To return to things themselves is to return to that world which precedes knowledge, of which knowledge always *speaks,* and in relation to which every scientific schematization is an abstract and derivative sign-language, as is geography in relation to the countryside in which we have learned beforehand what a forest, a prairie or a river is."

While stressing the "primacy of perception," Merleau-Ponty was unwilling to renounce the task of reflection and analytical scrutiny. He readily admitted that "we cannot rest satisfied with the description of the perceived world" and that "it appears as a psychological curiosity if we leave aside the idea of the true world, the world as thought by the understanding." As an attentive student of Husserl's opus, Merleau-Ponty fully appreciated the importance of "bracketing" and of the temporary suspension of familiar involvements; in his view, however, the aim of such suspension was not to sanction retreat into an ivory tower but to bring everyday life into fuller view and to rekindle amazement and "wonder" in the face of the world: "Reflection does not withdraw from the world towards the unity of consciousness as the world's basis; it steps back to watch the forms of transcendence fly up like sparks from a fire." Bracketing and experience thus were intimately linked; far from contradicting Heidegger's "being-in-the-world," Husserl's procedures were destined "to bring back all the living relationships of experience, as the fisherman's net draws up from the depths of the ocean quivering fish and seaweed." The movement from perception to valid cognition, against this background, was not so much a straight or linear progression as a complex process of clarification in which experience "gradually rectifies itself and proceeds by dialogue with itself and with others"—a dialogue which is not aimless chatter but enveloped by a common horizon of truth.[16]

Regarding types of knowledge or cognitive orientations, Merleau-Ponty's early writings concentrated especially on the relationship between philosophical-hermeneutical inquiry and exact empirical science. Strict science, he wrote in "The Philosopher and Sociology," designates "the effort to construct ideal variables which objectify and schematize" the lessons of experience, while philosophy refers to reflective awareness "of the open and successive community of alter egos living, speaking, and thinking in one another's presence and in relation to nature." Husserl's great merit, in Merleau-Ponty's view, was "to mark out a realm and an attitude of inquiry where philosophy and effective knowledge could meet." Despite his insistence on the "rigorous distinction" between the two cognitive dimensions, his investigations of the life-world and especially his notion of a "psycho-phenomenological parallelism" led him in the end "to the idea of *reciprocal envelopment.*" In application to social inquiry, the problem was how social life "can be both a 'thing' to be acquainted with without prejudices, and a 'signification' which the societies we acquaint ourselves with only provide an occasion for—how, that is, the social can exist both in itself and in us." Sociology, Merleau-Ponty insisted, could not restrict itself to a "mere recording of facts" devoid of interpretation and a concern for the meaning of data: "If objectivism or scientism were ever to succeed in depriving sociology of all recourse to significations, it would save it from 'philosophy' only by shutting it off from knowledge of its object." Conversely, hermeneutical interpretation could not sever its ties with empirical knowledge without deteriorating into empty speculation: "The philosopher thinks about his experience and his world. Except by decree, how could he be given the right to forget what science says about this same experience and world?"[17]

During the later years of his life Merleau-Ponty came to appreciate increasingly the significance of Freudian psychoanalysis as a key for decoding human experience. The Freudian approach, in his view, diverged both from positivistic scientism and from a hermeneutical phenomenology limited to the level of conscious intentionality. In an essay published shortly before his death, Merleau-Ponty strongly endorsed the endeavors of those who "separate psychoanalysis from a scientistic or objectivistic ideology, who consider the Freudian unconscious as an archaic or primordial consciousness, the repressed as a zone of experience that we have not integrated." Phenomenology and psychoanalysis, he noted, were linked by close bonds of affinity—provided the thrust of phenomenology was broadened beyond the range of a simple "philosophy of consciousness." Given such a broadened conception, the basic terms of phenomenological inquiry were altered. Although consciousness was always "consciousness of something or of the world," this something or this world could no longer be treated as "an object that is what it is, exactly adjusted to acts of consciousness"; rather, consciousness emerged now as the "soul of Heraclitus," and "Being, which is around (consciousness) rather than in front of it," as "a Being of dreams, by definition hidden." Only by descending "into its own substratum" could phenomenology be reconciled with the Freudian enterprise. By contrast, a "phenomenological idealism" narrowly clinging to subjective intentionality was philosophically "insufficient" and a direct "threat to the Freudian heritage." Psychoanalysis, from this vantage point, appeared as a remedy both to the pretensions of hermeneutical thought and to the arid myopia of empiricism; by delving into the realm of unconscious or preconscious experience, it successfully bypassed "idealist" as well as "objectivist" deviations—and perhaps the two dangers were "not so opposed at that."[18]

At this point, the parallel with Habermas' "anthropology of knowledge"—and especially with his notion of a critical recovery of distorted or repressed meanings through reliance on psychoanalytic insights—comes clearly into view. As in Habermas' case, Freudian analysis in Merleau-Ponty's treatment combined the virtues of scientific knowledge and therapeutic insight; one should note, however, some differences of accent. As presented by Merleau-Ponty, depth psychology constituted a genuine synthesis rather than an amalgam of elements: knowledge and hermeneutical exegesis were able to blend because both perspectives were conceived from the beginning as congenial and mutually complementary. More importantly—and partly as a result of this convergence—psychoanalysis furnished not only critical weapons for combatting individual or social ills, but also an arsenal of coded or cryptic guideposts to recovery; viewed as an "archeology" of human experience, Freudian therapy emancipates from present constraints by uncovering submerged memories of the past. In all these respects, Merleau-Ponty's arguments are corroborated by Paul Ricoeur. In several of his writings, Ricoeur has insisted on the close linkage and complementarity between scientific explanation and hermeneutical interpretation. Science and exegesis, he has noted at one point, can no longer be rigidly separated as in Dilthey's time: "If understanding passes through explanation, explanation is completed in understanding." With regard to psychoanalysis, Ricoeur's *Essay on Interpretation* placed Freud's approach at the crossroads of two kinds of inquiry: a "hermeneutics of suspicion" concerned with the unmasking of systematic distortions and mystifications, and a "hermeneutics of reminiscence" aiming at the recovery of latent meanings and aspirations.[19]

The thematic range of the present volume, however, is not restricted to philosophical anthropology and its relevance for the epistemology of political inquiry. Parts Two and Three amplify these topics and, in doing so, branch out in new directions. Broadly speaking, the two parts elaborate on the two main legacies or intellectual currents which nourish the perspective of critical phenomenology: the first by exploring the implications of phenomenology and its two offshoots, existentialism and existential hermeneutics, for social and political investigations; the second by focusing on major contributions of critical Marxism and critical theory to such topics as the theory of social change or evolution, social-scientific epistemology and methodology, and the linkage between politics and ethics. In Part Two, the chapter entitled "Phenomenology and Social Science" provides general background by offering an overview of the successive phases of the phenomenological movement—from "pure" or "transcendental" phenomenology over existentialism to hermeneutics and the phenomenology of language—together with a synopsis of pertinent repercussions in the social sciences. After sketching the arguments of the leading philosophical spokesmen of the movement, the chapter traces the development of phenomenological social science from early "eidetic" versions articulated, among others, by Alfred Vierkandt and Max Scheler, over the writings of Alfred Schutz to more recent existentialist, "ethnomethodological," and "dialectical" formulations. A concluding appraisal briefly examines typical criticisms leveled at phenomenological social inquiry and some pitfalls or quandaries to which such inquiry tends to be exposed.

The emphasis of the following essay is on existentialism and existential phenomenology. Concentrating on such issues as philosophical anthropology or man's condition in the "state of nature," ethics or the theory of "natural law," and the origin of political institutions, the essay tries to uncover some similarities or "affinities" of outlook between a founder of modern political philosophy, Thomas Hobbes, and such leading French existentialists as Merleau-Ponty, Jean-Paul Sartre, and Albert Camus. The goal is by no means to portray Hobbes as an "existentialist"—his instrumental role in fashioning the modern "science" of politics is too obvious—but only to show existentialist overtones at some crucial junctures of his arguments. The chapter entitled "Hermeneutics and Historicism" addresses itself to a major problem or challenge beleaguering existentialism as well as contemporary hermeneutics and ordinary language philosophy: the challenge of maintaining cognitive and normative standards while being attentive to the diversity of cultural and political experiences. Two major attempts to meet the challenge and to avoid the perils of a linguistic or hermeneutical "descriptivism" are discussed: after nearly succumbing to relativism in some of his early writings, Peter Winch has tried to formulate "limiting notions" as universal parameters for social inquiry, while Karl-Otto Apel has stressed the role of "pragmatic universals" as benchmarks of rational discourse and as cornerstones of a "transcendental hermeneutics." The concluding essay of Part Two examines the complex relationship between the phenomenological movement and Marxist thought, directing primary attention to a leading spokesman of phenomenological Marxism in our time, the (late) Italian philosopher Enzo Paci.

Part Three begins with a tribute to the prominent critical Marxist thinker, Georg Lukács. The opening essay concentrates on one of the most innovative and seminal—albeit long ignored or repressed—Marxist writings of the interbellum period: Lukács' *History and Class Consciousness, Studies in Marxist Dialectics*. In opposition to the positivist orthodoxy of official communism, the book portrayed the defining characteristic of Marxism as being its commitment to a critical-dialectical method strongly inspired by Hegelian thought, rather than the endorsement of substantive economic doctrines. One of the remarkable features of this portrayal was its exegetic perceptiveness, for the book was written and published several years before the discovery of Marx's early manuscripts which corroborated the suggested Hegelian affinities.

The book also had a considerable impact on subsequent intellectual developments; the sections on "reification" and alienation in particular anticipated crucial themes of existentialism. The essay in this volume compares Lukács' conception of social change with prevalent social-scientific models, especially with the structural-functional framework articulated by Talcott Parsons. The main argument is that such models tend to transform social dynamics into quasi-naturalistic causal sequences construed in analogy with biological or mechanical processes. By contrast, Lukács' book stresses the role of purposive human agency—but an agency which is not divorced from economic structures and social conditions.

The central focus of the third part is on the program of a "critical theory of society" as propounded by members of the Frankfurt School, especially by such younger representatives or sympathizers as Habermas and Apel. The chapter on "Reason and Emancipation" offers an introduction to Habermas' major writings and in particular a discussion of his *Knowledge and Human Interests* and its import for the epistemology of social and political inquiry. Referring to some critical comments advanced mainly by Apel, the chapter explores the nexus between theory and practice and, more specifically, the issue of the relative autonomy of valid knowledge or cognition from immediate practical concerns. The next essay, entitled "Critical Epistemology Criticized," presents a panoramic survey of reviews and commentaries written in the aftermath of *Knowledge and Human Interests*, reviews proceeding from a broad spectrum of vantage points, including idealist, realist, and materialist positions. Besides assessing the cogency of criticisms, the chapter also mentions some clarifications and reformulations advanced by Habermas in response to his critics. The concluding chapter seeks to elucidate the normative thrust of the Frankfurt School's program and thus to pave the way toward a "critical reconstruction of ethics and politics." After outlining dominant trends in recent ethical and metaethical thought, the chapter examines Apel's endeavors to escape the descriptivist bias of contemporary hermeneutics and to unearth the "ideal" normative yardsticks implicit in human interaction and discourse—yardsticks which, properly articulated, serve to reconcile survival needs with the quest for the "good life."

The latter quest, to be sure, is not unique to critical theory, but has been shared by many or most spokesmen of the phenomenological movement. Among French phenomenologists, Merleau-Ponty in particular has expressed views which are generally compatible with Apel's arguments. Opposing the reduction of moral considerations to the description of prevailing habits or empirical preferences, Merleau-

Ponty strongly insisted that ethics is inconceivable without the premise of human autonomy and free choice: "If I can say yes or no to my destiny, then the Good is not my good unless I agree to it." However, freedom of choice in his view was not synonymous with arbitrary whim or private taste, since the conception of normative standards could not be segregated from the fabric of human interaction and discourse: "If we admit that our life is inherent to the perceived world and the human or social world, even while it recreates it and contributes to its making, then morality cannot consist in the private adherence to a system of values." Merleau-Ponty's writings also are helpful in illuminating the linkage between ethics and politics. In criticizing private or abstract value systems, he also castigated the equation of the political "good life" with the invocation of formal principles detached from concrete human agonies and oblivious of prevailing power constellations. "Whatever one's philosophical or even theological position," he observed at one point, "a society is not the temple of value-idols that figure on the front of its monuments or in its constitutional scrolls; the value of a society is the value it places upon man's relation to man." From the perspective of critical phenomenology, politics thus revolves basically around concrete intersubjective experience and around the way people actually treat each other in a morally relevant sense in everyday life: "To understand and judge a society, one has to penetrate its basic structure to the human bond upon which it is built; this undoubtedly depends upon legal relations, but also upon forms of labor, ways of loving, living, and dying."[20]

PART ONE

Politics and the Human Condition

1. Political Science and the "Two Cultures"

ABOUT TWO DECADES HAVE PASSED since Lord Snow formulated the "two cultures" idea in his famous Rede Lecture at Cambridge. Certainly in this lecture Snow did not invent or freshly discover the conflict of "cultures"; he merely highlighted a well-known phenomenon by expressing it in a catching phrase. In the meantime, his phrase has been subjected to many criticisms and comments. Some writers have charged that Sir Charles stipulated too many, others that he stipulated too few "cultures." In his *Science: The Glorious Entertainment,* Jacques Barzun challenged Snow's conception, arguing that the various groups described by Sir Charles "together with those for whom the issue does not even begin to exist, belong to one culture, the scientific culture of the western world in the twentieth century." To Barzun this unified outlook established by natural science was a cause of anxiety and grave concern. To Edward H. Carr, by contrast, the same unity of scientific culture appeared as a most desirable arrangement and he denounced the "rift between the so-called 'two cultures'" as a product of "ancient prejudice, based on a class structure of English society which itself belongs to the past."[1] Some writers, on the other hand, have attacked Lord Snow as too parsimonious, claiming that there are not two, but a great variety, perhaps "*n* cultures." In his *Second Look,* Snow acknowledged that he may have overlooked the possibility of a "third" culture (including social and political science). Otherwise, however, I think Snow made a fairly good case in his comments on the "two thousand and two cultures" school of thought when he described it as an "attempt at excessive unsimplicity" which "goes happily away into nullity."[2]

Obviously, every distinction can be broken down into numerous sub-distinctions, in an exercise of the "technique of the intricate defensive." However, Snow was not concerned with petty traits or idiosyncrasies, but rather with general intellectual habits and forms of thought which he called "cultures." The social sciences—and especially political science—certainly cannot claim to be strangers to this bifurcation of cultures. During the past decades the literature of political science has frequently resounded with the conflict. More recently, the furor has somewhat declined, and the various camps appear willing to view each other with more patience and equanimity. Nevertheless, I do not believe that the conflict has been reduced to, or ever was, a mere "nonsense fight," as James Prothro has suggested. In the words of Lord Snow, I think that "something serious" is intended in the matter. Somewhere behind the scene there lurks the specter of Laplace and of the *"machine à gouverner"* referred to by Norbert Wiener.[3]

The conflict involves the age-old problem of the unity of knowledge and the unity of human experience. I have no intention of disparaging the spirit of toleration wherever it may exist today in our profession—although it is difficult to escape the impression that gestures of tolerance sometimes reflect a condescending benevolence toward a supposedly vanquished enemy. Patience and good will are highly desirable in any academic pursuit. However, unless one were to endorse the equality of all opinions, the merits of the case cannot be settled merely by well-intentioned sentiments. The chief problem remains how the relationship between the "two cultures" can be conceived as logically possible and intelligible; connected with this problem is the question (also raised by Snow) of how political science has to be construed in order to function as a "third" culture.[4] In the following I want to review the development of this problematic both in the distant and the more recent past, in order finally to explore the possibility of a structural correlation of diverse types of inquiry within the parameters of the study of politics.

I.   Classical Heritage: The "Stoic Triad"

The relationship between the "two cultures" or—to descend from the level of metaphors—the relationship between science (meaning exact science) and the humanities belongs in the larger context of the interrelation of forms of knowledge and intellectual pursuits. From time immemorial mankind has been justly preoccupied with this interrelation, probably partly in an effort to ward off large-scale schizophrenia. In the past, the problem area was frequently referred to as the "classification of sciences" or as the system or "republic" of knowledge. It would be quite impossible here to trace the entire history of classification efforts. What I propose to do in the present context is merely to sketch briefly the outlines of the classical heritage and then to highlight some of the recent taxonomic explorations, with special emphasis on the place of political science.

There are many ways in which forms of knowledge can be correlated, depending on the criteria chosen for the operation. The most enduring approaches have been those which focus on subjective or objective criteria, that is, approaches which concentrate either on the "knower," on man's various faculties of mind and feeling, or on the "known," the various subject areas of study, or on a combination of the two. Among ancient philosophers, Plato has sometimes been credited with the invention of various taxonomic schemes; however, the only classification which clearly emerges from his writings is the hierarchical arrangement of human faculties and of the levels of the world corresponding to these faculties.[5] Plato divided reality into the visible and the intelligible world, with the visible world being amenable to sense perception and leading to "opinion" either in the form of conjecture or belief, and with the intelligible world being reserved to reason either in the form of discursive reason (comprising some of the natural sciences and mathematics) or of dialectical reason aiming at the ultimate realm of ideas. This scheme manifests a strong dichotomy between the phenomenal and the ideal world or (using the terms with some hesitation) between the concrete-empirical and the abstract-theoretical realms, a dichotomy which can be found as a recurrent feature in many subsequent attempts at classification. The process of "enlightenment," in the Platonic sense, consisted in the ascent from the level of sense and opinion to the intelligible world; this process was also the hallmark of a proper understanding of politics, as is illustrated in the "allegory of the cave" in the seventh book of the *Republic*.

In accordance with his more diversified interests and more systematic outlook, Aristotle devised a somewhat more complex taxonomy which, at least in part, amended the abstract-concrete bifurcation and differentiated between the "theoretical," "practical," and "productive" branches of philosophy, dealing respectively with forms of being, actions, and the making of tools or products. Theoretical philosophy included natural science and was assumed to proceed, in an ascending scale of generality and abstraction, from psychology and physics over mathematics to metaphysics. Practical philosophy focused on actions promoting either the individual or the public good and comprised chiefly ethics, economics, and politics.[6] Aristotle's taxonomy was destined to exercise a profound influence on subsequent developments, though it was perhaps not entirely free of ambiguities. One question concerns the relationship of theoretical and practical philosophy. Action and theory or analysis can be well enough distinguished for some purposes; but one may wonder whether, at least in some respects, the performance of an action might not be amenable to empirical and theoretical analysis. This question also reflects on the position of politics in the Aristotelian scheme. Politics was raised by Aristotle to the status of an "architectonic" discipline because statesmen and politicians must view all forms of knowledge in relation to the common good. This conception seems plausible enough (at least to a political scientist); but the proclaimed status is insufficiently supported by the classification scheme, where politics appears as one subdivision of one branch of philosophy.

Aristotle's distribution of knowledge gained its widest currency in a modified or simplified version, a version developed by the Stoics and Epicureans which consisted in the triad of logic, physics, and ethics. In Aristotle's scheme, logic had served mainly as a propaedeutic to metaphysics while physics was a major branch of theoretical, ethics a major division of practical philosophy. The simplification was probably due to the more pragmatic orientation of the Stoics and Epicureans, who viewed philosophy chiefly as an instrument to guide human life and who for this purpose required, as Robert Flint observed, "a logic to guide the reason, a physics to explain the world, and an ethics to rule the moral life."[7] It was precisely its compelling simplicity which enabled the triad, sometimes called the "Stoic triad," to function as cornerstone of classification attempts through the ages and down to our own time.

Medieval writers and especially scholastic philosophy built upon this triad, although several important changes were introduced. The most prominent of these modifications was the hierarchical arrangement of forms of knowledge, an arrangement culminating at its apex in the "mistress science" of theology which embraced some elements of ethics and to which all other forms of knowledge were only ancillary or preparatory. The lower echelons of the pyramid were occupied by a sequence of studies known as the seven "liberal arts," a concept which can be traced back to Cassiodorus and Martianus Capella. The liberal arts were again subdivided, for pedagogical and curriculum purposes, into two "paths" or "ways": the so-called *trivium* which included grammar, dialectic, and rhetoric, and the *quadrivium* comprehending arithmetic, geometry, astronomy, and music. As Robert Flint informs us, it was customary for medieval students to pass slowly through the *trivium* (which corresponded largely to the logic of the Stoic triad) and rapidly through the *quadrivium* (corresponding to the Stoic physics), sometimes omitting the latter entirely, so as to advance directly from the *trivium* to theology. This aspect, he thinks, accounted largely for the character of scholasticism, its intimate combination of language and metaphysics. In the late Middle Ages, the scholastic classification of knowledge was frequently merged with neo-Platonic and other forms of speculation. Thus Dante represented the distribution of sciences as corresponding to the divisions of the heavens, while St. Bonaventura, the "Seraphic Doctor," arranged it in an ascending scale of inspiration, ranging from an external "light" over an inferior and internal to the superior "light" of theology.

The period of the Renaissance and Reformation brought a reaction mainly against the excessive speculation of the late Middle Ages and against the relative neglect of the *quadrivium* studies. As a result, the scholastic scheme underwent several significant transformations. One of these changes consisted in the removal of the apex of the medieval pyramid, revealed theology, to a realm of faith separate from human reason. With the removal of this domain from the republic of knowledge, there remained the realm of rational "philosophy" or "science" broadly conceived,[8] a realm which, in the tradition of the Stoic triad, comprised commonly the provinces of metaphysics, physics, and ethics. It should be noted, however, that the survival of the Stoic triad under the aegis of rational philosophy was more apparent than real: with the unfolding potential of the natural sciences, the traditional components of the triad were increasingly assimilated or incorporated into the canons of "theoretical" knowledge (now reinforced by the method of experimentation and technical reproduction of natural processes). Of a very different character and more limited immediate impact was another innovation in the republic of knowledge, a change which related, so to speak, to the preparatory echelons of the scholastic pyramid, to the level of the *trivium*. At least in the case of some Renaissance and post-Renaissance writers, the pedagogical reliance on language and rhetoric was supplemented or replaced by an emphasis on philological and historical exegesis and related humanistic studies. The turn to history is exemplified especially by such Italian writers as Mario Nizolio, Tommaso Campanella, and Giambattista Vico. Dividing the republic of knowledge into the two areas of "oratory" and "philosophy," Nizolio assigned the study of history to the first domain, along with such traditional disciplines as rhetoric and grammar; in the second domain he distinguished between natural and civil philosophy (a distinction preceding Hobbes's *Leviathan* by almost a hundred years), with civil philosophy comprising ethics, politics, and other studies which today

we would call "social sciences." Campanella accorded to history an
even more prominent place, treating it virtually as the foundation of
all knowledge. On the eve of the Enlightenment, Vico proclaimed the
preeminence of historical and social studies over other sciences, deriving this preferred status from their roots in "practical" knowledge, from
the fact that society and history are the work of man and thus more
readily intelligible (*verum et factum convertuntur*).

By the time of Vico's writing, however, historical and social studies
were already placed on the defensive by other "modernizations" in the
republic of knowledge, innovations typified by the classification system
of Francis Bacon. In common with other Renaissance writers, Bacon
insisted on a strict bifurcation between knowledge and faith, between
the natural world of sense perception and the divine or spiritual world.
In itself, this aspect was not particularly novel or astonishing; however,
Bacon carried the bifurcation into the heart of man, distinguishing between a divine rational soul made in the image of God and a sensible
or animal soul which alone was subject to scientific (or "theoretical")
inquiry. This distinction had a profound effect on his taxonomic system and, as will be seen, resulted in the virtual obliteration of at least
the ethical (or "practical") component of the Stoic triad.

The realm of all possible human knowledge was divided by Bacon
into the three fields of history, poetry, and philosophy which, in turn,
were correlated to three basic human faculties. History—assigned to the
lowest level—was supposed to correspond to the faculty of memory
which collects sense impressions and images of individual objects;
poetry was viewed as the work of imagination which combines and
changes received impressions while, in the field of philosophy, human
reason was given the task of analyzing and classifying the impressions
in systematic form. It is especially in this highest field that Bacon's system exerted its lasting impact, chiefly through his stipulation of a
linear sequence or unified method of analysis in which reason was
assumed to proceed from natural theology to philosophy of nature and
finally to the philosophy of man. Philosophy of "nature" included physics
and metaphysics (which, however, consisted merely in general axioms
and abstract laws of nature). Human philosophy or philosophy of
"man" was divided into the analysis of individual man, including his
body and his internal or mental faculties, and the analysis of civil affairs
or the body politic. Ethics was merely an empirical treatment of psychic phenomena (such as will, passions, and affections), while moral
judgment properly speaking was relegated to revelation and hence outside rational scrutiny. Politics was treated in a similar manner; viewing the political community as a body among others, Bacon's civil phi-

losophy consisted chiefly in the examination of the natural appetites of that body, especially the arts and techniques of power.[9]

The implications of Bacon's system, especially for the study of politics, were developed with consistency and originality by one of his contemporaries, Thomas Hobbes. Although an admirer of Thucydides and the author of a history of the English civil war, Hobbes accorded very little weight to historical knowledge, relegating it to the mere accumulation of facts. As with Bacon, his chief preoccupation was with science or theoretical philosophy which, in his view, revolved around a strict causal method ("demonstrations of consequences of one affirmation to another") and which branched into natural and civil philosophy, the former dealing with nature and its products, the latter with the body politic as the chief product of human reason. The Baconian system was partly reinforced and partly counteracted by another philosophical current of his time: the Cartesian mind-body dualism. Descartes's philosophy corroborated the tenor of the Baconian method by treating the entire external nature as a mechanism or as matter extended in space. At the same time, however, Descartes separated from external nature the idea of mind or a thinking substance—a substance which he did not simply relegate to revelation, thereby reclaiming vast areas for philosophical or metaphysical speculation. His classification of knowledge might be described as a combination of the Baconian emphasis on faculties and the traditional Stoic triad. Like Bacon, he distinguished several human faculties; but three of these—sense, memory, and imagination—were ascribed to the body, while the fourth faculty of understanding or reason was said to belong to the mind or thinking substance.

The juxtaposition of Baconian and Cartesian thought reveals some profound tensions and ambiguities concerning the nature of human understanding, tensions which pervaded intellectual developments throughout the Enlightenment period. Some philosophers pursued the more empirical and naturalist orientation, while others inclined toward rational speculation and metaphysics. John Locke generally continued the Baconian lines of argument, while placing more explicit emphasis on the classical triad of physics (dealing with things), ethics (dealing with actions), and logic (called "semeiotics" and dealing chiefly with signs).[10] Condillac, in turn, followed Locke and Newton, thereby leaving a strong imprint on French Enlightenment philosophy. On the other hand, Christian Wolff developed a system of metaphysical rationalism which relied heavily on deductive argumentation and which, very characteristically, included psychology (or the philosophy of mind) within the branch of cognitive metaphysics. Eclecticism or a blending of philosophical positions prevailed in the French Encyclopedia whose classification scheme, though strongly patterned after the Baconian system, made significant concessions to spiritualism and metaphysics.[11]

It is probably against this background of conflict between empirical and metaphysical systems—and also of the relative neglect of practical thought—that one should assess Kant's philosophical contribution. The problems concerning the nature of human knowledge had given rise to belligerent camps favoring either broad metaphysical speculation or narrow empiricism, unless refuge was taken in the leaning tower of mental solipsism. The chief aim of Kant's critiques was to overcome these onesided orientations, by portraying at once the wealth and dignity and the limitations of human reason. To a considerable extent, traditional metaphysics had consisted of an effort to populate pure reason with empirical data, thereby in a sense duplicating the world and producing such hybrids as a rational but substantive physics and a rational but substantive psychology (or "pneumatology"). In order to overcome these hybrids, Kant distinguished between a priori and a posteriori knowledge, the first referring to the principles or categories of pure reason unpolluted by sense experience, the other containing the world of empirical or phenomenal existence. Within the confines of this distinction, Kant's philosophy still maintained the basic categories of the Stoic triad, especially the categories of theoretical and practical knowledge. In the realm of theoretical knowledge, once the pure principles of reason were identified, the whole of a posteriori experience lay open to empirical and scientific investigation. In the field of practical philosophy, dealing with the "kingdom of ends," reason was charged with supplying the principles of a metaphysics of morals or ethics. One should add, however, that in Kant's thinking the domains of theoretical and practical philosophy were only precariously related: the transcendental freedom of the individual remained juxtaposed to the strict causality and necessity of nature. It was this gulf that dialectical thinking (especially Hegelian and Marxist dialectics) tried to remedy by establishing a much closer connection between reason and experience and between theoretical and practical thought.

II. Positivism and the Dichotomy of
"Natur- und Geisteswissenschaften"

During the last century, some of the historical tendencies I have mentioned came to fruition; as a corollary, new conflicts and battle lines emerged in the republic of knowledge. After the interlude of idealism, the chief orientation of the nineteenth century was clearly in the direction of empirical and scientific studies. It seems correct to say that the Baconian system came here finally into its own, especially his linear sequence of scientific disciplines (and also his comparative neglect of practical philosophy). Nevertheless, the legacy of the Cartesian mind-body dualism still continued to raise serious problems and uncertainties. Jeremy Bentham generally followed the empirical tradition, but thought it necessary to make the mind-body dichotomy an integral part of his classification scheme. The philosophy of the sensible world, as distinguished from metaphysics, was divided into a science of body ("somatology") and a science of internal or mental states ("pneumatology"). The latter science was again subdivided into a branch dealing with the more intellectual pursuits ("nooscopy") and a branch devoted to affections and passions ("pathoscopy"), comprising such areas as aesthetics, ethics, and political science. In a similar vein, John Stuart Mill maintained that the "whole field of human knowledge" separated itself "obviously, and as it were spontaneously" into the two divisions of "physical science and moral or psychological science."[12]

Despite their prominence, however, utilitarian writings were overshadowed by Auguste Comte, at least in the field of the system of sciences or taxonomy of knowledge. Comte adhered more strictly to the Baconian idea of a linear filiation of sciences, although he permitted himself some digressions. While Bacon had separated theology and metaphysics from human knowledge, without thereby denying their inherent significance, Comte added a historical twist to this arrangement, claiming that theology and metaphysics characterized earlier stages of human development, while the present and future belonged to empirical or "positive" knowledge. Despite this historical perspective, however, Comte did not elaborate greatly on the Baconian faculty of memory (history); nor did he contribute significantly to the realm of imagination (poetry or arts). His emphasis rested on positive philosophy or science ("theoretical" knowledge) and it is in this area that linear filiation or continuity of analysis played its dominant role. In developing the concept of filiation, Comte showed very little regard for the mind-body dualism; another distinction appeared to him more significant: that between abstract (or general) and concrete (or descriptive) sciences. The former were assumed to focus on general laws abstracted from empirical data, while the latter were derivative disciplines involving the explanation of particular phenomena by means of general laws. In the field of abstract or general sciences, Comte included mathematics and the natural or physical sciences. The natural sciences were divided into inorganic and organic physics, the two disciplines being bridged by chemistry. Inorganic physics was said to branch into astronomy and physics proper, while organic physics subdivided into physiology (or biology) and social physics (or sociology). Physiology included phrenology and psychology (as sciences of the mind), while sociology comprehended "social statics," or the theory of order in society, and "social dynamics," dealing with change and progress in society. The filiation of sciences was thus: mathematics, astronomy, physics, chemistry, biology, and sociology—a sequence which, Comte maintained, was one of decreasing generality and increasing complexity in which subsequent sciences depend on preceding sciences, but not vice versa.[13]

Comte's classification has been sketched here in some detail mainly because of its rather consistent adherence to a naturalist or natural science orientation, and because of its widespread repercussions in subsequent developments. Herbert Spencer initially launched an attack on the concept of linear filiation, but ended up with a system very much like Comte's. Spencer's chief objection seems to have been to filiation in the sense of an actual historical evolution of the sciences; but, of course, Comte never maintained such a view. Spencer relied even more strongly than Comte on the abstract-concrete dichotomy, stipulating the existence of three groups of disciplines: abstract, abstract-concrete, and concrete sciences. Many other examples of the period could be cited to illustrate the same trend of thinking. Thus, Karl Pearson in his famous *Grammar of Science* acknowledged that he took his cues entirely from Bacon, Comte, and Spencer when he distinguished between abstract and concrete sciences and related them in a logical sequence. In the United States in 1882 Professor Charles W. Shields of Princeton defended a very similar linear arrangement, in which logic and mathematics appeared as a propaedeutic to the "sciences" which ranged from physics, chemistry, biology, to psychology and sociology.[14]

On the whole, these developments signified the expansion and virtual predominance of "theoretical" (or scientific) thinking in the republic of knowledge. To be sure, this trend did not remain unchallenged; one of the strongest objections or counter-arguments was voiced by Wilhelm Dilthey and his followers. As Dilthey himself asserted on frequent occasions, his endeavors were largely prompted by the progressive domination of all forms of human thought by the canons of natural science. The aim of his writings was to rescue and defend another realm of thought, apart from natural science: the realm of internal or mental experience, apprehended by means of *Geisteswissenschaften.*

In choosing the term *Geisteswissenschaften* (or mental sciences), Dilthey acknowledged that he simply followed the practice of Mill and other writers and that the term was not fully satisfactory, since mental states can only with great difficulty be separated from the unity of psycho-physical reality. Beyond this dissatisfaction, however, Dilthey made it clear that he interpreted the term in a very different sense from Mill and other empiricists whose dichotomies had by no means exempted mental experience from the naturalist method; the barrier to claims for natural science, in his view, derived from the qualitative difference of internal awareness, a difference grounded in "unity of consciousness" and "spontaneity of will." As he emphasized, it was not his intention to return to a precritical stage of philosophy or to the old metaphysical or "rational psychology." Instead of the precritical distinction between material and spiritual substances, he relied on the dichotomy between the realms of external sensation and internal or psychic experience—both part of empirical reality and amenable to systematic treatment. *Geisteswissenschaften* were anchored in direct, immediate, internal human experience. The social sciences, history, and the humanities all belonged legitimately to this branch, since all dealt with phenomena which were or had been forms of human experience and mental life; the aim of these disciplines was to translate documents and petrified records back into the original language of human life and psychic experience. The phenomena of these disciplines were more directly accessible to man than any other forms of knowledge since, to quote Dilthey, "only what mind has produced, mind can fully understand." The physical world of the natural sciences, by contrast, was not as immediately a part of human experience. The only way to render nature intelligible was to subject it to the constructs of natural science, its abstract laws of uniformity and causality. "Nature," Dilthey said, "we explain; psychic life we understand [*verstehen*]."[15]

Much has been written about *Verstehen*, a concept which obviously was quite central to Dilthey's theory of mental sciences. One should acknowledge that Dilthey tried to overcome the purely subjective implications of the concept by insisting on careful, systematic treatment and analysis. Nevertheless, despite his stand against precritical philosophy, it is hard to avoid the impression that his distinction between natural and mental sciences tended to relapse into the bifurcation of material and spiritual substances. If, in defense against this charge, Dilthey insisted that psychic states were part of empirical reality, it was permissible to ask why, from this perspective, psychic experience was not amenable to scientific treatment (according to canons of natural science). Such scientific treatment of internal expe-

rience was already emerging during his own time and its feasibility
became increasingly manifest. The most famous illustration of this trend
was probably Wilhelm Wundt. In several of his writings Wundt elaborated on the problem of the classification of knowledge; his approach
in this matter appeared similar to that of Dilthey, as he, too, divided
empirical knowledge into natural sciences and *Geisteswissenschaften.*
The difference between the two branches, he argued, was not to be
construed as one between substances or objects, but rather as one between objects and the psychological subject.[16] Like Titchener and
other structuralists, Wundt still relied very strongly on introspection, a
method which enabled psychology to serve as pillar or basic discipline
of *Geisteswissenschaften*; however, he also founded the experimental
method of psychology, which was difficult to confine to the narrow
limits of introspection. The emergence of experimental analysis, in turn,
provided important impulses to the subsequent rise of psychological
"behaviorism," a perspective wedded to the empirical analysis of psychic processes and to the explanation of human behavior in terms of a
causal, stimulus-response framework.

As soon as the possibility of a scientific psychology was acknowledged, the dichotomy between external and internal or between "nature" and "mind" was rendered ambiguous and the respective classification of knowledge subject to re-evaluation. Several intellectual movements of the time sought to overcome Dilthey's quandaries by shifting
from the level of empirical psychology to that of a purified consciousness exempt from the stimulus-response nexus; foremost among these
movements were neo-Kantianism and transcendental phenomenology.
The neo-Kantian camp was internally subdivided into a number of
groups or circles, with some favoring the abstract-theoretical scrutiny
of logical and mathematical symbols and others concentrating more
on the traditional humanities, including the study of history and society. The humanistic branch was represented chiefly by the so-called
"Southwest German" school led by Wilhelm Windelband and Heinrich
Rickert. In their taxonomic inquiries, both philosophers started from
the premise that the bifurcation of natural sciences and *Geisteswissenschaften* was no longer entirely satisfactory. As Windelband pointed
out in his famous Strassburg address of 1894, the dichotomy between
nature and mind possessed great strength in the Middle Ages and continued unabated in Cartesian metaphysics. However, with Locke's empirical treatment of external sensation and internal reflection the distinction began to appear doubtful, while Kantian philosophy challenged the notion of a strictly "internal perception." It was therefore
no longer obvious that knowledge in the *Geisteswissenschaften* was

simply based on such internal experience; in any event, psychology as an empirical discipline could no longer be accommodated in such a distribution of sciences. In place of this distribution Windelband proposed a distinction between natural science and history. Both branches, he argued, aimed at rigorous knowledge, but their distinction revolved around different cognitive objectives. Natural sciences could be viewed as attempts to extract the persistent uniformities and abstract laws from phenomena, while historical disciplines sought to retain the concrete, particular content of these phenomena: "the former are sciences dealing with laws, the other sciences dealing with events; the former teach what is always, the other what was once the case."[17]

While Windelband's observations were highly suggestive sketches (and offered as such), Rickert proceeded to subject taxonomic questions to a more thorough and systematic examination. Paraphrasing Kant, he defined "nature" as empirical reality with reference to general laws (or at least general principles). Due to its "nomothetic" orientation, he noted, natural science persistently tries to transcend concrete perception; in its most perfect state, it would culminate in a completely abstract conception in which all sensible and qualitative aspects are resolved in mathematical or quantitative relationships. This perfection would correspond to the Laplacean formula of the world as a system of simultaneous differential equations and would satisfy Condillac's statement that all true propositions are "the same." The only element which sets a limit to this universal formula is the realm of concrete, particular, or individual experience or activity—a realm reserved to historical and related humanistic disciplines. However, in stressing the uniqueness of historical phenomena and the "idiographic" character of humanistic studies, Rickert tried to avoid the danger of cultural relativism and particularism. In order to generate rigorous and systematic knowledge, he pointed out, historical and humanistic inquiries had to rely on concepts or guiding ideas of a "general" nature. Drawing at least in part on Kant's critique of "practical reason," Rickert found these general concepts or ideas in the domain of trans-empirical norms and values as embedded in religious teachings, constitutions, and legal codes. The impregnation of historical phenomena with such norms and values could be termed "culture"; it thus became possible, in a limited sense, to delineate a special subject area of study and to designate the historical and humanistic disciplines as "cultural sciences" or *Kulturwissenschaften.*[18]

Although unorthodox in their preoccupation with the humanities, the discussed "Southwest German" circle still remained heir to important traditional bifurcations and dichotomies: especially to the Kantian distinctions between a priori mental categories and external nature (a reformulation of the Cartesian dualism) and between the domain of natural necessity or natural laws and the realm of internal freedom discovered by practical reason. Some of these bifurcations were called into question—albeit at first obliquely and cautiously—by the phenomenological movement inaugurated by Edmund Husserl. Like the neo-Kantian thinkers, Husserl was staunchly opposed to "psychologism," especially to attempts to submerge all types of cognitive endeavors in empirical stimulus-response processes. Countering positivist and behaviorist pretensions, he appealed to the power of reflection to transcend all contingent empirical constraints; as he insisted, the study of psychic processes and of *any* empirical phenomena could never yield valid scientific knowledge as long as scientific propositions were themselves products of psychic conditioning. The phenomenological method of "bracketing" or *epoché* was designed to grant access to a layer of consciousness which—while not itself a contingent factor—was presupposed in all cognitive pursuits and in the examination of all phenomena.

As formulated by Husserl, phenomenology was a Janus-faced enterprise: in accentuating the role of transcendental reflection, he paid homage to the central thrust of the Kantian and Cartesian tradition; at the same time, however, his preoccupation with the attentive inspection of phenomena laid the groundwork for new departures. In stressing "intentionality" as the crucial link between noetic faculties and perceived phenomena, Husserl's perspective pointed the way (potentially) toward a narrowing of the gulf between mind and matter or between cognitive structures and the world of "things-in-themselves." In a tentative fashion, the intentional quality of consciousness was invoked by Husserl for taxonomic purposes or the classification of cognitive pursuits: different intentional orientations were assumed to provide the underpinning for inquiries into different "regions" of experience. Yet, despite the broad range of investigations opened up by the phenomenological method, one cannot overlook a certain restrictiveness in Husserl's outlook, at least as it was articulated during the early decades of this century: predicated on intentional consciousness, phenomenological research was bound to carry a distinctly theoretical or contemplative character, while practical human concerns and aspirations tended to be bypassed or de-emphasized. Concerns of this kind only surfaced during his later years, as a corollary of his efforts to uncover the human "life-world" as the precognitive infrastructure of knowledge. Once the life-world was seen as the matrix of everyday activity and interaction, the road was cleared for expanding phenomenological attention from descriptive and theoretical analysis ultimately to the full range of human life, including individual and social practice.

While Husserl's departure from theoretical reflection was hesitant and somewhat ambivalent, Heidegger in *Being and Time* (1927)—one of his first major publications—resolutely relinquished the focus on consciousness in favor of precognitive "existential categories" characterizing and shaping the distinctive manner of human experience. In defining human existence as "being-in-the-world," *Being and Time* took a decisive stand against the mind-matter dualism and also against the dominant epistemological traditions of the modern era: empiricism (with its attempt to derive thought from external conditions) and rationalism (with its stress on the "constitutive" role of reflection). As presented by Heidegger, man—without being a product of his environment—was from the beginning enmeshed in a dense fabric of common perceptions and life patterns; his linkage with the world resided neither in causal connections nor in a purely cognitive "intentionality," but rather in the category of "care"—a term denoting chiefly man's need to be concerned with the "point" or meaning of his existence. As structured by care and other existential categories, human life gave rise to a number of distinct cognitive orientations which were briefly alluded to in *Being and Time*: apart from scientific explanation and technical manipulation of external nature, the study mentioned chiefly understanding of others through practical interaction and the endeavor to gain deepened self-understanding. Almost simultaneously with the appearance of *Being and Time*, Max Scheler—another student of Husserl and advocate of an "anthropological" phenomenology—presented a detailed taxonomy of types of knowledge as rooted in deep-seated, precognitive dispositions and endowments. According to Scheler, the broad spectrum of cognitive endeavors could be subdivided into three main branches: the field of empirical science, dedicated to the control of nature; the domain of cultural and normative insights; and the quest for ultimate or transcendental meaning.[19]

Despite their references to culture and human interaction, neither Heidegger nor Scheler elaborated specifically on the implications of a post-rationalist epistemology for the humanities and social sciences. This elaboration was one of the objectives and accomplishments of the Frankfurt School of Social Research which emerged during the subsequent decade. From the beginning, members of the school were committed to the development of a "critical theory"—which can be viewed, in part, as a further radicalization and self-scrutiny of the Kantian legacy of critical philosophy. In his programmatic essay on "Traditional and Critical Theory" (of 1937), Max Horkheimer differentiated between two basic types of knowledge and cognition: theoretical-empirical science, concerned with the analysis of existing reality, and critical-dialectical thought dedicated to the practical transformation of society (a distinction which added a dialectical dimension to the bifurcation between nomothetic and historical disciplines). Horkheimer's taxonomy was refined and reformulated by younger representatives of the Frankfurt School, with particular attention to the prereflective underpinnings of cognitive endeavors. In his *Knowledge and Human Interests* Jürgen Habermas delineated three different types of inquiries, linking them with three basic orientations or "interests" rooted in the human condition: thus, empirical science and technology were traced to the human desire for instrumental control of the environment; historical and cultural interpretation or "hermeneutics" was connected with the need for intersubjective collaboration and understanding; while critical-dialectical analysis was tied to the interest in emancipation and self-transparency. A similar conception—utilizing the rubrics of science, hermeneutics, and critique of ideology—was articulated by Karl-Otto Apel in several of his writings; stressing the nexus of prereflective experience and cognition, Apel redefined and reoriented the task of epistemology in the direction of an "anthropology of knowledge."[20]

III. "Behavioralism" and Its Alternatives

After this somewhat lengthy review of past skirmishes and recent realignments in the republic of knowledge, let me now return to the more immediate concern of this chapter: political science and its place in the "two cultures" conflict. A dominant trend in recent decades, at least in the United States, has been the attempt to apply "scientific" or natural science standards to all social disciplines, including the study of politics. This development, sometimes referred to as "behavioralism," is by no means a sudden or whimsical phenomenon, but a resolute effort to transform social and political inquiry into a branch of "theoretical" (or scientific) knowledge. Although sources for behavioralism can be found in the doctrines of Comte and Spencer and in nineteenth-century scientism, its major impetus and almost puritanical rigor arise from intellectual trends of our own era. The first steps toward a "scientific" politics occurred roughly at the time when Russell and Whitehead, in the *Principia Mathematica*, explored the convergence of logic and mathematics and when the Vienna circle initiated the rigorous analysis of formal language. Numerous additional influences have played a role, including the growing rationalization and technical perfection of industrial society, the policies of research institutions and philanthropic foundations, and the experiences and operational needs of two world wars.

I do not propose, in this context, to trace the development or assess the accomplishments and failings of the "behavioral movement" during recent decades; this story has been told several times.[21] For present purposes I limit myself to the observation that a political science identified exclusively with behavioral or natural science seems ill-equipped to fulfill the task of a "third culture" suggested by Lord Snow. In the remainder of this chapter I intend to sketch briefly some alternatives or countertrends which have been opposed or juxtaposed to the behavioral orientation by contemporary theoreticians or practitioners of social or political science. Sometimes these alternatives rely strongly on internal or mental phenomena and thus seem indebted to the dichotomy between *Natur- und Geisteswissenschaften.* In other instances the inspiration seems to derive from the differentiation between empirical-nomothetic and hermeneutical-historical disciplines or (more rarely) from the classical distinction between theoretical and practical knowledge.

Countertrends reminiscent of the legacy of *Geisteswissenschaften* assume a variety of shades and formulations. To some extent, echoes of this legacy can be found in Eric Voegelin's *The New Science of Politics* (although the author's argument is too complex to permit easy labelling). Despite its seemingly fashionable title, the central aim of the study was a frontal attack on behavioral or scientific political inquiry and, more generally, on "positivistic destructiveness" and "perversion." The destructiveness of positivism, according to Voegelin, was the "consequence of two fundamental assumptions": first, "the splendid unfolding of the natural sciences" which suggested that "the methods used in the mathematizing sciences of the external world were possessed of some inherent value"; and secondly, the "assumption that the methods of the natural sciences were a criterion for theoretical relevance in general." From the "combination of the two assumptions," he added, followed "the well-known series of assertions that a study of reality could qualify as scientific only if it used the methods of the natural sciences, that problems couched in other terms were illusionary problems, that in particular metaphysical questions which do not admit of answers by the methods of the sciences of phenomena should not be asked." The detrimental effects of these premises were illustrated by Max Weber in whom—as Voegelin claimed—the scientific movement "ran to the end of its immanent logic." In order to rescue the study of society and politics from positivism, it was necessary to rediscover the "ontological" difference between the objects of inquiry. According to *The New Science of Politics,* such a rediscovery presupposed a more comprehensive effort of "restoration" involving a "return to the consciousness of principles" and a willingness to rely "on the methods of metaphysical speculation and theological symbolization."[22]

In a more emphatic and unequivocal manner the mentalist thrust of the tradition of *Geisteswissenschaften* emerges in Friedrich Hayek's methodological writings. In his study *The Counter-Revolution of Science,* Hayek contended that the extension of the methods of natural science to social inquiry was a dangerous aberration and an "abuse of reason." The inapplicability of these methods to social inquiry was attributed chiefly to a qualitative distinction of subject matters. Natural science, he maintained, examines external data independently of human thoughts and beliefs; the subject matter of social science, on the other hand, revolves around the human mind, human opinions, feelings, and attitudes. In formulating the desirable approach to social science phenomena, Hayek recommended the method of introspection which, in his treatment, appeared as a narrow version of *Verstehen* theory based on the argument that only mind can know mind. "So far as human actions are concerned the things are what the acting people think they are," he wrote. "Our data must be man and the physical world as they appear to the men whose actions we try to explain."[23] Occasionally mentalist overtones can be detected even in the case of writers whose major focus is on language and intersubjective communication. An example is Peter Winch, whose study *The Idea of a Social Science* was strongly influenced by the later Wittgenstein and ordinary language analysis. Winch showed convincingly that human thought and conduct are embedded in language and social patterns of discourse. However, in an effort to ward off positivist or behavioralist inroads into social inquiry, he strongly insisted on the "internality" of social life: "If social relations between men exist only in and through their ideas, then, since the relations between ideas are internal relations, social relations must be a species of internal relation too."[24]

Among contemporary students of politics, Michael Oakeshott is by far the most eloquent and most respected proponent of a historical-hermeneutical type of inquiry. In one of his essays, Oakeshott defined politics as "the activity of attending to the general arrangements of a set of people whom chance or choice have brought together." As used in this phrase, political activity was synonymous neither with an automatic response to psychic impulses nor with the enactment of abstract postulates. In his words, politics proceeded "neither from instant desires, nor from general principles, but from the existing traditions of behaviour themselves"; its central concern was "the amendment of existing arrangements by exploring and pursuing what is intimated in them." The exploration of intimations was akin to learning a language or type of discourse, to interpreting the meaning of statements, and eventually to participating in a "conversation." Raised to the level of an academic discipline, "political education" or the study of politics had to have an appropriately interpretive character. The "governing consideration," according to Oakeshott, was "that what we are learning to understand is a political tradition, a concrete manner of behaviour. And for this reason it is proper that, at the academic level, the study of politics should be an historical study." In another context, Oakeshott delineated political study as a type of "practical knowledge"—a term which he differentiated from pragmatic "vocational" training but placed in particularly marked contrast to "technical" or instrumental-scientific knowledge. The latter type—which was favored by modern "rationalism"—was "susceptible of formulation in rules, principles, directions, maxims" and lent itself ultimately to planning and social engineering. By contrast, practical knowledge could not be "learned by heart, repeated by rote, and applied mechanically," but only be "imparted and acquired" in a concrete manner: "It exists only in practice, and the only way to acquire it is by apprenticeship to a master—not because the master can teach it (he cannot), but because it can be acquired only by continuous contact with one who is perpetually practising it."[25]

The notion of a practical type of knowledge—with specific reference to the classical legacy—has been articulated in more detail by Wilhelm Hennis in his *Politics and Practical Philosophy*, a study dedicated to the "reconstruction of political science." In his treatise, Hennis challenged the prevailing tendency of submerging political inquiry in "theoretical" or analytical knowledge; his main goal was to uncover the linkages relating the contemporary study of politics to the tradition of "practical philosophy" in the Aristotelian sense of the term. In trying to clear a path toward "reconstruction," he emphasized three main ingredients of politics conceived as practical knowledge: its foundation in human activity; its orientation toward a normative goal or *telos*; and its reliance on "topical" inquiry. While natural science aims at explanation and theoretical analysis, the study of politics cannot remain satisfied with detached observation, since it revolves around concrete actions and interactions guided by human values and aspirations. The exploration of political activity, Hennis observed, requires a special approach: the approach of "topical" discussion or practical-hermeneutical discourse which aims at the elucidation and disentanglement of social or communal problems in concrete, historical situations. "That politics is a practical science," he noted, "is the most important taxonomic heritage of the past, its rejection the basic reason of the crisis of our discipline."[26]

In a tentative fashion, steps in the direction of a critical-dialectical perspective have been undertaken, among others, by such writers as Christian Bay and Peter Bachrach. The distinctive feature of this perspective is the effort not only to probe normative aspirations and historical meaning patterns, but also to uncover the overt or subterranean constraints obstructing meaningful and equitable social interaction. In the formulation of Christian Bay, politics refers or should refer "to all organized activities aiming at resolving social problems, including the problems of keeping order ('government') and of protecting the weaker, or the less secure and free, against the stronger, or the more powerful and privileged ('justice')." Generally speaking, he adds, "the problems of politics are posed by the discrepancies between what is and what ought to be"; in investigating any given political system, the student of politics is bound to encounter "manifest or, more pervasively, enduring latent or hidden conflicts" between "ideals of justice" and "realities of deepening injustice." In terms of academic inquiry, this insight implies—in Bay's view—that "political science education must aim at liberating the student from the blinders of conventional wisdom, from political totems and taboos, so that he may make the basic choices of how to live and of political ideals as an independent person with optimal critical powers" and with maximum resistance to "alternative political dogmatisms." In a similar vein, Peter Bachrach observes that the political theorist—especially the theorist of democracy—cannot remain content with explanatory models, since in doing so he would "accept as unalterable the configuration of society as shaped by impersonal forces." Deprived of normative guideposts, political theory "cannot perform the crucial function of providing direction to man's actions." Yet, as Bachrach adds, "to lose sight of reality in political theorizing is to invite indifference and boredom." In analyzing present-day political arrangements, in particular, the student of politics cannot ignore or bypass "the elite-mass nature of modern industrial society and the implications of this fact for democratic theory."[27]

By way of conclusion, I would like to draw some inferences from the preceding overview for the constitution of political science, its branches and territories. I am very much aware of the hazards of such an undertaking; certainly, in the following I do not intend to establish watertight compartments. It is unfortunate, but probably beyond remedy, that the discipline has come to be known as "political science" (with a somewhat brazen emphasis on science); perhaps terms like

"politics" or "politology" would be less presumptuous and more comprehensive. The broad field of political science or politology, it seems
to me, can be divided roughly into three major branches: analytical or
behavioral political science; practical-hermeneutical politology; and
critical-dialectical political analysis and philosophy.[28]

Analytical or behavioral political science can be broadly defined as
inquiry centering on the observation and analysis of empirical political
phenomena in accordance with general principles of explanation. The
great majority of contemporary students and practitioners tend to con-
gregate under this banner. One reason for this tendency resides in the
immense amount of empirical data available in our contemporary global community; another reason may be found in the prevailing intellectual climate in industrial societies, a climate which, somewhat like the
force of gravity, seems to incline students toward "theoretical" or analytical knowledge. In general terms, the behavioral approach starts from
hypotheses and proceeds to the elaboration of abstract or general, but
empirically testable, laws or principles; wherever possible, the approach
aims at quantification and mathematical formulation. On the basis of
Popper's doctrine of the "unity of method" (or continuity of analysis),
behavioralism may be viewed as a connecting link between our discipline and natural science.

The explanatory thrust of behavioral or analytical inquiry reaches
the limit of its competence in the domain of purposive human activity
and practical political experience. In the words of Mulford Sibley, understanding politics "includes trying to comprehend not only how the
parts are related to one another in hypothetical situations but also how
the parts interact in actual history"; the student of politics thus is required not only to formulate "theoretical scientific propositions" but
also to articulate practical "judgments" about past and present issues.
Practical-hermeneutical inquiry is designed to further judgmental capacities; its chief aim is to assist in the elucidation of intentional human
conduct and concrete social meaning patterns. Such an effort involves
not only a careful study of social and political conditions, but an interpretive assessment or *Verstehen* of human aspirations in the context
of these conditions. If one were to follow Eric Weil, one might include
in this branch also the formulation of "practical" political theories, that
is, theories which are meant to provide guidance for the solution of
political problems in given historical constellations. Such theories, Weil
asserts, have always attempted to clarify "the contradiction between
procedures of the past and the exigencies of the present, the exigencies
of circumstances under which human aspirations must be pursued, but
can only be reached at the price levied by these circumstances."

While practical-hermeneutical inquiry ties the study of politics to the humanities, the third branch or perspective reveals some of the "architectonic" qualities ascribed to the discipline by Aristotle. As previously indicated, critical-dialectical investigations seek to link the empirical explanation of law-like, social or behavioral processes with the exploration of intentional aspirations—in other words, the domain of natural or quasi-natural necessity with the dimension of human freedom. In any given political system, quasi-natural constraints are operative on the level of available means and instruments of production and also in the prevailing distribution of power. Critical research aims not only to uncover such constraints, but also to assess them against the prospects of intersubjective understanding and equity. To guard against ideological bias, such endeavor has to be nurtured by broad-gauged philosophical reflection—a reflection which ponders not only the intrinsic postulates of thought but also the subterranean premises of cognition. In contradistinction to other kinds of inquiry, critical reflection does not engender positive knowledge or information, but rather a perspective or oblique commentary on such information. In the words of Merleau-Ponty, philosophy is not so much a particular body of doctrines as "the vigilance which does not let us forget the source of all knowledge." Returning to the original theme of these pages, the conception delineated here may point the way beyond the "two cultures" conflict. Connected though not narrowly identified with natural science or the humanities, the study of politics—while perhaps not qualifying as a "third culture"—may at least begin to meet Lord Snow's challenge by helping to repair channels of communication and to restore a freer flow of ideas between the branches of the republic of knowledge. This republic, moreover, is not isolated from the larger political context. From this vantage point, the acceptance of Snow's challenge may also contribute to the maintenance of public discourse and to the recognition of the common humanity of the members of the political community.

2. Empirical Political Theory
and the Image of Man

IN PAST CENTURIES SOCIAL SCIENCE was commonly designated as the science or study of man, a usage which lingers on in contemporary literature.[1] Despite changes in terminology, it remains a fond belief of many professionals and most laymen that the basic objective of social science is the comprehension of man and of the diverse patterns of man's conduct. While other disciplines may investigate his biological and physiological dimensions, social science boldly seems to grasp man at his core, as a thinking, feeling, and acting creature. To be sure, the tools and strategies of inquiry have varied over time. It is now a commonplace to assert that the social sciences, including political science, have experienced a revolution in recent decades, a revolution bent on reshaping these disciplines in accordance with the canons of natural science. This development has resulted not only in the careful collection and rapid accumulation of empirical data, but also in efforts to absorb empirical findings into new conceptual and explanatory schemes. As in other social disciplines, one of the most intensive endeavors of recent political science has been the search for a general framework of explanation, for an "empirical" or scientific theory of politics. My purpose here is not to lament or praise these developments and innovations. What I would like to explore is one aspect of the described revolution: its implication for the study and comprehension of man. Has science brought us closer to the perennial focus of social inquiry? What image of man is reflected in the mirror of recent political science and to what extent are we able to recognize ourselves in this mirror?

Unhappily this task is encumbered at the outset by impressive obstacles. Even a cursory acquaintance with contemporary political science literature reveals not one, but a great variety of conceptual frameworks, theories, and approaches. There is considerable dispute over the requisite ingredients of a scientific or empirical "theory," and the adherents of one persuasion are by no means eager to grant the label to their opponents in other camps. Also, the "empirical" foundations of some current theories are by no means obvious or beyond question. I cannot hope to resolve these questions or controversies; nor do I wish to insist on a narrow definition. For my own purposes I would tend to assign the label of "empirical" or "analytical" theory to a coherent set of researchable propositions which, at least within a hypothetical framework, possess explanatory and predictive capacity. In the present context, however, I am quite willing to concede the label to conceptual frameworks or approaches which approximate the preceding criteria.[2] The stipulation of such broad boundaries, of course, does not significantly reduce the thicket of prevailing orientations. Fortunately, a path or clearing has been cut into the underbrush by means of a distinction aptly expounded by Maurice Duverger. Political theory, Duverger pointed out, has always "oscillated between two dramatically opposed interpretations. According to one, politics is conflict, a struggle in which power allows those who possess it to ensure their hold on society and to profit by it. According to the other view, politics is an effort to bring about the rule of order and justice." In the first interpretation, he added, politics "serves to maintain the privileges of a minority against the majority"; in the second, it is a "means of realizing the integration of all citizens into the community."[3]

The dichotomy of integration and conflict, to be sure, is not Duverger's invention. Using a variety of labels and formulations, many contemporary social scientists subscribe to a similar distinction of theoretical perspectives. According to this dichotomous scheme, some social and political theories focus on the integration, consensus, and stability of a community, while others are preoccupied with conflict, constraint, and dynamic change.[4] The scheme clearly has the advantage of simplicity and may be adequate for purposes of broad orientation. However, as it seems to me, the dichotomy is too blunt an instrument to capture the richness of contemporary social and political theories. Cutting across the categories of integration and conflict, another distinction can be discerned: a distinction deriving from different units of analysis. As I intend to show, some contemporary theories focus on the system or political community as major unit of investigation, while others accord primary status to individual actors or groups and their interrelationships. A combination or pairing of the above criteria would seem to result in at least three types of theoretical orientations: an orientation which, proceeding from a system focus, is preoccupied with systemic integration and stability; a perspective which, while largely concerned with consensus, starts from the analysis of individual actors and groups; and finally an approach which, relying on individual actors and groups, explores their discord and dynamic interactions.[5] Adhering to this typology I shall try to delineate the main premises and propositions of the three perspectives, using the labels of *systemic, exchange,* and *conflict* theories; in each case I shall make an effort to trace, as far as possible, the human features implicit in the theoretical framework.

I. Systemic Theories

Among the great variety of contemporary empirical approaches, one perspective has probably exercised a dominant influence, at least in political science, during recent decades. This perspective is characterized by its focus on the social or political "system" as the unit of analysis and by its ambition to identify the determinants of system stability, equilibrium, and integration. Despite differences in usage, the term "system" in this context refers commonly to a set of elements standing in close interaction, although writers are not agreed on whether their unit of investigation is a physically concrete or a purely analytic structure. Apart from and connected with the identification of a system as an investigative unit, the perspective also attempts to explain the persistence of the unit over time and under changing environmental conditions. As Morton Kaplan informs us, systems analysis refers to "the study of a set of interrelated variables, as distinguished from the environment of the set, and of the ways in which this set is maintained under the impact of environmental disturbances."[6] Explanation of system stability may rely on various interrelated factors, including functional requisites and value consensus. While conceptually distinguishable from system persistence and equilibrium, "integration" frequently serves as an overarching or unifying theme, denoting "those characteristics of a unit system's structure which explain the maintenance of the system as a stable and distinct (i.e., cohesive) entity under a range of boundary conditions."[7] The perspective delineated here is exemplified in several contemporary frameworks, including that ambitious product of scientific synthesis called general systems theory. However, due perhaps to its abstract and elusive character, general systems theory has received only scant attention in political science. Professional interest has focused on other systemic approaches some of which, according to

Oran Young, "are ultimately derivatives of general systems theory in an analytic, if not an historical, sense":[8] structural functionalism, Easton's input-output model, and cybernetics and communications theory.

Deriving from anthropological sources, structural functional theory has been developed chiefly by Talcott Parsons and Marion Levy. Subsequently, the theory was adopted by political scientists, primarily (but not exclusively) for purposes of comparative analysis. The starting point and basic unit of analysis of structural functionalism is commonly a system or a set of interlocking systems. As its name indicates, the theory tries to explicate the operation of a system by means of certain basic "functional" and "structural" patterns—terms which, unfortunately, are not devoid of ambiguity. Some writers have tended to define "function" as any consequence or effect of a pattern of action; but, as critics have noted, this definition could lead to strange or spurious conclusions.[9] More careful partisans of the approach, therefore, have limited the term to effects relevant to or required for the operation and continued existence of the system. As Marion Levy points out, structural functional analysis involves a series of basic steps or procedures: determination of the unit of analysis and of the general limits of its variability; identification of functional requisites or of the conditions necessary for the unit's persistence; and finally some indication of the structural arrangements or patterns of action through which functions are performed.[10] Functionalists differ in their treatment of requisite conditions. Following Parsons' example, Robert Holt has identified four major requisites: pattern maintenance, related primarily to "maintenance of conformity to the prescriptions of the cultural system"; goal attainment, concerned largely with system survival; adaptation to environmental influences; and integration or the promotion of solidarity and cohesiveness among system elements. Other writers have produced more elaborate schemes; but the emphasis is commonly on system stability and integration.[11]

In contrast to structural functionalism, political input-output analysis is largely a homegrown product of our own discipline; but there are significant linkages between the two approaches. As in the functional model, the focus of input-output theory is on the "system" as the basic unit of analysis. According to David Easton, political life can be viewed as "a system of behavior operating within and responding to its social environment as it makes binding allocations of values." Opting against a reliance on concrete or physical criteria, Easton presents the political arena as an "analytic" structure operating within the overall membership system of society, and more particularly as "that system of interactions in any society through which binding or authoritative allocations are made and implemented."[12] Input-output analysis implies that the political community is embedded in an environment of diverse components, that it receives stimuli and challenges both from intra- and extrasocietal sources, and that its major task is to transform and convert this stream of inputs into authoritative outputs involving rewards and sanctions. Again akin to functionalism, the system focus of this model is coupled with a stress on system stability. Easton in any event has left little doubt about his preoccupation with systemic persistence—an aspect, to be sure, which need by no means be equated with immobility or stagnation. As he has pointed out, the basic objective of his framework is to uncover "the life processes of political systems—those fundamental functions without which no system could endure—together with the typical modes of response through which systems manage to sustain them. The analysis of these processes, and of the nature and conditions of the responses, I posit as a central problem of political theory."[13] A corollary of Easton's preoccupation with system persistence is his concern with stress avoidance or regulation. Severe stress or disturbance is said to occur whenever the system or its essential processes are pushed beyond their critical range of variability; one of the means of obviating disturbance consists in circular connections or "feedback" mechanisms through which output performance becomes available as information to the system for purposes of readjustment.

The notions of information flows and feedback mechanisms are equally crucial to another contemporary framework whose inspiration derives primarily from recent advances in electronics and computer designs: communications theory and cybernetics. Although unique in some respects, the framework can easily be viewed as an example of systemic theory.[14] According to Karl Deutsch, the central focus and starting point of cybernetics is the general concept of a self-controlling and self-modifying communications system or "learning net"; this concept, he explains, refers to "any system characterized by a relevant degree of organization, communication, and control regardless of the particular processes by which its messages are transmitted and its functions carried out."[15] As in Easton's model, the political system defined as a learning net operates through a series of input and output processes; but demands and allocations are conceptualized in terms of information flows whose complexity is enhanced by a variety of storage, coding, and steering devices. The main goal of such mechanisms is to promote the viability and persistence of the net—a goal which, again, is by no means identical with a freezing of existing patterns. Deviations from the viability objective are countered by elaborate feedback controls designed to readjust the system's actual to its expected performance and to overcome communications pathologies and distortions. A strong assumption in cybernetic theory is that the maintenance of information flows contributes not only to overall effectiveness, but also to the cohesion and integration of system elements. In the words of Deutsch, once we conceive of a political system as a network of communication channels and chains of command, "we can measure the 'integration' of individuals in a people by their ability to receive and transmit information on wide ranges of different topics with relatively little delay or loss of relevant detail."[16] This statement is reminiscent of Norbert Wiener's view that communications in society are "the cement which binds its fabric together."[17]

As can be seen, systemic approaches share a series of common accents and preferences which differentiate them from other theoretical postures; as a rule, leading exponents have been quite explicit about such accents. Talcott Parsons, for example, has persistently maintained that the functioning of social and political communities should be explained in systemic terms, rather than from an individual or group perspective. Reserving the concept of "political system" to value allocations on the level of whole societies, Easton has relegated internal subgroups to a secondary or "parapolitical" status; he has also criticized theoretical efforts proceeding from an actor focus as a partial if not parochial enterprise.[18] Similarly, systemic theorists have not been greatly attracted to questions of power and domestic conflict. In Deutsch's theory, power appears as but one of the currencies of politics, while conflict is explained largely in terms of information and "switchboard" pathologies.[19] A frequently voiced objection to systemic approaches concerns their presumed static character; in this general form, however, the stricture seems unwarranted. From his earliest writings, Parsons had been attracted to the concepts of equilibrium and homeostasis; but the terms were said to apply both to static, repetitive operations and to "orderly" patterns of development. In later years, he has paid increasing attention to processes of social "evolution" and "growth," processes defined largely in terms of a system's expanding faculties of adaptation and integration. Both Easton and Deutsch have attacked the narrow restrictions of equilibrium models; through feedback and other homeostatic devices, both have sought to incorporate adaptive change and growth into their theoretical frameworks. Nevertheless, apart from leaving the impulses of change somewhat opaque, evolution and growth are usually conceived as quasi-biological or teleological processes involving an enhanced capacity of survival; in any event, major cleavages and upheavals tend to be neglected.[20] In a synoptic study of empirical theories, Oran Young has assessed the strengths and weaknesses of systemic approaches; while prolific in discussions of system stability and moderate change, such approaches in his view are relatively mute on questions of power, goal selection, and radical transformation.[21]

Due to their particular focus, systemic models seem to be equally silent on questions of human motivation and personality. Is it nevertheless possible to discern some human features behind the imposing but abstract edifice? Fortunately, systemic theorists have provided many clues for such an enterprise. Easton, it is true, has disclaimed any implication of his theory for a conception of human behavior and motivation; but his empirical studies of political socialization are indicative of his main concerns.[22] Moreover, as Young has noted, Easton's model displays a significant tendency or bias. "Since the political system is a consciously analytic construct," he writes, "roles and patterns of roles are much more nearly the basic unit of analysis than individuals and groups of individuals. And even in the discussion of roles, the flow of analysis is directed toward the contribution of various role patterns to the persistence of the system, rather than toward the contribution of the system to the well-being of the role holders."[23] According to Morton Kaplan, each social or political system specifies for its members certain expected forms of behavior or roles; "thus John Jones has both nuclear and extended family relationships, a role in the business in which he is employed, a social and recreational role, and perhaps a religious role among many others." To insure stable behavior patterns, the participant of a system "must be motivated to act in ways consistent with the critical limits and the other actors must be motivated to induce him so to act."[24] The mechanisms of role compliance have been specified in considerable detail by Talcott Parsons. For purposes of systemic stability, he observes, individuals have to be inducted into the common culture and motivated to conform with expected behavior patterns. This task is accomplished largely through "internalization," a process through which "the norms or values (or role-expectation goals) defined in a culture come to be constitutive parts of the personality" of individuals. "Once socialized," he writes, "and making due allowance for elements of conflict and malintegration on both the personality and the social system levels, a person cannot act otherwise than in conformity with his internalized values."[25]

What we have discovered so far are some intriguing fragments or glimpses of human features; what seems needed at this point is an attempt to combine these fragments into a coherent and compelling human profile. Such an attempt has already been made. As it seems to me, many of the above arguments can be fitted, with some adjustments, into an image of man delineated with great care by Ralf Dahrendorf: the image of *homo sociologicus,* of man the role-player and compliant social actor. As Dahrendorf observes, most research and theoretical work in modern sociology proceeds implicitly or explicitly from the assumption that "man behaves in accordance with his roles," that man becomes relevant for analysis "only to the extent that he complies with all the expectations associated with his social positions. This abstraction," he adds, "the scientific unit of sociology, may be called *homo sociologicus.*"[26] According to Dahrendorf, there are two central sociological concepts which pinpoint the intersection between individual and society: "It is by positions and roles that the two conceptually distinguishable facts, the individual and society, are mediated; and it is in terms of these two concepts that we describe *homo sociologicus,* sociological man, the basic unit of sociological analysis." Of the two concepts, however, role in his view is by far the more crucial. Positions "merely identify places in fields of reference," while roles "tell us about how people in given positions relate to people in other positions in the same field." Basically, social roles "represent society's demands on the incumbents of social positions"; they are "bundles of expectations" whose violation entails a variety of sanctions and deprivations. Yet, before an individual can comply with these expectations, he must know them; thus, "like an actor, man as a social being must learn his roles, become familiar with their substance and the sanctions that enforce them." Role learning constitutes a "process of socialization by the internalizing of behavior patterns." The individual, Dahrendorf writes, "must somehow take into himself the prescriptions of society and make them the basis of his behavior; it is by this means that the individual and society are mediated and man is reborn as *homo sociologicus.*"[27]

There can be little doubt that Dahrendorf's image of sociological man pervades much of contemporary social science. Yet, the argument could be made that the profile is still somewhat vague, that—at least with reference to systemic approaches—some of its lines need to be sharpened. Above all, "role-playing" is a rather complex and generic concept, a concept which seems applicable to many human masks and images, above and beyond *homo sociologicus.* What distinguishes systemic approaches from other current theories is their treatment of man as a relatively docile ingredient of a larger unit, their emphasis on man as "role-taker" rather than "role-maker."[28] An argument along these lines has been advanced primarily by Dennis Wrong. Attentive to sociological convention, Wrong agrees that "the sociologist's point of departure is an established social structure," that his initial concern is "with those attributes of human nature which sustain consensus, conformity, and role behavior"; he even finds it acceptable to equate "major attention to psychological processes sustaining social conformity with the sociological perspective *per se*." However, in his view, some current approaches have excessively narrowed this perspective; in particular, "the tendency of structural functional sociologists to stress the primacy in society of consensus on values over conflicts of interest and to define society itself as a 'boundary-maintaining system' with built-in processes preserving its equilibrium, inclines them to reliance on a generalized view of man as a thoroughly oversocialized, conformist creature." As Wrong observes, all social theory is prompted by vital questions, especially by the "Hobbesian question" of how social order is at all possible. Confronted with the Hobbesian query, much of current theory has taken refuge not only in an "overintegrated" view of society, but also in an "oversocialized" model of man, a model which depicts human beings as dominated by internalized social norms and as "essentially motivated by the desire to achieve a positive image of self by winning acceptance or status in the eyes of others."[29] Wrong's assessment is supported by the argument of Hans Zetterberg that the quest for social approval comes close to qualifying as "the major motivational theorem in sociology"; against this background, the maximization of approval or of "favorable attitudes from others" could be viewed as "the counterpart in sociological theory to the maximization of profit in economic theory."[30]

II. Exchange Theories

While occupying a predominant position, systemic theories have not been unchallenged in contemporary political thought. Champions of alternative theoretical avenues are by no means in full agreement on premises or conclusions; but most tend to place greater weight on the initiative of participant actors or social groups than is customary in systemic approaches. To be sure, by itself a focus on the individual actor as primary unit of analysis is hardly sufficient for the development of a coherent "empirical theory," even under a liberal construction of this term.[31] To produce researchable propositions, the actor focus has to be modified and refined through the introduction of additional parameters and stipulations, especially the stipulation of human interaction in a social context. This emphasis on human interaction is one of the central features of current "exchange" theories or approaches, theories which have been developed primarily, but not exclusively, by politically concerned economists. In an address to the political science fraternity in 1967, William Mitchell announced good tidings for partisans of such views by presenting exchange models as "the shape of political theory to come" and by predicting an impending shift "from political sociology to political economy." As Mitchell explained, the starting point of the "new political economy" is a conception of politics as an exchange process not very different from economic exchange. This conception, he added, involves a focus on the choices and decisions of interacting individuals, groups, and organizations as they are engaged in the more or less rational pursuit of their subjective self-interests; such decisions, moreover, are assumed to be made under varying degrees of uncertainty concerning the goals of others, their strategies and the rules of the game.[32] While concentrating on the pursuit of subjective self-interest, however, exchange theory commonly does not anticipate cleavage and chaos as the result of this pursuit; rather, competitive interaction is viewed as the harbinger of progress leading to higher levels of happiness, social harmony, and integration. In this respect at least, the new political economy rejoins the perspective of systemic approaches. The peculiarity of exchange models, as Mitchell noted, resides not so much in their views on equilibrium and consensus, but in their method of explanation: instead of deriving from agreement on common values, integration is assumed to emerge from bargaining and limited competition.[33]

In its recent rise to prominence, the new political economy has animated a variety of conceptual formulations and substantive concerns; a relatively pure example of the approach can be found in the work of James Buchanan and Gordon Tullock, especially in *The Calculus of Consent*.[34] As Buchanan and Tullock observe, the adoption of a political exchange model is justified by the fact that economic and political interactions "represent co-operation on the part of two or more individuals," that "the market and the state are both devices through which cooperation is organized and made possible." In defending their choice, the two authors are also relatively careful in identifying competing approaches or counter-models. One of these counter-models is the "organic conception" of the state in which the political system has "an existence, a value pattern, and a motivation independent of those of the individual human beings claiming membership." Despite a certain limited usefulness, the organic view is rejected as "essentially opposed to the Western philosophical tradition" and as largely irrelevant to a theory of modern democracy. Although they refrain from doing so, the authors' argument could easily have been extended to some systemic approaches where persistence is postulated as a goal inherent in the collectivity.[35] The other major counter-model identified by Buchanan and Tullock places the spotlight of attention on domination, coercion, and conflict. "In quite similar fashion," they write, "we shall also reject any theory or conception of the collectivity which embodies exploitation of a ruled by a ruling class. This includes the Marxist vision, which incorporates the polity as one means through which the economically dominant group imposes its will on the downtrodden." As the authors make clear, their objection applies to coercion in every form "whether the ruling class is supposed to consist of Marxist owners of productive factors, the party aristocracy, or the like-minded majority." Equally proscribed are notions of class struggle and class-based motivation: "The point that has been largely overlooked is that it remains perfectly appropriate to assume that men are motivated by utility considerations while rejecting the economic determinism implicit in the whole Marxian stream of thought."[36]

Having rejected the notions of organic collectivity and of class dominance, Buchanan and Tullock are left with an individualistic premise. As they explain, their model is "methodologically individualistic" in the sense that, for purposes of analysis, it "begins with the acting or decision-making individual as he participates in the processes through which group choices are organized." In analogy to the economic theory of the market, the individual entering the political arena is expected to follow his self-interest in a more or less rational fashion; rationality, moreover, is assumed to apply not only to the choice of means but also to the selection of ends to the extent that the individual is able to rank alternative goods according to a consistent scale of preferences. To be sure, in political life rational behavior is handicapped by risk and uncertainty, especially in view of the absence of a "one-to-one correspondence between individual choice and final action." Nevertheless, according to Buchanan and Tullock, the significance of this handicap is greatly reduced once political choice is seen as a continuous process in which risk is evenly distributed among all participants. This aspect of reciprocity points to another central feature of the authors' model: their emphasis on harmony and mutual gain. Consensus, in fact, appears as the cornerstone of their political edifice. In agreement with versions of the social contract theory, all individuals are viewed as initially "free and equal"—or at least as equally free to participate in the adoption of basic political decision-rules. Similarly, changes or improvements in such decision-rules are predicated on the possibility of general acceptance—an arrangement loosely akin to the economist's rule of "Pareto-optimality." These and related stipulations support the authors' conclusion that, instead of engendering cleavage and strife, the political market is primarily a cooperative and integrative enterprise. Arguing against the hypothesis of exploitation, Buchanan and Tullock assert that the perspective of the new political economy "does not require that one individual increase his own utility at the expense of other individuals. This approach incorporates political activity as a particular form of *exchange*; and, as in the market relation, mutual gains to all parties are ideally expected to result from the collective relation." In the terminology of modern game theory, the political process thus appears largely as a "positive-sum" game, rather than a "zero-sum" contest in which the winnings of one party are the losses of the opponent.[37]

The development of exchange theory has not been the exclusive domain of political economists; some contributions have also been made by sociologists, notably by George Homans and Peter Blau. Like political economists, Homans starts from an individualist, rather than a systemic perspective. As he points out in *Social Behavior: Its Elementary Forms*, his concern is with the explanation of the actual, rather than the expected, social behavior of individuals in direct contact or interaction with one another; more specifically, social interaction is viewed as "an exchange of activity, tangible or intangible, and more or less rewarding or costly, between at least two persons." For purposes of explanation, Homans finds it possible to rely on "two bodies of general propositions already in existence: behavioral psychology and elementary economics"; both sets of propositions, he writes, "envisage human behavior as a function of its pay-off: in amount and kind it depends on the amount and kind of reward and punishment it fetches."[38] To be sure, both theories need extrapolation when applied to social interaction. This need, however, does not jeopardize a basic analogy. Thus, the economic law of supply can be translated into the sociological proposition that "the more valuable the reward gotten by an activity, the more often a man will emit it"; likewise, the law of demand is equivalent to the statement that "the higher the cost incurred by an activity, the less often a man will emit it." As in the case of Buchanan and Tullock, social exchange for Homans is primarily a cooperative and integrative experience. Defining psychic "profit" as reward less cost, he argues that "no exchange continues unless both parties are making a profit." Also, the stability of social interaction is said to depend on the fairness of its terms or the just distribution of rewards and costs between persons, an arrangement threatened by a one-sided power monopoly.[39] While not denying their importance in social life, Homans views conflict and coercion as basically inimical to exchange since trading of punishments, "when at all damaging, puts an end to social behavior."[40]

Drawing to some extent on Homans' propositions, Peter Blau has constructed an ambitious model of exchange in social life. In Blau's terminology, social exchange "refers to voluntary actions of individuals that are motivated by the returns they are expected to bring and typically do in fact bring from others." Like Homans, he explores both the similarities and the differences between economic exchange and social interaction; the major distinction in his view resides in the unspecified character of social obligations. One valuable aspect of Blau's argument consists in his careful demarcation of the exchange model from alternative perspectives and concerns. As he points out, social exchange properly speaking can and should be differentiated from a variety of interactions, especially from "two limiting cases." In one instance, an individual may give away money because his conscience demands that he help support the underprivileged without expectation of gratitude. While this situation "could be conceptualized as an exchange of his money for the internal approval of his superego," Blau considers it "preferable to exclude conformity with internalized norms from the purview of the concept of social exchange." In the other case, an individual may surrender money in a holdup at gun point; despite the apparent trading of money for life, the author argues again in favor of excluding "the result of physical coercion from the range of social conduct encompassed by the term 'exchange.'" Above and beyond physical violence or its threat, differences in power are recognized as having a pervasive impact on exchange processes, "since established power enables an individual to compel others to provide services without offering a fair return." Generally speaking, Blau's model supports a distinction between coercive power founded "on the deterrent effect of negative sanctions" and "influence based on rewards, as that characteristic of exchange transactions."[41]

Apart from the contributions of political economists and sociologists, some affinities with exchange models can be detected in versions of interest-group theory. According to Buchanan and Tullock, the economic "conception of democratic process has much in common with that accepted by the school of political science which follows Arthur Bentley in trying to explain collective decision-making in terms of the interplay of group interests." In their opinion, a group calculus could be substituted for an individual calculus "without significantly affecting the results."[42] An important parallel between exchange theory and such a group calculus consists in the conception of pressure politics as an integrative process resulting in harmony and mutual adjustment; instead of reflecting a conflict between rulers and ruled, the political system in this view appears as a conglomeration of specialized interests whose strength corresponds roughly to group size. As is well-known, exchange in this sense was a central feature of Bentley's theory, which treated government "as the adjustment or balance of interests"; a similar emphasis on balance and adjustment is characteristic of many neo-Bentleyan arguments.[43] Some of the premises of group theory have also been injected into community power studies and empirical analyses of democracy. Thus, a prominent student of community power pictured American society as "fractured into a congeries of hundreds of small special interest groups, with incompletely overlapping membership, widely differing power bases and a multitude of techniques for exercising influence on decisions salient to them."[44] The limits or limitations of this vision have not gone unnoticed. In the words of Elmer Schattschneider, "the vice of the groupist theory is that it conceals the most significant aspects of the system. The flaw in the pluralist heaven is that the heavenly chorus sings with a strong upper-class accent." As he added, the overwhelming majority of the people "cannot get into the pressure game."[45]

The human features underlying the above arguments and models are not very hard to discern. Underneath its formulas and equations, exchange theory presents to us a relatively familiar human profile: the profile of *homo economicus,* of man the gain seeker and maximizer of utilities. To be sure, portions of this profile have been redrawn and its sharp contours tempered in most contemporary writings. As Buchanan and Tullock observe, even orthodox economic theory does not depend for its validity on the assumption of an individual propelled by a single-minded ambition for private gain. By the same token, the calculus of political exchange does not rely for its logical coherence "upon any narrowly hedonistic or self-interest motivation of individuals"; rather, the basic requisites of this calculus are satisfied as long as different individuals are assumed to pursue different goals or interests in both their private and their social actions.[46] Similar sentiments are expressed in Anthony Downs' *An Economic Theory of Democracy.* In his view, the behavioral premises of traditional economics are not tailored to "a man whose thought processes consist exclusively of logical propositions, or a man without prejudices, or a man whose emotions are inoperative"; what is postulated in market theory is simply an individual "who moves toward his goals in a way which, to the best of his knowledge, uses the least possible input of scarce resources per unit of valued output." As Downs adds, the behavioral dimension of his own model does not claim to embrace the whole personality of an individual, the "rich diversity of ends served by each of his acts" or the "complexity of his motives." Moreover, in view of ineradicable uncertainties about the future, the individual of his model is bound to display a less "calculating-machine-brained character" than the personality construct of traditional economic theory.[47]

Despite initial qualifications or disclaimers, however, the characteristic features of *homo economicus* still emerge vividly in contemporary political economy. Downs' model carefully replicates the "two major steps" of orthodox economic analysis: discovery of a decision-maker's ends, and explanation of the most reasonable means of attaining these ends. With regard to the first step, Downs by and large accepts the self-interest axiom of economic theory; only the content or direction of self-interest is modified. While in market relations the individual participant is assumed to maximize material benefits, the actor in the political arena is expected to calculate his advantages in the selection of governments in the same manner as governments and political parties seek to formulate policies which will maximize political support. The most rational means of reaching these goals, according to Downs, are actions which are efficient in the sense of "maximizing output for a given input, or minimizing input for a given output." More particularly, rational behavior in both the economic and the political arena refers to an individual's ability to arrange his preferences in a transitive rank order and to choose consistently the most advantageous alternatives. Through a more protracted line of reasoning Buchanan and Tullock reach almost identical results. The mere assumption of differing utility functions, they concede, does not permit the development of fully operational and testable hypotheses. In order to increase the explanatory power of the exchange model, additional restrictions have to be placed on individual utility functions, restrictions which are "precisely analogous to those introduced in economic theory." Specifically, the model has to incorporate the working hypotheses "that the average individual is able to rank or to order all alternative combinations of goods and services that may be placed before him and that this ranking is transitive"; behavior is said to be rational "when the individual chooses 'more' rather than 'less' and when he is consistent in his choices."[48] As the authors make clear, the behavioral dimension of exchange theory—especially the acceptance of the self-interest axiom—can be viewed as an application or adaptation of utilitarian principles.[49]

More significant alterations in the discussed personality type have been introduced by sociological theorists. George Homans, for example, combines the perspectives of economics and behavioral psychology in an explicit attempt to elucidate elementary social behavior and to "rehabilitate the 'economic man.'" As in the case of his economic colleagues, Homans' rehabilitation effort is at the same time a defense against simplifications and misrepresentations. The trouble with traditional economic man, he writes, "was not that he was economic, that he used his resources to some advantage, but that he was antisocial and materialistic, interested only in money and material goods and ready to sacrifice even his old mother to get them." What was wrong with this individual in other words were his goals and ambitions, since "he was only allowed a limited range of values." By contrast, "the new economic man is not so limited. He may have any values whatever, from altruism to hedonism, but so long as he does not utterly squander his resources in achieving these values his behavior is still economic."[50] In rehabilitating economic man, Homans manages not only to broaden his horizons but also to shift some accents of his profile. While political economists tend to limit their arguments to the axiomatic level, Homans tries to uncover the psychological underpinnings of human behavior. Relying on the findings of experimental psychology and of the "operant conditioning" of animals, he explores the extent to which exchange of human activities depends on rewards and deprivations conceived as positive and negative "reinforcements." A corollary of his greater reliance on psychological factors is his relative de-emphasis of long-range calculation and rationality; in the main, this de-emphasis derives from his concern with explanation rather than exhortation. "For the purposes of explaining how men have indeed behaved," he asserts, "it is seldom enough to ask whether or not they were rational. The relevant question is what determined their behavior."[51] The same concern with the explanation of actual conduct accounts also for Homans' differentiation of economic man from the dimension of social roles and the enactment of expected behavior patterns.[52]

III. Conflict Theories

Among contemporary theoretical preoccupations in political science, power and political conflict occupy a relatively subordinate if not obscure position. This obscurity is puzzling both in view of the history of social science and of the concrete lessons of experience. At least since the dawn of the modern age, the attention of leading social theorists has been absorbed by the dilemmas of power. The "Hobbesian question" of how society is at all possible was posed against the stark background of conflict and destruction.[53] The political experiences of our own age would seem to lend support to this formulation of the question. Yet, during recent decades, social scientists have tended to elude the Hobbesian query and to concentrate almost exclusively on the quasi-organic functioning of society or the rational behavior of its participants. To be sure, despite this temporary shift in focus, the more disquieting features of political life have not gone unnoticed. As Robert Dahl observed some time ago, because of the absence of complete homogeneity "an important element of coercion" is liable to exist in human society; "government by unanimity" seems unattainable. More recently, there has been a growing stress on the importance of such elements and on the need to reincorporate them in the study of politics. Among others, Francis Wormuth has exhorted political science to return "to its proper theme, the study of power." As he added: "The dangers and the promises of the future are the dangers and the promises of power."[54]

Statements to a similar effect could be multiplied without difficulty; in fact, the literature of political science abounds with references to the themes of power, domination, and conflict. Nevertheless, the use of this vocabulary alone is insufficient evidence of a coherent theoretical framework. By and large, the development of contemporary conflict theory has been the work of sociologists, aided by some political scientists conversant with the theory of games.[55] In the terminology of game theory, political conflict can be formulated as a "zero-sum" contest, in contrast to cooperative encounters involving mutual gain; William Riker's study of political coalitions is built solidly on this theoretical basis. In his study, Riker concentrates on the "authoritative allocation of values" by decision-makers, focusing on groups as primary units of analysis; as he explains, conscious decision-making in groups is essentially "a process of forming coalitions." For the examination of this process, Riker adopts the parameters of game theory, especially two basic assumptions. The first of these is the postulate of "rationality." In his formulation, rational behavior in the political arena consists in the effort to maximize power or, more precisely, in the adoption of a "winning" strategy. Although such conduct may not be characteristic of all individuals, those "institutions that work by coalitions" select and reward behavior which is rational in the specified sense. The second major assumption is the zero-sum axiom—the requirement that the gains of the winners equal the losses of their opponents. Riker readily admits that political life is not always a condition of pure and unrelieved conflict and that bargaining in particular "involves some sort of gain for both parties." However, although in the long run all participants stand to gain from society and civilization, there are occasions when winning is the paramount objective. In contrast to money, which can be divided and distributed among the contestants, victory in the political arena is frequently "an indivisible unit." Thus, "by emphasis on winning what is often an indivisible prize in these matters, as in games, the common imagination abstracts pure conflict for which the zero-sum model is entirely appropriate."[56]

While impressive in its mathematical elegance, Riker's study is circumscribed by its formal axioms and its focus on coalition formation. The broader connotations of social conflict have been elaborated by contemporary sociologists, most notably by Ralf Dahrendorf. The contribution of sociologists in this area is not surprising in view of the heritage of their discipline; Dahrendorf is quick to acknowledge his debt to this tradition. "From Marx and Comte to Simmel and Sorel," he writes, "social conflict, especially revolution, was one of the central themes in social research."[57] It may be instructive to note some parallels between the arguments of the game theorist and the sociologist. Like Riker, Dahrendorf concentrates on social groupings or "structural elements" of society as primary targets of his analysis;[58] these groupings, in his case, are the product of the differential distribution of power and authority, of the fact that all societies are divided into positions of dominance and subordination. Also like Riker, Dahrendorf stresses the "zero-sum" element implicit in the power relationships of the political arena. While income and money can be divided and distributed throughout society in a continuum ranging from the lowest to the highest rank, power remains recalcitrant to complete diffraction. "Wealth is not and cannot be conceived as a zero-sum concept," he asserts. "With respect to authority, however, a clear line can at least in theory be drawn between those who participate in its exercise in given associations and those who are subject to the authoritative commands of others."[59]

True to the tenor of his approach, Dahrendorf has carried the battle to opposing theoretical frameworks or perspectives; structural functionalism has been the most frequent target of his criticism. In a now famous essay, he compared the structural functional scheme to the literature of utopias, basing his analogy on such common utopian features as universal value consensus, absence of conflict and disruptive processes, and isolation in time and space. Like utopias, he noted, structural functionalism was disengaged from society, representing instead a "superstructure of concepts that do not describe, propositions that do not explain, and models from which nothing follows." The assumption of shared values offered little help for research, since the thesis "that societies are held together by some kind of value consensus" constitutes "either a definition of societies or a statement clearly contradicted by empirical evidence." Above all, the thesis was detrimental to the explanation of structurally generated conflicts: "By no feat of the imagination, not even by the residual category of 'dysfunction,' can the integrated and equilibrated social system be made to produce serious and patterned conflicts in its structure." While not intrinsically static, the structural functional model reduced social change to the regular occurrence of homeostatic processes which, "far from disturbing the tranquility of the village pond, in fact *are* the village pond."[60] More recently Dahrendorf has extended his criticism to other types of systemic theories, including cybernetics and Easton's input-output model. While differing in their formulations, he observes, all these theories tend to minimize constraint and to stress integration, continuity, and adaptation; disturbances or conflicts are either ruled out as extraneous to this type of analysis or introduced as unexplained accidents. Typically in these models, "the system is regarded as persisting through time by virtue of the equilibrium created either by its internal cycles of power and support, or by the flow of communications, or by the interchange between subsystems as mediated by the currency of power."[61]

Systemic theories have not been the only targets of Dahrendorf's critical acumen; some indication of the distinction between exchange and conflict models can be gleaned from his comments on "market rationality" and its implications for social organization. From a market-rational perspective, he writes, the market appears as "a place of exchange and competition, where all comers do their best to improve their own lot. The starting point of any market-rational attitude is the assumption that a smoothly functioning market is in fact to the greatest advantage of the greatest number." The beneficial operation of the market is predicated on rules of the game or formal procedures, rather than substantive norms; as Dahrendorf tries to show, however, there are at least two grave difficulties inherent in this conception. First of all, the market does not operate in a vacuum; in all social fields "there are social structures that undermine the effectiveness of the rules of the game, arrangements by which certain players are in fact distinguished from others by being put at an advantage or a disadvantage." Thus, rules of the game require a compensating device; specifically, market-rational politics presupposes substantive norms and decisions, "unless it is to remain an ideology of systematic privilege for those who are already in a position to participate." The second difficulty resides in the hazy borderline between procedures and substantive norms and in the tendency of rules to degenerate into discriminatory devices. Both difficulties, according to Dahrendorf, derive from the same source or origin. "Plainly," he writes, "there is some force that persistently interferes with the pure realization of market-rational principles, something that makes it impossible to play the market-rational game according to purely formal rules. This force can be identified: it is power, and the social consequences of power." Because of power, because of the division of rulers and ruled, "there are always inequalities of participation in the regulated game of the political process, and there are always people interested in translating the rules of the game into substantive norms that create or perpetuate privilege."[62]

Against this background, the rudiments of Dahrendorf's own approach can now briefly be sketched. This approach is formulated as a counter-model to prevailing integration or consensus schemes. While the latter rely on the assumption of stability, integration, value consensus, and functional coordination of elements, conflict theory is based on the ubiquity of social change and conflict, the "dysfunctionality" of all the elements of social structure, and the constraining character of social unity. The element of constraint is particularly significant because of its dynamic implications. "Power," writes Dahrendorf, "always implies non-power and therefore resistance. The dialectic of power and resistance is the motive force of history." This means that every political organization exhibits a differential and in fact dichotomous distribution of power and authority; in Max Weber's terminology, the political community is an "imperatively coordinated association." The dichotomous distribution of power in society gives rise to at least two opposing social groups: the groups of the powerful and the powerless, the carriers of "positive" and "negative dominance roles." From this starting point, conflict theory proceeds to the exploration of group formation and group conflict. Initially, the carriers of positive and negative dominance roles constitute merely two structurally defined quasi-groups with opposite "latent interests." In certain situations, however, the bearers of these roles organize themselves into groups properly speaking with "manifest interests"; among the factors which promote or obstruct this transition are technical, social, and political conditions of organization. Once organized, interest groups generated in this manner engage in conflict over the preservation or change of the *status quo*, with the form and intensity of the conflict being determined by empirically variable circumstances. Subject to variations in speed and extent, the conflict among interest groups produces changes in the structure of social positions, through changes in dominance relations.[63]

As in previous instances, the question which I want to raise now concerns the behavioral implications of the discussed perspective. What human features can we discern in the stipulations of struggle and constraint? Despite the usual need of extrapolation, the profile presented to us in this theory is no stranger to political scientists: it is the image of *homo politicus*, of man the power seeker and maximizer of self-determination. While seemingly simple and straightforward, this image is by no means one-dimensional. Of the epithets which I have selected, the latter referring to self-determination is probably the more significant. As has frequently been observed, power is a somewhat elusive possession which is rarely sought for the sake of its own pleasure; but this objection does not touch the central issue. The image of political man reminds us that politics is not simply or not only a matter of convention or rationality, but a matter of will and action. Yet, though all human beings are endowed with some will power, not all are equally capable of implementing their wills and thus determining the courses of their lives. In all known political communities, at least, some layers have had an advantage over others in shaping both their own lives and the direction of society; in other words, social positions granting this kind of autonomy have traditionally been scarce. From this scarcity arises a struggle of wills, a struggle which is primarily a contest over the extent and direction of self-determination and self-realization.

While he is reluctant to resort to behavioral arguments, Dahrendorf's analysis provides at least some glimpses of political man. As a sociologist, Dahrendorf tends to explain social conflict primarily in terms of structurally defined social positions and corresponding role expectations; the major conflict groups in his theory are the carriers of positive and negative dominance roles. Yet, his concept of roles points beyond the strictly structural domain. As he emphasizes, social roles are a constraining force on individuals due to the availability of sanctions attached to role expectations. Since sanctions, however, are decreed by ruling groups and since conflict theory postulates imperfect compliance, Dahrendorf's role-player would seem to acquire some of the troubled features of *homo politicus*.[64] Despite the limiting parameter of "rationality," traces of these features can also be found in Riker's model; the prime ambition of political man in this model is to win over others. "Politically rational man," Riker comments, "is the man who would rather win than lose, regardless of the particular stakes." This formulation, he adds, is quite consonant with definitions of power prevalent in social science: "The man who wants to win also wants to make other people do things they would not otherwise do, he wants to exploit each situation to his advantage, and he wants to succeed in a given situation."[65] The darker, nonrational forces operative in this quest have not escaped the attention of political scientists. In a study contrasting scientific and political man, Hans Morgenthau asserted that political conflict cannot be dissolved through rational adjustment or scientific formulas. "The failure of the dogmatic scientism of our age to explain the social and, more particularly, the political problems of this age and to give guidance for successful action," he wrote, "calls for a re-examination of these problems in the light of prerationalist Western tradition. This re-examination must start with the assumption that power politics, rooted in the lust for power which is common to all men, is for this reason inseparable from social life itself."[66]

Morgenthau's statement alluded to motivational constants, to a psychological infrastructure of political conflict; concern with this infrastructure has been shared by many social scientists. In fact, political man on this level shades over into and blends with another image or profile of social science, the image of "psychological man." This man—fashioned largely from the building blocks of Freudian analysis—remains torn between the dictates of society and his antisocial impulses; in the words of Philip Rieff, he has "withdrawn into a world always at war, where the ego is an armed force capable of achieving armistices but not peace."[67] From his original habitat, the psychological model of man has invaded and permeated other disciplines. As Max Marc has argued, the model looms large in current social theory and "underlies much of contemporary political science." In his portrayal, the Freudian image embraces primarily the following tenets: that man is driven by instincts, while society and civilization are possible only at the price of instinctual frustration; that frustration in man's instinctual life leads to displacement or is translated into aggression; that society is held together through constraint and through the bonds between leader and led; that, since the establishment of society involves instinctual frustration, "all history is made up of repression and rebellion."[68] As Marc has also noted, however, an excessive emphasis on psychoanalysis is bound to obfuscate political reality. Where politics is seen as an illness to be cured, knowledge and psychiatric insight are likely to replace social conflict.

The convergence of psychological and political man is exemplified nowhere better than in the writings of Harold Lasswell. Integrating Eduard Spranger's notion of the power seeker with Freudian personality theory, Lasswell in *Psychopathology and Politics* sketched a developmental physiognomy of *homo politicus*. The core of his conception was the stipulation that political man is propelled by private motives which he displaces onto public objects and rationalizes in terms of public interest.[69] More detailed features of this physiognomy were presented in *Power and Personality*. As Lasswell endeavored to show in this study, the basic idea underlying the notion of political man was "that some personalities are power seekers, searching out the power institutions of the society into which they are born and devoting themselves to the capture and use of government"; moreover, the political individual had to be grasped as a "developmental type who passes through a distinctive career line in which the power opportunities of each situation are selected in preference to other opportunities." The driving motive of the power seeker was identified as an intense craving for deference which remains unsatisfied in the private sphere. Political man, in other words, was said to pursue power as a means of compensating for psychological deprivations, such as lack of respect and affection, suffered during childhood. This quest was not necessarily conscious or deliberate; but yearning had to be accompanied by at least a minimum degree of skill and effectiveness. The human profile which thus emerged was that of an individual who accentuates power, demands influence for himself or those with whom he identifies, possesses and inspires confidence in his capabilities, and acquires at least a minimum proficiency in the skills of power.[70]

The preceding journey through our discipline leaves us in a discomforting condition. We started from an examination of empirical or scientific political theory, and we soon discovered that there is a variety of such theories or frameworks in contemporary political science. Investigating these theories and their human dimensions, we found again that our discipline is populated not by one, but a diversity of human images and models of man. One after the other, we saw *homo sociologicus, homo economicus,* and *homo politicus* enter the limelight of our profession and deliver their prepared monologues. What are we to make of these stylized performers, of these familiar yet elusive characters whom Dahrendorf calls the "glass men of social science"? As it seems, we have entered a difficult labyrinth, a complex cabinet of mirrors whose oddly bent surfaces confront us with a procession of *doppelgänger.* How can these divergent images be reconciled with each other? And more important: what is our relationship to them? Can we still recognize ourselves in the mirrors of contemporary science?

Clearly, the divergence of images is a manifestation of the identity crisis of modern man, a result of his alienation from the world and his products. Against this background the models of empirical theory reveal themselves as the projections and reflections of man in an estranged universe.[71] While the symptoms of the crisis are relatively evident, however, the remedy is not. How can man's alienation be overcome and his sense of identity restored? At least two sweeping solutions have been suggested to this query; both, one might say, consist in the destruction of the mirror relationship. According to one argument, the dilemma itself is illusory: we are the glass men of science. In a strictly logical sense, we are told, there is no reality, at least no intelligible reality outside the scientist's mirrors. Therefore, what can be known or said about human beings is portrayed and explained in these mirrors, an explanation which is potentially complete. This ambition of completeness seems to be the scientist's peculiar temptation; most of the approaches discussed in these pages claim or aspire to be "general theories" of society and human behavior.[72] However, at least if generality is meant to suggest comprehensive coverage, the claim is demonstrably spurious. Ever since social disciplines have decided to emulate the sciences of nature, man's practical strivings have been slipping from their grasp. The dichotomy of facts and values—a distinction which "empirical" political theory is bound to support—imposes an irremediable restriction on the scientist's legitimate range of explanation; for the same reason, his models cannot hope to absorb the man of common sense experience. Where this limitation is ignored, social science quickly deteriorates into ideology, a doctrine in which prescription masquerades as analysis and empirical propositions assume normative control over human behavior.[73]

The other solution acknowledges the dilemma of alienation but puts the blame on the scientist's doorsteps. As we are told by enthusiasts—some of them members of our profession—the identity crisis of modern man was precipitated by scientific mirrors and will be cured with their demolition. In this view, the glass men of social analysis are simply arbitrary disfigurements; their removal, we are assured, will quickly restore man's pristine integrity. There is little point here in embellishing the artifacts of scientific imagination; their blemishes and incongruities have been noted even by their friends. Yet on closer inspection, some of these defects may turn out to be virtues. His artificiality, for example, has not prevented *homo economicus* from strengthening the explanatory arsenal of economic theory; a similar intellectual service may be performed by his companions. Viewed in this manner, the glass men of science are not merely distortions, but *doppelgänger* whose stylized profiles reveal and magnify some of the traits of our complex physiognomy. Little would be gained in this case from the destruction of mirror images. Although an urgent task, the restoration of man's identity can hardly be accomplished through amputation and truncation; instead of promoting human wholeness, such a method can only result in the forced poses of a petty dogmatism.

If we reject amputation, we will somehow have to live with our stylized artifacts; in the absence of compulsion, the acquisition of human wholeness can only be the work of dialogue and patient interrogation. One phase of this dialogue is of an intramural character, involving as participants the glass men of empirical theory. Probably not all these artifacts possess equal stature and explanatory capacity. It can plausibly be argued, I think, that conflict theory has special significance for some crucial areas of our discipline; *homo politicus* seems to speak with particular cogency to an age of upheaval and rapid transformation.[74] However, I want to forego invidious comparisons at this point and concentrate on the prospect of amicable relationships. One way of conceptualizing these relationships is through reliance on Freudian imagery. In this imagery—passingly invoked by both Wrong and Dahrendorf—sociological man appears as the representative of man's conscience or "superego," while economic and political man are expressions of his "ego" and "id" components. Advancing beyond the level of suggestive metaphors, Mancur Olson has reflected on the interrelationship of scientific models, especially models of sociological and economic provenance; as he explains, sociology is primarily concerned with "the formation and transmission of wants and beliefs of all kinds," while economics explores the means through which people strive to obtain their goals most efficiently. The diversity of available models, he adds, is bound to broaden and enrich our discipline; since different perspectives imply divergent strategies and conclusions, we should hope not only "for a great deal of disciplinary overlap" and communication, but for a similar confrontation inside the domain of political science.[75]

The dialogue to which I am referring, however, cannot be restricted to the glass men of science; in this intramural setting, their discourse would be empty and pointless. If they are to be more than crisis symptoms, our artifacts have to face not only each other, but also their moral counterpart, the man without mirrors. This man—integral and free despite the testimony of his detractors—has some of the traits of the "tenth character" described by Robert Musil, a character marked by "the passive fantasy of unfilled spaces."[76] Although relatively silent and elusive, this individual is yet the most influential partner in our dialogue; in fact, our glass men have to remain poised in his direction, unless they are to degenerate into the phantoms of closed societies and a closed universe. Thus, the models of empirical theory are neither self-sufficient nor eternal; their profiles resemble the rough contours of a statue still in the making. Underneath their stylized masks and awkwardly frozen gestures there are glimpses of an unfinished man—an individual embarked on a fantastic adventure, the adventure of reassembling a broken creation.

3. Social Role and "Human Nature": Plessner's Philosophical Anthropology

THE STORY OF SOCIAL and psychological inquiry during the past two centuries constitutes a striking mélange of success and frustration. The application of empirical techniques to the human and social sciences has engendered an enormous amount of tested or testable propositions regarding human behavior in diverse social and cultural contexts. Yet, the accumulation of behavioral data is not directly synonymous with a growth in comprehension. Scientific specialization has tended to compartmentalize knowledge and to fracture man into a series of sharply delineated but unrelated facets; even where broad explanatory formulas are proposed, such schemes hardly disclose a coherent and recognizable human face. While prolific in generating detailed information about man, behavioral analysis is mute on the sense of being human. The disparity between methodology and purpose has not gone unnoticed; in recent years, discontent with research technology and methodological predominance has encouraged the resurgence of a "humanist" perspective in all social and behavioral disciplines. To be sure, the task of a humanism in our time cannot simply be to resurrect a compact and apodictic model of "human nature"—divorced from empirical findings and concrete experience. The proliferation of information suggests a more modest aim: to explore and delineate patiently the elusive contours of man in the midst of cultural diversity. For many decades this aim has been the motivating incentive of "philosophical anthropology," a branch of inquiry cultivated in Europe since the early part of this century. Not long ago, Helmuth Plessner—a founder and leading representative of this type of investigation—celebrated his eightieth birthday. The present chapter is meant as a tribute to his work.[1]

The intent of the following pages, however, is not solely commemorative or retrospective. Apart from attempting to portray some of Plessner's central teachings, the chapter tries to derive lessons from his writings for contemporary social and political thought. For this purpose, an effort is made to relate his arguments to prominent conceptions of man's role in society and to the political implications of such views. Thus, Plessner's notion of man's instinctual deficiency will be compared to a position according to which this deficiency can be overcome only by the resolute institutionalization of cultural patterns and by the standardization of role expectations; human frailty, from this vantage point, urgently needs to be compensated through social stability. An opposing outlook—endorsed by segments of the so-called "counter-culture"—pictures man as basically a fugitive from the constraints of roles and institutional settings; established cultural patterns are viewed as inimical and even antithetical to authentic human life and man's search for self-fulfillment. The intended comparison entails a three-part outline: a first portion dealing primarily with Plessner's writings; a second part devoted to an examination of institutionalism and role conformity; and a last section reviewing the arguments counseling a retreat from roles and a return to privacy or at least to a socially unstructured mode of life.

I

As a broad-gauged exploration of man, philosophical anthropology owes its inspiration not only to the development of empirical science but also to the rise of phenomenology and interpretative philosophy.[2] To a significant extent, its impulses can be traced to Husserl's injunction to turn to "the things themselves," to take a fresh look at the world unencumbered by time-honored explanations. In application to the study of man, Husserl's stress on intentionality implied a rejection or at least radical modification of traditional mind-body dichotomies, especially of the Cartesian bifurcation of matter and thinking substance. In this sense, the two founders of philosophical anthropology—Max Scheler and Helmuth Plessner—were both equally indebted to the phenomenological perspective. Yet, in Scheler's case, the departure from past dualisms was at best precarious; moreover, the relationship between empiricism and interpretation remained haphazard and obscure. While accepting the findings of biology regarding man's unspecialized instinctual apparatus, Scheler viewed man's "openness" chiefly as an indication of his superior destiny. Emulating Husserl's (temporary) attachment to idealism, he located man's distinctive character in his ability to transcend his biological and ecological situation in the direction of a non-biological and even anti-biological realm of "spirit." Underneath the vocabulary of phenomenology, the Cartesian model thus re-emerged in the form of a hierarchical structure composed of distinct layers of reality.[3]

Plessner, by comparison, has always been much more resolute in his endeavor to overcome the Cartesian legacy—without lapsing into a one-dimensional scheme of either a materialistic or spiritualistic variety. While acknowledging the immense complexity of human experience, his writings seek to give a coherent account of man and his place in the world. Rather than recapitulating traditional teachings of man as a composite creature—with spiritual faculties superimposed on animal drives or reason grafted on passions—Plessner delineates the human condition as characterized by a peculiar nexus of nature and freedom, instinct and reflection. While biologically embedded in organic nature man, in his view, is able to observe and interpret his own situation—an interpretation which, in turn, becomes an integral part of his environment. An important access route to man's peculiar status is provided by phenomenological inspection: the patient scrutiny of modes of experience and patterns of reality. As Plessner tries to show, the nexus of instinct and reflection can be conceived as a distinct structure or mode of existence, as differentiated from other nonhuman modes of life. In reference to man, however, structure cannot simply mean an invariant dictate of nature, divorced from human participation; rather, man's continuing self-exegesis has to be seen as a constituent feature of his structural condition.[4]

Phenomenological inquiry, as practiced by Plessner, has by no means the status of a doctrinaire panacea; his perspective cannot simply be equated with a cultural hermeneutics devoted to the decoding of symbolic meaning. From the beginning his work reveals a close preoccupation with empirical science, especially with the findings of biological and ecological research regarding developmental divergences between man and animal and regarding their different relationship to the environment.[5] Jakob von Uexküll's demonstration of the closed ecological milieu of animals and of the fixed linkage between instincts and stimuli forms as much part of Plessner's outlook as Adolf Portmann's documentation of man's premature birth and initial developmental retardation. To be sure, human existence in his perspective is not simply a function of physical endowments; but the acknowledged danger of reductionism offers no warrant for an antibiological bias. As he insists, man has to be seen as an embodied creature—with the dual connotation that he both experiences the world through his bodily organs and that he "has" a body in the sense of being able to observe and reflect on his physical condition. Man, from this vantage point, thus appears simultaneously as the product and the questioning counterpart of nature. Although enmeshed in a physical habitat, he is not simply a finished or preordained segment of the natural order; nor is he a rootless adventurer or an arbitrary design.[6] Marked by a "natural artificiality" man, according to Plessner, is a creature lodged peculiarly at the crossroads of nature and history, of physical adaptation and the search for meaning.

The general thrust of this perspective was evident from his earliest writings. His dissertation at Heidelberg, submitted in 1917, explored the problem of an unconditional origin or starting point of knowledge and philosophical insight. As Plessner noted, the history of philosophy was replete with postulates of an absolute beginning or foundation of thought; since Descartes this focal concern had been radicalized, with philosophers opting either for a primeval material mechanism or for a constitutive consciousness as basic starting points—and sometimes for a combination of the two vistas. A follow-up study of 1918 abandoned historical exposition for critical scrutiny, challenging the adequacy of such unconditional premises for a proper understanding of man and his world.[7] In a preliminary fashion, outlines of Plessner's own conception emerged in his treatise on *The Unity of the Senses*, published in 1923. The study constituted a frontal attack on the Cartesian mind-body dualism, with its assumption of two irreducible principles underlying reality. How was it possible, the book queried, for objects to have an impact on human awareness and for awareness to transform things? The question, Plessner observed, was insoluble so long as man's sensory organs were seen purely as passive instruments transmitting external stimuli to a self-contained consciousness. Kant, it is true, had advanced the issue by arguing that human faculties shared in the construction of reality; but his concern had been limited to abstract cognitive categories. Going beyond the Kantian formula Plessner focused on the sensory apparatus and its role in human experience. Sense organs, he urged, played a vital part in man's interaction with his environment; instead of being treated simply as mute receptacles they should be viewed as sensible media in the articulation of purpose, in the attempt to make sense out of the multitude of opaque stimuli.[8]

A first comprehensive treatment of his position appeared in *The Stages of the Organic World and Man* of 1928. The notion of stages, as employed in the study, did not imply an evolutionary scheme to the effect that organic development involved the simple addition of new layers to the preceding set of faculties. As presented by Plessner, each stage of organic life—from plants through animals to man—constituted a morphological structure or organizational form, marked by a distinct pattern of relationships between organism and environment. In the case of plants, this relationship is immediate and automatic, since there is as yet no differentiation between subject and object, between the agent of experience and the surrounding world. Animals, by contrast, are able to interact with their environment, by digesting impressions and adopting a variety of behavioral responses. In Plessner's words, the life-world of animals is characterized by a "mediated immediacy" or "'indirect directness." Their experience is mediated through the body with its sensory organs and nervous system; at the same time, their contact with the environment is immediate in the sense that animals coincide with or are "centrally positioned" in their body and subject to the behavioral chain of stimuli and responses. In the case of man, the relationship is further complicated by his ability to be aware of and gain a distance from his situation. The human condition, Plessner notes, is doubly mediated and "reflexive" by virtue of man's "ex-centric position" in regard both to himself and his environment. Eccentricity, in this context, does not mean removal from physical and environmental bonds; but such bonds do not provide a stable ecology. Lodged at the boundaries of nature, human existence cannot be reduced to a fixed content. Facing his own alter ego man always points beyond himself, through his capacity to question every conception of himself and his situation. Rather than being safely enmeshed in a life-cycle or the stimulus-response nexus, man has to "lead" his life by designing a web of cultural and symbolic meanings—patterns which provide him at best with a fragile habitat.[9]

Plessner's portrayal of man's eccentric position, one should add, was by no means a mere philosophical speculation. Both in the *Stages* and in subsequent writings his conception was buttressed by detailed biological and physiological arguments. Together with Buytendijk and Erwin Straus he attributes a crucial importance, in the comparison between humans and animals, to man's erect position and its implications. Upright position, first of all, freed man's hands for diverse tasks, thereby bringing objects into his grasp and permitting the manipulation of instruments and utensils. More importantly, the erection of the body entailed the openness of man's visual and perceptual field, an openness which, linked with the unspecialized character of his instinctual apparatus, amounted to an emancipation from a fixed ecological milieu; such emancipation, in turn, enables man to observe his world from an eccentric vantage point and to articulate his findings through language.[10] Apart from physiological evidence, man's distinct status, in Plessner's view, is revealed also in peculiarly human types of gestures and expressive signals. As coherent structure, each stage of organic life is delimited against other configurations. For human beings, structure is circumscribed not so much by rigid limits as by open boundaries or horizons; moreover, man is peculiarly able to experience the boundaries of his existence. When the tension implicit in his embodiment—the strain to have a body and simultaneously to experience the world through it—can no longer be sensibly mitigated or reconciled, man takes refuge in laughter and tears: laughter, when the ambiguity of existence carries benign overtones; tears, when human ingenuity is overwhelmed by a hostile fate.[11]

Over the years, to be sure, Plessner's philosophical anthropology has not been free from modification or reformulation. For present purposes it must suffice to draw attention to a synopsis of his outlook: the treatise *Conditio Humana* of 1961. The study combines and restates many of the previously mentioned themes. The opening sections contain a strong critique of traditional speculative and epistemological assumptions, especially of the Cartesian mind—body scheme; a central aim of philosophical anthropology is to capture the juncture of internal and external dimensions in human experience. Plessner pays tribute to Bergson and Dilthey for having sketched a preliminary road map in this direction; further important steps were taken with biological investigations of alternative relationships between organism and environment. Together with the dualistic legacy the study protests against the rigid segregation of an invariant species from its historical and cultural manifestations. Given the interlocking character of nature and history, a general exploration of the "human condition" can reveal only a rudimentary structural blueprint which allows for such a linkage; among the key elements of this blueprint Plessner mentions man's retarded growth, his incongruous instinctual endowment, his erect posture, and the development of language. All these indicators combined point to a distinct mode of embodiment and a special relationship between human organism and the world. As he emphasizes, man is characterized by a unique blending of closure and openness:

> The customary assignment of fixed milieus to animals and open horizons to man oversimplifies and distorts matters, by failing to do justice to the ambiguity of human existence and by converg-

ing too readily, as in Scheler's case, with the traditional body-soul-spirit hierarchy.

Man's need to embody himself and his striving to make sense of his condition lead him to design cultural patterns which serve as temporary refuge and as a partial substitute for a fixed milieu:

> But what are these comforting patterns of our existence without the dimension of strangeness against which they protect us, without a world which is somehow beyond our reach and perhaps ultimately unfathomable? Only against the background of an open world transcending biological constraints—a world which, prone to unexpected turns, urges him into ever new and fragile compromises—is man able to maintain the precarious and vulnerable balance of cultural life.[12]

Centered on human experience, Plessner's opus does not offer a fully developed social and political theory; yet, his writings are replete with suggestive insights and crucial building blocks for such a theory. The notion of eccentricity implies that man faces not only himself and the world of objects but also other human beings. With the emergence of awareness and the growing mastery of language, man discovers himself in the first person, as an instance of personal and possessive pronouns both in the singular and the plural. More importantly, he is able to learn about himself only through the encounter with his fellowmen. As *Conditio Humana* asserts, in a passage reminiscent of George Herbert Mead: "Self-knowledge and self-interpretation are mediated through others and the world; the journey inside requires external support." Society arises from this nexus of ego and alter ego—though not without complications. Borrowing a term coined by Theodor Litt, Plessner sees the core of social relations in the "reciprocity of perspectives" among participants; reciprocity in this context, however, denotes not simply a mutual empathy or any other direct psychological bond. Going beyond immediate attachments or rivalries, men are able to question each other and to engage in a sustained discourse about their relationship—thereby suspending, at least in a partial manner, existing common-sense understandings and habitual contacts. In the terminology of Kant, human interaction is marked by an "unsociable sociability": by man's need to find himself in the eyes of others and by the simultaneous impulse to challenge the purpose and adequacy of existing arrangements. To remedy this incongruity societies are provided with normative and institutional structures—which, however, fail to secure permanent stability or social concord. As Plessner argued in one of his earliest writings, entitled *The Limits of Community*, the utopia of complete communal integration stifles reciprocal interrogation and thus the endeavor of human self-exegesis.[13]

The conception of society as a web of reciprocal perspectives has distinct repercussions for role theory; Plessner has been eloquent in delineating this connection. Roles, in his view, are the nodal junctures through which men are able to interact in society and to lead a socially relevant life. Role patterns share in the ambiguity of the human condition. On the one hand, such patterns are bundles of normative expectations which channel and control human behavior; on the other hand, however, roles have a liberating effect by allowing man to gain a distance from his context and to differentiate a zone of privacy and personal liberty from the realm of public demands. Enactment of roles, in any event, is not by itself synonymous with alienation or loss of "selfhood." On the contrary; the arsenal of social roles enables man to embody himself and thus to learn about both himself and others:

> Only through contact with others can man grasp himself; these others, however, he encounters through the medium of roles, just as they find access to him in the same medium.

If man were either a strictly biological organism or a pure spirit, mutual ties would not require the complex mediating fabric of roles; his peculiarly broken relationship to himself and the world, however, is mirrored in his social experience. In the words of Plessner, man in his social bonds is destined to be a "doppelgänger," a hybrid creature combining, in a unique and intricate fashion, public postures and private aspirations.

Social relations anchored in the role nexus are exposed to numerous hazards and vulnerable to corruption and deformation. The chief hazards result from contraction or the eradication of the tension between man and his roles. Such contraction can occur either through reification—the attempt to collapse man in existing social structures—or through a rejection of roles and a withdrawal into private "authenticity." In either case, man as *doppelgänger* is leveled into a one-dimensional mold. Actually, reification and retreat are bound to condition and reinforce each other: the more man's core is internalized, the more the social fabric is liable to degenerate into a hollow and opaque artifact. In modern times, Plessner notes, these twin dangers have been growing in prominence. Historically, he differentiates be-

tween three main types of role conceptions: (1) an organic view according to which roles denote ascribed status and reflect the scale of embodiment and representation available in the community; (2) a theatri-
cal conception which sees role carriers as performers in a *theatrum
mundi,* a drama infused with mythical or metaphysical significance;
and finally (3) a purely functional notion which treats individuals as
exchangeable agents in the pursuit of mundane tasks. The succession
of perspectives and especially the emergence of modern functionalism,
he argues, implies an increasing chance of individual autonomy, but
also a growing complexity and frailty of social bonds. In our age, the
refinement of bureaucratic and technological efficiency, coupled with
the rise of social engineering and manipulation, threatens to absorb
man into a self-sufficient network of institutional controls. The remedy
against this peril, in Plessner's view, cannot be found in "inner emigra-
tion" or private self-indulgence, but only in the active endeavor to restore a tenable linkage between privacy and public life. "Identified
with privacy in an extra-social sense and supposedly rendered unassail-
able," he notes, "freedom loses touch with reality and thus any chance
of social implementation. By contrast, freedom must be able to matter
and to 'play a role,' and this is possible only as long as individuals con-
strue their social performance not as a mere mummery in which participants confront each other behind impenetrable masks."[14]

Embodiment in social roles and institutional structures, from
Plessner's perspective, is an eminently political task; an essay of 1931
deals specifically with the political dimension of human experience.
As he emphasizes, philosophical anthropology and politics cannot be
treated as two neatly segregated domains; throughout history, conceptions of man have influenced political practice and vice versa. The
reciprocal impact can be traced back ultimately to man's eccentric
status, his position at the juncture of nature and history. Due to this
status, human existence is not simply a fixed or pre-ordained destiny, but embedded in man's ongoing self-interrogation and self-
interpretation; as an "open question" human nature remains in principle inexhaustible. Self-interpretation, however, is not merely a theoretical or speculative but a practical undertaking. On a purely contemplative level, diverse and even incompatible views could conceivably
coexist without colliding; but, in reality, men are placed in concrete
situations and have to adopt a definite perspective or course of action—
a selection which necessarily excludes competing alternatives. Politics,
Plessner suggests, is thus a distinctly human enterprise: a result of
man's search for meaning in an unfinished and equivocal history. Given
the constraints of action, the selection of goals involves a differentia-

tion between friends and foes, partisans and strangers; where social purpose is at stake, the choice entails a struggle for political power, a contest over the official boundaries between familiarity and strangeness. Once drawn, to be sure, such boundaries are not perennial; friendships and rivalries can be suspended and subjected to scrutiny, but only as a step to new commitments and new partnerships. Struggle for power, moreover, does not mean a glorification of force or its elevation to a general goal. On the contrary; the relationship between partner and foe is also a struggle for mutual recognition and the search for purpose a striving for a just and equitable society. However, the power differential among men attests to the risks of the social venture and to the tentative character of human justice.[15]

In its general thrust, Plessner's argument is not without philosophical parallels in our century; there are striking similarities between his outlook and existentialist thought. Like Plessner, Heidegger seeks to overcome traditional dichotomies; pursuing the intimations of Husserl's work, he formulates a view of human *Dasein* which departs radically from customary conceptions of man as a tool-making animal or as a composite of instinct and reason. The notion of "being-in-the-world," above all, pictures man in a condition of incongruity which closely approximates eccentricity. In the words of one observer, man in Heidegger's view is not so much a substance as a relation: "Man is the gap which separates and at the same time unites subject and object"; he "stands over against the world while at the same time being tied to it." As he adds, *Dasein* from this vantage point is not simply a fact but "a rift within Being"; prompted by "care" for meaning, man is led to question himself and his world, in an open-ended inquiry.[16] Similarities of this type, however, cannot obliterate important differences of accent—differences on which Plessner has insisted on numerous occasions. In his judgment, Heidegger's existential vision of man is articulated largely in an apodictic fashion relying on intuitive insight; despite the focus on historicity, his vision seems to be immune from the inroads of concrete historical experience. Above all, Plessner suspects the stress on individual "authenticity" of being an invitation to a retreat into privacy and a denunciation of modern mass democracy.

Perhaps, a closer parallel can be detected with the writings of Merleau-Ponty. While preoccupied with philosophical and hermeneutical understanding, Merleau-Ponty was never rigidly hostile to empirical studies; rather, a central ambition throughout his life was to trace the emergence and disintegration of "sense" against the background of an opaque and unconscious nature. At the same time, his concern with man was never a subterfuge for private indulgence—as is evident from his essays on social and political issues and his careful attentiveness to the question of power. Together with Plessner, Merleau-Ponty stressed both human embodiment and the inexhaustible quality of experience; his characterization of the human condition as "*être-au-monde*" captures man's ambiguous position between a finite environment and an open-ended horizon of meaning. As he writes at one point, man is neither an object nor a "constituting consciousness" but a special "intentional" creature—"oriented towards all things but not residing in any." Arguing against those who, relying on a preordained order, "wish for man, like things, to be nothing but a nature heading toward its perfection," he depicts man as a "creature who never achieves completion"—"a rift, as it were, in the peaceful fabric of the world." There is a type of "Pascalian piety," he adds,

> to which we owe the profoundest descriptions of man as an incomprehensible, contradictory monster whose old, self-imposed habits are the only nature he possesses and who is grand because of his wretchedness, wretched because of his grandeur.[17]

II

As a distinct type of inquiry, philosophical anthropology has not been limited to the work of its founders, Scheler and Plessner, but has attracted numerous other practitioners. Among this group, one of the most prominent and challenging is the sociologist Arnold Gehlen. A comparison between Plessner and Gehlen is particularly instructive since, starting from roughly similar premises, both have arrived at starkly divergent conclusions. Gehlen's approach to philosophical anthropology was first sketched, in a broad fashion, in a study entitled *Man* of 1940. Like Plessner the study takes its point of departure from man's relative "openness," resulting from the unspecialized character of his instinctual and organic apparatus; deprived of a direct physical habitat, man, in contrast to animals, appears as an incomplete and unfinished creature. In Gehlen's view, however, this incompleteness is primarily a deficiency or strain to be remedied. His instinctual disorientation leads man into multiple environments and into unforeseen, possibly threatening situations; at the same time, his open posture renders him vulnerable to excessive excitation, exposing him to the risk of being inundated and overwhelmed by random stimuli and impressions. A physically handicapped creature, man thus finds himself in a situation fraught with perils and unpredictable surprises; in order to secure

his survival, he has to turn his deficiency into an asset and to use his
openness for the invention of corrective measures. In trying to overcome the strains of his physical condition, man cannot simply trust
nature but has to rely on artifice and ingenuity: "Through his own
efforts man seeks relief from stress and attempts to transform the
deficiencies of his existence into an improved chance of survival."

The struggle against deficiency furnishes the key to man's special
position in the world and to his cultural accomplishments. According
to Gehlen, the search for relief from stress constitutes the basic
"structural" principle governing all modes of human experience—
from perceptual selection through symbolization to consciousness;
whenever man confronts the world he seeks to reduce and subdue
the randomness of impressions and impulses. Language is a particularly effective instrument of stimulus reduction and regulation. By
means of language man is able to gain a distance from the impact
of immediate impressions and the constraints of the stimulus—response
nexus; through symbolic articulation he can obtain an overview over
seemingly disconnected events and thus control his situation. All
the various efforts and activities through which man dominates nature
for his benefit can be summarized under the term "culture." In
Gehlen's words, culture is man's "second nature," the only condition in
which he can live with a measure of safety. Man's cultural achievements, from this perspective, are essentially means of stress management and tension relief. Precisely because of the diffuseness and plas-
ticity of his instinctual apparatus, man is capable of mastering himself
and his world; whatever he is lacking in physical endowments he
acquires through diligence and disciplined training. Cultural patterns—
especially normative and institutional structures—compensate man for
his natural handicaps; they provide him with a viable habitat, equivalent to the animals' environmental milieu.[18]

In subsequent writings, Gehlen explicated more clearly the social
and political implications of his approach. In a study published in
1956 he contrasted the solidity of primitive or archaic cultures to the
flaccidity and effervescence of modern, especially advanced Western
civilization. The study started again from the diffuse character of
human endowments and from the need to seek relief from stress; in
lieu of the previous focus of human inventiveness, however, the accent
now rested on man's cultural dependence. Without abandoning the
distinction between nature and artifact, Gehlen emphasized the
autonomous operation and objectivity of cultural products and their
emergence from unreflected imperatives of the human condition;
although owing their genesis to human interaction, he noted, cultural

institutions are prone to acquire an independent authority capable
of "extending its dominion into the very core of human experience."
Where institutions operate effectively, culture channels and habit-
uates human behavior with the same unquestioned reliability as
does a natural milieu. The value of culture, however, resides not only
in its replication of the stimulus—response nexus. According to Gehlen,
stable institutions permit man to become part of a lasting purpose
which vastly excels individual goals and aspirations; they also grant him
a freedom from instinctual constraints which is superior to arbitrary
whim and subjective license. Given these cultural advantages, Gehlen's
preferences among the examined historical epochs were readily
apparent. Archaic cultures were distinguished by solid institutional
structures in which human life was securely embedded; modern
civilization, on the other hand, is marked by the corrosive effects of
subjective speculation and petulant agitation. For people in primitive
times public positions were not simply roles which could be shed or
exchanged at will. "Individuals," he writes,

> who are so completely congruent with their status have no alterna-
> tive to being absorbed by prevailing institutions; they have no
> external reference point to which they could retreat. This is the
> kind of dignity which is so largely lacking in our time where 'sub-
> jects' are in constant rebellion against all institutions.[19]

Gehlen's preferences are equally evident in some of his more recent
writings, especially in his treatise on ethics of 1969. The study differentiates between four major ethical conceptions or systems, all of
which are said to be traceable to distinct biological roots: (1) an ethics
of reciprocity; (2) an instinctual ethics tending toward happiness; (3)
a family ethics; and (4) an institutional or public ethics relating to the
State. According to Gehlen, there is a biologically sanctioned balance
between these various ethical systems; the viability of human life is
jeopardized once this balance is seriously disrupted or undermined.
The basic thesis of the study is that such disintegration is well under
way. As he tries to show, the modern era is characterized by the progressive weakening and dismantling of institutional ethics in favor of
its competitors—especially in favor of an expanded family ethics. The
latter type, he notes, cultivates and institutionalizes the values of peaceful coexistence: love, charity, and solidarity. Originating in blood relations, this conception—under the impact of Enlightenment thinkers and
other speculative intellectuals—has steadily been broadened and generalized into an encompassing "humanitarianism" devoted to universal

peace and brotherhood; conversely and in precise measure as this expansion progressed, loyalty to State and nation has declined and
atrophied. In its assault on public institutions, humanitarianism has
been assisted and reinforced by hedonism or the ethics of happiness,
with its stress on private comfort and social welfare. The frantic pursuit of high living standards has tended to substitute private ambition
for the public interest. Jointly, hedonism and humanitarianism have
destroyed the values traditionally associated with the State, such as
honor, service, performance of duty—values whose institutional cultivation is required for the maintenance of the species.[20]

Institutionalism, as expounded by Gehlen, is a somewhat unique
and even idiosyncratic doctrine; yet, in less emphatic form, aspects of
his perspective can be found in contemporary social thought. For present purposes a brief reference to structural-functionalism and systems
theory must suffice. What is normally lacking in such approaches, to
be sure, is both Gehlen's biological erudition and his distinct historical
vantage point. An affinity can be detected, first of all, in the notion of
tension management and stress relief; most functionalists and systems
theorists see a central task of the social and political order in the management of stress, the screening and regulation of inputs, and the struggle against randomness.[21] Another point of contact, at least with functionalism, resides in the normative dimension—to the extent that normative values are intimately linked with the goal of system maintenance and survival. A final similarity can be detected in the emphasis
on the institutionalization of norms and the conception of society as a
web of roles—although, in functionalist terms, this web includes indi-
vidually achieved status. In the words of Talcott Parsons, the basic
concern of functionalist theory is with "what we have called for social
systems the institutionalization, for personality systems the internalization of norms or values." The task of institutional structures and role
patterns, in this view, is to stabilize behavioral expectations and to ex-
pedite the integration of the social fabric. Assuming an adequate internalization of role requirements, the hazard of deviant behavior is
virtually banished. "Once socialized and making due allowance for
elements of conflict and malintegration on both the personality and the
social system levels," Parsons notes, "a person cannot act otherwise
than in conformity with his internalized values."[22]

Gehlen's arguments have elicited comments and critical evaluations from many quarters—notably from other practitioners of philosophical anthropology. While appreciating the biological background
of his views, Plessner has voiced reservations regarding the narrowness
of Gehlen's approach. "To apply—as Gehlen does—the notion of en-

vironment to man's open position in the world," he states in *Conditio Humana*, "is an intriguing attempt, but one which is bound to subordinate spiritual achievements to biological imperatives: to imperatives of stress relief, economy, and stabilization for purposes of action." What is ignored both by traditional and Gehlen's "pragmatic" anthropology, he adds, is the "possibility that, in man's case, openness and confinement collide and are locked in an intimate, but never completely stable nexus." While the environment of animals is fixed and species-specific, man has the ability "to live everywhere and to adjust to all milieus, if necessary through artificial means." The difference is not one of degree but of kind: "What emerges if man is reduced to a biological creature—even if only to a creature of habit—is a torso" and at best a "pseudo-environment." The situation is not remedied, Plessner argues, if the term "environment" is tailored specifically to the cultural domain and the latter designated as "second nature." Although it may be true that man "finds himself" only in a cultural context, this context furnishes a special and precarious habitat. Culture is a "nurtured and cultivated one-sidedness" to which men "succumb if they lose sight of the limitations of their norms and habits." In contrast to biological milieus, cultural patterns despite their uniqueness "point beyond themselves—as illustrated by the possibility of translation among languages—and remain linked with other patterns of the past and present."[23]

On a broader theoretical basis, Gehlen's outlook has been scrutinized by adherents of a critical philosophy and critical social science; among members of the Frankfurt School, Jürgen Habermas has paid particularly close attention to his teachings. Addressing himself to Gehlen's general anthropological perspective—especially as outlined in *Man*—Habermas criticized the merger of culture and biology and the tendency to reduce human aspirations to instrumental activity in the service of survival needs. "The standard of biological utility," he commented,

> is patently unable to exhaust the meaning of social conduct. A blind reproduction of life for its own sake is indifferent toward barbarism and humanity and toward the purpose of an existence exposed by nature on the threshold between truth and untruth.

Turning to Gehlen's comparison of primitivism and modernity, he objected to the elevation of archaic conditions into an invariant model of human life. "What may have been appropriate for primitive cultures," he observed, "surreptitiously is treated as a corollary of human existence"—with the intimation that "human nature entails the necessity of an authoritarian society." According to Habermas, Gehlen's presentation involved an illegitimate fusion of historical contingency and apodictic judgment: a given historical era, marked by its bent toward discipline and institutional repression, was singled out as the yardstick of "natural and therefore desirable" social arrangements. The relationship between nature and history, however, was more complex:

> While there may have been, and may still be, situations in which institutions of this type are indispensable for human guidance, other circumstances are historically possible and perhaps already prevalent in which man, by sublimating his instinctual energies and thus gaining control of himself, is released from the institutional harness of the past whose power and dignity Gehlen extols.[24]

More recently, in a review of Gehlen's study on ethics, Habermas has delineated in more detail the divergence between critical theory and institutionalism. The review first of all noted various inconsistencies and incongruities in Gehlen's argument. In Habermas' view, the linkage of "humanitarianism" with family ethics, and the confrontation of the latter with an institutional ethics, was spurious and misleading since both family and nation cultivate peaceful coexistence among group members while instilling hostility toward outsiders. In order to promote loyalty, both groups insist on the values of honor, service and sacrifice: "both demand pacific virtues in internal and polemical virtues in external relations." The limitation of the term "institution" to the public domain, moreover, was arbitrary since the family was equally entitled to this designation. As Habermas tried to show, family and State were not so much rigid opposites as part of a pattern of ethical development in which the predominance of blood relations was progressively challenged and "mediated" by the authority of the territorial State. Instead of mirroring a biological antagonism, the two types of ethics, thus, reflected a historical conflict or "historical stages of moral awareness." Ethical development, moreover, did not terminate with the establishment of the nation State; since the rise of the market economy and the "Protestant ethic," Western culture has aimed in the direction of a global ethics—a trend adumbrated in Kant's categorical imperative. The entire development is marked simultaneously by the universalization of norms and their internalization: by an expanding range of application and by a growing reliance on moral autonomy. In the absence of apodictic insight, Habermas suggests, universality and autonomy can be reconciled only through open discussion; instead of

being rooted in family ethics, modern "humanitarianism" therefore is
linked with or aspires to an "ethics of reciprocity." Against this background, the test of an ethical conception resides not so much in its
contribution to institutional stability as in its capacity to grasp man's
relationship to his fellow-men in an increasingly complex and interdependent world.[25]

Gehlen's outlook has also been assessed by Karl-Otto Apel. Concentrating on the historical comparison of archaic and modern cultures,
Apel noted with approval Gehlen's struggle against Cartesian dualism
and his concern with concrete embodiment. The stress on institutions,
he observed, was distantly reminiscent of Hegel's preoccupation with
distinct cultural structures; Gehlen's fascination with objectivism, however, entailed a serious curtailment of this legacy. While, for Hegel, the
core of culture resided in the complex mediation between subjective
experience and "objective spirit," Gehlen's approach treated institutions
as empirical data amenable to sociological and biological analysis. In
contrast to dialectical philosophy, Apel wrote, "Gehlen recognizes only
the necessity of institutional alienation, but not the need for its ever
renewed transcendence." Man's dependence on institutional embodiment offered no warrant for the canonization of archaic life-styles—
especially since such an attempt was bound to clash with Western
civilization's basic thrust toward internalization and critical reflection,
a thrust initiated by monotheistic religion and Greek philosophy. As
he added, the rigid attachment to ritual was not entirely congruent
with Gehlen's own historical account in which spiritual transcendence,
encouraged by monotheism, was presented as a possible cultural avenue rather than as a synonym for "subjectivism" and instinctual regression. The dilemmas of our age including the hazard of subjective self-
indulgence, in any event, could be remedied not by an abdication of
consciousness in favor of a return to primitivism, but only through a
strengthening of critical thought and responsible intersubjective discourse; in this manner alone could social and cultural institutions obtain justification and broad-based support.[26]

III

Under present-day conditions, institutionalism as advocated by
Gehlen is bound to have a polemical edge. In our century, the conception of man as a representative of public functions and normative
structures has been strongly challenged by a counter-image according

to which roles are at best ill-fitting costumes or disguises in the human quest for self-fulfilment; condemned to improvisation, man from this perspective adopts social postures only in order to disavow them. In recent decades, this Protean view of man has gained wide currency as part of the Western "counter-culture" and the revolt against established institutional and cultural patterns; sometimes, especially among advocates of psychic experimentation, an introverted humanism is extolled as an antidote to social sclerosis. From biological teachings the mentioned view adopts the distinction between organic milieus and human openness, but openness in this case denotes a complete malleability and indeterminacy; endowed with infinite freedom human existence appears as a reservoir of unlimited possibilities. Together with the stress on indeterminacy, moreover, the argument is frequently advanced that "authentic" existence can be found only in the domain of internal freedom, as contrasted to the impersonality of public life-styles. Occasionally, portrayals of Protean man carry overtones of Robert Musil's *Man Without Qualities*—but without the grim and harrowing features of Musil's sketch.[27]

The view of man as a free agent, to be sure, is not simply a temporary fad but has a long and reputable philosophical lineage; what is at issue here is merely the equation of autonomy and detachment. In our age, the philosophical lineage has been continued chiefly by the existentialist movement. Plessner is inclined to adopt a summary outlook, charging not only Heidegger but existentialism as such with a bent toward private introspection; given the diversity of individual formulations, however, this judgment is probably in need of qualification. Among leading existentialists, Karl Jaspers—at least in some of his writings—seemed to approximate or intimate a Protean conception. Thus, in discussing the "authentic" mode of awareness called *Existenz*, he insisted that ultimate selfhood is an open-ended possibility radically distinct from all empirical manifestations. In contrast to other modes of experience, he writes, *Existenz* is "not something which could be replaced, as if everything were a playing by means of roles and masks, in which no one really performed"; rather, the term designates "the self which is unrepresentable in intuition, in which I am one with myself, behind all my roles, a self which supports and carries these roles."[28] Some critics have made this notion of selfhood the central target of their attack—a focus which de-emphasizes perhaps unduly Jaspers' view of the situational character of freedom and his concern with human communication. Thus, Frederick Heinemann characterizes him as a "gliding philosopher" and his approach as one of "evanescence." As he notes, Jaspers' central preoccupation is with the fate of the person who is in danger of becoming a mere cog within the enormous machine of the modern welfare state and who loses his substance, self, and his spiritual center.

The counsel, however, which emerges from his writings is one of non-commitment: as a thinker, "he follows the principle of moving in nothing but possibilities," wishing to remain free for all options "without ever making a final decision." Gliding through alternatives, Heinemann concludes, Jaspers gets caught in Hegel's "bad infinity," an endless succession of experiences without results.[29]

While Jaspers' case may be in doubt, the thrust of the contemporary "counter-culture" is less ambiguous. Two examples may serve to illustrate the general direction. In his *The Making of a Counter Culture,* Theodore Roszak launched a frontal attack on modern "technocratic" society, marked by an "objective mode of consciousness," in an effort to vindicate the values of visionary experience and private spontaneity. Objective consciousness, as enshrined in scientific method, he argued, begins by opposing the observer's mind to the surrounding world and concludes by crushing internal sensitivity in favor of the compactness of external data:

> Objectivity leads to such a great emptying-out operation: the progressive alienation of more and more of In-Here's personal contents in the effort to achieve the densest possible unit of observational concentration surrounded by the largest possible area of study.

The final triumph of objectivism, according to Roszak, lies in the replacement of internal insight by mechanical devices such as the computer; unlike man, such a device seems completely dependable since it "acts without involvement in what it does." At this point, instead of serving as a mere instrument, the mechanical artifact turns into "its maker's ideal": "The machine achieves the perfect state of objective consciousness and, hence, becomes the standard by which all things are to be gauged." Against the dangers of mechanization implicit in technocracy Roszak invoked the broad range of spiritual experience. The "primary project" of the counter-culture, he writes, is

> to proclaim a new heaven and a new earth so vast, so marvelous that the inordinate claims of technical expertise must of necessity withdraw in the presence of such splendor to a subordinate and marginal status in the lives of men.

Once the shackles of objective mentality are left behind, we are faced
with

> the scandalous possibility that wherever the visionary imagination
> grows bright, magic, that old antagonist of science, renews itself,
> transmuting our workaday reality into something bigger, perhaps
> more frightening, certainly more adventurous than the lesser ra-
> tionality of objective consciousness can ever countenance.[30]

The appeal from objectivism to deeper and richer layers of consciousness can also be found in another leading manifesto of the
counter-culture: Charles Reich's *The Greening of America*. As presented by Reich, technocratic rationality actually constitutes a secondary stage or level in American cultural development, superimposed on
the original "American Dream." Designated as "Consciousness I," the
original American outlook—which remained in effect throughout much
of the last century—was centered on individual achievement and self-
sufficiency. Escaping from the constraints of class status operative in
Europe, the American settlers and their descendants placed their trust
in the "sovereign individual" and in the virtues of hard work and self-
restraint; presupposing widely dispersed resources, the perspective was
suited to a "society of small towns, face-to-face relationships, and individual economic enterprise." With industrialization and the ascendency
of scientific method this idyllic vision was progressively undermined
and replaced by a mentality shaped by the needs of large-scale organizations and subservient to the dictates of technical and managerial
efficiency. Styled "Consciousness II" and reaching its apex in our own
age, the new mentality "believes in the central ideology of technology,
the domination of man and environment by technique"; accordingly,
"science, technology, organization, and planning are prime values."
While the preceding era focused on "the fiction of the American Adam,
the competitive struggle, and the triumph of the virtuous and strong
individual," Consciousness II "rests on the fiction of logic and ma-
chinery; what it considers unreal is nature and subjective man." The
values of efficiency and technocratic control, Reich argues, are not restricted to business corporations but tend to be applied to society at
large. "Throughout all of Consciousness II," he notes, "runs the theme
that society will function best if it is planned, organized, rationalized,
administered." The chief aim of public policy, from this vantage point,
is conflict-management and "conflict resolution."

A corollary of the reliance on technology, in Reich's view, is a
strong institutional bias:

One of the central aspects of Consciousness II is an acceptance of the priority of institutions, organizations, and society and a belief that the individual must tie his destiny to something of this sort, larger than himself, and subordinate his will to it.

Apart from being requisites for social management, institutions provide an indispensable framework for human fulfilment; the individual "relies on institutions to certify the meaning and value of his life, by rewarding accomplishment and conferring titles, office, respect and honor." Instead of being a self-reliant agent, man under the sway of technocratic rationality is basically an other-directed conformist, an "artificially streamlined" and "smoothed-down" creature. "Under the domination of the Corporate State," Reich asserts, man is condemned to lead a "robot life" in which he is "deprived of his own being" and reduced to "a mere role, occupation, or function"; harnessed to assembly lines and organizational structures he is transformed into an "uptight" person—"with a coating or crust over him, so that he can tolerate impersonal relations, inauthenticity, loneliness, hassling, bad vibrations." Integrated into institutions, individuals do not so much mold their lives as accept prefabricated behavioral patterns; they are "role-players" with a keen awareness of "what is fitting to their roles." By forcing individuals to adjust their interests and tasks to standards set "outside themselves," roles place a straitjacket on human experience: "The role-prison drastically restricts such fundamental aspects of personality as relationships with others, personal expression, modes of thought, and goals and aspirations." The most corrosive result of role-constraint, Reich adds, is "the fact that the individual's own 'true' self, if still alive, must watch helplessly while the role-self lives, enjoys, and relates to others."

The situation is not entirely hopeless, however; suddenly and without advance notice, a rampant technology during the past decades has engendered its own corrective in the form of the youth culture and its reverberations. In contrast to the "loss of self" characteristic of technocracy, the youth movement seeks to restore human integrity and self-hood; while the older generation accepted society and institutions as the objective world, the new attitude—"Consciousness III"—proclaims "that the individual self is the only true reality." The emergence of this attitude involves a spontaneous emancipation, an act in which "the individual frees himself from automatic acceptance of the imperatives of society and the false consciousness which society imposes"; as a consequence of such liberation, "the individual is free to build his own philosophy and values, his own life-style, and his own culture from a new beginning." According to Reich, concern with selfhood does not imply selfishness; the aim is "not an 'ego trip' but a radical subjectivity designed to find genuine values in a world whose official values are false and distorted." The search for authentic experience requires a retreat from opaque institutions and stereotyped role patterns; Consciousness III "rejects any relationship based wholly on role, relationships limited along strictly impersonal and functional lines." To gain internal autonomy, an individual has to cultivate distance or the mental attitude of being an outsider:

> Only the person who feels himself to be an outsider is genuinely free of the lures and temptations of the Corporate State.

Detachment of this type is not easily accomplished; on the contrary, "escape from a role is painfully difficult for most people, which shows how important an effort it is." In turning toward selfhood, the individual discovers not so much a compact human "nature," as rather a faculty of improvisation, an arsenal of infinite possibilities. "The basic stance of Consciousness III," Reich notes, "is one of openness to any and all experience. It is always in a state of becoming." The Protean vista is illustrated in the entire life-style of the young generation, including "their culture, clothes, music, drugs, ways of thought." The "lasting essence" of the new mentality is "constant change, and constant growth of each individual."[31]

Like its institutionalist counterpart, the conception of man as *bon sauvage* and as a fugitive from social roles has been exposed to probing criticism. According to Plessner, the identification of authenticity with an extra-social selfhood encourages the danger of private self-indulgence and the tendency to treat society and public responsibilities as external vexations. The opposition of role-self and authentic self, in his view, constitutes a remnant of the Kantian distinction between intelligible or "noumenal" and "phenomenal" man—with a distinct bias in favor of mental retreat. "To accept the existentialist claim and to seek freedom and authenticity in an internal realm," he writes, "means to promote the reification of man in public life." Addressing himself more directly to the implications of the counter-culture, Habermas corroborates and expands Plessner's argument. Gehlen's denunciation of subjectivism, he observes, could find ready ammunition in the contemporary youth revolt with its bent toward "cultural anarchism." In trying to dismantle established social structures, this revolt "accentuates spontaneity and face-to-face contacts and, with the aid of drugs, experiments with forms of a better, if not the 'good life'." While acknowledging the intent to restore genuine interaction under the debris of corporate manipulation, Habermas deplores the withdrawal into a spurious state of nature with its concomitant of moral regression. To the extent that a social life-form coincides with ordinary language, the escape from society conjures up the peril of a lapse into private speech—a condition which Maurice Natanson once described as "social aphasia." Pushed to its logical conclusion, Habermas states, the counter-culture denotes an attempt to return to a pre-linguistic stage and to accomplish the "conscious production of palaeosymbols"; given this thrust, "love of wisdom is not surprisingly replaced by a sympathy for madness." The disintegration of public discourse is linked with an abdication from politics. Removed from the "concrete parameters of public communication," the counter-culture continues and reinforces the trend toward depolitization and leisure-time privacy fostered by corporate society.[32]

After this excursion into contemporary controversies it may be well to glance back at the original theme of these pages. The discussion of competing images of man was designed to sharpen the contours of Plessner's position. In contrast both to the institutional and the Protean vision, Plessner's view of the interlocking character of openness and confinement presents man basically as a *doppelgänger*—a creature never completely congruent with his roles and yet unable to find himself except through public embodiment and through patterned interaction with his fellow-men. The notion of man as a *doppelgänger* does not imply a mere combination of opposites, a juxtaposition of "noumenal" man and his "phenomenal" manifestations—such as prevails in Ralf Dahrendorf's portrayal of "*homo sociologicus*."[33] What is involved in the view is not simply a paradox or contradiction, but rather an intrinsic tension which needs to be faced and sustained as a continuous challenge in individual and social life. Against this background, Plessner's writings contain traces of at least an incipient dialectical outlook— by pointing to the unfinished historical dialectic between sense and nonsense, intentionality and decay of meaning.[34]

As practiced by Plessner, however, philosophical anthropology is not restricted to historical or cultural experience in a narrow sense. Placing man at the juncture of nature and history, his perspective remains attentive to the biological and physiological dimension of human existence; as he wrote at one point: "There can be no philosophy of man without study of nature." In comprehensiveness and breadth of concern his outlook is reminiscent of Freudian thought; by incorporating the findings of both natural science and the humanities, his philo-

sophical anthropology resembles Freud's effort to link interpretation
with empirical research, therapeutic dialogue with scientific analysis.
To some extent, the resemblance extends to the domain of social and
political thought—especially if *Civilization and Its Discontents* is taken
as point of reference. Together with Freud, Plessner acknowledges that
social interaction and cultural development involve the establishment of
normative and institutional structures. Given the lack of a stable environment, however, cultural patterns are bound to rest on a precarious
foundation. "Each regulation," he writes,

> contains restrictions and thereby creates its opposite. Wherever
> processes of channeling are introduced, the development of energy
> becomes restricted, whether in the physical or in the social world.

The unspecialized character of man's instinctual apparatus militates against a completely successful containment:

> Experience shows that wants can be created and that human de-
> sires are not only unlimited but also undetermined. Each *nomos*
> overcomes an anomie only to create a new one in its place.[35]

Apart from its dialectical and Freudian overtones, Plessner's perspective also displays an affinity with the legacy of critical philosophy
and critical social thought, as cultivated in particular by the Frankfurt
School. Habermas' delineation, in *Knowledge and Human Interests*, of
a deep structure of human cognition and experience is not incompatible with Plessner's outline of a basic human morphology; as presented
in the study, cognitive "interests" denote both a common patrimony of
the human species and acquisitions of a cultural and historical learning
process. Habermas' discussion of Freudian psychoanalysis in the same
context bears witness to his endeavor to reconcile scientific investigation with cultural hermeneutics—an endeavor further corroborated by
his subsequent elaborations on linguistic and communicative competence.[36] Similarities of this kind, to be sure, do not amount to convergence. Whatever differences of accent may persist, however, are
overshadowed by Plessner's endorsement of a critical perspective in
social inquiry. As he observed in his presidential address before the
German sociological association, social science signifies and is possible
only as "an institutionalized and permanent scrutiny of social conditions in scientific form and with a critical intent." Due to its reflexive
character—the prevailing nexus between the observer and his subject
matter—social inquiry cannot be entirely indifferent to social objectives:

There can be no theory in this sensitive domain which is not a critical theory and which, as critique, does not take an implicit stand for or against the premises of an open society.[37]

PART TWO
Phenomenology, Existentialism, Hermeneutics

4. Phenomenology and Social Science: An Overview and Appraisal

THE RELATIONSHIP BETWEEN SOCIAL SCIENCE and social reality seems infinitely more complex than that between tool and object of analysis. In our time, the subterranean linkages of knowledge and experience have been vividly exposed: the crisis features of social reality have produced, or at least are accompanied by, an identity crisis in many academic disciplines—notably in social science. The manifestations of this malaise are familiar; they range from scholarly reassessments of specific research procedures to confrontations in the context of professional organizations. Occasionally, such agonies have even surfaced in official pronouncements. In his presidential address to the political science fraternity in 1969, David Easton diagnosed professional unrest as a "new revolution" following closely on the heels of the behavioral or scientific renovation. As he pointed out, the preceding behavioral transformation had scarcely run its course before it was "overtaken by the increasing social and political crises of our time." Although not diametrically opposed to its predecessor, the new insurgency involved a profound challenge to professional orthodoxy: "The essence of the post-behavioral revolution is not hard to identify. It consists of a deep dissatisfaction with political research and teaching, especially of the kind that is striving to convert the study of politics into a more rigorously scientific discipline modelled on the methodology of the natural sciences."[1]

Despite its dramatic vocabulary, however, Easton's address did not contemplate a radical departure from prevailing conventions. The diagnosis of "revolutionary" unrest was coupled with a plea for implementation rather than critical reassessment of the behavioral paradigm. Apart from counseling greater awareness of normative bias and

97

apart from urging "boldly speculative theorizing"—which, of course, would build upon "the findings of contemporary behavioral science"— Easton's catalogue of remedies centered primarily on a moderate shift in professional priorities from pure to applied research. There is reason to question the cogency of this line of argument. Considering the insistence of the behavioral model on explanation and prediction, the conspicuous failure of its adherents to explain and anticipate contemporary crises—a failure conceded by Easton[2]—dampens confidence in the remedial qualities of applied knowledge. Moreover, the dearth of "basic" findings seems to militate against accelerated implementation. Considerations of this sort suggest at least the possibility of an alternate assessment of "post-behavioral" ferment: as an invitation to a more direct exploration of social reality, in place of or alongside the behavioral model. The legitimacy of such an undertaking is vindicated by the behavioral model itself. If it is correct, as most practitioners tend to agree, that behavioral science aims at general and necessarily abstract propositions, at the formulation of analytic theories amenable to objective measurement and validation, then there would seem to be ample room for an approach concentrating on the concrete configurations of experience in an effort to render them meaningful and transparent for purposes of practical, everyday life. By and large— and neglecting for the moment intricacies of definition and detail—this aspiration is at the basis of phenomenological investigation.

Obviously, the suggestion of an alternative to the behavioral model runs counter to time-honored professional convictions. There is a deeply ingrained belief, approaching certitude, that any departure from the straight and narrow path of scientific method leads inevitably into the abyss of arbitrary bias, into the quagmire of undisciplined and idiosyncratic speculation. According to this belief, a belief backed by the sanctions of academic repute, the scholar venturing beyond the scientific encampment is condemned to aimless and solitary peregrinations in an inhospitable wilderness. It seems fair to point out, however, that—far from being self-evident—the demarcation between haven and wilderness, between scientific certitude and arbitrary choice is itself a result of behavioral convention. The following pages seek to reduce the dread of solitude by drawing the attention of professional colleagues to a different convention or paradigm, constructed in the supposed wilderness. No doubt, the phenomenological "movement" lacks the comforts of well-established routines and domesticated thought patterns; but it is more than an assemblage of unrelated monologues. While falling short of the cumulative research enterprise envisaged by Husserl, phenomenology can be conceived as an ongoing process of conversation and mutual interrogation. In this conversation, some themes are central and recurrent, others more peripheral; also, the involvement of participants is far from uniform. These pages cannot hope to capture more than the basic contours of the complex dialogue. After briefly tracing main lines of the philosophical argument, the presentation proceeds to a review of prominent contributions in the social science domain in order to glance, finally, at some critical assessments and appraisals of the phenomenological enterprise.

I. Philosophical Background:
From Pure to Existential Phenomenology

Explorations and forays beyond the encampment of science are not peculiar to our time; intellectual history is replete with skirmishes about the provinces and boundaries of knowledge. For present purposes it must suffice to trace these forays back to the generation of explorers at the turn of the century, and principally to the work of Wilhelm Dilthey.

Although not himself a phenomenologist, Dilthey raised a series of important questions which have remained a challenge to phenomenological inquiry. Alarmed by the incessant advances of natural science and the sweeping claims of positivism, Dilthey boldly set out in search of an area of investigation immune from the scientist's measurements. The territory which he finally staked out was the domain of internal experience, a domain reserved to interpretive or "hermeneutical" understanding as cultivated by humanistic or mental sciences (*Geisteswissenschaften*). While nature—the subject matter of the natural sciences—was a realm of external objects constituted independently of human effort and only indirectly intelligible through artificial constructs, mental phenomena offered privileged access to human inspection since "only what mind has produced, mind can properly understand."[3] Dilthey's own studies, his careful portrayals of historical epochs and intellectual currents, were admirable illustrations of the potency of this type of inquiry. Yet, despite the richness of his insights, his explorations were fraught with grave perplexities. If, as he seemed to suggest, human life was deeply enmeshed in a social and historical matrix, how was it possible to decipher the records of other societies and epochs? Moreover, what was the nature of mental phenomena and of the recommended decoding device of hermeneutical interpretation? Were such phenomena simply empirical processes, occurrences in "subjective consciousness" at a given time and place? If so, were psychic states not legitimate targets of scientific psychology, instead of being set aside for humanistic treatment?

Dilthey grappled with these issues and was able to meet some of them in his later writings; but to a considerable extent he remained vulnerable to empiricist rejoinders. Having borrowed the concept of mental sciences from the positivist tradition, his arguments readily lent themselves to psychological misinterpretation. Some efforts to obviate this dilemma were made at the time by the neo-Kantian school of thought, especially by Wilhelm Windelband and Heinrich Rickert. As both philosophers insisted, the steady progress of experimental psychology involved a profound challenge to the segregation of internal and external experience, jeopardizing the corresponding dichotomy of types of investigation. Trying to guard against the pitfalls of "psychologism," Windelband and Rickert replaced Dilthey's scheme with the distinction between natural science and history or (to use Rickert's terminology) between "generalizing" and "individualizing" disciplines. To be sure, the exploration of concrete, individual reality was not identical with the mere collection of random data. As Rickert in particular tried to show (in this respect implementing Dilthey's intentions), there are different means of integrating data in a general framework: instead of subsuming a particular factor under a general category or principle, "individualizing" inquiry seeks to grasp the essential significance of phenomena in a meaningful context, a context of normative values, symbols, and beliefs. To the extent that phenomena reflect such values, concrete reality can be designated as "culture" and historical disciplines as "cultural sciences" (*Kulturwissenschaften*).[4]

While settling some issues, the neo-Kantian argument stirred up a flurry of new quandaries. What was the relationship of consciousness to the data of concrete experience? More specifically, how was a "cultural" realm accessible to a subject hopelessly split into a priori structures and passive sense impressions? It is at this point that phenomenology, in the modern sense of the term, enters the scene. To be sure, the basic thrust of this philosophical perspective is not easy to identify; as previously indicated, the phenomenological "movement" is far removed from constituting a homogeneous phalanx. Behind the multiplicity of definitions, however, the rudiments of a common ground can still be discerned. From this synoptic vantage point, phenomenology implies attentiveness to the broad range of experience, a radical openness to all kinds of phenomena irrespective of their scientific validation; as a corollary, the perspective counsels patient exploration of phenomena and a reluctance to prejudge or truncate their significance through enclosure in rigid and definitive systems of explanation. Unfortunately, this rudimentary sketch runs counter to the very spirit of attentiveness, by ignoring an inordinate amount of individual and historical variation. Without intimating sharp discontinuities, it is feasible and customary to differentiate between at least two successive phases or patterns of focal concern: a first, pioneering phase characterized by reliance on a purified transcendental consciousness and a relative disregard of social contingency—a phase associated chiefly with the name of Edmund Husserl; and a second phase—exemplified in the work of Martin Heidegger and some representatives of the French school of phenomenology—in which attention shifts to the existential dimension of human experience and to the predicaments of intersubjective relations. Today, it may already be possible to identify a third phase of the development: a phase in which the investigation of social contingency has produced a decisive preoccupation both with dialectical thought and with the hermeneutics of human dialogue.

While reflecting a persistent line of inquiry, Husserl's own work shows considerable variability and marked shifts in emphasis; in the present context the barest outline of his endeavors must suffice. Parallels to Rickert—to whose chair in Freiburg he succeeded later in life—can be found primarily in his first major contribution, the *Logical Investigations* published around the turn of the century. Drawing on his extensive training in mathematics, Husserl in the first volume of this work launched a vigorous attack against psychologism, interpreted as a doctrine deriving logical propositions from empirical psychic processes. This attack, however, was only the starting point of his analysis. Instead of pursuing the intimations of a pure logic, Husserl in the second volume turned his attention to a "phenomenological elucidation of knowledge" focusing on the nonsensory foundation of human awareness. In this manner, he arrived at the conception of a transempirical, but fertile, consciousness: a consciousness marked by a basic "intentionality" or directedness pointing toward the essential features of phenomena. The inspection and intuitive grasp of such features (*Wesensschau*) was to be the task of "phenomenological" inquiry. Small wonder that this conception should have captivated the imagination of his contemporaries, including Dilthey who greeted it as a possible philosophical underpinning of his own efforts. In contrast to established school doctrines, Husserl's perspective contained an invitation to take a fresh new look at the world, to pierce the grey mist of explanations and theories about theories in an effort to return "to the things themselves" (*zu den Sachen*). Loosely akin to William James's radical empiricism, phenomenology in this sense promised a *restitutio ad integrum,* a restored access to phenomena in their pristine splendor and variety.[5]

During his early years in Göttingen, Husserl exemplified the merits of his perspective in a sequence of careful analyses, especially the investigation of internal time consciousness. Progressively, however, he became preoccupied with a refinement of his method and its presuppositions. In the course of this development he steadily moved closer to Kantian transcendentalism—and away from the historical school and Dilthey's concerns. A clear signal of this change was the essay on "Philosophy as Strict Science" of 1910; but the new focus reached its first culmination in a landmark study whose title announced a program: *Ideas Concerning a Pure Phenomenology and Phenomenological Philosophy.*[6] As an access route to pure inspection, Husserl now elaborated the procedure of "reduction" or "*epoché,*" a procedure which could be further differentiated into at least two operations: "eidetic" reduction, or the disregard of empirical contingencies in an effort to grasp essential structures; and "transcendental" reduction, involving a suspension or "bracketing" of questions of empirical existence in an effort to focus on the source of experience in transcendental consciousness.

The pursuit of purity was intensified during Husserl's active years at the University of Freiburg. Increasingly he came to equate phenomenology with transcendental "idealism"—although there is dispute over the propriety of the term in this context. His idealist bent found climactic expression in his studies on logic and on Descartes's meditations, published or conceived around 1929, the year of his retirement. Despite his striving for purity, Husserl's later writings bear ample testimony to his efforts to evade the dangers of transcendental solipsism. Some of these efforts led him into the proximity of existentialist concerns, although his formulations were not free of ambiguities. Perhaps the dominant issues in Husserl's later thought were the themes of intersubjectivity and of the "life-world" of everyday experience. The life-world (*Lebenswelt*) in particular was conceived as the immediate horizon of individual and social experience, a terrain marked by distinct patterns of action and life styles. Yet, one could ask, what was the phenomenological status of this terrain? Was the life-world merely a prima facie evidence waiting to be distilled through the channels of transcendental reduction? Or was it a primordial matrix for any phenomenological investigation?[7]

As Husserl's own development suggests, the turn toward an existentialist perspective was prompted at least in part by the predicaments of pure inspection. The initial call "to the things themselves" had encouraged broad-scale explorations of phenomena, explorations devoid of coherence or focal concern. To some extent, Husserl's resort to idealism was a response to this dilemma, although the transcendental ego in his treatment remained largely a source of knowledge. Against this background, existentialism provided chiefly a dominant set of problems, a framework of investigation; but in the long run, the focus on human existence was bound to affect the design and character of the phenomenological enterprise. In an intriguing fashion the transition from pure cognition to a man-centered outlook was illustrated in the work of Max Scheler, a work which added moral conviction and a certain inspirational zest to phenomenology. According to his own account, the issue which preoccupied Scheler from the very beginning was the question of man's nature and status in the universe.[8] Reality to him was not simply a neutral target area for research but a field encountered in a concrete human pursuit. "Phenomenological experience," in his treatment, signified an immediate intuitive insight into the essential structure of phenomena as they offered themselves in their qualitative richness and diversity; as a guide to this experience, "reduction" involved a spiritual act liberating man from the bonds of contingent reality. On the basis of this conception Scheler ventured into the domain of ethics, developing a catalogue of nonformal but a priori values amenable to phenomenological inspection. A similar foundation supported his "philosophical anthropology," an ambitious effort to assess man's place in the hierarchy of creation. Mindful of the dangers of psychologism, Scheler located the distinctive quality of man neither in his psyche nor in his instrumental intellect, but in his "spirit" (Geist): a term denoting not only consciousness and reason but also intuition and even certain refined affections like love and devotion.[9]

The actual convergence of phenomenology and existentialism is frequently identified with the name of Martin Heidegger, Husserl's successor in Freiburg; but at a closer look, the convergence seems quite precarious. There are some parallels between Scheler and Heidegger, arising mainly from their common concern with man. However, Heidegger was never tempted by the notion of a full-fledged or substantive anthropology; in addition, man in his writings served increasingly as a gateway to the exploration of transpersonal meanings. A student of Rickert, Heidegger quickly underwent Husserl's pervasive influence, an influence which reached its peak with the latter's arrival in Freiburg. To be sure, emulation soon gave way to autonomous, even radical reformulation: in Being and Time Husserl's transcendental ego was dislodged from its pivotal position in favor of the focus on human existence (*Dasein*). As in Scheler's case, this dislodgement implied a reassessment of the phenomenological enterprise, including the method of reduction. Eidetic inspection of essences conflicted with the individuality of phenomena (a point for which Heidegger was indebted to Rickert), while transcendental reduction was suspect because of its egological overtones. Probing beneath the cognitive level, Heidegger transformed Husserl's method into a relentless "destruction" or purge, a purge designed to pierce the screens of false objectivity and theoretical speculation and to reveal the hidden meaning of experience through fresh interpretation. This procedure formed the core of a "hermeneutic" or interpretive phenomenology applied chiefly to existential analysis. Defining "existence" as openness to alternative possibilities of self-realization, *Being and Time* unraveled a series of structural categories and modes of experience, including man's insertion in the world, his tendency to lapse into inauthentic complacency, his anxiety in the face of the deceptive compactness and "uncanniness" of the universe, and his concern (*Sorge*) about his own significance.

There is no need, in the present context, to pursue Heidegger's subsequent development or to settle the question whether it involved a departure from or an intensification of his initial perspective.[10] Many of the insights or arguments of *Being and Time* were further developed and more concretely profiled by the French school of phenomenology as it emerged since World War II. To be sure, the background of French phenomenology is extremely complex. The primary source, both in time and importance, was undoubtedly Husserl, probably because of a certain affinity of his arguments to the Cartesian tradition. Yet, Husserl's phenomenology was fused from the beginning with other intellectual currents of the time. The publication of the "Paris manuscripts" had revealed a strong Hegelian legacy in Marx's early thought. At the same time, Hegel's *Phenomenology of Mind* was being reinterpreted in a manner which stressed its concrete, anthropological qualities, thus rendering it compatible both with existentialism and with Husserl's injunction "to the things themselves." From this confluence of sources derive various features characteristic of French phenomenology, including the preoccupation with the "lived body" and with the domain of intersubjectivity. The main feature, however, is the merger between Husserl, Heidegger and Hegel, a merger exposing phenomenology to the drama of negation and contradiction and, ultimately, to the drama of history.[11]

As developed by the French, "existential phenomenology" was not devoid of complications. In Sartre's early writings the elements of his thought seemed almost irreconcilably pitted against each other. His prewar essay on "The Transcendence of the Ego" intensified Husserl's method by "reducing" even the absolute ego and ejecting it from the realm of transcendental consciousness. This intensification had a dual result. On the one hand, the ego was now more firmly embedded in the world of empirical contingency and concrete experience; on the other hand, transcendental consciousness emerged entirely cleansed of encumbrances—a prey to nothingness and at the same time a constitutive source of human designs. In *Being and Nothingness,* transcendental reduction entered into an uneasy alliance with Hegel's dialectic: consciousness or the "for-itself"—characterized by privation and yet the root of man's haunting freedom and responsibility—was shown locked in relentless combat with the world of things or the "in-itself," a fateful embrace in which consciousness was constantly striving to find objective fulfillment but could reach this goal only at the price of self-destruction.[12] Sartre's stark antinomies were mitigated and their terms reformulated by Maurice Merleau-Ponty, whose work revealed the rich potential of a phenomenology sensitive to concrete existence. Drawing chiefly on Husserl's later writings—and also an intimate familiarity with Hegel's phenomenology—Merleau-Ponty depicted existence as "incarnated" consciousness, a consciousness not merely thrust into an alien universe but enmeshed and participating in a life-world and its unfinished fabric of meaning. Reduction, from this vantage point, became an act of amazement and wonder in the midst of this world, stimulated by a loosening of habitual ties; instead of concentrating on anonymous man, phenomenology delved into the perspectival dimensions of experience rooted in perception.

In the meantime, phenomenology has branched out in several directions, animating a variety of pursuits. The most prominent tendencies are the further development of historical and dialectical inquiry and, more or less closely linked with this inquiry, the elucidation of the hermeneutics of intersubjective meaning. With the turn from the absolute ego to embodied existence, phenomenology could no longer be shielded from the pressures of social and historical experience; in proportion to the intensity of these pressures, Hegel tended to give way to Marx. In his *Critique of Dialectical Reason,* Sartre produced a morphology of social development, integrating the existentialist theme of human choice and design with the parameters of a Marxist dialectic. Sartre's work is not the only example of an existentially oriented Marxism; one could also point to Lucien Goldmann's sensitive investigations of historical "structures" and to Leszek Kolakowski's discourse on historical responsibility.[13] However, dialectical argument is no longer a matter of apodictic assertion. With the demolition of the pretense of a scientific history, the articulation of historical purpose has to rely on communication and mutual interrogation; it is at this point that the dialectic makes room for human dialogue. The elucidation of this dialogue is the task of hermeneutics, a hermeneutics no longer confined to the silent discourse between man and his destiny but extended to embrace the interpretation of concrete life-worlds of meaning. To some extent this task is furthered by ordinary language analysis, especially by Wittgenstein's focus in his later writings on concrete "language games" as contrasted to the artifice of a universal scientific vocabulary; yet, hermeneutics seeks not only to grasp internal meaning structures but also to break their code in an effort of interpretation and open communication. Linguistic analysis nevertheless serves as a useful reminder of the dominant medium of meaning assignments; at this juncture a hermeneutics of purpose enlists the support of the phenomenology of language.[14]

II.   Phenomenology and Social Science

The phenomenological enterprise has never been the exclusive domain of philosophers. From the inception of the "movement," its arguments have radiated into a broad spectrum of intellectual and scientific endeavors; due to its primary concern with the search for meaning, repercussions have been strongest in the humanities and social sciences. To be sure, the demarcation between philosophy and adjacent disciplines is frequently hazy and ill-defined; in regard to phenomenology, academic boundary lines have persistently been ignored both by professional philosophers and by their colleagues in other fields. For this reason, a review of the impact of phenomenology cannot rigidly segregate descriptive (or broadly empirical) from philosophical inquiries; committed to open horizons, phenomenology militates against narrow compartmentalization. Yet, for present purposes, some limitations have to be established: using the term in a somewhat narrow sense, the focus will be on the "social sciences." Apart from certain border areas overlapping with sociology, this focus excludes the broad domain of psychology and psychoanalysis—a domain in which the perspective of phenomenology and existentialism has proved remarkably fruitful.[15] Without aiming at comprehensive coverage or a sharp differentiation of disciplines, the following presentation seeks to trace phenomenological repercussions or echoes in sociology, political science, and some versions of social psychology.

There are striking affinities between the phenomenological perspective and the arguments of some of the "founders" of modern sociology. In the case of Max Weber, the parallels have frequently been noted. To be sure, Weber was not directly affiliated with any of the phenomenological circles of the time. His philosophical frame of reference was provided by Dilthey and Rickert or rather the historical school as reformulated by Rickert; thus his thinking was deeply permeated by the distinction between natural and "cultural" sciences. In his early methodological studies the influence of Rickert was particularly pronounced, especially his emphasis on "individualizing" study. As Weber argued at the time, the goal of the cultural (including the social) sciences was not simply to subsume data under general and necessarily abstract laws—although such laws could serve as subsidiary tools—but to grasp the richness of concrete reality in its cultural significance, a significance derived from the embeddedness of phenomena in a context of values.[16] Only to a limited extent were these sciences amenable to general formulation: through the design of condensed meaning structures or "ideal types." In *Economy and Society*, the chief accent was still on the search for significance although the conceptual arsenal was vastly expanded. As Weber insisted, physical occurrences and merely reactive behavior, even if subsumed under laws, were not the primary targets of social science; rather, the central focus was on social "action," a term denoting human behavior "when and insofar as the acting individual attaches a subjective meaning to it." Consequently, sociology was defined as an inquiry aiming at the "interpretive understanding (*Verstehen*) of social action"—an understanding involving chiefly the elucidation of the "complex of meaning in which an actual course of understandable action thus interpreted belongs," but not necessarily an act of psychic reproduction.[17]

In an indirect manner, a linkage between Weber and early phenomenology can be traced in the work of Adolf Reinach, a close associate of Husserl and a leading figure in the Göttingen circle. Although his work has remained a torso, it is possible to extrapolate suggestive propositions relevant to sociological analysis. The starting point of his conception was a theory of "social acts," referring primarily to acts intentionally directed toward social partners and "in need of being received and understood" by these partners. In social experience, a series of such acts tended to coalesce in characteristic patterns and configurations. The purpose of phenomenological inquiry, in Reinach's view, was not simply to explore the psychological motivations of social agents. Under the impact of Husserl's *Logical Investigations* and the injunction against psychologism, he aimed at an inspection of the essential features or pure structures of social patterns, an inspection aided by intuition and theoretical idealization.[18] Possibly, the notion of pure structures also provides a connecting link between early phenomenology and Georg Simmel's "formal" sociology, as Edward Tiryakian has attempted to show. Like Weber, Simmel built his theory on the bedrock of social action and interaction, on the view that society is the product of a complex web of interlocking pursuits. While "general" sociology ranged over the broad fabric of social life, the function of "formal" sociology was to investigate the pure "social forms" of interaction—such as competition, division of labor, and stratification—independently of special contents and motivations. "Although he diverged from Husserl in some respects," Tiryakian claims, "Simmel's study of social life may be viewed as an *eidetic one,* in the sense that he sought to reduce manifestly different forms of social phenomena to their underlying essential characteristics ('forms')."[19]

While Simmel's position may be in doubt, Alfred Vierkandt is commonly recognized as a leading exponent of phenomenological sociology. In common with Weber and the historical school, Vierkandt differentiated between natural and cultural sciences. In his formulation, natural sciences dealt with the world of things mute or indifferent to human purpose, while cultural sciences probed the realm of social interaction, a realm resonant to questions of meaning. Sociology in particular was defined as science of the essential forms or structures of social interaction and culture. In developing his theory Vierkandt acknowledged a certain indebtedness to Simmel's insights; yet, as he emphasized, these insights required a more solid philosophical and methodological underpinning. Regarding method, he adopted in large part the arsenal of pure phenomenology, especially "eidetic" reduction: the phenomena of social interaction were to be reduced to their essential structures through intuitive inspection. Actually, Vierkandt proceeded to reduce social forms further to a deeper layer—a layer of basic social dispositions or "categories" of social experience. As he observed, dispositions of this kind were innate or natural endowments which, for their activation, required the presence or responsiveness of other human beings. On this categorial basis, Vierkandt then constructed a typology of major forms of social interaction, relying to some extent on Ferdinand Toennies' dichotomy of "community" and "society"; the distinction between these types derived primarily from the degree and intensity of intersubjective communication and concord. Considering his reliance on phenomenological reduction, he seemed little perturbed by the peril of solipsism: quite apart from psychic reenactments, intentionality seemed directly accessible to intuitive understanding and empathy.[20]

Vierkandt's categories of social experience can be viewed as a rudimentary outline of a "philosophical anthropology"—a type of study launched at the time by Max Scheler (whose influence he credited at several points). Actually, Scheler's rank as a sociologist was hardly inferior to his philosophical standing; his combined endeavors reached a peak during his later life when he taught in both disciplines at Cologne. His general sociological outlook showed the imprint both of phenomenology and the historical school, an imprint reflected primarily in his distinction between empirical and cultural sociology. While empirical research dealt with "real" factors such as drives and impulses, cultural sociology was concerned with the realm of essential structures, the realm of ideas and values. This distinction formed also the basis of his philosophical anthropology, with its bifurcation between biological drives and a metabiological "spirit." Yet Scheler was by no means content with the statement of antinomies. In his view, a major task of sociology as well as of philosophy was to investigate the interaction between real and ideal factors, the convergence of vitalistic and normative elements in society and history. This objective led him to another new field of research: the sociology of knowledge, designed to analyze the concrete matrix of culture. The new focus, to be sure, had little effect on his basic philosophical outlook; socio-historical genesis did not jeopardize the essence and validity of knowledge.[21]

Scheler's sociological legacy is impressive and diverse; his major impact, however, has undoubtedly been in the areas of "philosophical anthropology" and the sociology of knowledge. Regarding the former, a broad "school" of thought has emerged in the wake of his analysis— a school, it is true, whose members have departed considerably from his example and are far from sharing a uniform outlook. The leading representatives of philosophical anthropology in this sense are Arnold Gehlen, Erich Rothacker, and Helmuth Plessner; among these, Plessner deserves special mention in this context, chiefly because of his proximity to the phenomenological movement, a proximity dating back to his association with Scheler at Cologne. Since his perspective has been discussed in the preceding chapter, I can limit myself here to a brief summary. Trained as a biologist but deeply affected by Dilthey and the historical school, Plessner shared Scheler's overriding concern with man's nature and status in the order of the universe; yet, he was comparatively less inclined toward metaphysical speculation or a substantive ontology. Drawing partly on the theory of multiple biological environments developed by Jakob von Uexküll, Plessner defined man as a broken and elusive creature, a creature deprived of a natural habitat or ecology and compelled to a continuous search for meaning under open horizons. In the stress on openness and "ec-centricity," his conception resembled to some extent Heidegger's analysis of existence (*Dasein*). However, Plessner's anthropology included from the beginning a concern with man's body as well as the dimension of historical experience; more importantly, society was not relegated to the level of bland anonymity.[22] Although devoid of a natural ecology, man was constantly engaged in the construction of an artificial or cultural habitat of norms and institutions—a habitat, to be sure, which always remained fragile and tentative. Instead of being diverted from his goal, man discovered himself and his tasks through social interaction and through the reciprocal effort of role interpretation and role assignment.

In the domain of the sociology of knowledge, Scheler's legacy was cultivated primarily by Karl Mannheim. To be sure, Mannheim's work is multifaceted and entirely resists a brief summary, a circumstance related to the diversity of his philosophical inspirations. A student of both Rickert and Husserl, he was closely acquainted during his formative years with Weber, Scheler, and Georg Lukács; the same intellectual versatility accompanied him throughout his life. To some extent, Mannheim's development illustrates the transition from pure to existential phenomenology. While his early writings reflected a fusion of pure inspection with neo-Kantian formalism, his exposure to Marxism—chiefly mediated through Lukács—turned his attention to more concrete human and historical dimensions. As he wrote in "Competition as a Cultural Phenomenon," phenomenology has increasingly come to realize that "certain insights concerning some qualitative aspects of the living process of history are available to consciousness only as formed by certain historical and social circumstances, so that the historico-social formation of the thinking and knowing subject assumes epistemological importance."[23] In the construction of his sociological theory, this perspective was corroborated by his broad training in the "cultural sciences." Together with Weber he conceived society as a network of purposive social actions; at the same time he transformed Weber's ideal types into less formalized "structures" of meaning—structures dynamically emerging from social interaction and continuously open to reinterpretation. These structures were also the matrix of values and ideas, sometimes condensed into *Weltanschauungen*. While unwilling to embrace a simplistic doctrine of economic determinism, Mannheim took seriously Scheler's (and Lukács') view of the interpenetration of real and ideal factors. This view, dominant in his sociology of knowledge, led him to the conception of "relationism," denoting an interlocking web of life-worlds and perspectival dimensions. In the end, of course, his neo-Kantian training reasserted itself, in the stipulation of a neutral scientific domain, guarded by "socially unattached" intellectuals.[24]

From the vantage point of contemporary social science, the most prominent representative of a phenomenology sensitive to existential concerns is undoubtedly Alfred Schutz. Through his activity on both continents Schutz's writings constitute an important link between European phenomenology and American sociology and social psychology. His thought represents a nodal juncture in other respects as well. Philosophically, he developed major insights implicit in Husserl's later writings and, in doing so, foreshadowed some of the arguments of the French school of phenomenology. Regarding social science, he constructed a bridge between phenomenological inquiry and Weber's theory of social action. To be sure, the integration of these diverse facets was not a sudden accomplishment, nor was it exempt from revision; despite a remarkable internal consistency, Schutz's life clearly was a journey in more than a geographical sense.

His early endeavors showed the pervasive imprint of the transcendental reduction, combined with residues of a neo-Kantian epistemology. In his *Phenomenology of the Social World*, first published in 1932, he subjected Weber's interpretive sociology to a sympathetic but searching analysis, in an effort to clarify the core notion of meaningful social action. In undertaking this task, Schutz enlisted the help of Henri Bergson and chiefly of Husserl's transcendental phenomenology for, as he wrote, "the meaning-structure of the social world can only be deduced from the most primitive and general characteristics of consciousness." By means of phenomenological reduction he found the source of meaning in the stream of lived experience or internal time-sense, and more specifically in the reflective glance of the ego upon such experience. Against the background of lived experience in general, "action" was differentiated in terms of the prospective assignment of meaning, an assignment orienting behavior toward a goal or "project" envisaged "in the future perfect tense"; in motivational terms the project could be described as the "in-order-to motive" of the action as distinct from "because-motives." Turning to the social world—and replacing the strict method of reduction with the "attitude of the natural standpoint"—Schutz defined "social action" as project-oriented experience or behavior whose in-order-to motive contains reference to another self. Regarding intersubjective relations, he argued that genuine understanding of behavior was possible only in a limited domain, the domain of directly experienced social reality (*Umwelt*), especially in face-to-face encounters with immediate consociates. However, there were other horizons of experience beyond direct encounter: especially the dimensions of contemporaries (*Mitwelt*), predecessors (*Vorwelt*), and successors (*Folgewelt*). In these dimensions understanding was possible only through typifications of behavior, typifications endowed with greater or lesser anonymity and including, in the case of contemporaries, mutual role assignments and interpretations. Social science dealt primarily with such typified meaning structures. Despite his emphasis on horizons of experience, Schutz shared Weber's conception of the social scientist as neutral observer capable of penetrating, through the construction of ideal types, the diverse meaning dimensions of social reality.[25]

Subsequent experiences broadened and enriched Schutz's perspective. In a series of essays he examined in detail the theme of intersubjectivity as treated by Scheler and existentialists like Sartre. Also, especially after his arrival in the United States, he began to probe affinities between phenomenology and the thought of William James, Alfred North Whitehead, George Herbert Mead, and others. The most important development, however, was his growing concentration on *Lebenswelt*, the world of "daily life" and "common sense" experienced from the perspective of the "natural attitude." Although the paramount reality for every individual, this domain was by no means anonymous or undifferentiated. For the individual the everyday world was first of all a system of coordinates centered around his body and his "biographical situation"; but this system was not a private invention. Individual experience included from the beginning a "stock of knowledge at hand," a stock made up of typifications of behavior and sustained by a general "reciprocity of perspectives." Instead of being a fixed premise, the individual ego was the result of interaction and reciprocal role interpretations. Intersubjective understanding, quite apart from its epistemological and methodological connotations, thus emerged as a primary type of experience: as "the experiential form of common-sense knowledge of human affairs." Reflecting its openness, individual awareness also tended to be fragmented and elusive, due to the individual's involvement in a variety of social contexts and role structures. According to Schutz, this involvement was governed by the individual's active pursuits and framework of relevance. Even at this point, however, a reciprocity of perspectives prevailed: the diverse frames of relevance were all derived from a basic existential source, man's "fundamental anxiety" in the face of his mortality. As a result of his intense concern with *Lebenswelt*, Schutz developed a more reserved attitude toward egological arguments; correspondingly, his perspective became sensitive both to questions of "philosophical anthropology" and to the diversified historical dimensions of experience.[26]

To be sure, the focus on *Lebenswelt* did not resolve all quandaries. Was everyday life merely a surface feature to be purified through transcendental reduction, or was it presupposed by such an enterprise? This question was intimately related to the task of analysis. Was the social scientist a universal observer immune from the constraints of his life-world? Or was he immersed in the "natural attitude," but to the detriment of articulation and interpretation?[27] Recognition of such quandaries does not affect the merit of Schutz's main contributions, nor the pervasiveness of his impact. Largely as a result of his activity, mutually beneficial contacts have been established between phenomenology and American social science and social psychology, especially with the school of symbolic interactionism inspired by Mead—a contact which is hardly surprising in view of Mead's emphasis on meaningful "social acts" and on the formation of the self through a process of reciprocal role interpretations.[28].

In contemporary social science, the impulse of Schutz's work is most prominently displayed in "ethnomethodology" and recent developments in the sociology of knowledge. Of the two trends, the former is perhaps more ambitiously conceived, but also more ambiguously formulated; its chief representatives are Aaron Cicourel and Harold Garfinkel. The basic aim of ethnomethodology—loosely akin to "ethnoscience" in anthropology—is to explore the arena of common-sense experience, to understand the world as perceived and acted upon by participants in everyday situations. Stimulated by Schutz's distinction between typifications and common-sense perception, Cicourel has attempted to remedy the arbitrary features of social science constructions through an analysis of the life-world. In his view, only a developed "theory of culture," aiming at the rules and meaning-structures of ordinary life, can provide a legitimate basis for scientific analysis and measurement.[29] Garfinkel, who frequently voices his indebtedness to Schutz, has elaborated a series of experimental devices for testing the parameters of the life-world; unfortunately, his endeavors tend to be obscured by cumbersome language. According to a competent observer, he is chiefly preoccupied "with the practical everyday activities of men in society as they make accountable, to themselves and others, their everyday affairs, and with the methods they use for producing and managing these same affairs."[30] A major technique employed by Garfinkel in his investigations is the "demonstration experiment," a procedure relying on the disturbance or disruption of ordinary situations in an effort to uncover implicit common-sense assumptions. Clearly, this technique is designed to penetrate the life-world without submerging the observer in the "natural attitude."

Broadly related to ethnomethodology, but more cogently stated, are recent reassessments of the sociology of knowledge. The main protagonists in this domain are Peter Berger and Thomas Luckmann, former students and collaborators of Schutz. In their formulation, the sociology of knowledge is concerned primarily with the range of common-sense, prescientific "knowledge" in a society—with whatever members of that society accept as the "reality" of their everyday situation. Since such knowledge, however, is not privately invented but is developed in social interaction, the task of this sociology becomes "the analysis of the social construction of reality." By concentrating on everyday perceptions the authors redefine and expand the enterprise initiated by Scheler and Mannheim: instead of limiting themselves to ideal factors or ideologies, their perspective comprises "everything that passes for 'knowledge' in society." In developing their conception, Berger and Luckmann acknowledge various sources of inspiration: apart from Schutz, these sources include Mead and the school of symbolic interactionism, "philosophical anthropology" as practiced chiefly by Plessner and Gehlen, as well as the young Marx and elements of Durkheim's thought. Against this theoretical background the authors find the core issue of sociology in general—and the sociology of knowledge in particular—in the relation between society as an "objective" and a "subjective" dimension, in the question of how society can be the result of meaningful human action and at the same time confront man as objective reality congealed in institutions and typifications. As they try to show—following a careful phenomenological investigation of the life-world—this dilemma can only be resolved dialectically: "Society is a human product. Society is an objective reality. Man is a social product."[31]

As described by Berger and Luckmann, the life-world is not simply a natural ecology, but assumes dynamic and disquieting features. In their assessment, there is a definite need "to bring to bear a dialectical perspective upon the theoretical orientation of the social sciences." Although not abundant, there are examples in contemporary social thought pointing in the direction of a dialectical phenomenology and even a phenomenological Marxism. In *Search for a Method*, Sartre outlined a "progressive-regressive" method inspired partly by Henri Lefèbvre, a method including among its steps phenomenological description and the "understanding" or interpretive comprehension of phenomena in the context of an evolving synthesis. A similar intent is reflected in Kolakowski's query whether Marxism can be adapted to an interpretive type of investigation.[32] In the sociological domain, the main representative of a dialectical phenomenology is Georges Gurvitch, although his perspective combines a variety of heterogeneous (including positivist) ingredients. Despite the complexity of his views, his work reflects at least in a broad sense the transition from a transcendental to a dialectical phenomenology. Attracted to phenomenology chiefly through contacts with Scheler, he sketched in his early writings the outlines of a "microsociology" concerned primarily with forms of sociability or basic modes of social experience. At the same time, a combination of Husserl's transcendental reduction with Durkheim's morphology of social reality led him to the formulation of an ambitious "depth sociology," designed to trace social experience back through a series of layers to the bedrock of consciousness. More recently, the preoccupation with reduction has been replaced or at least fused with the emphasis on dialectical method. Far from implying a closed system of explanation, however, the dialectic to Gurvitch signifies only a tool for open-ended inquiry; on the basis of a radical empiricism this inquiry probes the dynamic transformations of meaning-structures, the continuous differentiation and integration of phenomena in the broader synthesis of social experience.[33]

The notion of an open dialectic is bound to remain opaque unless it is grounded in an ongoing intersubjective assessment of situations; such assessment presupposes communication and articulation. Basing himself to a large extent on Wittgenstein's later writings, Peter Winch, in his *Idea of a Social Science,* developed a sociolinguistic perspective focusing on the linkage between social action and ordinary discourse. In his view, intelligible behavior implies adherence to the explicit or implicit rules characteristic of the grammar of a language community; the task of social science is to understand or decipher the meaning of behavior by viewing it in the context of this grammar which, in turn, reflects a particular way or "form" of social life.[34] Yet, the social scientist is not exempt from the parameters of ordinary discourse; understanding, thus, would seem to imply an effort of translation aiming at the elucidation of perspectival life-worlds. Traces of such an effort can be found above all in contemporary social psychology; among others, Anselm Strauss has portrayed individual life as a story of successive reinterpretations of actions and episodes. A hermeneutics of this kind seems equally congenial to the explication of diverse social and historical dimensions of experience.[35]

III.   Comments and Appraisals

In the course of its development phenomenology has given rise to a long line of commentaries and more or less animated evaluations; both its more strictly philosophical and its sociological formulations have been the target of summary endorsements or condemnations. For present purposes it must suffice to draw attention briefly to some of the issues confronting a phenomenological social science. In this domain, the lines of debate have frequently—but not exclusively—been drawn by philosophers of science; to a large extent, the debate revolves around the relationship between the natural and social sciences, with the opponents of phenomenology asserting a basic symmetry or methodological convergence between the two arenas of investigation. There is no intention here to rekindle the animosities surrounding the controversy about behavioralism. It seems fair to point out, however, that—apart from isolated gestures of reconciliation and good will—there has been remarkably little communication between the protagonists of the dispute. Generally speaking, spokesmen of the symmetry thesis have been unduly assertive about the solidity and monolithic firmness of their position, thus ignoring dissenting views among philosophers of science who recognize the need for contextual analysis.[36] Also, buttressed by the vogue of professional opinion, these spokesmen have been reluctant to consider the phenomenological argument seriously and on its own terms. Defects of this kind could easily be demonstrated with reference to such recurrent sources of contention as the desirable degree of "objectivity" in the social sciences and the character of typifications and "ideal" structures;[37] at this point the notion of interpretive understanding may serve as an illustrative example.

The main charge leveled against phenomenology in the social sciences concerns the supposed unreliability of its method of inquiry, especially the hopeless subjectivism deriving from its reliance on understanding (*Verstehen*). Critics commonly have made little or no effort to differentiate among phenomenologists, although there are distinct variations of accent between such types of investigation as the eidetic inspection of essences and the hermeneutic scrutiny of life-worlds. Apart from this lack of discrimination, critical comments frequently display a strange unfamiliarity with the topic under discussion. Even a cursory acquaintance with the relevant literature reveals that phenomenologists are far from equating understanding with simple introspection or psychic reproduction; as Weber already insisted, interpretive social science by no means presupposes adherence to the maxim that "one has to be Caesar in order to understand Caesar." Nor does phenomenology assume that psychic states are more readily accessible than physical objects. What these and similar charges ignore is the origin of phenomenology in the revolt against psychologism. In the social sciences, the aim of interpretive reconstruction is not an indulgence in psychic idiosyncracies but the elucidation of social action in a meaning context intelligible from the actor's perspective.[38] Moreover, as Schutz has pointed out, understanding is not only a methodological device, but a common-sense experience involved in intersubjective encounters of everyday life; viewed in this sense, an interpretive endeavor precedes and is at the basis of the most rigorous scientific pursuits. This aspect also has a bearing on the issue of validation. In Ernest Nagel's assessment, understanding serves at best the purpose of generating imaginative hypotheses, but lacks entirely the capacity of validating explanations. While it would certainly be misleading to confuse imaginative insight with demonstration, scientific method hardly constitutes the only means of intersubjective verification. As an example, Schutz points to the interpretive assessment of a defendant by his jury; others have suggested a broader analogy to the justification of moral conduct where "testing" normally involves an attempt to provide adequate reasons.[39] Without such forms of intersubjective validation, ordinary social life would seem impossible.

Misconceptions about phenomenology are not always the result of hasty reading; sometimes they are provoked by shortcomings of its practitioners. The quandaries and hazards inherent in the phenomenological enterprise have been candidly discussed by such sympathetic critics as Stephan Strasser and Jürgen Habermas. In Strasser's view, there are a series of peculiar "dangers" or temptations to which phenomenologists tend to be exposed. The chief danger is the lure of arbitrary and undisciplined speculation, the indulgence in private monologues; a formidable obstacle to the search for valid knowledge, this lure frequently manifests itself in a disdain for rigorous inquiry, in the haughty presumption of being exempt from the constraints of methodology, scientific or otherwise. Among other temptations he lists the pitfall of a "phenomenological impressionism," reflecting a naive trust in superficial observation and in the virtues of the "natural attitude"; at least equally damaging is the resort to rhetoric and stylistic subterfuge, the practice of camouflaging the dearth of insights behind a smoke screen of sentimentality or verbal obscurity.[40] Habermas' comments are addressed more directly to the predicaments of the phenomenological method. Identifying phenomenology somewhat narrowly with pure inspection, he questions the competence of transcendental consciousness, its supposed ability to disentangle the meaning structures of life-worlds while being sovereignly immune from perspectival constraints. A similar query applies to sociolinguistic analysis, particularly to the observer's ambition of decoding language games. Turning to hermeneutics and stressing the merits of this type of inquiry, Habermas cautions against the perils of a unidimensional methodology and against the neglect of such limiting parameters as technology and political power.[41]

Perhaps this is the place for a personal appraisal. In my estimate, phenomenological social science would do well to heed the comments of its friendly critics; its endeavors can only benefit from a determination to resist the embrace of spurious allies. Above all, phenomenology should not be confused with private phantasy or with the search for peculiar psychic experiences; at least in this respect practitioners must always be mindful of Husserl's example, the example of careful, modest, and painstaking investigation. Uncontrolled subjectivism also leads phenomenology into the danger of ignoring the limits of purposive social action. Although a product of continuous human design, society is capable of subverting well-meant intentions; as Berger and Luckmann have shown, the social world tends to confront its agents as an objective reality condensed in institutions and typical life styles. To the extent that objective reality in this sense is the target of exact science, phenomenology is ill-advised to be contemptuous of scientific pursuits. The conflict between rigorous science and philosophical or humanistic inquiries has been deplored by leading phenomenologists; as Merleau-Ponty observed at one point: "We have to show that science is possible, that the sciences of man are possible, and that all the same philosophy is possible. It is necessary in particular to end the rift between systematic philosophy and the advancing knowledge of science."[42] The neglect of science seems particularly inappropriate at a time when social reality is increasingly saturated with technological devices and when the fruits of science are in the process of permeating man's life-world and his everyday vocabulary. Science and technology, however, are not the only factors impinging on ordinary life; their impact is matched and perhaps overshadowed by the chronic effects of power and domination. Far from representing a uniform natural ecology, the life-world implies vastly different experiences for people at different levels of the social and political hierarchy. In an age of worldwide social ferment, phenomenology can ill afford to indulge in idyllic portrayals and "picture book" illustrations of the human condition.

With this emphasis on the fragmentation of the social life-world, the discussion returns to the crises of our time. These crises constitute a challenge not only to man's practical resourcefulness, but also to deeply cherished intellectual habits. Many of the current dilemmas have been fomented or at least aggravated by an intellectual myopia which, while insisting on the complete purity of scientific research, ignored the human and social ramifications of the scientific enterprise. According to the approved canons of methodology, both the scientist's inventiveness and intuition and the social and political purposes served by this work are outside the range of his professional concern; hopelessly tainted by arbitrary preferences, these domains are placed beyond the pale of intelligible conversation. It is at this point that phenomenology breaks decisively with established convention, by reclaiming the vast areas of prescientific "knowledge" and common-sense assumptions as legitimate topics of inquiry. In its effort to recover even the dark residues of reason for human dialogue, phenomenology appears as the proper heir of the European enlightenment—as Husserl has tried to show in the *Crisis of European Sciences*. To be sure, ambitions tend to be more subdued in our time; enlightenment in its present sense does not imply commitment to the myth of a total rationality, but only to the elementary standards of common decency and social discourse. Due to their focus on human interaction, the social sciences are peculiarly destined to participate in this heritage. By keeping open the horizons of his inquiry, the social scientist remains faithful to Husserl's injunction: "We are ... through our philosophical activity the servants of humanity."

5. Hobbes and Existentialism: Some Affinities

FROM THE DISTANT SHORES of Stuart England Thomas Hobbes still speaks to us in a strangely familiar and captivating idiom. Having traversed the rugged expanse of three centuries, some of his words are obviously muffled and obscure, but whatever the obstacles, our generation seems willing to strain in order to perceive more clearly the subtle inflections of this voice.

During the past decades the literature devoted to Hobbes has expanded rapidly both in volume and in breadth of focus, covering the most diverse topics of his natural and civil philosophy. The reasons for this preoccupation are complex and elusive. To some extent the preoccupation may stem from the fact that Hobbes stood at the beginning of various intellectual and social trends that have culminated or have been eclipsed in our own time. According to Crawford Macpherson, Hobbes was one of the first advocates of "possessive individualism," an anthropological doctrine that concentrated on the accumulation and protection of property as man's primary motives and became a cornerstone of the market economy and modern industrial society. Taking a broader view, Jürgen Habermas identified Hobbes as one of the ancestors of technological rationalism, a rationalism that in its combination of rigorous analysis and technical invention continues to animate the "scientific revolution" of our age.[1] These and similar interpretations undoubtedly possess great plausibility and persuasiveness, but they hardly tell the entire story. Neither Hobbes's vocabulary nor our own seems restricted to this range of discourse. While attractive to the scientific mentality of a technological era, Hobbes's voice also reaches us on a different level of frequency—the level of basic human experience. From this vantage point one may

120

legitimately query whether and to what extent Hobbes's idiom bears resemblance to that of contemporary existentialist literature. The following pages seek to explore this question, on the assumption that a comparison should contribute to the mutual clarification of the arguments of both partners.

The attempt to trace a linkage between Hobbes and existentialism is likely to seem whimsical or extravagant. One may object that the enterprise is excessively subjective and that violence is done to the "original" Hobbes in an effort to render him our contemporary. But this charge exaggerates the ambition of these pages; the intent here is not to present Hobbes as an "existentialist," nor even as a spiritual parent in a direct historical lineage, but merely to suggest a certain affinity, a feasibility of developing some of his statements in an existentialist direction. To part of the charge, however, I plead guilty without embarrassment: any interpretation proceeds from the perspective of one's own experience. My interest is, in any event, not antiquarian; if it could be shown that Hobbes was merely a remote ancestor living in a world totally alien to our own, I would simply conclude that I have no business with him. In a slight reformulation of the same charge, one might object that the proposed exploration ignores the lapse of time and implies an immutable anthropology or the postulate of a constant human nature behind the flux of social configurations. The argument presented in these pages, however, does not properly involve a fixed human ontology, but at best suggests a certain way of viewing the world and man in the world. Moreover, despite profound fissures and upheavals, the passage of three centuries has hardly produced the irreparable breach that would preclude the intended comparison.

Another query that cannot be escaped concerns terminology: to present Hobbes from the perspective of "existentialism" is to assume an obligation to clarify the use of this notoriously ambiguous concept. To some extent, I must resort to a stipulative procedure. No effort will be made here to delve into the recesses of religious existentialism or into the intricacies of Heideggerian ontology; the discussion will instead be limited to a certain secular and progressive version, a version exemplified in the writings of Maurice Merleau-Ponty, Jean-Paul Sartre, and, to some extent, Albert Camus.[2] At this point the content of this version will be outlined only roughly. In the thinking of all three writers, existentialism proceeds at least in a loose way from the proposition that existence precedes essence, that human life is not channeled by a preordained teleology inherent either in nature or in reason. Human experience, in this view, is intimately wedded to concrete phenomena and situations; man is expelled from the refuge of a transcendent spirituality but, nevertheless, constantly eludes the world of objects through an act of withdrawal or denial. Existence thus is a state of breach or estrangement and at the same time an incessant search to remedy the breach. Alienation and anxiety have frequently been identified as basic existentialist concerns, but exclusive reliance on these concerns may tend to submerge existentialism in sentiment and psychic peculiarities. Perhaps Merleau-Ponty offered a corrective to this tendency when he wrote:

> A more complete definition of what is called existentialism than we get from talking of anxiety and the contradictions of the human condition might be found in the idea of a universality which men affirm or imply by the mere fact of their being and at the very moment of their opposition to each other, in the idea of a reason immanent in unreason, of a freedom which comes into being in the act of accepting limits and to which the least perception, the slightest movement of the body, the smallest action, bear incontestable witness.[3]

I.   Anthropology and Social Conflict

For purposes of the proposed comparison it seems appropriate to follow the road Hobbes takes in developing his philosophical argument. After having delineated principles of analysis and the basic properties of inanimate and animate bodies, Hobbes embarks on an examination of human attitudes and dispositions in their "natural" state or in the absence of a civil community. Some of the propositions advanced at this point have received wide currency as distinctive trademarks of his thought, but their basis is less frequently explored. The thesis of man's "perpetual and restless desire of power after power, that ceases only in death" and the portrayal of "natural" human life as "solitary, poor, nasty, brutish, and short" are sometimes ascribed to the pessimism, if not the base disposition, of the philosopher. His anthropology is thus reduced to a personal idiosyncrasy. To be sure, the context in which these propositions are advanced does not always enhance their persuasiveness. The argument that perception and sensory experience result from bodily movements and countermovements might lead the reader to the conclusion that, far from being compelled to a restless search, man could be sufficiently constrained and contented by this circulation of movements. The situation is not remedied by the assumption of a basic fissure in Hobbes's view of man and by the appeal from a "mechanistic" to a "vitalistic" or spiritualistic version of anthropology; in the latter version, man might still find repose in an unlimited internality and transcendence.[4] Although it is probably true that Hobbes never fully clarified his thoughts on this point, many of his observations seem to indicate a view that is by no means unfamiliar to existentialism: the conception of the congruous incongruity of human experience, of man as a deficiency constantly in quest of reality.

The contours of this incongruity emerged only slowly in Hobbes's writings. In the first sketch of his philosophical position, the thesis of the dependence of human motivation and of animal motion in general on external impacts was joined almost abruptly with the conception of a restless competition and discord; the nexus remained largely implicit.[5] Yet the treatment of human sensation in terms of a quasi-mechanical motion seemed to preclude at least the metaphysical notion of a human essence, of a preordained teleology gently directing man's path with the promise of fulfillment. Some implications of man's predicament were developed in *De Cive*. Arguing against Aristotle's view of man as a "political animal," Hobbes in the opening chapter maintained that nature had not provided man so conveniently with a goal or haven. While admitting that it might seem "a wonderful kind of stupidity" to place this stumbling block in the threshold of his doctrine, he insisted that man's inclinations and desires, even when ultimately directed at social commerce, did not by themselves procure peace. Civil society was, in short, the result less of natural inclination than of design and planning. The nexus between natural inclinations and human discord was explored more fully in the *Leviathan*. Although alluded to in earlier writings, the divergence between animal and human experience was now specified in greater detail and the borderline demarcated; almost invariably, the distinctive criterion was placed in the peculiar structure of human consciousness and imagination. Thus while signals of command were found to be intelligible to most animate creatures, man was assigned the special capacity of "understanding not only his will, but his conceptions and thoughts, by the sequel and contexture of the names of things into affirmations, negations and other forms of speech." Moreover, man could go beyond the immediate confines of perception by trying to determine the likely consequences and possible uses of an object—a faculty, Hobbes writes, "of which I have not at any time seen any sign but in man only; for this is a curiosity hardly incident to the nature of any living creature that has no other passion but sensual." Coupled with this inventiveness was man's rational potential, his ability developed through training to "reduce the consequences he finds to general rules," to "reason or reckon, not only in number, but in all other things."[6]

Largely on the basis of these arguments Hobbes then advanced his general thesis of the deficiency and restlessness of human life. The absence of a preordained essence and the incongruity between man's imagination and the world supported the conclusion that man on earth could not find ultimate fulfillment or a *finis ultimus*, that the "felicity of this life" resided not "in the repose of a mind satisfied" nor in the attainment of an object, but rather in the "continual progress of the desire from one object to another, the attaining of the former being still but the way to the latter." The further proposition of human conflict and discord could be attached to this thesis without great difficulty, for in the pursuit of his goals, man cannot avoid encountering others engaged in a similar endeavor. This general search or race, however, is dominated not only by a (historically variable) scarcity of desired goods, but above all by a scarcity of positions in front or on top, and from this scarcity derives the danger of hostility and even physical destruction. Moreover, man in the pursuit of his ends has to assure himself constantly of the necessary means, and, due to their diverse abilities, other human beings are liable to be employed as such objects or instruments or to be subdued or destroyed in case of resistance. As Hobbes suggests, there are three principal sources of human conflict—competition, diffidence, and resentment: competition to use and subdue others as objects, diffidence of being used or subdued as such, and resentment for being valued more as an object than as a person.[7]

As will readily be admitted, the discussed issues continue to reverberate strongly in contemporary existentialist thought; indeed, man's predicament in a disenchanted universe is sometimes identified as existentialism's chief concern. In the writings of Albert Camus, man is portrayed as a wandering stranger, an exile in a silent and inhospitable land. While perhaps transparent to a divine intelligence, the world does not disclose a meaning *for man*, a justification of his presence. "In a universe suddenly divested of illusions and lights," Camus writes, "man feels an alien, a stranger. His exile is without remedy since he is deprived of the memory of a lost home or the hope of a promised land." In the absence of a preordained teleology, human life becomes a defiant adventure, a voyage without the promise of a safe harbor; "man is the only creature who refuses to be what he is." On this voyage, the longing for rest and fulfillment has to be abandoned as an illusory hope. The man who realizes his predicament, the "absurdity" of his condition, is also "that individual who wants to achieve everything and live everything," whose ambition is "first and foremost being faced with the world as often as possible."[8] From this general quest, the likelihood of human conflict would seem to follow as a natural consequence. Curiously, despite his emphasis on rebellion and revolt, Camus never devoted much attention to conflict. The rebellion which preoccupied him was more a protest against man's predicament than an actual contest between men. His thoughts, it seems, were always impatient to reach the stage of general human concord and understanding.

In a more patient and methodical manner, other contemporary thinkers have examined the evidence and consequences of man's predicament. In a comment on Hegel's *Phenomenology*, Merleau-Ponty observed that "man, as opposed to the pebble which is what it is, is defined as a place of unrest (*Unruhe*), a constant effort to get back to himself, and consequently by his refusal to limit himself to one or another of his determinations." The source of this unrest was assigned precisely to the incongruity of human experience, to the discrepancy between consciousness and the objects of the world. "Whatever relationships may be shown to exist between consciousness and the body or brain," he argued, "all the discoveries of phrenology will not suffice to make consciousness a *bone*, for a bone is still a thing or a being, and if the only components of the world were things or beings, there would not be even a semblance of what we call man—that is, a being which is not, which denies things, an existence without an essence." According to Merleau-Ponty, however, human experience was distinguished not only from a "bone," but also from animal life because of the different structure of awareness. Consciousness, he wrote, "implies the ability to step back from any given thing and to deny it. An animal can quietly find contentment in life and can seek salvation in reproduction; man's only access to the universal is the fact that he exists instead of merely living. . . . Life can only be thought of as revealed to a consciousness of life which denies it." Yet, the view of existence as denial and negation remains elusive on the level of definition; negation becomes concrete experience only in man's encounter with other human beings. At this point, phenomenology adds a philosophical criterion to Hobbes's anthropological argument of human conflict. Due to the incongruent juncture of consciousness and the world, the awakening of individual awareness is bound to reduce other human beings to the status of objects of awareness, a reduction that may proceed from the denial of their human quality to the level of violence and physical destruction. In the words of Merleau-Ponty: "The only experience which brings me close to an authentic awareness of death is the experience of contact with another, since under his gaze I am only an object just as he is merely a piece of the world under my own. Thus each consciousness seeks the death of the other which it feels dispossesses it of its constitutive nothingness."[9]

Sartre's writings abound with descriptions of human incompleteness and insufficiency. Already one of his earliest studies explored man's vertigo or anguish before the recognition that nothing in his past or personality structure ensured or excused his pattern of conduct. In the novel *Nausea*, the protagonist is overcome by the lack of a preordained meaning or purpose, by the realization that existence is contingent and unjustifiable. "We are a heap of living creatures, irritated, embarrassed at ourselves," Roquentin observes; "we hadn't the slightest reason to be there, none of us; each one, confused, vaguely alarmed, felt *de trop*, in relation to the others." In *Being and Nothingness* this deficiency was investigated and corroborated from the perspective of consciousness. Man, Sartre now argued, is "the being through whom nothingness comes into the world," the being whose life implies an incessant withdrawal and negation. The relation of existence to essence in man is "not comparable to what it is for the things of the world" since "human freedom precedes essence in man and makes it possible." Incapable of taking his cues from a prearranged destiny, man has to chart his own course; his present has meaning only in the light of a future which is his own project. In Sartre's terminology, man as the "for-itself" is a nothingness in constant pursuit of definite being or the "in-itself." This pursuit, however, remains futile, since man tries in vain to escape his nihilating awareness; ultimate synthesis eludes him in this world. As Hazel Barnes comments: "For the for-itself to be one with the in-itself would necessitate an identification of fullness of being and non-being—an identification impossible because self-contradictory. The only way by which the for-itself could become in-itself would be to cease being for-itself, and this we have seen can happen only in death."[10] Sartre's later writings still reflect the same concern with man's elusive search. "Man," he writes in *Search for a Method*, "defines himself by his project"; in continually surpassing his condition "he reveals and determines his situation by transcending it in order to objectify himself—by work, action or gesture." This projection, he adds, "is what we call existence, by which we do not mean a stable substance which rests in itself, but rather a perpetual disequilibrium, a wrenching away from itself with all its body."[11]

As in the case of Merleau-Ponty, Sartre's view of human existence is intimately connected with the theme of social conflict. The famous phrase in *No Exit*, "l'enfer c'est l'autre," has startled (though perhaps not enlightened) audiences for some time. In *Being and Nothingness* conflict is discussed largely in terms of awareness. In the eyes of another person an individual is necessarily turned into a strange object, into something which he has not chosen to be. "Beneath the other's look," Sartre writes, "I experience my alienation and my nakedness as a fall from grace which I must assume." This experience, however, is reciprocal because in looking at the other, "by the very fact of my self-assertion I constitute him as an object and as an instrument, and I cause him to experience that same alienation which he must now assume." As a result, conflict is "the original meaning of being-for-others."[12] In the *Critique of Dialectical Reason* the discussion of the subject-object dilemma is expanded and deepened through the notion of scarcity. Since man must design his project in a given situation and since the world known to us is characterized by a shortage of desired goods and positions, "scarcity defines a particular relation of the individual to his environment." Through his involvement in the material environment, however, man's activity "rebounds against man himself"; he becomes part of an objective and inhuman dimension. In this dimension, every individual constitutes for others an object among objects, an obstacle to be overcome or subdued; thus everyone carries in himself for all others "the menace of death." In the words of Wilfrid Desan, scarcity is the element of negativity built into social relations "by which one is capable of killing or vulnerable to being killed."[13]

II.   Natural Law and Ethics

No part of Hobbes's writings is more intensely controverted than his theory of moral obligation. Lodged at the juncture between the "state of nature" and the commonwealth, his moral philosophy clearly occupies a crucial place in his entire argument. Broadly speaking, two main alternative interpretations have emerged in this area—interpretations that, though conceived as radical opposites, are perhaps not entirely incompatible. According to the first and more traditional view, Hobbes's moral theory coincides with his psychology of natural dispositions and constitutes in essence a doctrine of self-interest adorned with prudential admonitions. The second view—originating in the "Taylor thesis" formulated before the last war—regards Hobbes's moral tenets as entirely divorced from his psychology or anthropology, as a true deontology based on nonempirical, transcendent values. Among other adherents of the latter view, Howard Warrender at one time argued that Hobbes subscribed to a prescriptive ethics strictly independent of any notion of self-interest and self-preservation, an ethics deriving its ultimate sanction from divine injunctions. Combining the two alternatives, Leo Strauss has championed a dualistic interpretation patterned after the neo-Kantian "*Sein-Sollen*" dichotomy. Unable or unwilling to resolve the dilemma, Hobbes is in this view assumed to oscillate perpetually between a naturalistic and a prescriptive morality, with great damage to the coherence of his thoughts.[14] It is at this state of the argument that existentialism questions the foundation and ineluctable character of the stipulated dichotomy. For why—one can legitimately ask—must human life be unproductive of responsibility? And how can transcendent principles be morally relevant without regard to human concerns and needs? In this writer's view, Thomas Hobbes intervenes at the same point by postulating the search for peace as a standard compatible with human experience.

To a reader anxious for hidden mysteries, Hobbes's argument must appear dry and uninspiring; his terse sentences never soar to the heights of eternal vistas or awesome revelations. His starting point—life and its continuous affirmation—is almost offensively mundane. Human existence to Hobbes is a simple original fact unsupported by teleological justifications. Human life can neither be derived from nor be explained in terms of a higher reason or immutable principles; rather, whatever principles can be found are linked to this humble and dark origin. Even when life is traced to the fiat of divine omnipotence, this omnipotence neither owed nor offered man a justification of his act. Life is, however, not only a simple fact but also an act of affirmation. By his mere presence—by breathing and consuming food—man affirms life and his desire to live. A contrary intention is not truly demonstrated until the successful completion of suicide; at this point, death silences man's argument. While alive, man necessarily confirms and seeks life and its preservation; he also endeavors to obtain the means that seem conducive to this goal. Thus man—not hypothetically, but in reality and inevitably—seeks to undertake what he thinks good for himself (*bonum sibi*) and to avoid what he considers harmful, "but most of all the terrible enemy of nature, death, from whom we expect both the loss of all power and also the greatest of bodily pains in the losing." Such behavior is not only inevitable, but also legitimate in its basic intent. Reason, unproductive of life, cannot veto the affirmation of life. But since what is not against reason is called "right" or "blameless liberty," everyone must be conceded the original privilege or, as Hobbes says, "the right of nature" to "preserve his own life and limbs with all the power he has" and with all available means.[15]

Pursued as a prompting of nature, the affirmation of life carries within itself the seeds of contradiction and destruction. In the absence of additional safeguards, man's pursuit of life rebounds against himself; in seeking the means of his preservation, he encounters others as objects and obstacles and is liable to endanger both their lives and his own. As such or as an outgrowth of nature, this conflict is beyond judgment. Nature cannot be described as wicked without absurdity (or, if one likes, impiety), because nature merely seeks preservation without regard to human standards or to the damage inflicted. It is only to man that this conflict can appear offensive because man, although a part of nature, is also conscious of its processes. To human consciousness, however, nature's blind conflict reveals itself as an intolerable contradiction. As has been shown, man demonstrates by his mere presence his intention to live; also, since he cannot disregard the presence of others, he demonstrates his intention to live with others. But if, in the pursuit of his aims, he provokes the danger of mutual destruction, he acts as if he intends to be killed.[16] The realization of this contradiction—indifferent to nature—becomes a sting to man's awareness and the first signal of rebellion: the signal for an attempt to overcome nature's haphazard condition through creative design, through the establishment of a peaceful and civilized life.

The road leading from conflict to peace, however, is slow and arduous. In Hobbes's argument, reason never rises far above nature's contradiction; rational awareness remains linked to the unrational contingency of existence and human passion. Even when designing a civil remedy, man does not simply abandon his natural inclinations; rather, compelled to seek his own good (that is, his preservation) by an apparently careless nature, he can be reconciled with himself and his awareness only in a condition in which nature's aim is more stably secured against avoidable dangers.[17] Moreover, the realization of nature's contradiction is not an inspiration with the power of sudden transformation. Although implanted in man by nature, reason in Hobbes's view is a tender faculty requiring cultivation and industry. Especially in the state of nature where passions abound, rational awareness is liable to be a fragile gift.[18] If reason requires cultivation, the pursuit of its precepts demands diligence and foresight, for reason cannot effect the immediate removal of nature's dilemma. It is only with a view toward the future or in the context of time that this dilemma can be remedied, because only in this context is man able to subordinate his short-range good to the long-range good of a more secure life.[19] Finally, in Hobbes's argument, the task of building a civil life is not assigned to reason alone but is shared by various

natural inclinations which can be enlisted in support of the enterprise.[20] Despite its fragile condition, rational awareness nevertheless
imposes on man the burden of responsibility. With the emergence of
consciousness, man learns that nature's dilemma should be overcome
because it *can* be overcome, at least to some extent. Once this voice of
consciousness is perceived, man can no longer in good faith pretend
his utter helplessness at the hand of nature; he can no longer blame
his acts entirely on nature without offending his consciousness or conscience. Hobbes's statement that man, in the state of nature, is bound
in foro interno suggests that even at this stage man can contravene his
conscience by acting in bad faith.[21] To be sure, in the absence of
further safeguards, man's outward conduct cannot entirely follow the
precepts of peace without endangering his life and thereby continuing
the contradiction; however, good faith requires man even under these
circumstances to abstain from senseless violence and to direct his endeavors—and his actions to the extent that safety permits—toward the
emancipation from nature's dilemma.

Among the selected existentialist writers, none has been more preoccupied with moral questions than Albert Camus. In fact, it has been
observed that his style at times evokes the tradition of classical French
moralists. In the *Myth of Sisyphus,* it is true, Camus protests that
"there can be no question of holding forth on ethics"; but the entire
essay is a defense of man and of his struggle against his predicament,
against the absurdity or incongruity of existence. Man's predicament
derives not simply from the blind indifference of nature, from the
silence of a universe that does not disclose a meaning to man, but
from man's awareness of this condition and from his desperate longing
for rationality and lucidity. Nature, Camus observes, is not reasonable,
but this by itself does not matter; "what is absurd is the confrontation
of this irrational world and the wild longing for clarity whose call
echoes in the human heart." In this confrontation, two apparent solutions offer themselves to man: complete affirmation and complete
denial, the one assigning a hidden meaning to nature, the other si-
lencing man's query through suicide. According to Camus, however,
both alternatives are roads of escape; both the "leap" and suicide are
forms of surrender in the face of man's predicament. The only coherent
attitude is one that meets the challenge, an attitude of defiant revolt
and perseverance. Revolt, to Camus, means the "constant confrontation
between man and his obscurity. It is an insistence upon an impossible
transparency." What emerges from the revolt is not an affirmation of
transcendent meanings and higher values, but a sober and dry assertion of human existence. The only truth convincing at this point

"comes to life and unfolds in men. The absurd mind cannot so much expect ethical rules at the end of its reasoning as, rather, illustrations and the breath of human lives." But this "breath of human lives" is not entirely impotent as a guide of behavior, because its continuance is not easily assured: "Let us say that the sole obstacle, the sole deficiency to be made good, is constituted by premature death."[22]

While the *Sisyphus* essay concentrated on the individual's revolt against his predicament, Camus's *Rebel* examines man more closely in his social context; while the former remained tentative and aphoristic, the latter is more confident (at times overconfident) in its assertion of rules of behavior.[23] The central question of the *Rebel* is whether, in view of man's absurd condition, killing and violence can be accepted as coherent patterns of conduct. Again, two radical answers—absolute acceptance and absolute negation—suggest themselves: the first postulating a higher meaning in the world or in history in whose name men can be sacrificed, the other using the blindness of nature as an excuse for violence and destruction. Both answers, according to Camus, are unacceptable because both fight against their own premises. By the simple act of living, man manifests his intention to live and to render life possible; by persevering in his dilemma he "admits that human life is the only necessary good since it is precisely life that makes this encounter possible and since, without life, the absurdist wager would have no basis." In asserting his existence, man, who is not alone in the world, also admits the need to live with others. But when embracing violence and death, man embroils himself in contradiction; as Camus writes, assertion of life "when it develops into destruction, is illogical." Once brought to awareness, the contradiction cannot persist without offending man's consciousness or conscience, for to sustain the absurdist encounter, "the conscience must be alive." Thus, "from the moment that life is recognized as good, it becomes good for all men. Murder cannot be made coherent when suicide is not considered coherent." Together with the prohibition of murder, a host of other rules of behavior follow from man's original affirmation, rules that promote the possibility of civil life and communication.[24] All these rules, however, find their basis in the fact that man cannot in good conscience maintain his life and at the same time make himself an accomplice of (physical) death. Although his capacities are limited and although violence may be inevitable in exceptional cases, he cannot postulate destruction as a general principle of conduct. In Camus's words, human existence "in its exalted and tragic forms, is only and can only be a prolonged protest against death, a violent accusation against the universal death penalty."[25]

Merleau-Ponty has been less expansive on his moral views than Camus; but he has not been silent. His essay "Man, the Hero," written at the end of the war, probed themes similar to those developed in Camus's *Rebel*. The starting point of the essay was again man's confrontation with a disenchanted and silent universe: "If one ceases to believe not only in a benign governor of this world but also in a reasonable course of things, then there is no longer any external support for heroic action; it cannot gather strength from any divine law or even from a visible meaning in history." In this situation, the only coherent attitude of man is sober perseverance: "to be and think like a living person for as long as he does live, to remain poised in the direction of his chosen ends."[26] Yet, in comparison with Camus, Merleau-Ponty's arguments have always been more subtle and complex, more attentive to concrete reality. In Camus's presentation, the success of man's rebellion, the progress from contingency to rational harmony was hardly in doubt, largely because of the theoretical character of man's predicament. To Merleau-Ponty, by contrast, violence was a reality that could not be overcome by theory alone. As he observed in his *Humanisme et terreur,* "history is terror because there is a contingency"; violence, therefore, "is the situation with which every regime begins." Thus the movement from terror to humanism, from violence to the recognition of man by man involves not a sudden ascent, but an incessant labor without the promise of final victory. One of the major roadblocks—Merleau-Ponty pointed out at the time—consists in the denial of the ambiguity and openness of history, in man's submergence in a ready-made destiny.[27] While inextricably involved in the world, man is also the conscious witness of his involvement; consciousness, however, is first of all an awareness of contingency and death. As he stated in another context: "To be aware of death and to think or reason are one and the same thing, since one thinks only by disregarding what is characteristic of life and thus by conceiving death." This awareness is not a simple gift nor an unearned privilege of "man" in general; its sting is felt primarily by the underprivileged and oppressed, those concretely threatened in their existence. From this vantage point, however, awareness can turn into a sober plea against terror: "There are two ways of thinking about death: one pathetic and complacent, which butts against our end and seeks nothing in it but the means of exacerbating violence; the other dry and resolute, which integrates death into itself and turns it into a sharper awareness of life."[28]

Among all existentialist writers Sartre has been most reluctant to express his moral views. The demand for authenticity has sometimes been described as the only moral criterion of his philosophy,[29] but perhaps it is possible to extract from his arguments further implications which are not entirely at odds with Hobbes's position. In Sartre's view, human life is a simple fact, devoid of ontological necessity: both my own existence and the existence of others are not derived from or justified in terms of permanent reasons or principles. Moreover, human life as such is beyond judgment; existence cannot be assigned a good or evil "nature" without absurdity (that is, without treating the for-itself as an in-itself). Human existence, however, is engaged in a constant search for fulfillment, in a quest of its own good. While poised in its pursuit, it cannot choose evil or its own destruction without denying itself as pursuit. As Sartre writes, to will myself as evil "would mean that I must discover myself as willing what appears to me as the opposite of my good and precisely because it is evil or the opposite of my good. It is therefore expressly necessary that I will the contrary of what I desire at one and the same moment and in the same relation; that is, I would have to hate myself precisely as I am myself. I would have to approve myself by the same act which makes me blame myself." This contradiction, however, prevails in man's original encounter with others at the point where existence is in principle endangered or denied. Since man cannot knowingly choose evil, the contradiction can persist only in the absence of awareness. Once raised to the level of consciousness, the simultaneous assertion and denial of existence becomes an act of bad faith. In Sartre's terminology, bad faith or the "spirit of seriousness" consists in blaming one's behavior on eternal principles or the world of objects, in refusing responsibility for one's future.[30] In order to overcome bad faith, consciousness has to perform a "purifying reflection," a purification or catharsis which can become the basis of a coherent moral behavior. This purification, however, is not an emotional inspiration; it is an act of reason, since rationality and knowledge are the only coherent links between man and his world. Bad faith is essentially irrational because it maintains the contradictory principles that one is free and not free. In the words of Hazel Barnes, Sartre's philosophy "includes the irrational among its data and recognizes that man's irrational behavior is an important part of him. But the final appeal, the standard of judgment is reason."[31]

III.   Social Contract and Commonwealth

Hobbes's properly "political" theory, his theory of sovereignty and the commonwealth, can only be sketched at this point. In the absence of further safeguards, moral rules are in Hobbes's view unable to extricate man from nature's dilemma, from the conflict of preservation and destruction. To remedy this conflict, a further step is required—the establishment of a civil society and a common government. Except in case of immediate danger or overwhelming force, this undertaking is the work of foresight and design. Properly speaking, civil authority is always the result of conscious assent and recognition, regardless of whether assent precedes the exercise of power (government "by institution") or follows after the fact (government "by acquisition" or conquest). It should be noted, however, that in Hobbes's theory mutual recognition or understanding does not simply emanate from a transcendent source, nor is it by itself a secure basis of civil life. Agreement is commonly accompanied or encouraged by natural inclination, especially by fear of harm. In this respect the main types of government differ only in the source of danger and in the origin and immediacy of possible violence.[32] Yet apprehension, while active as midwife, is not properly the parent of the civil bond. All social or civil obligation involves an act of consciousness and mutual consent, which requires at least some degree of trust,[33] but neither trust nor consent are unmotivated. In addition, mutual agreement alone does not sufficiently guarantee the observation of its terms. In Hobbes's poignant phrase, "covenants without the sword are but words, and of no strength to secure a man at all."[34] Thus, having prodded the growth of social concord, natural inclination—especially fear of sanctions and retaliation—becomes also its jealous protector and guardian. In times of excitement, it is true, a multitude may gather and, without established authority, jointly perform actions that seem to proceed from a common will; this union, however, is the result of quick enthusiasm and prone to quick disintegration.[35] To overcome this hazard a more durable type of commitment is required, a commitment that combines the expression of mutual consent with the simultaneous appointment or acceptance of a common power of whose actions every partner considers himself the joint author. This commitment, writes Hobbes, is "the generation of that great Leviathan, or rather (to speak more reverently) of that mortal god," the civil community or commonwealth.[36]

Without embracing a uniform political outlook, French existentialists have focused their attention strongly on questions of civil and political life. Partly as a result of concrete experiences, the genesis and maintenance of a political community have been prominent topics in their writings. In Camus's view, the basis of civil cohesion resides in the universality of man's predicament. "The first progressive step for a mind overwhelmed by the strangeness of things," he writes, "is to realize that this feeling of strangeness is shared with all men and that human reality, in its entirety, suffers from the distance which separates it from the rest of the universe." In challenging this common predicament, the defiant man also challenges the silent hostility between human beings, between oppressor and oppressed, and clears the path leading to mutual recognition and understanding. The rebel, by opposing man's absurd condition, "therefore pleads for life, undertakes to struggle against servitude, falsehood, and terror, and affirms, in a flash, that these three afflictions are the cause of silence between men, that they obscure them from one another and prevent them from rediscovering themselves in the only value that can save them from nihilism—the long complicity of men at grips with their destiny." With this emphasis on mutual recognition and accord as the basis of civil life, however, the parallel between Camus's and Hobbes's argument comes to an end. As portrayed by Camus, consensus seems disengaged from concrete motivation and impervious to human frailty. While insisting that "the part of man which cannot be reduced to mere ideas should be taken into consideration—the passionate side of his nature that serves no other purpose than to be part of the act of living," he refrains from exploring the implications of passion and violence. Agreement seems to be consummated in a higher region "where minds meet and, in meeting, begin to exist," a region isolated from the ravages of desire. Rather than creating human concord, revolt in Camus's description simply discovers the realm of a common human nature, a realm which, far from requiring the protective shield of a political power, dictates its standards to political life. Rebellion, he writes, "is the affirmation of a nature common to all men, which eludes the world of power"; it thereby "brings to light the measure and the limit which are the very principle of this nature."[37]

Camus's divergence from Hobbes's argument also demarcates his departure from fellow existentialists who refused to segregate consensus and passion by a rigid barrier. While finding the basis of civil life in mutual recognition, Merleau-Ponty ties the emergence of such recognition closely to the experience of conflict, to the subject-object dilemma where man's reduction to an object or instrument would not constitute violence without the simultaneous intercession of awareness. "I do not feel threatened by the presence of another," he writes, "unless I remain aware of my subjectivity at the very moment his gaze is reducing me to an object; I do not reduce him to slavery unless he continues to be present to me as consciousness and freedom precisely when he is an object in my eyes. We cannot be aware of the conflict unless we are aware of our reciprocal relationship and our common humanity." Thus, just as mutual recognition proceeds from mutual denial, human denial involves the seeds of its supersession: "Just as my consciousness of myself as death and nothingness is deceitful and contains an affirmation of my being and my life, so my consciousness of another as an enemy comprises an affirmation of him as an equal. If I am negation, then by following the implication of this universal negation to its ultimate conclusion, I will witness the self-denial of that very negation and its transformation into coexistence."[38] The linkage between civil life and discord in Merleau-Ponty's thought can also be gleaned from his comments on Machiavelli (which seem to apply with equal force to Hobbes). "What he is reproached for," he notes, "is the idea that history is a struggle and politics a relationship to men rather than principles. Yet is anything more certain?" As he adds, Machiavelli's starting point did not preclude mutual agreement but clarified the prerequisites of civil commitment: "By putting conflict and struggle at the origins of social power, he did not mean to say that agreement was impossible; he meant to underline the condition for a power which does not mystify, that is, participation in a common situation." Machiavelli's emphasis on the role of power and passion extended from the genesis to the continued maintenance of civil life. His originality, Merleau-Ponty observes, resided precisely in the fact that "having laid down the source of struggle, he goes beyond it without ever forgetting it"; for power, while not identical with naked force, cannot simply be resolved in the "honest delegation of individual wills, as if the latter were able to set aside their differences." The merit of this reminder was to prevent obfuscation and to delineate more clearly the challenge of building a properly human community.[39]

Proceeding from a similar perspective Sartre has attempted a more detailed scrutiny of the formation and operation of civil communities. The connection between consensus and discord has been a major preoccupation of this endeavor. In *Being and Nothingness* awareness was portrayed as generating the instrumental treatment of other human beings, a treatment experienced as offensive and incongruous precisely because of the presence of mutual consciousness.[40] In the *Critique of Dialectical Reason* the subject-object dilemma was translated into the relationship between human praxis and its repercussions in the objective world. As the *Critique* tries to show, human interaction initially takes the form of a mere multitude or "series," of a juxtaposition of individual actors whose projects, pursued in the material environment, rebound against themselves and other actors. The frustration and internal or external dangers resulting from this condition lead to a realization of "the impossibility of life which threatens the serial multiplicity" and to an attempt to transform the series into a more cohesive union. Especially under the threat of immediate violence, in times of "high historical temperature," the multitude may be galvanized into a "group in fusion," an intimate collectivity in which each member, guided by a common objective, acts as "third man" or synthesizing agent. Sartre calls this step the "beginning of humanity," an event which "pulled us out of the earth." Fusion in Sartre's treatment, however, does not involve a transcendental meeting of minds or the discovery of an abstract human nature; rather, it derives from a mutual recognition of complicity, from joint participation in the pursuit of a common goal. A product of converging activities, the group in fusion does not constitute a biological organism, nor is it possessed of ontological substance or permanence; with the accomplishment of the original objective the cohesion of the group is liable to disintegrate. At this point, various protective devices—devices designed to combat atomization—are likely to be employed. Thus, under threat of punishment or "terror," an oath or other form of pledge may be imposed to secure the continued loyalty of group members. In this manner, the group enters the process of organization and institutionalization, a process that includes the establishment of a common authority and the allocation of functions to members of the community.[41]

The preceding pages have explored the affinity between Hobbes and existentialism at significant junctures of their argument. Now, with the establishment of the state or commonwealth, the two finally seem to part company. In Hobbes's presentation, the establishment of a common power seems to inaugurate a reign of relative tranquility and rationality, a reign whose continued maintenance depends chiefly on the skill and circumspection of the sovereign. It is true that he rejects the possibility of complete security and describes the commonwealth as a "mortal god"; but the sources of this mortality or vulnerability remain largely obscure. Despite the restraining impact of the common power, the exercise of this power obviously requires at least the tacit consensus or acquiescence of the majority of the population. Yet while Hobbes notes the ineradicable flux of passions and sentiments, he simply appeals to the ready intelligibility of the advantage of public order without specifying how abstract understanding and acceptance are translated into practical loyalty in concrete situations. Moreover, acceptance and consensus are conditioned by governmental performance. Again, Hobbes acknowledges that governments and representative bodies are by no means "free from human passions and infirmities"; but in discussing the "internal causes tending to the dissolution of any government" he concentrates almost entirely on seditious opinions and erratic emotions of the people.[42] It is at this point that Hobbes seems to have left or abandoned his argument without pursuing its further implications. The stipulation of a common power whose decisions ultimately derive from human will clearly introduces an element of contingency into the operation of the commonwealth. Far from embodying a transcendent or perennial rationality, governments inevitably pursue particular human designs and programs; likewise, popular loyalty and obedience are due not to authority in general but to actual rulers with concrete policies. Thus, rather than reflecting solely the immaturity and flightiness of the people, a measure of discord and change seems to be endemic to political communities.

The ambiguity and effervescence of political life, only implicit in Hobbes's argument, have been eloquently stressed by existentialist writers. In Sartre's argument, political communities are engaged in a constant search for synthesis and unity, without being able to accomplish this goal on a permanent basis. The process of organization and institutionalization injects into group relations an element of rigidity and confinement. While acting as supreme regulator, the sovereign remains a human individual with special goals and ambitions; governmental decisions are thus necessarily limited both in objective and appeal.[43] To an even greater degree Merleau-Ponty has been sensitive to the elusive character of political efforts. "Our times," he observes at one point, "have experienced and are experiencing, more perhaps than any other, contingency." There is no assurance of the success of the human adventure, of the quest for a properly human society; one cannot even "exclude in principle the possibility that humanity, like a sentence which does not succeed in drawing to a close, will suffer shipwreck on its way." But though unaided by a preordained destiny and plagued with constant reversals, men can remain guardians of their future "provided they will measure the dangers and the task."[44] Viewed in this subdued light, Hobbes's writings may still speak to us with the voice of a contemporary. Our generation, like his, has been nearly overwhelmed by violence. How can we fail to appreciate his serenity and quiet perseverance in an age in which the potential of destruction has reached global proportions and in which civil life reveals more than ever its extreme fragility?

6. Hermeneutics and Historicism: Reflections on Winch, Apel, and Vico

FOR NEARLY THREE CENTURIES, Vico's name remained virtually unknown outside narrow philosophical and literary circles; indications are, however, that he is beginning to emerge from this obscurity.[1] His resurgence, it seems to me, is by no means fortuitous or the result of mere antiquarian interests. In a striking manner philosophical developments in our time have revived central themes of the Neapolitan thinker; his preoccupation with practical-historical experience and its exegesis reverberates in many facets of contemporary thought—even bypassing the barrier between Continental and Anglo-Saxon perspectives. On the Continent, Vico's legacy had been preserved to some extent in Dilthey's "life-philosophy"; in a more rigorous fashion, the implications of this legacy were explored by existential phenomenology and hermeneutics with their focus on the human "life-world" and on the significance of prereflective understanding for cognitive operations. Comparable concerns have surfaced in analytical philosophy. Abandoning (or at least modifying) the quest for an artificial symbolism capturing the structure of the empirical universe, linguistic analysis during recent decades has shifted attention increasingly to ordinary language as the underlying matrix of practical and theoretical endeavors. In a similar vein, philosophers of science have tended to turn from logical calculation and empirical verification to the concrete "context of discovery"—the paradigmatic frameworks in terms of which investigative procedures are sanctioned and research goals formulated.[2]

The sketched developments, it is true, have by no means been greeted with universal acclaim. On the contrary, the notion of an experiential matrix of thought has engendered alarm among defenders of objective knowledge, both inside and outside the logical-empiricist camp. Among nonpositivists, Leo Strauss and his followers have for some time waged a vigorous polemic against the danger of historicism —denoting by this term the submergence of universal truth in the flux of contingent historical conditions.[3] Apprehensions of this kind cannot lightly be dismissed, given the magnitude of the issues involved; undeniably some writers—both among existentialists and linguistic analysts—betray a strong bent toward the relativistic abyss. Yet, the mentioned polemic is perhaps overly sweeping. It seems somewhat farfetched to suspect a large group of philosophers of building their case on a basis fragile enough to erode their theories the moment they are articulated. Moreover, even the champions of objectivity have not always managed to bypass the nexus between knowledge and experience. On repeated occasions, Strauss has stressed the importance of prepredicative or "prescientific" awareness—but without clarifying the transition from the "life-world" to absolute cognition.[4] The following pages intend to trace a path through the tangled web of everyday understanding and knowledge, by reviewing (in an admittedly cursory fashion) the arguments of two contemporary philosophers concerned with the exegesis of everyday life: Peter Winch and Karl-Otto Apel. Drawing on the Wittgensteinian conception of ordinary language as a social "life-form," Winch has developed a theory of sociological understanding which is at least incipiently hermeneutical in character. In Apel's case, on the other hand, the combined influence of existential phenomenology and recent linguistic theory has given rise to a unique and complex blend of critical hermeneutics. In both cases—it will be seen—Vico's legacy plays a prominent role as a barrier against relativistic reductionism.

I

Among contemporary students of ordinary language Peter Winch occupies a prominent and perhaps unique position due to the comprehensive thrust of his investigations; while a number of thinkers have explored the ramifications of particular linguistic usages, Winch has tried to develop arguments of the later Wittgenstein into a broad theory of social inquiry. In *The Idea of a Social Science*, first published in 1958, everyday language was presented as a basic matrix structuring human experience and thought in a social context. As he pointed out, the goal of cognition—and of philosophical inquiry in particular—was to render reality intelligible and this goal was "inseparably bound up" with the "question of how language is connected

with reality, of what it is to *say* something." Far from serving as a
mere tool of analysis, language in Winch's view was the indispensable
access route to reality, since "in discussing language we are in fact
discussing what counts as belonging to the world. Our idea of what
belongs to the realm of reality is given for us in the language we use."
As a corollary, instead of proceeding in a vacuum, the quest for knowledge was inevitably imbedded in the framework of everyday discourse
and thus in the "context of the relations between men in society." The
nexus between knowledge and discourse was particularly intimate in
the social sciences, since in this case both the observer and the observed phenomena were guided in their conduct by linguistic usage.[5]

Philosophical reliance on language, according to Winch, was by
no means an invitation to arbitrary whim. Taking his cues from Wittgenstein, he insisted that ordinary language disclosed a regular pattern
and that to engage in meaningful speech was basically synonymous
with the notion of "following a rule." As he observed, however, the
"rules" of ordinary discourse could not simply be identified either with
abstract, logical formulas or with empirical generalizations, since both
conceptions neglected the practical or pragmatic dimension of speech.
Logical formulas alone could not govern meaningful discourse in the
absence of concrete implimentation: "we must always come to a point
at which we have to give an account of the application of the formula." Even logical reasoning, taken by itself, could not be coherently
analyzed without reference to human involvement or participation:
"Learning to infer is not just a matter of being taught about explicit
logical relations between propositions; it is learning *to do* something."
Far from being the result of a logical syllogism, human experience was
indispensable to logical criteria which "arise out of, and are only intelligible in the context of, ways of living or modes of social life."[6] In
the same manner, normative principles of conduct and human action
had to be viewed as *"interwoven,* in much the same way as Wittgenstein spoke of the notion of a rule and the notion of 'the same' being
interwoven." As invoked in these examples, human action was not
merely a private pastime but an intersubjective or public enterprise;
adherence to the rules of discourse presupposed a social practice or a
common "life-form." "It is only in a situation," Winch wrote, "in which
it makes sense to suppose that somebody else could in principle discover the rule which I am following that I can intelligibly be said to
follow a rule at all."[7]

Just as discourse was irreducible to logical inference, rules of
language were not simply factual occurrences amenable to empirical
investigation and verification. Such a view, Winch pointed out, was

predicated on an inadmissible segregation of language from the real world. Commenting on T. D. Weldon, a spokesman of analytical positivism, he objected to the assumption that philosophical problems were basically the result of linguistic confusion which could be remedied through a closer adjustment of language to factual data. In the eyes of empiricists of this type, he noted, "all statements about reality must be empirical or they are unfounded, and *a priori* statements are 'about linguistic usage' as opposed to being 'about reality.'" As he tried to show, the task of scientific inquiry was not simply to depict reality but to render it intelligible—an aim which could not be pursued in the absence of intersubjective communication. In the case of the natural scientist two sets of relations had to be taken into account: the relation to the phenomena investigated and the relation to his fellow scientists. While the phenomena furnished the occasion for experiments and analysis, the investigation presupposed that the scientist had "a mode of communication in the use of which rules are already being observed." Due to its peculiar subject matter, sociology was doubly tied to communication since both the studied phenomena and sociological investigation constituted a human activity "carried on according to rules." Social inquiry for this reason was basically a philosophical rather than factual or empirical discipline, since philosophical exegesis alone was able to integrate data into patterns of meaningful conduct: "To describe what is observed by the sociologist in terms of notions like 'proposition' and 'theory' is already to have taken the decision to apply a set of concepts incompatible with the 'external,' 'experimental' point of view. To refuse to describe what is observed in such terms, on the other hand, involves not treating it as having *social* significance. It follows that the understanding of society cannot be observational and experimental in one widely accepted sense."[8]

Although cogently and lucidly argued, Winch's *Idea of a Social Science* was not free of weaknesses and ambiguities. A host of critics quickly descended on the most vulnerable aspects of the study. Given contemporary trends of inquiry, easily one of the most provocative features was the presentation of social science as a reflective rather than empirical enterprise. Undeniably, many passages of the study carried not only antiempiricist but broadly idealist overtones. Repeatedly, Winch stressed that the central issues of social science were philosophical and "conceptual" in character—a thesis deriving chiefly from the aspect that "a man's social relations with his fellows are permeated with his ideas about reality" and that, in fact, "social relations are expressions of ideas about reality." One of the most frequently quoted statements boldly formulated a mentalist program of inquiry: "If social relations between men exist only in and through their ideas, then, since the relations between ideas are internal relations, social relations must be a species of internal relations too." The mentalist theme, it is true, was not uniformly maintained throughout the book. On several occasions, Winch specified that an adequate understanding of society could not simply rely on "introspective experience" or psychological "intuition." In other contexts, he endorsed the Freudian notion of unconscious behavior and even agreed that it may sometimes be useful to adopt an external or empiricist point of view in order to gain a distance from familiar interpretations. Concessions of this kind, however, were at best incidental or subsidiary facets of the study. Weber's effort to combine interpretive understanding with empirical analysis was denounced as entirely misleading, since what was needed in case of misunderstanding was "a better interpretation, not something different in kind." In a similar vein, Pareto's (and Marx's) endeavor to trace ideological "derivations" to underlying "residues" was treated as a pointless empiricist venture.[9] In a subsequent essay, written in response to some of his critics, Winch tried to mollify the speculative thrust of his work—but without clarifying completely the relationship between philosophy and social science as well as the linkage between a priori and empirical statements.[10]

Perhaps more important than its antiempirical overtones was the proclivity of Winch's *Idea of a Social Science* to succumb to the quandaries of relativism. Once the pursuit of social knowledge and cognition in general were tied to a given ordinary language, the question arose how different languages and "life-forms" could be compared and, above all, how social inquiry was able to aspire to generally valid propositions. Winch's comments on the issue, scattered through the study, were not particularly reassuring. The investigation of social phenomena, he noted at one point, presupposed judgments regarding their meaning and relevance—judgments which were "intelligible only relatively to a given mode of human behavior, governed by its own rules." Human actions and beliefs were tightly embedded in a social context and the relation between meaning and context was an "internal one"; consequently, it was "nonsensical to take several systems of ideas, find an element in each which can be expressed in the same verbal form, and then claim to have discovered an idea which is common to all the systems." Different types of phenomena were subject to different criteria of intelligibility, and the social scientist had to be careful not "to impose his own standards from without." For example, it was quite illegitimate to deprecate magic in comparison with modern science; for "to try to understand magic by reference to the aims

and nature of scientific activity" was necessarily "to *mis*understand it."
Needless to say, comments of this kind were unsettling both to science
and traditional philosophy; in particular, it was not clear how they
could be reconciled with scientific "progress" understood as the steady
approximation of human knowledge to external objective reality—a
goal cherished not only by confirmed positivists but also by adherents
of Karl Popper's "criticist" or experimental approach to scientific inquiry.[11] Ostensibly, it is true, Winch's arguments paid homage to objective analysis; but his notion of objectivity was at best elusive. Despite the pervasive effect of language contexts and the intimate linkage
of understanding and participation in ongoing practices, he imposed
on the researcher the task of a detached exegesis of "life-forms." "To
take an uncommitted view of such competing conceptions," he wrote,
"is particularly the task of philosophy; it is not its business to award
prizes to science, religion, or anything else."[12]

As it seems, Winch himself was not entirely content with his treatment of the mentioned issues; in any case, the topic of cultural and
linguistic diversity received a more careful and circumspect treatment
in his subsequent writings. "Nature and Convention," an essay published two years after the initial treatise, explored mainly the moral or
normative implications of the topic; for the first time, Vico's legacy
emerged as a crucial guidepost in the discussion. The essay launched
a frontal attack on some of the most basic premises underlying Popper's approach (and positivism in general): the rigid distinction between facts and values and the notion that moral or social norms rest
on arbitrary decisions or preferences. As Winch tried to show, at least
some normative standards could not be described as conventional in
this sense, since they were presupposed in the very notion of social
interaction or a social practice. Addressing himself first to the fact-
value relationship, he argued that the distinction was neither as clear-
cut as supposed nor could it be predicated on the arbitrary and
changeable content of norms (in comparison with scientific laws);
rather, both scientific findings and moral judgment relied on a conceptual and experiential framework, although the nexus was more intimate in the latter case. Moral judgment, in any event, was not simply
a matter of individual preference or commitment, since "a decision
can only be made within the context of a meaningful way of life and
a moral decision can only be made within the context of a morality."
Normative standards, moreover, were linked with cultural contexts not
in a randomly variable way, since not all social practices were the
result of agreement. While not denying "an irreducible historical contingency in the norms that a society adheres to," Winch protested

against "the idea that there need be no fixed points in all this change and variety, that there are no norms of human behavior which could not be different from what they are in fact, and that everything in human morality is therefore ultimately conventional in character."

In trying to elucidate moral conceptions "which, in one form or another, must be recognized in any human society," Winch returned to the crucial role of language in human interaction. Implicit in the notion of a "social community," he stated, was that such a community should have a shared language and that the members could intelligibly communicate in everyday life. Intelligibility of communication, from this perspective, was an integral condition of social relations, just as "rationality" meant not so much a private tool as the ability of members of society to follow the "rules" of ordinary discourse. In Winch's view, further notions, more distinctly normative in character, could be derived from these premises. Meaningful interaction, in particular, implied that discourse was guided generally by the norm of truthfulness— since otherwise true and untrue statements could not be differentiated. "One can say," he wrote, "that the notion of a society in which there is a language but in which truth-telling is not regarded as the norm is a self-contradictory one. The conception of a distinction between true and false statements (and therefore the conception of statements *simpliciter*) could not *precede* a general adherence to the norm of truth-telling." Conceivably, Winch added, the argument supporting this norm could be expanded to cover other key principles of ethics, including those of justice and "integrity"—with the latter having the same relevance to "human institutions generally" as truthfulness to the "institution of language." The broad linkage between language and virtue implicit in the argument, moreover, could gain support from Vico's notion of a "natural law of the peoples" as delineated in the *New Science*. "There must in the nature of human things," one reads there, "be a mental language common to all nations, which uniformly grasps the substance of things feasible in human social life, and expresses it with as many diverse modifications as these same things may have diverse aspects. A proof of this is afforded by proverbs and maxims of vulgar wisdom, in which substantially the same meanings find as many diverse expressions as there are nations ancient and modern."[13]

In a subsequent essay, Winch attempted to draw the lessons from his excursion into ethics for comparative social inquiry. Unfortunately, the thrust of the moral argument was not entirely preserved; at least, its sociological implications were not fully elaborated. Entitled "Understanding a Primitive Society," the essay examined the magical practices and beliefs in witchcraft prevalent among the Azande tribe in Africa; a major aim was to shield such practices against the presumptuousness of Western researchers and, above all, to exempt Azande magic from the confining canons of modern science. Winch was by no means willing to embrace subjectivism or to plunge "into an extreme Protagorean relativism"; he readily agreed that "men's ideas and beliefs must be checkable by reference to something independent." Yet, as he insisted, great care had to be taken in fixing the "precise role" of such independent checks; moreover, science constituted by no means the only possible or pertinent yardstick. According to some students of primitive cultures, the criteria of scientific experimentation were alone able to establish the "true link between our ideas and an independent reality"; this posture, however, was not persuasive—if only for the reason that expressions like "true link" and "independent reality" were not themselves derived from scientific criteria. In Winch's view, Azande magic belonged to a realm of discourse distinct from the scientific analysis of external reality—a realm reserved to religion and mythology and ultimately rooted in the matrix of practical-existential experience. The investigation of primitive "life-forms," from this vantage point, was not simply a study of scientific backwardness or naiveté. "What we may learn by studying other cultures," he observed, are not merely "other techniques" of empirical explanation; "more importantly we may learn different possibilities of making sense of human life, different ideas about the possible importance that the carrying out of certain activities may take on for a man, trying to contemplate the sense of his life as a whole." As he added: "Our blindness to the point of primitive modes of life is a corollary of the pointlessness of much of our own life."

The domain of existential experience, Winch suggested, was not a completely elusive or unstructured dimension. The concluding portion of the essay tried to delineate basic guideposts or "limiting notions" pertinent to this domain—guideposts which again harked back explicitly to Vico's legacy. "I wish to point out," he stated, "that the very conception of human life involves certain fundamental notions—which I shall call 'limiting notions'—which have an obvious ethical dimension, and which indeed in a sense determine the 'ethical space,' within which the possibilities of good and evil in human life can be exercised. The notions which I shall discuss very briefly here correspond closely to those which Vico made the foundation of his idea of natural law, on which he thought the possibility of understanding human history rested: birth, death, sexual relations." Together with Vico, Winch stressed that human life was not merely a chain of random events, but was pervaded by a concern for sense: "Unlike beasts, men do not merely live but also have a conception of life." When talking about the life of man, it was possible to "ask questions about what is the right way to live, what things are most important in life, whether life has any significance, and if so what." The mentioned limiting notions, from this perspective, were crucial impulses and parameters for such questioning. When seriously probed, the experiential boundaries of life could not simply be resolved like mathematical riddles; resisting integration into a ready-made theoretical system, they pointed beyond themselves to a transcendental horizon: "The point is that a concern with one's life as a whole, involving as it does the limiting conception of one's death, if it is to be expressed *within* a person's life, can necessarily only be expressed quasi-sacramentally. The form of the concern shows itself in the form of the sacrament."[14]

In comparison with *The Idea of a Social Science,* Winch's essay on primitive cultures contained a number of significant revisions or specifications. In countering more forcefully the lure of relativism, the essay—at least in some passages—adumbrated the conception of open-ended "life-forms" amenable to critical evaluation. Stressing the "open character" of the rules of social discourse, he admitted at one point that "there may well be room for the use of such critical expressions as 'superstition' and 'irrationality' "; in another context he cautioned against the tendency to treat "life-forms" as "isolated language games" with "mutually exclusive systems of rules." Statements of this type clearly pointed in the direction of hermeneutical exegesis, understood as struggle and confluence of divergent horizons of experience.[15] Yet, failing to cling to the sketched outlook, the essay was marred in many respects by ambiguity and vacillation. Paraphrasing Wittgenstein, the paper maintained that criteria of evaluation take on "as many different forms as there are different uses of language"; applied to the issue at hand, this view virtually congealed Azande beliefs into a self-contained universe of discourse. In Winch's presentation, it seemed illegitimate not only to juxtapose magic and science, but also to confront those aspects of Azande ritual which claimed to have explanatory relevance with the "more sophisticated practices" of modern scientific analysis. What is more, Winch appeared reluctant to compare primitive magical practices both with modern notions of magic—which were termed "parasitic"—and with broader religious standards. To some extent, ambiguity also prevailed with regard to the "limiting notions" mentioned at the end of the essay. When treated as implicit in "the very notion of human life," experiential boundaries easily acquired the status of purely logical or conceptual principles; at the same time, the focus on birth, death, and sexual relations was suggestive of general biological criteria susceptible to empirical confirmation. Seen in either a logical or empirical light, however, how could limiting notions qualify as universal "rules" of human discourse—given the presentation of such rules in Winch's earlier work?[16]

II

Historical and cross-cultural comparison is a lively issue not only among ordinary language thinkers but also in European philosophical and sociological discussions. As has frequently been observed, there are many striking parallels between Anglo-Saxon and Continental philosophical trends in our time; in particular, affinities between the later Wittgenstein and existential phenomenology and hermeneutics have repeatedly been explored.[17] Broadly speaking—and focusing on one major intellectual perspective—Continental thought in our century has moved from the detached inspection of phenomena, relying on the potency of a solitary transcendental consciousness, to a concern with the intersubjective "life-world" or the domain of everyday experience. Motivated in part by Husserlian insights, Heidegger in *Being and Time* delineated a nucleus of existential categories structuring man's practical relationships with the world and with his fellow-men. Proceeding from a common level of prereflective and pretheoretical understanding, man's search for knowledge in this view involved a complex hermeneutical learning process in which everyday understanding was clarified or purified in the same measure as encountered phenomena disclosed new dimensions of significance. While, in his later work, Heidegger turned his attention increasingly from mundane interaction to the ontological matrix of human experience and discourse, some of his students—in particular Hans-Georg Gadamer—pursued his initiative in the direction of a philosophical hermeneutics devoted to the elucidation of man's ongoing quest for meaning in diverse cultural and historical contexts. In the following I shall briefly sketch related arguments advanced by Karl-Otto Apel—a philosopher influenced in some measure by Heideggerian existentialism but equally conversant with the central issues in contemporary linguistic philosophy.

In developing his own version of a philosophical hermeneutics, Apel on several occasions commented on trends in recent Anglo-Saxon thought, including the contributions of Wittgenstein and Winch.[18] An essay of 1965, entitled "Analytical Philosophy of Language and the

'Geisteswissenschaften,' " presented a broad panorama of the successive phases in the development of linguistic analysis—from the "logical atomism" endorsed by Russell and the early Wittgenstein, over the constructivism of Carnap and other logical empiricists, to the ordinary language approach initiated by Wittgenstein's later writings. As outlined in Wittgenstein's *Tractatus,* the quest for objective knowledge was predicated on the growing approximation and eventual congruence of the structural elements of language with the world of empirical facts—a congruence which, once achieved, was designed to eliminate all metaphysical and normative quandaries and also any need for an observer's interpretive exegesis of propositions. Exempt from metalinguistic reflection, the logical structure of language served as the horizon of knowledge and ultimately as a substitute for the discarded framework of transcendental subjectivity or consciousness. Subsequently, growing disenchantment with the notion of an absolute or universal calculating language gave rise to the constructivist approach of logical empiricism—an approach according to which scientific analysis had to rely on artificially designed and at best heuristically useful linguistic instruments, although all such instruments were expected to produce the same kind of empirically verifiable knowledge. In both stages, truth consisted basically in a correlation of logical syntax and the empirical or semantic content of statements; in Apel's view, the conception of knowledge reflected in the two stages harked back to the Leibnizian juxtaposition of *vérités de raison* and *vérités de fait* (with the first stage corresponding roughly to Leibniz's postulate of a *mathesis universalis*). Both the logical and the factual poles of truth, from this perspective, were essentially self-contained and perennial dimensions, while human participation in cognition and exegesis appeared superfluous or as a simple source of error. In the meantime, inaugurated both by Charles Morris' discovery of a third, "pragmatic" dimension of language (in addition to syntax and semantics) and by Wittgenstein's turn to the description of everyday discourse, the development of linguistic analysis had reached a new stage in which the aspect of human participation had regained at least a measure of significance in the pursuit of knowledge.

As Apel indicated, the posture of analytical philosophy toward the Continental *Geisteswissenschaften,* and especially toward hermeneutics, had in the past been reserved if not decidedly hostile. Only recently, the emergence of ordinary language philosophy encouraged a progressive rapprochement between the two perspectives; Winch's *Idea of a Social Science* in particular had to be viewed as an important step in this rapprochement. Although not flawless, Winch's study in Apel's judgment contained important building blocks for a hermeneutical social inquiry. A central premise, he noted, was the close linkage between ordinary language rules and social "life-forms" and, as a corollary, between understanding and everyday experience; moreover, going beyond Wittgenstein, the study rehabilitated philosophy by assigning it a crucial function in the interpretive decoding of "life-forms." A particularly valuable feature of the book was the treatment of interpretive "understanding" as key investigative strategy. Countering the purely descriptive and quasi-behavioristic leanings of some of Wittgenstein's followers, Winch rejected the reduction of social conduct to blind habit or to a result of external conditioning and manipulation—a reduction compatible only with causal analysis. At the time, while stressing the purposive or intentional character of conduct, he refused to submerge understanding in psychic empathy or subjective intuition, concentrating instead on the correlation of meaning and the matrix of public discourse. In exploring the nexus between knowledge and everyday life, Apel observed, Winch moved into the proximity of philosophical hermeneutics as initiated by Heidegger and developed by Gadamer. Together with Heidegger (and Wittgenstein) Winch took a stand against psychologism and introspection and ultimately against the Cartesian subject-object dichotomy. Another affinity resided in the common focus on language as medium of communication and interpretation: "Due to this reorientation hermeneutics ceased to be a mere adjunct to epistemology; in the case of Winch as in that of Heidegger, knowledge presupposes a public understanding of the world deriving from a shared life-experience."[19]

Despite its considerable merits, Apel discerned in Winch's *Idea of a Social Science* a series of shortcomings and inconsistencies. One quandary concerned the "empirical" status of Winch's arguments or their relevance to the investigation of concrete social contexts. By emphasizing the reflective and philosophical thrust of social inquiry, his presentation seemed restricted to the a priori conditions of understanding as such, bypassing the diverse manifestations of social experience. On a procedural level, access to such manifestations in any event depended on the prior grasp of the general "rules" pertinent to the examined behavior. As Apel countered, this strategy was barely tenable in the observer's own habitat, but of little or no help in the investigation of unfamiliar "life-forms" where the relevant rules themselves have to be unearthed by means of a laborious interchange between a tentative prejudgment of the fabric of life and the scrutiny of concrete actions or incidents. In contrast to the subordination of content to general rules, Apel thus counseled reliance on the "hermeneutical circle," the dialectical linkage of formal and substantive aspects of understanding in an open-ended search for meaning across cultural and historical barriers. A corollary of the focus on established rules was the tendency of Winch's study to encapsulate social inquiry in conceptual categories and ultimately in self-enclosed frameworks of social discourse. In Apel's view, human conduct could not entirely be deciphered by reference to purposive maxims or to an "internal" nexus of ideas; once unconscious or repressed motivations were taken into account, social science could not refuse the assistance of explanatory and statistical models of analysis—especially if the goal of such methods was "to understand man better than he understands himself." Winch's resistance in this matter was bound up with his aversion to interpretive cross-cultural comparisons, an aversion strangely incongruent with his attachment to philosophical reflection. Viewing language games as "boundaries of knowledge"—Apel stated—he arrived at a "monadology of diverse cultural systems conceived as cognitive contexts (and at a corresponding relativism in his philosophical approach to social science)." To overcome this defect, philosophy had to be revived as a comprehensive realm of discourse, foreshadowing at least in a tentative sense the evolving synthesis of human experience.[20]

The notion of a comprehensive and unrestricted discourse was further elucidated in a subsequent essay of 1972, entitled "Universal Communication as Transcendental Premise of Social Inquiry." Apart from recapitulating the synoptic overview of analytical philosophy, the essay offered a critical commentary on some of Winch's more recent writings. As Apel recognized, Winch's "Nature and Convention" constituted an important advance over the narrow descriptive concern with self-contained language games. The standard of truth-telling, in particular, was presented not as a variable and culturally contingent preference, but rather as a basic condition for the functioning of any discourse or social interaction. In a similar vein, "integrity" was portrayed as performing the same crucial role in the operation of social institutions as truth-telling in communication and "fair play" in games. Arguments of this type, Apel noted, pointed broadly to the hermeneutical and ethical parameters of an "ideal language game"—parameters which, although deformed and inadequately implemented, "must be presupposed in every actual discourse and social 'life-form.'" Unfortunately, the perspective adumbrated in the paper was not fully maintained in the later essay on primitive culture. By shielding Azande magic against critical evaluation, "Understanding a Primitive Society" virtually precluded the possibility of cross-cultural anthropological comparison. By treating culture as an internally coherent web of ideas, moreover, the paper ascribed to contingent empirical "life-forms" a degree of rational transparency and intelligibility which could at best be postulated on the plane of unlimited communication.[21]

The antidote to descriptivism, in Apel's view, could be found not so much by resorting to an extralinguistic "logic of science," but by pursuing the implications of language for social inquiry. The differentiation of language games, he argued, was plausible only against a broader interpretive background; language and discourse, thus, had to be viewed not as fixed enclosures but as open-ended contexts pointing beyond themselves to a universal framework or synthesis of communication. Far from constituting another contingent "life-form" or even an amalgamation of "life-forms," this framework was presupposed in every actual language game as its transcendental horizon or ideal standard. The invocation of Vico's legacy, Apel conceded, went a long way toward overcoming the descriptive isolation of cultures; however, the thrust of the reference was not unambiguous. When treated simply as biological uniformities, it was not clear how "birth, death, and sexual relations" could function as intelligible "institutions" in social life and as cornerstones of Vico's *New Science*. Instead of focusing on empirical generalizations (or purely logical premises), Apel preferred to interpret the "limiting notions" as "pragmatic universals" or basic parameters in a universal discourse or language game—although these parameters had their empirical counterpart in biological conditions of the species. In application to social and anthropological inquiry, the notion of a universal discourse implied that individual cultures were amenable to critical evaluation both through the exposure of prevailing mystifications (via empirical analysis of unconscious factors) and through the scrutiny of life patterns in the light of broader standards. As far as they were meant to regulate empirical events, Azande practices could legitimately be compared to modern methods of scientific explanation and prediction. As far as the aim was existential self-knowledge, primitive beliefs had to be seen in the context of ethical and religious maxims. Distinguishing magic from the dimension of myth and religion, Apel concluded: "Although both tend to be fused in primitive cultures, myth may contain—in Ernst Bloch's term—an 'anticipatory spark' of truth, while magical practices can readily be defined as a perversion of technology."[22]

In interpreting Vico's categories as pragmatic standards, Apel was able to draw on his close familiarity with the Neapolitan philosopher, a familiarity demonstrated in his detailed monograph on the language theory of Italian Renaissance humanism. As the study indicated, it was possible to differentiate at least three major conceptions of language at the eve of the modern epoch: nominalism, logos-mysticism, and humanism. Inaugurated by Occam, nominalism postulated the rigid segregation of language from reality, of the conceptual apparatus of cognition from empirical data. In subsequent developments, this separation gave rise to the competing trends of empiricism and rationalism—with the former concentrating on the analysis of prelinguistic sensation and the latter aiming at the refinement of cognitive tools (a thrust culminating in the Leibnizian formula of a universal calculus or *mathesis universalis*). While, in the terminology of linguistics, the two trends were preoccupied respectively with "logical syntax" and "semantics," Renaissance humanism stressed the dimension of concrete interaction and pragmatic experience; in contrast to the classical tradition of "theoretical" knowledge (comprising mathematics and natural science), humanist thought revived the legacies of practical insight and of ordinary speech or rhetoric. In their effort to resist the challenge of abstract analysis, humanists were able to derive support from the Ciceronian dictum regarding the natural priority of the "art of discovery" (*ratio inveniendi*), rooted in everyday knowledge, over the procedures of logical-empirical demonstration (*ratio iudicandi*). Yet, commonsense arguments tended to be philosophically vulnerable as long as discourse referred simply to contingent speech patterns. For this reason, the stress on rhetoric was accompanied, at least to some extent, by an undercurrent of thought nurtured by Platonic and biblical impulses: the tradition of logos-mysticism. According to this tradition, language was neither a detached tool nor haphazard usage, but the medium of a transcendental act of communication; conceived as kerygma or disclosure of meaning, language participated in the ongoing and unfinished creation of the world. The alliance between humanism and logos-speculation, Apel noted, reached its climactic expression in Vico's conception of a transcendental or universal "philology."[23]

In Apel's presentation, Vico's attachment to Roman-Italian humanism was clearly revealed in his early pedagogical essays dealing with academic instruction. Opposing the rising tide of Cartesian rationalism, these essays endorsed the notion of the precedence of discovery over analytical demonstration, expanding the classical distinction into a broad confrontation between deductive-rational knowledge and the domain of prereflective awareness or the *sensus communis* of everyday discourse. Ordinary language, Vico insisted, furnished a basic preunderstanding of the world which was presupposed in every type of scientific inquiry or critical analysis. In his *New Science,* the precedence of discovery received a more solid theoretical underpinning. According to Apel, Vico's famous maxim *"verum et factum convertuntur"* signaled not the surrender of truth to arbitrary commitment but highlighted the relevance of practical participation to the search for knowledge—especially in the realm of human affairs. Although creative involvement, to some extent, was the hallmark of mathematics and experimental science, the maxim reached its full significance in the study of history and philology (or the humanities)—since only in these disciplines was human understanding able to participate in the concrete unfolding of the studied phenomena (rather than replicating or reconstructing an abstract design). Historical experience, from this perspective, was not simply a web of random data, but the reflection of an ongoing epiphany of meaning in successive events mediated through human action. While focusing on concrete epochs and countries, the *New Science* adumbrated an "eternal ideal history," rooted in a "common spiritual vocabulary" of mankind. Although not synonymous with absolute knowledge, everyday language and experience pointed toward a universal discourse as its horizon of truth. In Apel's words: "Every manifestation of truth in symbols or concrete speech refers back in a perspectival manner to truth as such, just as every 'internal language form' refers to the general human 'form' of truth as to its regulative principle."[24]

Apel's monograph was not merely an exercise in historical scholarship, but also a contribution to the clarification of contemporary thought. While the two offshoots of nominalism—empiricism and rationalism—have coalesced again in our time to form the pillars of logical empiricism and of the positivist philosophy of science, Vico's fusion of humanism and logos-tradition has paved the way to transcendental-hermeneutical inquiry. On several occasions, the study traced the repercussions of Vico's legacy over Hamann to Herder and Humboldt and ultimately to Heidegger; in particular, Heidegger's stress on pre-reflective understanding and his conception of truth as "revealing-concealing" advent of Being (*aletheia*) were presented as philosophical culmination of a long line of development stretching back beyond Renaissance humanism to the mysticism of Böhme as well as to Augustinian and Platonic sources.[25] In other contexts, Apel has focused in greater detail on Heidegger's relationship to Vico's philology and to the pragmatic turn in contemporary linguistics, devoting particular attention to the implications of his arguments for the meaning of "truth"; as he noted, a loose parallel could be drawn between the development of Vico's perspective (from his pedagogical essays to the *New Science*), on the one hand, and the line leading from the pragmatic-existential focus on "care" in *Being and Time* to Heidegger's later delineation of an ontological conception of language.[26] More recently, Apel has tended to view the nexus of experience and cognition in a somewhat more subdued and complex light; accepting (within limits) the differentiation between genesis and validity of propositions, he has come to interpret preunderstanding and ordinary discourse as vital premises (rather than as synonyms) for knowledge. In a sense, however, this outlook is still compatible with Vico's legacy—in particular with his teachings relating to the two domains of "philology" and "philosophy" and their mutual interdependence.[27]

As it seems to me, Apel's philosophical perspective is not entirely isolated in our time. To a considerable extent, his hermeneutics can be compared with views articulated by Paul Ricoeur, especially in the essays collected in *History and Truth*. For both philosophers, the search for knowledge involves, in St. Paul's words, a *"cognoscere ex parte, per speculum, in aenigmate"*—a slow and arduous approximation from the level of everyday experience toward truth (or from "philology" to "philosophy"). Commenting on the history of philosophical thought, Ricoeur notes the antimony between, on the one hand, the immense diversity of worldviews and, on the other, the notion of knowledge as a timeless and impersonal web of assertions. If attention is centered on diversity, the observer is likely to be gripped by a "vertigo of variation," with history turning into a "lesson in scepticism"; approached from the vista of immutable solutions, by contrast, the sequence of theories is bound to appear as a "history of errors" and truth as the suspension of questioning. In Ricoeur's view, human inquiry is stretched between two poles: a temporal situation, reflecting the "narrowness of my condition," and a perennial goal; thus, "the search for truth is itself torn between the 'finitude' of my questioning and the 'openness of being.'" Thanks to the open horizon of truth, the history of thought is not simply a "parade of scattered monographs" or an "imaginary museum," but a common discourse "heading toward self-clarification." Extending his argument to the domain of actual history, he finds a similar universal thrust in the interaction between diverse national cultures and "life-forms"—"a kind of harmony in the absence of all agreement." It is in this light that he interprets Spinoza's dictum: *Quo magis res singulares intelligimus eo magis Deum intelligimus* (the more we understand individual objects, the more we understand God).[28]

7. Phenomenology and Marxism: A Salute to Enzo Paci

A CONVERGENCE OF ILLS may justify resort to a battery of remedies or antidotes—provided the antidotes are mutually compatible and do not coalesce into a toxic compound. In our century, Marxism has been widely heralded as a basic remedy to the corrupting effects of a market economy geared to corporate profit and a technology obtuse to social concerns. However, as interpreted by communist hierarchies, Marxism itself has tended to be submerged in the dictates of industrial expansion and technological efficiency. Faced with this official interpretation, proponents of change have frequently sought to reinvigorate the salt of the dialectic by blending Marxism with newer philosophical perspectives; phenomenology and existentialism have served as preferred means to recapture the human dimension and purposive thrust of Marx's teachings.

At a first glance, the attempted merger seems unlikely and ill-starred—given the Marxist focus on economic explanation and phenomenology's preoccupation with intuitive understanding. Even where the two orientations are seen as broadly complementary rather than conflicting, their alliance is fraught with numerous hazards; a merger, for example, which simply superimposed apodictic intuition upon the self-assurance of a scientific determinism would accomplish little but the escalation of reciprocal defects. Recently, one of the milestone efforts in this domain has become available to English-speaking readers: Enzo Paci's *The Function of the Sciences and the Meaning of Man.*[1] By exploring the humanist premises of Marxism and the social implications of a phenomenological analysis of experience, the study demonstrates the rich potential and stimulating vistas of a philosophical and practical reconciliation of the two perspectives. At the same time, however, the publication can be said to illustrate better than any other the inherent hazards of such an undertaking.

In large measure, the dilemmas of a phenomenological Marxism can be traced to latent ambiguities in both elements of the merger. As it seems to me (and as I shall try to argue in these pages), the alliance can be mutually beneficial only to the extent that both partners are able to assume a critical posture, a posture which, without lapsing into skeptical indifference, employs criticism not only as a weapon against opponents but as a means of self-scrutiny and self-reflection. On this score, however, the legacy of both orientations tends to be ambivalent.

In the case of Marxism, the basic thrust of the founders was undeniably critical in a comprehensive manner. All of Marx's writings involved an exposure of the congealed masks and ideological camouflages of existing social arrangements; such exposure, moreover, was intended as a preparatory step to the broad-scale emancipation and critical self-awareness of all members of society.[2] Yet this general outlook has been uneasily mixed with unexamined premises and assumptions— and this not only in the writings of Marx's successors. Marx's emphasis on labor and the development of productive forces has encouraged the streamlining of the dialectic into a synonym for industrial progress and technological evolution. Similarly, his observations on the relationship between infrastructures and superstructures, between material life and cognition, sometimes exhibit a doctrinaire flavor averse to further clarification; thus the statement that "the production of ideas, conceptions and consciousness is at first directly interwoven with the material activity and the material interaction of men" conceals the complex character of the nexus between thought and immediate experience. Also, the stress on the intimate linkage of theory and practice tends to short-circuit inquiry into the intricate liaison between knowledge and action, between exigencies of nature and standards of practical conduct. "It does not matter what this or that proletarian, or even the proletariat as a whole, *imagines* to be its goal at any particular moment," *The Holy Family* asserts. "What is important is what the proletariat is and what it must historically accomplish in accordance with its nature. Its goal and its historical action are irrevocably predetermined by its own life-situation."[3]

The legacy of phenomenology is hardly less ambivalent; moreover, the situation is aggravated by the diversity of definitions and interpretations. According to a competent student of this legacy, phenomenology should be conceived as a radically critical enterprise, as an effort to rekindle or reactivate the Socratic dialogue.[4] This is definitely an attractive and, in the long run, very promising view. However, the question remains whether such a definition can be squared in every respect with the phenomenological movement as inaugurated by Husserl and whether it does not perhaps blur some distinguishing traits of this movement.

In the works of Husserl and most of his followers, one can hardly neglect the central role assigned to personal intuitive "evidence" as final criterion of true experience and valid cognition.[5] Moreover, in Husserl's writings this stress on personal evidence was connected, at least during major phases of his work, with a monadic conception of consciousness—with the result that intersubjective relations tended to be seen as a series of analogous experiences and dialogical interaction as a synchronization of monologues. However, this is clearly only part of the story. Husserl's turn to evidence and away from preconceived opinions was itself a decisive step in the direction of a critical reconstruction of philosophy. More important, his later focus on the life-world (*Lebenswelt*) disclosed the intersubjective matrix of personal experience and thus laid the groundwork for sustained mutual interrogation and critical dialogue. The implications of this focus are abundantly manifest in the *Crisis of European Sciences* (and appended manuscripts). There, Husserl at one point describes genuine philosophy as "a new sort of praxis, that of the universal critique of all life and all life-goals, all cultural products and systems that have already arisen out of the life of man," a praxis whose aim is "to elevate mankind" and "transform it from the bottom up into a new humanity." In another passage, he directly reflects on the intersubjective dimension of individual cognition:

> Scientific propositions are formed by individual scientists and founded as scientific truths—but being and the verification of being are claims only as long as other scientists can put forth opposing reasons, and as long as these are inconfutable. This means that the realization of the cognitive purpose of the individual scientist is authentically scientific only if he has taken into account the universal horizon of co-scientists as real and possible coworkers.[6]

The discussed vacillation has significantly conditioned past attempts to promote a rapprochement between Marxism and phenomenology. Paci's *Function of the Sciences* deserves attention because it epitomizes both the potential virtues and the intrinsic problems of this rapprochement. This chapter is intended primarily as a critical salute to Paci—critical in the sense delineated by Husserl himself—presented in three main stages. In order to provide a context or foil for Paci's study, the chapter initially sketches a synopsis or historical overview of prominent encounters or confrontations between the two theoretical orientations. Projected against this background, Paci's arguments are subsequently reviewed and their major strengths and weaknesses assessed. To round out the presentation, a final section compares his views briefly with various parallel endeavors in contemporary sociology and social thought.

I. Encounters: from Lukács to Habermas

Paci's work is by no means the first example of a contact or liaison between Marxism and phenomenological inquiry. Actually, in large portion, his study takes the form of a sustained and occasionally critical commentary on the writings of philosophical precursors in this area. As he suggests, contacts between the two perspectives can be traced back to the early decades of this century, to the time of Husserl's first major publications. As one may recall, Marxism during this period experienced a striking revival of dialectical thinking—a revival which, nourished largely by the rediscovery of Hegelian sources, stood in stark contrast to the positivist and neo-Kantian interpretations of the preceding era.

There are important reasons that account for the mutual attractiveness or at least partial affinity of Marxist and phenomenological thought during this time. Both movements, it seems to me, were attempts to overcome the despair and relativistic confusion characteristic of the *fin-de-siècle* epoch and of a disintegrating liberalism. Reacting against positivist reductionism and compartmentalization of knowledge as well as against neo-Kantian antinomies, both perspectives sought to recover the unifying source of all knowledge and experience behind the dichotomies of nature and history, subject and object, external and internal, contingent and transcendental domains. In the case of phenomenology, this search led through a bracketing of received explanations and categories to the exploration of a substratum of intentional consciousness embedded in the life-world. Dialectical Marxism, in a similar manner, sought to restore the vision of a coherent totality or synthesis of experience buried under the disparate ruins of an objectified universe and arbitrary subjective impulses.

Among the pioneers pointing broadly in the direction of his own version of a phenomenological Marxism, Paci mentions Georg Lukács, but without specifying the character of the claimed relationship. Lukács' early contact or affinity with phenomenology has, of course, frequently been noted; the contact definitely preceded his affiliation with Marxism or with dialectical thinking in general. During his studies in Berlin and Heidelberg, he came under the influence of the dominant philosophical tendencies of the time—without, however, becoming the docile disciple of any school.[7] Whatever fascination phenomenology held for Lukács seems to have derived chiefly from its concentration on metaempirical, ideal "essences." To a considerable extent, his early preoccupation with literary and esthetic questions was an expression of his passionate longing for a realm of absolute or pure experience transcending contingent reality and the confining splits of subjective and objective, normative and empirical dimensions. This longing was clearly evident in one of his first major writings, *The Soul and the Forms,* published in 1911. According to Lucien Goldmann, Lukács' thinking at the time stood at the crossroads of three philosophical currents: Southwest-German neo-Kantianism, Dilthey's historical hermeneutics, and Husserl's phenomenology. *The Soul and the Forms,* in Goldmann's view, constituted basically a merger of "two central notions of phenomenology and Dilthey's school: those of a *transtemporal essence* and of *Verstehen.*"[8] The fusion of the two notions resulted in the concept of a transtemporal meaningful "form" designating an ideal structure accessible to pure understanding. At the same time, Lukács contracted the neo-Kantian juxtaposition of empirical world and absolute norms into a stark and uncompromising confrontation, a confrontation which, in the absence of mediations, was bound to culminate in a tragic vision of life. Thus, on the eve of the European conflagration, *The Soul and the Forms* expressed both the revolt and the inevitable failure of authentic existence in the midst of a corrupt and fragmented society.

His next work, *The Theory of the Novel,* written at the beginning of the war, showed a slight shift in perspective. While still clinging to the notion of transtemporal forms, Lukács now concentrated on the *entre-monde* between human aspirations and social environment; in contrast to the stark conflict peculiar to tragedy and the idyllic harmony characteristic of epic tales, the novel appeared as the medium portraying the tension and precarious interaction between authentic life and society, a tension intimating at least dimly the possibility of reconciliation. The acceptance of such a possibility implied a step in the direction of dialectical thinking and especially of a Hegelian phenomenology of experience—although the prospect of reconciliation was still relegated to a distant utopia. World War I and the outbreak of the Russian revolution in 1917 triggered Lukács' interest in Marx's writings and his association with the communist movement.

A few years later he published one of his most brilliant, and also most controversial, books: *History and Class Consciousness, Studies in Marxist Dialectics.* The book lacked none of the uncompromising ardor and élan of his earlier works. Written at the height of revolutionary ferment and expectations, *History and Class Consciousness* boldly aimed to unravel the meaning of human development by focusing on the progressive transparency of social antagonisms and their impending *dénouement* in a classless society. To be sure, the turn to dialectical thought entailed an important change in vocabulary and philosophical conceptualization: instead of the previous stress on transtemporal essences, the study focused on the evolving synthesis of historical experience, on the total fabric of meaning emerging out of dispersed and possibly opposed fragments. In semi-Hegelian fashion, history was seen as the alternation of estrangement and self-discovery. Capitalist society signified a growing objectification of human relations, with the laboring class suffering the highest degree of estrangement due to its transformation into a commodity on the market. Yet the worker was not only a victim but also an avenger and possible redeemer: by becoming conscious of its condition, the proletariat was destined to abolish exploitation and usher in a new era permitting free and authentic existence to all members of society.

History and Class Consciousness remains one of the most remarkable documents of the period; in a philosophical sense, its virtues are many and continue to provide yardsticks for Marxist thought. One of the chief assets of the study was the delineation of a dialectical Marxism. By reviving an almost forgotten dialectical legacy, the book overcame both positivist and subjectivist distortions of the past; in the words of Goldmann: "Lukács' outlook restored to Marxism its internal coherence and swept aside with one stroke all the imputed 'dualisms,' 'inconsistencies,' 'confusions,' and 'philosophical inadequacies.' "[9] Equally significant was the stress on estrangement and alienation—aspects that were soon to become major themes in existentialist literature. For present purposes a central value of the study resided in its incipient critical posture, in the author's repeated emphasis that Marxism should be viewed as method and key to further inquiry rather than as compendium of fixed propositions.[10] Unfortunately, statements to this effect remained undeveloped and were counteracted by the bold venture to gain absolute or total comprehension. At least in this respect, the book's outlook was subterraneously linked both with Lukács' previous writings and with the thrust of phenomenological inquiry. Just as (early) phenomenology was marked by a "leap into evidence," by the claim of an intuitive grasp of essences, *History and Class*

Consciousness can be said to betray a "leap into synthesis," a plunge into the full meaning of historical experience.

Although understandable and valuable as a reaction against positivist fragmentation, the leap in both cases had the effect of discouraging critical inquiry into crucial mediations and linkages. Despite his portrayal of Marxism as a method, Lukács described the nucleus of this method as the focus on the total fabric of history—a fabric which seemed accessible to immediate inspection without requiring the patient labor of intersubjective interrogation and corroboration. Contrary to the author's intention, historical development thus appeared subject to a predictive calculation only partially different from positivist determinism. In the same manner, the contraction of the dialectic prevented investigation of the nexus between theory and praxis. To the extent that the proletariat was presented as both the object and the subject or sovereign agent of social change, revolution and emancipation seemed the direct result of social exploitation and practical conduct immediately deducible from observed conditions.[11]

As is well known, *History and Class Consciousness* suffered a peculiar fate: eclipsed and bypassed by political developments, it was soon repudiated not only by official communist circles but also by its author. Whether for tactical or philosophical reasons, Lukács soon moved from his early concerns into almost the opposite direction, toward a moderate realism or objectivism which seems difficult to reconcile with dialectics and definitely incompatible with phenomenological inquiry. In his writings published during his Moscow years and the immediate postwar period, he actually adopted a vehemently hostile attitude toward phenomenology and existentialism—a posture that may in part have been a reaction against some of his own early leanings. In *Existentialism or Marxism?*, phenomenological and existentialist thought was portrayed as manifestation of the progressive disintegration of bourgeois culture during the "phase of imperialism"; both movements, Lukács claimed, were based on the method of subjective intuition and thus entirely at odds with rational inquiry—an inquiry whose relationship to, or distinction from, scientific objectivism was unfortunately not clarified.

In *The Destruction of Reason*, the attack on intuition was expanded into a broad overview of the decline and degeneration of German philosophy from Schelling to Hitler's time. Phenomenology and existentialism were treated as appendices or special types of an irrational "life philosophy"; as in the previous essay, the phenomenological reliance on "bracketing" or *epoché* was castigated as a subjectivist maneuver to elude the question of objective social reality.[12] More recently, in a treatise completed shortly before his death, Lukács slightly relaxed his categorical opposition. His *Ontology of Social Life* draws very heavily on the work of Nicolai Hartmann, a thinker who was at least partially influenced by phenomenology. Like Hartmann, the study accepts, within limits, the legitimacy of a plurality of individual concerns and subjective perspectives; however, all such perspectives are ultimately rooted and combined in a complex hierarchy of reality independent of human awareness.[13]

Not all of Lukács' friends and followers share his hesitations and scruples with regard to phenomenology. Not long ago, one of his students explored the affinities between Marxism and phenomenological inquiry, through the medium of a friendly, imaginary dialogue between a number of participants, including a Lukácsian thinker and a phenomenologist whose views closely resemble Paci's.[14] The topic of phenomenology and existentialism is treated with little suspicion, and sometimes with moderate sympathy, also by other East-European writers today, especially by members of the so-called *Praxis*-group. Gajo Petrović, a Yugoslav philosopher and leading member of the group, observed more than a decade ago that "the contemporary philosophy of existentialism is concerned with humanistic problems about which the young Marx wrote but which were neglected by Marxists afterwards. Its conception of man is, on the whole, different from the Marxist one, but on some points they come near each other."[15] A Marxist perspective at least partially reminiscent of Husserl's phenomenology has been developed by the Czech philosopher Karel Kosík. In his *Dialectic of the Concrete*, Kosík distinguished between the dimension of phenomenal appearances, comprising unexamined objects and ideological opinions, and the basic structure of reality or the concrete essence of the "things themselves." In contrast to phenomenological formulations, however, appearances and essence were seen as intimately linked and the piercing of "pseudo-concreteness" was to be accomplished not through a return to pure intuition but through the method of dialectical thinking—a method which, moreover, was seen as chiefly a critical enterprise.[16]

The mentioning of the *Praxis*-group evokes the memory of an earlier reformulation of Marxist thought: Antonio Gramsci's "philosophy of praxis." A brief consideration of this precedent is indicated in this context, since Paci understandably devotes considerable attention to the founders of Italian Marxism, Gramsci and Antonio Labriola. Both writers are notable for their reactivation of a dialectical and non-positivist conception. Their outlook, in this respect, parallels closely that expressed in Lukács' *History and Class Consciousness*; their relationship to phenomenology, however, is considerably more indirect and tangential. Both Labriola and Gramsci objected strenuously to the reduction of Marxism to a naive naturalism or objectivism; valid cognition, in their view, depended not merely on the reflection of objects in passive minds but on the purposive interchange between man and the world.[17] Historical development, above all, could not be conceived as the mechanical operation and unfolding of natural laws; rather, social innovation presupposed the active intervention and praxis of the proletariat. On all these points their writings exhibited the same promise, as well as the same shortcomings, as Lukács' early position. Yet, as it seems to me, there are at least a few aspects where Gramsci's arguments point beyond these confines. Valid cognition, he noted, was not simply the result of isolated observation or insight, but the fruit of universal consultation and confirmation. What Marx called the "structure" or "infrastructure" of society was a set of given and taken-for-granted factors that effectively conditioned human aspirations. Dialectical thinking, from this perspective, was the movement from an opaque evidence over speculative interpretation to full comprehension.[18]

The relationship between structure and superstructure, thought and matter, also was a central preoccupation of the French or French-speaking school of existential phenomenology during subsequent decades—a school comprised of Sartre, Merleau-Ponty, and, at least for a brief time, the Vietnamese theorist Tran Duc Thao, whose interest in Husserl seems to have resided primarily in the distinction between appearances and essence. In an essay of 1946 entitled "Marxism and Phenomenology," Tran Duc Thao reformulated the Marxist nexus of infrastructure and superstructure in terms of the opposition between a basic layer of experience and awareness—revealed through bracketing—and the realm of opinions and institutional objectifications. Husserl's fascination, however, seems to have waned quickly, for a few years later the same author tried to demonstrate the inferiority of intuitive inspection to the method of dialectical materialism with its stress on labor as source of human values; at least in part, the change derived from disenchantment with the nonapodictic implications of Husserl's turn to the life-world.[19]

Despite obvious parallels, Sartre's intellectual development deviates in many respects from that of the Vietnamese philosopher: the attempt to reconcile Marxism and phenomenology constitutes a late rather than a preliminary phase in his thinking; moreover, his interpretation both of Marxism and of existential phenomenology acquired increasingly critical and self-critical connotations. Until the end of World

War II, Sartre's writings reflected a purely phenomenological outlook devoid of Marxist overtones, an outlook combining the teachings of Husserl and Heidegger together with some Hegelian vocabulary. His major studies of the period, including *Being and Nothingness,* further radicalized the pure inspection of essences by purging consciousness of any substantive elements—an operation that transformed phenomenology into a stark dichotomy between awareness and the world of things or, in Hegel's language, between the domains of the "for-itself" and the "in-itself." In contrast to the dialectic of synthesis elaborated by the young Lukács, Sartre thus developed a dialectic of antithesis and negation. Both the plunge into synthesis and the reliance on absolute freedom and negation, however, produced the same result: the neglect of intersubjective mediations.

During the postwar period Sartre slowly sought to repair the breach between human awareness and the world that characterized his earlier works. This search led him to a more attentive examination of dialectical thinking in general and of Marxism in particular. An important step along this road was his essay "Materialism and Revolution," published in 1946. In this essay, Sartre defined Marxism essentially as a philosophy of praxis and revolutionary action, while relegating both materialism and idealism to the status of contemplative or metaphysical doctrines; in doing so, he boldly cut through the entangled knot of structure-superstructure relations, opening the way for a fresh reexamination of the issue. Despite the boldness of formulation, however, the essay still bore the imprint of earlier arguments and doctrinaire assumptions: Largely identified with labor and completely absorbing theoretical reflection, revolutionary praxis was depicted as an act of total transcendence and self-realization on the part of the proletariat.[20]

Some ten years later, Sartre made another move toward a rejuvenation of Marxism. The opening section of his *Search for a Method* affirmed not merely the possibility but the urgency of a combination of Marxism and existential phenomenology. Although Marxism was recognized as the dominant and unsurpassed "philosophy" of our age, superior to other trends or "ideologies," existentialism (at least its nonreactionary variety) was portrayed as a vital corrective in view of the stagnation of official Marxist thought. While "living Marxism," Sartre complained, was "heuristic" and its concepts exploratory "keys" or "interpretive schemata," official doctrine had degenerated into ritual: "The totalizing investigation has given way to a scholasticism of the totality. The heuristic principle—'to search for the whole in its parts'— has become the terrorist practice of 'liquidating the particularity.'"

Since existentialism "reaffirmed the reality of men" and focused on "experience in order to discover there concrete syntheses," it could serve as an antidote to Marxist sclerosis.[21]

Unfortunately, Sartre's subsequent writings did not quite live up to the promise contained in these statements. The remaining part of *Search for a Method* was devoted to the methodological implications of dialectical thinking, in particular to the elaboration of a "progressive-regressive" method linking phenomenological description with theory and scientific analysis with synthetic comprehension. In 1960, the *Search* was attached as preface to Sartre's most ambitious theoretical undertaking, the *Critique of Dialectical Reason*. However, the title does not entirely match the content (at least of the portion published so far); starting from a primordial level of material needs and deriving the genesis of society from human labor and the struggle with scarcity, the study constitutes more a sociological application of the previously sketched method than an effort of dialectical self-scrutiny. The goal adumbrated by Sartre was pursued with greater perseverance and, perhaps, greater circumspection by Maurice Merleau-Ponty—although his early death prevented a full development of his thoughts. Actually, his writings frequently tended to anticipate Sartrean themes. Relying strongly on Husserl's life-world studies, Merleau-Ponty's early investigations of human behavior and perception completely avoided the antinomies of Sartre's dialectic of negation; by reconciling Husserl with the intricate pattern of Hegelian phenomenology, they pointed the way toward dialectical thinking and, ultimately, toward Marxism. Well in advance of Sartre's formulation, the *Phenomenology of Perception* depicted Marxism as a philosophy of human praxis—but without identifying praxis narrowly with labor or with a total act of transcendence. Over a decade before the *Search for a Method*, the essays collected in *Sense and Non-Sense* delineated a merger of Marxism and existential phenomenology.

By focusing on praxis, Merleau-Ponty suggested, Marxism bypassed both materialism and idealism as abstract doctrines; but the same focus could also be described as existential—provided existence was seen as "the movement through which man is in the world and involves himself in a physical and social situation which then becomes his point of view on the world." Existence, moreover, denoted not merely a general species or an elusive collectivity, but concrete human experience. To this extent, existentialism corroborated the critical and nondogmatic thrust inherent in Marxist thought from the beginning. "A philosophy," he observed, "which renounces absolute spirit as history's motive force, which makes history walk on its own feet and which admits no other reason in things than that revealed by their meeting and interaction, could not affirm *a priori* man's possibility for wholeness, postulate a final synthesis resolving all contradictions or assert its inevitable realization."[22]

The implications of these lines emerged more clearly ten years later, in a study which reviewed the developments of dialectical thinking in our century. Starting from Max Weber, whose outlook fully revealed the tensions of traditional liberalism, Merleau-Ponty credited Lukács with the formulation of a genuinely dialectical perspective—a perspective, moreover, which in large measure remained tentative and self-critical. Yet, infected by the revolutionary ebullience of the period and the trust in a ready-made proletariat, Lukács' work in important respects tended to encourage a visionary short-cut: "the revolution appeared as the *climax* in which reality and values, subject and object, opinion and discipline, individual and totality, present and future were destined to converge instead of being in conflict." Overtaken by political events, this vision soon disintegrated; Lenin's *Materialism and Empiriocriticism* marked the decline of dialectical thought and the return to dogmatic self-assurance. Since that time, Marxism constituted at best a coerced synthesis, concealing the survival of unresolved antinomies; stripped of crucial mediations the dialectic was identified either with a crude objectivism absorbing human praxis, or with a blind activism or voluntarism shunning reflection.

The task ahead, Merleau-Ponty suggested, was the cautious reconstruction of dialectical thought, a reconstruction which, instead of mutilating opposing elements, would permit scrutiny of their complex relationships. Among the themes requiring renewed attention were the linkages between thought and action, philosophy and practical life. Without lapsing into either a dialectic of synthesis or a dialectic of negation and total freedom, such an investigation would restore Marxism as a "questioning philosophy of history"; more important, it would revive its capacity of self-criticism, presenting it as a perspective "open even to those who challenge it and acquiring legitimacy precisely by facing such challenge."[23] Merleau-Ponty died while he was working at a comprehensive philosophical enterprise: an inquiry into the meaning of truth and its origins in opaque experience. In contradistinction to transcendental reflection, as well as to the dialectic of negation and the intuition of essences, the study portrayed philosophy as continuous interrogation—a quest that could not be exhausted "because the existing world exists in the interrogative mode."[24]

Merleau-Ponty's life-work remained a torso; but his inquiry has not been abandoned. As it seems to me, traces of his argument can be found in another brand of contemporary Marxism: the Frankfurt School, committed to the elaboration of a "critical theory of society." Paci completely bypasses this school—not without reason, for the attitude of Frankfurt theorists toward phenomenology has largely been hostile. This attitude, however, has not precluded encounters of both an obvious and a subterranean kind. An overt and direct liaison can be found in the early writings of Herbert Marcuse—most of which, it is true, predate his affliation with the Frankfurt group. A brief consideration of this encounter seems justified mainly because of certain affinities with Paci's work.

As a student in Berlin and Freiburg, Marcuse came under the influence of Husserl, Heidegger, and also Lukács; but whereas Lukács moved quickly from essences to dialectical synthesis, Marcuse tried to achieve a theoretical merger. In an essay of 1928 entitled "Contributions to a Phenomenology of Historical Materialism," Heideggerian phenomenology was presented as philosophical corroboration of Marxist aspirations. The nucleus of Marxism was seen in revolutionary praxis—in the "historical possibility of radical action which is to bring about necessarily a new reality that makes possible the total man." Action of this kind was termed necessary, for "every act lacking this specific character of necessity is not radical and need not happen"; it was also endowed with an overriding finality, "the determinate realization of human essence." The first concern of praxis, in the Marxist view, was with the "material needs required for self-preservation"; society developed in accordance with the different modes of production used to meet material needs. Division of labor made class antagonism the driving historical force: once conscious of its situation, "the chosen class matures to become the agency for historical action." All these Marxist notions were able to receive a solid theoretical grounding in phenomenology, especially in Heidegger's existential categories.

According to existential analysis, man was initially "thrown" into a world of ready-made concepts and social arrangements; but moved by "care" for the purpose of life, he was able to overcome this bondage and to realize his "essence" or "authentic existence." This realization occurred in a historical context, in the mode of "historicity"—"the decisive point in Heidegger's phenomenology"; moreover, steps in this direction were conditioned by basic existential "needs," including the need of production and reproduction. Yet, while providing a theoretical foundation, Heidegger's analysis remained abstract and elusive, refusing to proceed from general categories to the examination of concrete historical experience. In order to achieve a comprehensive perspective and to join general insight with concreteness, therefore, phenomenology had to be merged with dialectical materialism: "The phenomenological analysis of universal historicity becomes a theory of revolution only when it penetrates concrete historical conditions."[25]

After a few years of additional experimentation, Marcuse discarded the phenomenological focus in favor of other formulations—although one can plausibly argue that the quest for essences and apodictic insight was continued in later writings under different guises (e.g., the guise of Freudian instincts). Other members of the Frankfurt group never shared or condoned Marcuse's early infatuation. Theodor Adorno—together with Max Horkheimer a founder of the school—wrote a lengthy treatise denouncing Husserl's intuitionism as subjective speculation; on another occasion he harshly castigated Heidegger's verbal obscurities.[26] The same critical posture pervades the writings of Jürgen Habermas. In his *Theory and Practice*, which appeared in 1963, Habermas portrayed both phenomenological and existential interpretations of Marxism as essentially speculative or intuitionist distortions. Subsequent publications reiterated and reinforced this judgment. Thus, in an essay of 1965, Husserl's *Crisis* was singled out as an attempt to revive a purely contemplative outlook oblivious of its practical underpinnings.[27] Yet, despite these critical strictures, I think it is possible to discover some subterranean linkages with the intentions of both Husserl and Merleau-Ponty. As it seems to me, Habermas' formulation of a basic framework of interests underlying cognitive efforts is not entirely at odds with Husserl's notion of the life-world. In *Knowledge and Human Interests,* cognitive endeavors are depicted as rooted in a "life context," a context conditioning the character and the validation of knowledge claims. One should note, however, some important features of the postulated framework. First, cognitive interests as defined by Habermas are not merely endowments of a transcendental consciousness; rather, they are both the premises and the product of a concrete historical learning process. Also, interests of this type should not be conceived as private impulses but as parameters guiding the inquiries of an intersubjective "community of investigators." Finally, instead of denoting a uniform structure of needs, the framework is differentiated into a variety of basic orientations, especially those of work and interaction. Recently Habermas further refined his conception of the cognitive framework and of the linkage between thought and experience by stressing critical "discourse" as the medium of intersubjective interrogation and verification; reminiscent of Husserl's method of "bracketing," such interrogation is designed to loosen the grip of habits and unexamined opinions.[28]

II.   Paci's Function of the Sciences

Viewed against the background of the sketched story of encounters, Paci's arguments in *The Function of the Sciences* assume distinct contours and accents. As the story suggests, the merger of Marxism and phenomenology can produce different, even sharply divergent,
results. The admixture of phenomenological insights can help in re-
activating Marxism as an open theoretical and practical venture; it can
also corroborate or reinforce ideological self-sufficiency. Easily the
most ambitious example of the genre in contemporary philosophy,
Paci's work tends to reveal the entire range of implications.[29] The
overriding impression left by his study, however, is the immense sug-
gestiveness and fertility of the life-world focus; conceived as a realm
of concrete pretheoretical experience, the life-world poses a definite
challenge to doctrinaire enclosure. Over long stretches, *The Function
of the Sciences* offers a running commentary on Husserl's *Crisis* and his
elaborations of the *Lebenswelt* as a counterpoise to scientific objectivism. According to Paci, these elaborations unmistakably point in the
direction of dialectical materialism—but without reaching this goal.
Both the *Crisis* and Marx's analysis of the capitalist economy, he
argues, are critical efforts designed to rescue human experience from
reification and estrangement. Once the life-world is interpreted as incorporating the level of basic needs and of material production, phenomenology and Marxism are destined to converge.

The study abounds with statements testifying to the critical and
open-ended character of phenomenological inquiry. As a search for
the meaning of experience, phenomenology is an incessant pursuit;
since events are always embedded in a broader fabric with elusive
boundaries or horizons, their interpretation has to be constantly renewed. Although partial elements are pregnant with universal significance, Paci notes, "this universal horizon is never given in its totality";
consequently, "if phenomenology is an ontology, it is not so in a dogmatic or metaphysical sense." Although inquiry has to start from the
"evidence" available to individuals, the context surrounding such evidence extends in all directions, with the result that "the task of phenomenology is both temporally and historically infinite." Given the task
of constant renewal, it is clear that phenomenological findings have to
be amenable to challenge and correction. In Paci's words: "Verification
must always be perfected, rectified, and corrected. The life-world does
not leap once and for all from *doxa* to science." Seen from this per-

spective, phenomenology cannot be satisfied with momentary intuitions or spontaneous convictions; rather, infected by systematic doubt,
it recaptures the intentions of the Socratic dialogue. "Philosophy," we
read, "is the human activity in which life resumes the journey toward
truth by continuously returning to its own origin and by becoming
transformed in the horizon of truth, i.e., by always reconstituting being
into intentional meaning."[30]

The journey toward truth, moreover, is not a solitary adventure,
just as the discovery of meaning cannot be confined to private speculation. Experience is predicated on interaction and the decoding of
meaning thus involves the confluence and interchange of outlooks. The
world, Paci writes, "is a unity of horizons that I must constantly experience and relate in an open perspective. The representation of the
world is a synthesis that is always in process, a unification that is always making and correcting itself in the explication of the movements
of my body and other bodies, in the constant attempt to reach a unity
of the world." In the terminology of Husserl and Leibniz, the world
may be viewed as composed of monadic units and dispersed fragments;
but "the transformation and perfection of the world presuppose inter-
monadic life and reciprocal agreement between the monads." Interchange of perspectives and reciprocal agreement, to be sure, cannot
simply be presupposed or taken for granted. On the contrary, human
relations at present are characterized—as they have been in much of
the past—by incomprehension, antagonism, and manipulation. Intersubjective agreement and consensus thus is not so much an actual condition as an ideal standard of conduct; but "it is an ideal immanent in
the structure of the world." Ultimately the postulate of a universal community transcends even the boundaries of a given generation and
assumes a broadly historical connotation: "The 'unity of spiritual life' is
the intentional-historical meaning which is maintained in the totality
of human persons, in tradition and renewal and in the relation between the living and the dead. This totality is the totality of real men
who in their dialectic tend toward an open meaningful synthesis,
toward the meaning of truth that dialectically develops in the clashes
and encounters of men and cultures."[31]

This conception of phenomenology has definite implications for
social theory and practice, and especially for Marxism. Although the
vision of a universal community may never be fully attainable, social
relations are poised in this direction and cannot be abandoned to relativistic apathy; by the same token, however, the purpose of social life
cannot simply be divorced from actual human conduct and experience.
The goal, Paci notes, "is not *any* indifferent end"; rather, it involves

"action for the realization of a rational society which overcomes war and exploitations, along with 'naturalism,' fetishism, and slavery. This is the *horizon of truth*, although it is not the horizon of a philosophy understood as ideology or as a purely formal dialectic. It is the horizon of truth of a philosophy that is based on what men actually experience as they experience it and within the limits in which they experience it." A social theory incorporating this outlook is bound to assume a critical posture, a posture encouraging self-scrutiny. By rejecting both indifference and dogma, Marxism is able to regain its original momentum: "Each man contains the principle of truth; yet no man can ever be the truth: this would be idolatry. Critical Marxism could rediscover its own secret religious tone as the overcoming of every idolatry and as the movement of liberation from every type of alienation." As long as Marxism is treated simply as another type of scientism or objectivism, it falls short of its significance; while not rejecting technology in a romantic manner, Marxist praxis cannot be reduced to the mere application of scientific formulas. Once it is recognized that, contrary to the assertions of classical economists or Social Darwinists, society is not simply governed by naturalistic laws or by a crude "struggle for survival," social theory has to return to the human foundations of prevailing structural arrangements. The abandonment of objectivism, however, cannot mean indulgence in unprincipled speculation; rather, it demands a constant "critique of what is only illusory and apparent. In a rigorous sense, it demands the critique of ideology."[32]

In all these statements, it seems to me, the promise of a phenomenological Marxism is compellingly evident. Unfortunately, however, the statements are scattered and dispersed over the bulk of a lengthy argument that tends to be pervaded by a different tenor—a tenor more inspirational than Socratic in character. The two perspectives or styles of presentation, to be sure, are not neatly segregated; occasionally they merge in one and the same passage—but without effacing underlying fissures. Instead of stressing the need for patient exploration and consultation, many portions of the study present phenomenology—and Marxist phenomenology in particular—as an act of revelation, as a sudden glimpse underneath the covers of phenomenal appearances. The reality revealed in this manner is usually described as the dimension of the "precategorial" or pretheoretical life-world—a life-world seen from the angle of an experiencing subject who is both concrete and "transcendental," and which is directly endowed with a basic finality or teleology. As one will note, the hidden dimension is a somewhat complex scenery, and it may be well to examine its component elements in detail.

Probably the most recurrent and most emphatically expounded theme of the study is the stress on the subject as source of all insight and on the "return to subjectivity" as phenomenology's basic goal. "Phenomenology," the opening section proclaims, "wants to return his 'subjectivity' to man. It wants to return man to himself, freeing him from every fetishism, from the mask behind which humanity has been hidden or 'veiled.'" Somewhat later Husserl's work is described as a "founded philosophy that returns to apodictic subjectivity which is, as such, serious and rigorous." Paci does not tire to explicate the significance of this starting point. "The crisis," he writes, "is the forgetting of the origins, the human roots, the human subject, and the precategorial genesis." The implications for social, and especially Marxist, thought are correspondingly evident: "The center of the whole problem is, and remains, the return to subjectivity. We have alienation when social relations do not allow this return."[33] Assertions to this effect seem plausible enough as reaction against reification and exploitation and as reaffirmation of man's relevance as a thinking and experiencing subject. Complications arise quickly, however, when subjectivity is meant to serve as theoretical cornerstone and as foundation of a "first philosophy." That this is Paci's ambition can hardly be doubted. At one point, it is true, he seems to suggest that "the first person" is simply "a *fact*, a reality which cannot be altered by any theory or argument"; but he soon proceeds beyond the factual level. Phenomenology, he asserts, is "the only precategorial philosophy," adding that "as first philosophy," it is "a science of subjects and not objects." It seems clear, however, that, on a theoretical level, "subjectivity" immediately presupposes, and cannot be conceived without, the counterterm "objectivity" and that both can claim equal status.

Paci might counter that his argument aims not at the conceptual but at the preconceptual level of experience. In fact, he writes at one point that "the word 'subject' [is] but a category" and that one must return instead to the "original subject, i.e., the ego in flesh and blood." One wonders, of course, how the latter can be described and, more generally, how a first philosophy is possible without articulation. The quandary, in any case, remains: either the argument operates on a theoretical level, in which case "subjectivity" evokes objectivity as its partner; or it is meant to be "precategorial"—in which case the emphatic use of the term seems arbitrary or puzzling.[34]

A more serious dilemma deriving from the stress on subjectivity is the proximity to traditional idealism—a perspective according to which the "outside" world is either the result of a mental construction or the manifestation of an ideal core. Numerous statements seem to point in this direction. In several passages the subject is portrayed as an "internal" agent or consciousness contrasted to outside conditions. "If we depart from the 'internal' subject and analyze his operations," Paci contends at one time, "we find everything." Dialectical Marxism, we read in another context, is oriented "toward a maximum of the internal and a minimum of the external," that is, toward a "minimization of dependence" and a "maximization of the autonomy of each subject." To this may be added the notion that "the phenomenological subject is a conscious and therefore free subject," whereas unconsciousness characterizes the "external material world." More important are statements suggesting a far-ranging potency or creativity of the subject. "Philosophy, science, culture, and institutions are all human products," we are told; "they should not be extraneous objects turned against men. We are the subjects of historicity, the persons who create culture and function in the totality: the personal functioning mankind." On other occasions, man's creative role is expressed in even more dramatic language. A "transcendental" or philosophically radical attitude, Paci indicates, cannot simply accept the world "as already done and accomplished"; rather, rigorous reflection requires "taking a dialectical, revolutionary position on the intentional level." Phenomenological bracketing thus acquires a practical connotation: "The transcendental *epoché* is a total transformation."[35]

Paci, to be sure, is quick to reject any idealistic implications of his argument. Man's internality, we are given to understand, does not really contrast with outside conditions, and human creativity has to be understood at most in a figurative sense. "Man is internal while the world is external," he writes. "However, the internal man is within the external world, while the external world is within the internal man." As a result, one can say that "man is both internal and external." By returning to the subject, Paci adds later, "I discover in myself and in others the ways in which the external is given to me: Each one of us contains the external." In a similar manner, the stress on creativity is corrected by the reminder: "If we think about what Husserl says, we readily understand that consciousness discovers that it does not posit the world. Contrary to traditional idealism, consciousness discovers precisely that the world is pregiven." It may very well be that Paci with these assertions obviates the danger of subjective idealism; but at what price? While the merger of the external and the internal evokes the legacy of an absolute synthesis, the nexus of creativity and discovery

seems to be predicated on the assumption of an ideal core, a hidden
finality contracting theory and practice. The latter assumption is by no
means fortuitous.

In trying to avoid idealist subjectivism and at the same time a
naive realism according to which the mind simply mirrors an objective world, Paci is led to embrace the notion of a dynamic essence,
which, although discoverable, is not ready-made but awaits implementation through human involvement. This conception permits Paci
to write passages in which action and receptivity are intimately linked.
Thus the preceding reference to Husserl is followed by these comments: "We live in order to overcome the already constituted world, to
direct ourselves toward a new world that we can conceive and whose
realization we can seek to effect. Here the interest has changed, since
it is no longer concerned with the given world but with a world evolving from it by means of reflection"—a reflection aiming "toward a
teleological and intentional meaning." From this perspective, Paci
adds, "the world no longer interests us for what it is, but for the meaning it can have and for the meaning we can give to it and realize."[36]

The linkage of action and reflection is hardly conceivable without
the other feature: the merger of subject and the world. This fusion—
the notion that "each one of us contains the external"—is reiterated in
many variations. Thus, at one point, Paci affirms that "subjectivity is
the *entire world* to the extent that it is subjective, intentional activity."
In even bolder terms, another passage refers to "the total subject who
contains the world—even that world he does not knowingly contain
and the past that he ignores." This view has immediate relevance for
intersubjective relations; even if restricted to the "subjective, intentional" domain, the "world" contained by the individual would seem to
comprise his fellow-men. Paci tends to be explicit on this point. The
study speaks of "the structures of intersubjectivity which inhere in
every individual subject, in every monad" and of "the internal immanence of society in individuals." In a later section, Paci elaborates on
the aspect in greater detail. "The problem of the 'constitution of the
other' by the subject," he states, "is the phenomenological history of the
individual in relation to other individuals and the inherence of 'society'
in the individual. In fact, the individual finds others within himself
even if he becomes an absolute solipsist." Actually, he continues, the
individual has no choice but to start from "the *solus ipse* of solipsism";
by bracketing all external factors, including society and state, the individual "truly finds the others and society within himself." Social life,
it is true, is not simply deduced or extracted from individual awareness; repeatedly Paci stresses the importance of "coupling" or inter-

monadic contact. Such contact, however, tends to be presented either as an "immanence of monads and individuals in one another" or as the reciprocal discovery of affinity through "empathy";[37] what is missing is an actual confrontation or struggle with strangeness. As it seems to me, Paci's comments on this issue tend to fall short of Husserl's own insights, especially his endeavors in *Cartesian Meditations* to conceive a relationship between ego and others which would not efface their otherness. Most important, his view evades the task of interaction: on the premise of reciprocal immanence or affinity, social agreement does not seem to presuppose the arduous labor of intersubjective questioning and correction.

The conception of a subject-object convergence, however, extends beyond the social domain. Paci does not ignore the limits of conscious intentionality. "Matter," he acknowledges, "is given to me as matter in its impenetrability, opacity, passivity, and resistance. It provokes me, conditions me, and makes me experience what has not been done by me: being as such (*Sosein*) or matters of fact." Yet, even on this level, the gulf does not seem insurmountable, for he adds that "*Sosein* can be reduced to a lived modality. It is reducible to an *Erlebnis* that can be characterized as the *Erlebnis* of passivity of the hardness of things." Thus matter can be integrated into the life-world, the opaque into conscious experience. "The 'unconscious,'" Paci notes, "appears as the external material world and as the otherness not yet consciously constituted in my *Umwelt*." However, when viewed in the context of the life-world, "we become aware of the fact that even external and material nature is internal to the extent that it is life experienced by transcendental subjectivity." Man, in Paci's view, is able to incorporate matter chiefly through the medium of his body, which is anchored in inorganic nature and unconscious causality. Although the "phenomenological subject" has to be viewed as alert and aware, "it would not be conscious without its animated body: its soul or psyche and its organic body which is rooted in causality." By virtue of his body, he repeatedly stresses, man becomes the "point of insertion and encounter (*Umschlagpunkt*) of the internal and of the external," a notion he finds reflected in the "admirable phenomenological and Marxian concept of the nature which is *in me* as man's inorganic body." The vision of man's linkage with nature inspires Paci occasionally with rhapsodic formulations, reminiscent of the idealist philosophy of identity. Geological nature, he observes at one point, "has preceded me and continues to permeate me as if the planet Earth and the entire universe were the inorganic body of my individual, concrete, and transcendental ego. It permeates me as my material, organic, and animated individuality: as the body of intersubjective humanity, animals, plants, and the very minerals as material bodies. Inert matter is mine but I am also inert matter, the inert universe."[38]

A vision of this kind, it would seem, cannot readily be reconciled with dialectical thought: where subject and object become merged, a crucial dialectical tension appears suspended. Paci's comments on the topic are correspondingly elusive. The dialectic, he writes, "is the inclusion of the totality in the part, of the infinite in the finite, and of truth in individuality"; at the same time it is "the identification of the part and the whole, of actuality and rationality, and of individuality and totality." To be sure, inclusion and identification do not adequately convey the meaning of the dialectic as a process and Paci is fully aware of this circumstance. In trying to render his conception dynamic, however, he tends to present dialectical movement simply as a process of progressive revelation, as a struggle to remove the cloak of objectification from a hidden, purposive reality. Phenomenological dialectic, we learn, is "a dialectic of the hidden and the revealed," a dialectic "which unravels and persists." Discovery of the hidden occurs through a dual negation: the rejection of the negative veil of appearances. In Paci's words, phenomenological reflection "is a human operation of negating that negation which is appearance." While appearance "operates by negating and alienating man," *epoché* or the act of bracketing must "prevent these forms from once again becoming prejudicial." By collapsing or cutting through mediation, bracketing thus emerges as gateway to essential meaning and social transformation, the dialectic of negation as the harbinger of synthesis. "In the dialectic," we read, "we must bring about a *radical revolution* wherein each man and humanity deal with their own negativity while attempting to negate it (negation of the negation). In this revolution, quantitative operations must be transformed into qualitative ones. They must allow a qualitative change; they must permit a change of life's meanings and goals so that, ultimately, the paradoxes and contradictions become functions of a totalizing and constructive synthesis." Not surprisingly, the proletariat is invoked somewhat later as the chief motor of the dialectic, as the agency performing the dual negation: "It is insofar as it is not; and it is not insofar as it is."

What, in Paci's opinion, is crucial in dialectical thought, properly understood, is the dismantling of apparent objectivity in favor of authentic experience. "The fundamental point," he avows, "is the insertion of the dialectic into subjectivity and the penetration of subjectivity as a causal element into every dialectical modality." Such a view, he maintains, is entirely congruent with the outlook of the founders of

Marxism: "Dialectical modalities such as those presented as laws by Engels must necessarily begin with subjectivity, both as a point of departure and as living and operating presence." Taking his cues from Engels, Paci even speculates on the notion of a "dialectic of nature." By relying on life-world experience and the role of subjectivity, he claims to be able to clarify its significance; but his comments on the issue are at best puzzling. Orthodox proponents of the notion, in any case, would hardly appreciate his endeavors when learning that such a dialectic "must be constituted by us" and must necessarily begin "with us."[39] According to Paci, the focus on subjectivity also provides a reliable demarcation line between Hegelianism and genuine Marxist thought. As he tries to show, Hegel's dialectic—despite its pioneering value—was marred by overconceptualization, by an excessive indulgence in abstract categories; ultimately, this excess derived from a neglect of subjective life and of the method of bracketing. Hegel's philosophy, he says, "is a dialectic of abstract concepts, ideas, and constructions that have occluded their genesis in the precategorial world and in subjective and intersubjective operations." What is missing in Hegelian idealism "is precisely the subjective and precategorial point of departure"; in other words, "what Hegel lacked was the *epoché*: the first reflective dialectical operation of the subject living in the world." As he adds, this is a criticism that can be directed against Hegel's entire system, "as has already been done by the Left Hegelians."[40]

There are other reminders of Left Hegelianism in Paci's argument. A chief example is the intimate juncture of transcendental reflection with empirical contingency; one of the traits peculiar of the Hegelian Left was the assignment of absolute functions to empirical agents. "The transcendental reduction," he writes, "allows us to find what Husserl indicates as absolute subjectivity." However, the same reduction also reveals a "concrete living presence"; its aim thus is not an "abstract transcendental ego separated from the ego which we are or separated from that concrete world in which we have always been living." An "extreme" type of bracketing involves "reduction to an 'absolute' subjectivity," yet—since "subjectivity without the world contains it"—what emerges is not emptiness but a "new world" which is "to be found in subjectivity itself and is intentionally constituted by it." At other points Paci expresses himself even more succinctly. "The transcendental ego," he asserts, "is each one of us in his concreteness as a human being in flesh and blood"; by the same token, absolute subjectivity is "simultaneously the concrete ego."[41] Of course, Paci does not simply identify transcendental and mundane levels without further elaboration. However, as in the case of the dialectic, his elaboration takes the form of a two-layer theory according to which the mundane subject is merely a camouflage covering authentic man. Phenomenology, in his view, clears the way to a "transcendental foundation," provided the mundane is bracketed: "Objectivism and factuality are masks behind which man is hidden and fetishized. Therefore, the transcendental foundation requires the transcendental reduction to pure subjectivity, that is, to transcendental subjectivity." Properly performed, the transcendental reduction leads to "a subjectivity which is not mythological," to a "life oriented toward truth, the life which I somehow always live behind my masks"; once man "in the name of reason rejects his mask," he is able to discover "his own truth" and "his proper authentic nature." One may recall in this context what Merleau-Ponty wrote in 1960: "Man is hidden, well hidden, and this time we must make no mistake about it: this does not mean that he is there beneath a mask, ready to appear. Alienation is not simply privation of what was our own by natural right; and to bring it to an end, it will not suffice to steal what has been stolen, to give us back our due."[42]

As presented by Paci, the relationship between substance and mask is the basic key to historical development; although not presently accomplished, their convergence is the driving motor of mankind's teleology. In his words: "Our most secret nature, what we actually are in the most profound sense, first and foremost, is also the rational ideal, the teleological end and the final goal." Within man, he affirms, "there is a latent humanity—and here we interpret Husserl in a radical sense— a humanity which has not yet been born but which can be born if man so desires, if man assumes the responsibility for becoming what he can become." History, from this perspective, appears as "the progressive self-revelation and self-realization of what is hidden; and what is hidden is the authentic original man: both his meaning and his *telos*." While at present we do not yet live "according to our true life and therefore do not live according to reason" but rather "in a sort of pre-existence," our duty is "to realize our existence in history, to come really into being in history." By bringing to light and rendering manifest what has been concealed or latent from the beginning, teleological development links the past with the future. Historiography in its true sense, Paci comments, is "a process of continually bringing back to life," a persistent "rediscovery of the hidden historical meaning"; in this manner, "the historical-genetic origin becomes the goal: beginning and goal meet one another in a circle." This circle, however, is not merely pointless repetition; rather, it is an effort to resurrect and implement purpose in life, a constant "renewal in the present of the past for the future, of the *Lebenswelt* for the *telos*." In terms of human involvement, the renewal implies the investment of "will, decision, interest and praxis": the "return to subjectivity" is also a "return to action" entailing an "actual commitment directed toward a finality."[43]

The difficulty in these passages lies not in the general vision of a goal—which is bold and captivating—but rather in its formulation, and especially in the portrayal of history as teleological revelation. Such a portrayal tends to bypass or shortchange the complexity of meaning in concrete situations. Above all, the perspective implies a contraction of theory and practice, reflection and action—or, at least, it fails to elaborate sufficiently on their relationships. Paci emphatically insists on their intimate nexus; thus he finds the genuine character of Marxism in the aspect that "the historical and the scientific meanings of truth coincide." One may wonder, however, how a coincidence of this type can escape the lure of scientism and, in particular, how it can resolve the quandaries attached to the juncture of norms and observation.[44] More important, the notion of an immanent finality or *telos* in history tends to favor a posture of apodictic certainty, while dampening the taste for intersubjective discourse. Despite the recognition that mankind's goal is an "infinite task" which "is never completely realized," many statements in the study suggest that practical standards are the direct result of individual reflection. The transcendental reduction or *epoché*, we read, "has a moral aspect which, by freeing us from the mundane, must allow us to rediscover the 'natural' direction of the will toward the good and the evidence of the will 'pointed toward the ultimate meaning of determinate being.' " Transferred to the concrete political domain, the reduction has distinct implications—especially if coupled with a negative dialectic, the notion that "in the negation of the negation" the essence "becomes consciousness, will, and praxis." The apodictic character of these implications is reinforced when praxis is seen as rooted in, and basically conditioned by, material needs—needs which are universal and thus hardly amenable to dispute. "The proletariat fights and must fight for all, that is, for the *telos* and meaning of human history," Paci notes; in this case, "the subject, or groups of subjects, know and will according to a universal aim."[45]

The apodictic thrust of Paci's political outlook is predicated on, and supported by an important feature of early phenomenology: the notion of intuitive evidence as criterion of truth. Evidence, he writes, means experience and presence "in the first person." Although limited and finite, it is "the pledge and the proof that man can bring to light what is latent within himself, what he has hidden, what is not yet human, what is not rationally or philosophically grounded. For the philosopher who wants to constitute humanity and ground it upon philosophy, evidence is therefore the starting point, the beginning." Whatever can be experienced, he adds, "can be experienced directly through intuition"; the life-world in particular allows "an evident, convincing, and original experience in the first person." As universal science, phenomenology treats existential life "as the original source of verification and as the basis of truth." The basic principle of phenomenological inquiry is, in fact, "that it is always possible to depart from a presence, from actual evidence (an *Erfüllung*)." Paci realizes, of course, that individual evidence is restricted and that there is the possibility of deception and error in judgment. However, such error seems to be chiefly a failure of reflection and, as such, subject to the dialectic of substance and appearance. While surrounded by a penumbra like a source of light, evidence "must have a nucleus of certainty: it must be a basic revelation. Even though it is finite, it must be apodictic." The doubting ego "that has not yet reflected and recognized that it thinks while doubting" always "precedes the ego which is certain of its doubting"; thus "even while doubting, the preceding ego contains certainty."

At some points, especially when reporting on Husserl's notion of a community of investigators, the study seems to open up the prospect of corrective interaction; yet Paci's comments usually point back to the premises of reciprocal immanence and self-revelation. Phenomenological philosophy, he writes, is "rigorous because of its beginning anew and because of its continuous return to the factual and transcendental apodicticity of the human subject." On this level, "each man can discover in each part, beginning from himself and his own apodicticity, the meaning of the whole"; departing from the evidence in the first person, "he discovers in the universal correlation the possibility of knowing all that his evidence implies."[46]

The effects of this phenomenological starting point reverberate in many other facets of the study, not all of which can be mentioned in this context. One example is the formulation of the "precategorial" life-world: occasionally there is the suggestion of an apodictic knowledge on this level serving as groundwork for specialized inquiries. As a rule, the study is quite explicit in portraying the life-world as a domain of relative opinion or *doxa*—at least from the vantage point of immediate experience. The *Lebenswelt*, we read, conceived as "relative and prescientific life is the subjective world of the *doxa*." Paci, however, is by no means content with opinion, seeking instead grounded knowledge. Rigorous scrutiny, he notes, is required "insofar as the *Lebenswelt* needs techniques, theoretical praxis, and elaborations of teleological theories"; phenomenological bracketing must even "allow for a subjective science of the *Lebenswelt*." We may bypass here the question how a theoretical elaboration of a preconceptual domain is possible. As Paci repeatedly insists, a "science" of the life-world is not the investigation of a chimerical "thing-in-itself," but rather the search for the meaning and intentional purpose of life, a meaning inherent in practical conduct: "The science of the life-world is essentially praxis precisely because it is the science of the precategorial and of the operations performed and being performed by the subjects."[47] Passages of this kind, however, do not entirely banish the dilemmas endemic in the theory-praxis nexus. In his effort to show the cognitive potential of practical life, Paci is led to structural considerations. Without becoming an "objectified" discipline, he affirms, "the science of the *Lebenswelt* discovers a general structure," that is, a configuration of the "typical" and "invariable forms" of life. The task of phenomenology is to capture the life-world in its "essential forms" and in its "necessary and essential structure"; although life experience may be subjective, "its structures are not relative," but rather provide the nucleus for a phenomenological "ontology." At some points, the vision of a structural ontology acquires distinct connotations of a dual or two-layer reality, with the life-world providing the ideal forms of concrete phenomena. Despite his aversion against a naive realism, Paci's argument at these points tends to lend involuntary support to a "mirror" or correspondence theory of knowledge.[48]

The bent toward a more apodictic than critical outlook is also illustrated in Paci's comments on the various writers discussed in the study. Although painstaking and thorough, the commentary on the *Crisis* at important junctures tends to be obtuse to Husserl's subdued and careful formulations. This tendency has already been noted in regard to the concept of an investigating community, but examples could be multiplied. Usually, Paci's elaborations in such instances imply a de-emphasis of mutual correction in favor of experiential evidence and individual reflection.[49] Marx similarly undergoes occasional simplification. Thus, citing his statement of 1843 that "in the investigation of political conditions one is too easily tempted to overlook the objective nature of the relationships and to explain everything from the will of the persons acting," Paci concludes that its thrust does not affect "the person but only the person separated from the situation"; again, Marx's later stress on the precedence of economic categories—such as wage-labor or capital—over supposedly concrete initiatives is interpreted to mean that "the original concreteness from which Marx in fact departs, is the subjects."

Similar impressions can be gleaned from passages dealing with more recent Marxists or neo-Marxists. Lukács is commended primarily for his adherence to a dialectic of synthesis, with its insistence on dual negation and the movement toward totality under the aegis of the proletariat. Synthesis and emphasis on proletarian action are also the chief merits of Labriola and Gramsci; while Labriola is noteworthy primarily for his merger of subject and object, theory and praxis, Gramsci is singled out for his practical philosophy and for showing that "the humanly objective is grounded by the historically subjective, that is, by the universally subjective." By and large, Paci praises Sartre's endeavors—including his move toward an existentialist Marxism—but is slightly suspicious of his *Critique,* finding it insufficiently strict in terms of a reliance on subjective evidence: Only phenomenology, he observes, can offer "a rigorous and consequential foundation to Sartre's position." Criticism is heaped more lavishly on Merleau-Ponty, but basically for the same reason. Repeatedly, Merleau-Ponty is taken to task for favoring an abstract and ambivalent symbiosis of idealism and realism—a charge which finds little or no support in his writings; but the real complaint is readily apparent and involves another "ambiguity": a deficiency of apodictic firmness.[50]

III. Contemporary Sociology and Social Thought

As is well known, social science in Western countries is presently in a state of considerable ferment, a ferment characterized by the weakening of positivist predominance and the search for alternative methods and theoretical vistas. Increasingly, contemporary sociology and social thought are beginning to reflect the imprint of both phenomenological and neo-Marxist perspectives. While, in regard to phenomenology, the legacy of Alfred Schutz is exerting a growing influence, Marxist impulses are evident in the emergence of a "dialectical" or "critical" sociology with its emphasis on stratification, conflict, and social change. So far, however, sustained encounters between phenomenology and Marxism are infrequent; some of the pioneering works in the contemporary endeavor of reorientation do not indicate such a possibility.

Although informed and elaborate on Marxist trends in sociology, Norman Birnbaum's *Toward a Critical Sociology* makes only perfunctory reference to phenomenology as a quest for a trans-social human essence and authenticity. Similarly, Alvin Gouldner's *The Coming Crisis of Western Sociology* contains a sympathetic account of Marxist tendencies, but only an offhand allusion to Schutz during the discussion of one specialized type of inquiry; although reminiscent of phenomenological *Verstehen* and imbued with a Marxist concern for praxis, his "reflexive sociology" does not involve an articulate merger of the two perspectives.[51] Yet there are signs that the situation is changing—in no small measure due to the impact of Paci and kindred thinkers. Actually, phenomenological Marxism is not an entirely novel venture in Western social science. For several decades, the French sociologist Georges Gurvitch has experimented with such an alliance and his works have received a fair share of scholarly tribute and critical scrutiny.[52] For present purposes, I shall limit myself to more recent endeavors and briefly review the work of two American writers. The two examples, it seems to me, vividly illustrate the significance of phenomenological Marxism for social theory and sociological research, while at the same time disclosing instructive differences of accent and formulation.

The first example is Paul Piccone, one of the translators of *The Function of the Sciences* and chief editor of a social theory journal whose title, *Telos*, suggests its Husserlian inspiration. As translator and attentive student of the philosopher, Piccone to a large extent shares the ambivalence of Paci's outlook—including the bent toward apodicticity. The similarities in perspective are clearly revealed in the Introduction to the *Function*, which he coauthored with his fellow translator. The essay is strongly critical of "orthodox" Marxism, depicted as an abstract, objectified doctrine and as tool of manipulation in the hands of a ruling bureaucracy. The affinity between Marx and Husserl is seen precisely in their common struggle against objectivism and reification, with Husserl focusing on developments within the "European sciences." From this perspective, "capital, science, and Marxism are three different products of the *same* sociohistorical process of capitalist development." Analogous to the crisis of the sciences and capitalism, Marxist orthodoxy involves "essentially the separation of subject (workers) and object (their objective consciousness: Marxism), with the subsequent reification of the object to the level of an objective science." In his *Crisis,* Husserl had definitely pierced the cloak of scientific objectivity, laying bare the underpinnings of human knowledge: "The *leitmotiv* of Husserl's work is the return to the subject as the *real foundation.* Meanings are constantly referred to the human operations that constitute them." By returning to the subject—and to the life-world as its habitat—phenomenology boldly surpasses abstract philosophical systems and "categorial" schemes: "The life-world is fundamental to any philosophy that seeks to avoid naive realism or idealism and give an adequate analysis of knowledge." In contrast to realism, in particular, phenomenology insists that concepts "cannot be mechanically *derived* from the object, but must be constituted in terms of a *telos* that furnishes a precategorial criterion" of relevance and validity.

Although compelling in its domain, however, Husserl's phenomenology according to the authors is incomplete: his account of scientific developments ends abruptly at the point where he attempts to articulate the broader "roots of the crisis." At this point, Marxism can offer assistance by penetrating into the material infrastructure of social life. Husserl's analysis, it is true, "turns to the precategorial world as the world of human operations," but here "the world of materiality becomes central." Together with Paci, the authors consider "need" as "the precategorial foundation upon which everything else depends." Need, they write, is "determining. The life-world is the world of needs and of their satisfaction by means of labor." Thus Marxism is able to supplement phenomenology by integrating the question of scientific knowledge into a general social perspective: "A developed phenomenology coheres with Marxism as a dialectical account of how men make themselves and their institutions in the laboring process"; in fact, "phenomenology as a whole can already be found *within* Marxism as a necessary and essential moment of the whole structure, and the crisis of the sciences can be seen as a *special* case of the capitalist crisis."

While being supplemented and corroborated, phenomenology in turn offers a vital impulse destined to reactivate a stagnant Marxism. This impulse consists in the renewed focus on the crucial role of subjective experience: "What is needed is the development of a new subjective philosophy which, unlike the objectivistic systems developed since the Renaissance, would lay major stress on the subject, the lifeworld, and the all-important *telos*." In emphasizing the role of the subject, the authors occasionally seem willing to strain phenomenological vocabulary. Despite Paci's repeated avowal that "to constitute does not mean to create"—and despite the "determining" character of needs—they observe that "pseudo-rationalism camouflaged as 'scientific neutrality' is divorced from the creating subject who originally constitutes it."[53]

Many of Piccone's writings have been published in *Telos*. The mixture of criticism and apodicticity is strongly evident in his essay entitled "Phenomenological Marxism." The essay contains a vehement indictment of Marxist orthodoxy and an urgent plea for the adoption of a "critical" Marxist outlook. Reduced to an instrument of Soviet policy, Piccone writes, "orthodox Marxism as a theory has become an empty shell held together by dogmatic slogans—so empty that only the cynicism of its supporters can prevent it from being discarded as an intellectual aberration." The transformation of Marxism into an "ideological fossil," in his view, was not merely a vice of the Stalinist period, but continues to characterize official Soviet doctrine from Khrushchev's reversed "personality cult" to Brezhnev's "computerized Stalinism." Controlled by the party hierarchy and treated as unchallengeable dogma, orthodoxy has a philosophically and culturally stifling and even lethal effect: "All philosophy and culture is immediately reduced to the level of a weapon committed to fighting battles in which the sides are predetermined by the objective requirements of Soviet policy—which means, purely and simply, their destruction as philosophy and culture" and their degeneration into "apologetics."

This decay, Piccone adds, is not merely a fortuitous accident, but the expression of a deep-seated crisis involving the progressive reification of industrial society and the "disintegration of the working class as a revolutionary political force"; consequently, "any attempt at a critical Marxism today must start out in contraposition to the orthodoxy." In order to meet and overcome the crisis, "radical theory" must attempt "to rescue Marxism from the dogmatic stranglehold" by "developing a new critical Marxism." Such an effort implies, above all, a reexamination of the traditional conceptual arsenal: a Marxism "adequate to today's realities must start out by reconstituting first and foremost the notion of class and, specifically, of working class, in order to both capture and explain the myriad of phenomena that senile 'orthodox' Marxism cannot." Likewise, the relationship between base and superstructure must be reinterpreted in such a manner that base is no longer defined in a narrow economic sense as linked with "the physical means of production," but broadly as a "socio-economic situation which determines one's life style" and "the quality of life." If this is done, then revolution can be conceived primarily "as a qualitative change in this everyday life whereby today's fragmented and robotized workers would become subjects consciously (politically) engaged in concretely determining their destiny."[54]

As the essay emphasizes, phenomenology can significantly help in this critical endeavor by elucidating the crisis both of industrial society and of Marxist theory; in fact, "phenomenological Marxism is precisely the theoretical self-consciousness of the crisis of Marxism and an attempt to explain and overcome it." Phenomenology's contribution can be found mainly in Husserl's later writings; according to Piccone, "certain notions developed by the later Husserl can become extremely useful in the reconstitution of Marxism" by providing "fundamental categories of analysis which can adequately deal with the present socio-historical realities." Husserl's analysis of science in the *Crisis* revealed "the failure of this science to actually change reality by occluding it with its categories and thus checkmating man as the historical agent to the level of a mere passive object operating among similar objects." Basically, this analysis meant the recovery of the source of knowledge in preconceptual experience: "Phenomenology, critically understood, is the tracing back of all mediations to the human operations that constituted them." On a broader scale, the impulse of genuine Marxism points in a similar direction. "The difference between Marxist and bourgeois philosophy," Piccone notes, "does not concern the metaphysical quandary whether consciousness precedes matter or vice versa: on the contrary, the difference is between a dynamic, creative philosophy which explains man's making of himself by making the object and contemplative philosophies which contrapose an abstract subject to an abstract object, both equally inert." From this vantage point, the concerns of Marxism and phenomenology can be seen to be intimately meshed: "Phenomenological Marxism can be preliminarily described as that approach which constantly reduces all theoretical constructs—including Marxism—to their living context in order to guarantee the adequacy of the concept not only to the object it claims to apprehend, but also to the goals it seeks to attain. In fact, its point of departure is precisely the rejection of the theory of reflection so dear to 'orthodox' Marxists."

So far, the argument in its general outline appears clearly motivated by a critical intent, by the endeavor to reconcile "a relevant phenomenology and a non-dogmatic Marxism." However, Piccone's further elaborations raise serious doubts about the thrust of the proposed merger. These doubts emerge when one reads that Marxist philosophy, bent on changing rather than reflecting the world, "not only reconstitutes the world physically but conceptually as well" and that the basis of this reconstitution resides in class position—even though the term is redefined to mean a broad amalgam of underprivileged groups. Husserl's analysis is said to be congruent with this outlook because of its aim "to uncover the transcendental subjectivity which generated these concepts and which is constantly repressed in *mundane* experience." The theme, to be sure, was not fully developed in the *Crisis*; however, once it is realized that the "human operations to which phenomenology reduces all mediations" are historically and socially conditioned, "phenomenological analysis unavoidably ends up in Marxism as the class-analysis that explains the different kinds of consciousness in terms of class position (a result of social sedimentation) and labor (the teleological activity which allows the class engaged in it the *true* consciousness of its situation and the possibility of changing the world by means of the mediations that it itself creates)."

Regarding the question of validity, Piccone at this point resolutely endorses the phenomenological notion of the apodictic evidence of intentionality. "True consciousness," he writes, refers "simply to a consciousness that expresses the objective interests of the subjects possessing it; it is *true* because it is constituted by the subjects that have it." The same rule of evidence applies to all domains of knowledge and cultural experience. "The relation between concept and object," he continues, "is not one of reflection or symmetry, but one of adequacy"; consequently, "the criterion of truth cannot be correspondence between concept and object, but must be between the concept and its fulfillment of the goal for which it was originally devised." Since a concept cannot reflect reality, "it must be created"; but given the infinite number of possible concepts, the standard determining adequacy "is always a function of a social situation with its own needs and problems. In other words, the process of concept formation should not be seen as at all different from the process of commodity production; both processes are teleological and based on labor. Thus, it is possible to talk about all knowledge, including science, as class-determined."[55]

These passages conjure up a series of quandaries. If all knowledge is class-based and all science "class-science," then this statement is subject to the same standard and becomes a victim of the same relativity. More important, one may wonder whether, on these premises, philosophy and culture are not bound to be transformed into "weapons" in the class struggle and thus be reduced to "apologetics"—a result that was previously deplored. Piccone is eloquent in depicting the practical implications of phenomenological Marxism and of the reliance on primary evidence. Just as Marx "materialized" Hegel, he observes, "Marxism must 'materialize' Husserl by interpreting the base as the *Lebenswelt* and the worker as *transcendental subjectivity*"; only in this manner "is it possible to vindicate the need for revolution and the quest for a qualitatively different way of life." From the perspective of a revitalized Marxism, "revolution is necessitated not only by the exploitation and starvation of the proletariat, nor by cultural deprivation, but, more importantly, by its dehumanization whereby under capitalism men (both the capitalists and the proletarians) are limited to *mundane* experience." The proletarian, he explains, "ends up as the revolutionary agency not because of any inner superiority or higher moral character, but because in having to work he is always forced into the role of a *transcendental* subject who not only *mundanely* transposes pre-given categories into a pre-given reality, but also transforms that pre-given reality." While being treated as an object, the worker through his labor transcends and molds objective conditions; but this rift cannot endure: "Revolution is necessitated by the need to be an openly transcendental subject, that is, really human." Several questions arise again in this context. Does the portrayal of revolutionary praxis as "transcendental" constitution and creativity not transform phenomenological Marxism into the kind of ambitious "voluntarism" which is elsewhere denounced as the "construct of alienated intellectuals"? If revolution, on the other hand, is seen as implementation of objective interests and a latent teleology, is the rule of evidence not subtly changed into a "correspondence" of practical outcome and life-world conditions?[56]

As in Paci's case, some of the accents of Piccone's outlook are revealed in his comments on other writers. Lukács is credited for his effort to overcome the positivist scientism which dominated Marxism at the turn of the century—although *History and Class Consciousness* is criticized for resorting to a ready-made but irrelevant conceptual arsenal.[57] One also finds a sympathetic appraisal of Gramsci's contributions, including his stress on proletarian praxis and on the subject-object nexus. Strong endorsement is given to the early writings of Tran Duc Thao, especially his attempt to reformulate the structure-superstructure relation in terms of a dialectic of essence and appearance. Largely for the same reason, Kosík's *Dialectic of the Concrete* is singled out as "the high point" of the Marxist reawakening in Eastern Europe and as representing "a phenomenological Marxism of a quality unreached since Marx and Lukács' early work." By contrast, comments on Marcuse and the French phenomenologists tend to be much less favorable—a fact that may be connected with Piconne's somewhat summary dismissal of existentialism as a form of bourgeois decadence and escapism. Marcuse's Heideggerian Marxism is attacked for being a haphazard undertaking and, above all, for not penetrating sufficiently to Husserl's transcendental subjectivity; beset by "insuperable intrinsic difficulties," his "forced synthesis" of phenomenology and Marxism was "bound to fail from the very beginning." Sartre's work is dismissed as unreliable—but mainly for political rather than theoretical reasons, especially his "long history of flirting with the French Communist Party." Merleau-Ponty receives the least favorable treatment. In contrast to Marcuse's "forced" merger, his "philosophy of ambiguity" according to the author was a piecemeal amalgam which was "neither an exclusively phenomenological nor an exclusively Marxist perspective, but a phenomenology that paved the way for structuralism and a tamed Marxism that gave way to social democracy."[58]

Particularly relevant for present purposes are Piccone's observations on some key sociological theorists. In discussing Husserl's account of the life-world, he takes Alfred Schutz to task for inappropriately identifying this domain with the mundane or "common-sense" world and for bypassing the transcendental reduction. Such a treatment, he notes, "ends up by occluding precisely that crucial dialectic which makes the notion fruitful and relevant. The *Lebenswelt* does include the empirical and the common-sense world, but it also encompasses much more." Although ordinarily one may take features of the life-world for granted, "the *Lebenswelt* is also the domain in which concepts are invented and historical projects are formulated." Although it may be true that "most experience is of the mundane type," the "crucial point" is that "this mundane experience is parasitic on the original constitutive experience."[59] Even more severe strictures are leveled at Georges Gurvitch for his attempt to introduce a "dialectical realism" or "dialectical hyperempiricism" into sociology. By expelling reflection and intentionality, Piccone notes, Gurvitch's attempt shipwrecks on the "rocks of empiricism" and cannot "transcend the reified structure of the given, thus failing the acid-test of any meaningful dialectic." While the dialectic, properly understood, "draws its strength and dynamism from its ability to deal with teleology," which is "introduced by the omnipresence of subjectivity," the suppression of teleology in the name of realism "amounts to the attainment of a spurious objectivity which is scientifically trivial and socially useless." Rejecting "all a priori principles," the "empiricist dialectic" focuses "on the given in its phenomenal and reified form," with the result that "no radical change is either conceivable or required."[60]

The second example is John O'Neill, a sociologist and social theorist primarily (but not exclusively) known as a translator and interpreter of Merleau-Ponty.[61] Apart from their impressive stylistic flavor, O'Neill's writings are marked by their sensitivity for the nuances and intricate texture of concrete experience—and by a certain weariness with sudden ruptures and transcendental vistas. These qualities—and perhaps limitations—are clearly evident in a collection of his essays entitled *Sociology as a Skin Trade*. As the author notes in his introductory remarks, his "thinking represents a blend of Marxism with phenomenological concerns about language, embodiment, and intersubjectivity"; while his understanding of Marxism is indebted to recent French exegesis, including Jean Hyppolite, in phenomenology "the principal influences have been Maurice Merleau-Ponty and Alfred Schutz." There are many meeting points between his outlook and preceding discussions. Together with Piccone (and Paci), O'Neill laments and denounces scientific objectivism and the sway of technology. Many of his essays, he states in the opening section, seek to question "the restrictive code of objectivist science" and to demonstrate that "the basic norm of liberal capitalism is contained in the pattern of scientific and technological rationality which legitimates a corporate agenda of the over-privatization of all social resources, including individual knowledge and conduct." To a considerable extent, the interpretation of sociology as a "skin trade" is a reaction against the discipline's excessive concern with "scientism, value-neutralism and professional sociologism." In its scramble to gain professional status, "sociology has uncritically assumed all the trappings of science," lodging itself "in the bureaucratic organizations which are the institutional expression of the process of rationalization that has made the fortune of modern science and technology." In contrast to this sterilized self-enclosure, the author stresses the need of working with people and sharing their experiences: "Working with people creates a bewildering variety of practices which I shall call skin trades. . . . In my view sociology is a symbiotic science. Its promise is to give back to the people what it takes from them."[62]

O'Neill's criticism of scientific objectivism extends also to a positivist conception of Marxism—a conception which, in part, can be traced back to Marx himself. In his later writings, O'Neill notes, Marx "allowed the theory of historical materialism to harden into the form of a theory of economic, perhaps technological epiphenomenalism," thus giving it the cast of "an alienated (estranged) ideology of which he himself had been an early critic." Together with Piccone, he also favors a reexamination of Marxian concepts in the light of contemporary experience; for the "forms of power arising from the industrial and political system and their interrelations with the social class and stratification patterns of a given society" are matters for "empirical not logical" determination. In opposition to an objectified perspective, O'Neill stresses the human thrust of Marxist thought. Genuine Marxism, he contends, is neither a simple materialism nor idealism, and certainly not based on a correspondence theory of knowledge but rather an expression of practical concerns. At least in his early writings, Marx "rejected classical objectivist epistemology and sketched a phenomenology of a world-view based upon the creativeness of authentic personality"; this position, according to the author, is "the only positive path to the formation of a nonestranged world-view, in which the cultural world is considered a human project and human existence as an *Ecstasis,* as Heidegger, for example, has considered it." The stress on human purpose, to be sure, does not imply a leap into spiritualism. Like Paci, O'Neill insists on the bodily dimension of human experience—although his arguments hardly dispel the riddles surrounding the notion of embodiment. Actually, the focus on skin trades also reflects a preoccupation with the bodily aspects of human contacts, with the operation of social life conceived as a "body-politic."[63]

Affinities and convergences of this type, however, do not entirely efface significant—perhaps more weighty—differences of accent. Such differences emerge already from the choice of mentors and the tone of citations. O'Neill's sympathies for Merleau-Ponty and Schutz have already been mentioned. At one point, he even admits, in regard to phenomenology, an "underlying attachment to Hegel rather than Husserl" —a confession which is amply supported by his frequent reliance on the *Phenomenology of Mind* in many portions of the study.[64] As a previously quoted passage indicates, his attitude toward Heidegger tends to be favorable, if reserved; generally speaking, his comments on existentialism, although fluctuating, never approximate Piccone's vehemence. In his concern with embodiment and especially with the "libidinal" qualities of social relations one readily detects the imprint of Marcuse's *Eros and Civilization*. By themselves inconclusive, these differences of intellectual parentage and affiliation are matched by divergences of substantive outlook. In a subtle manner, Hegel's influence is noticeable in O'Neill's conception of the dialectic which, by comparison with the Husserlian return to subjectivity, tends to accord a somewhat more prominent status to the "object-pole," viewing the world and society as a result of the interchange "between intentionality and an irreducible ontological difference"; for, "if consciousness did not encounter the resistance of things and others, it could only know things perceptually and others by analogy and it would have no organic or social life." This view of the dialectic goes hand in hand with a more ready acceptance of objectification or externalization—as distinguished from alienation or estrangement—as a process indispensable for the manifestation of human purpose. "The process of externalization," he writes, "is the natural expression of the kind of being man is. Marx does not lament the external world, for it is the precondition of all human effort, the means to human expression." While from the perspective of Hegel and Marx, alienation or estrangement occurs only when social institutions "fail to achieve purposes which the participants intended," their position was "quite clearly that the necessity of objectifying man's natural capacities is not at all problematic."[65]

More important and telling than his view of objectification is O'Neill's stress on the crucial role of intersubjective relations. As he points out in his opening remarks, one of his central complaints against scientific objectivism is its contribution to "repressive communication," to the stifling of intersubjective contacts and understanding.

Easily the most attractive and intriguing passages of the study reflect the endeavor to counter this plight. "The error in modern communication and information theory," he states, "is that it overlooks the rhetorical vehicle of speech, reading, and writing. It does this because in turn it lacks any conception of the intention to institute solidarity and a just social order in the relations between the partners to human speech." Human action, he adds, "is essentially the unfolding of a cultural space and its historical dimensions, so that in a strict sense we never accomplish anything except as a collective and historical project. For the individual action involves, therefore, a constant dialogue with others, a recovery of the past and the projection of breaks which are never entirely successful."[66] In his attack on repressive communication, O'Neill claims to find an ally not only in Hegel's *Phenomenology*, with its emphasis on the struggle for recognition, but also in Marx. Despite previous reservations concerning the character of Marx's later works, the concluding portion of the study presents communicative interaction and the concern for moral recognition as cornerstones of Marxist thought, overshadowing economic considerations.[67] At this point, the author goes beyond Piccone in defending a broad interpretation of structure-superstructure relations in such a manner that the base refers generally to "human production which is *as such* rational and moral," while economics becomes "in fact a subculture within the total social culture." From this vantage point, material needs and the instrumental satisfaction of needs appear as a relatively subordinate aspect within the overall cultural matrix. By the same token, social life and development are no longer rigidly guided by economic class position or other structural factors, as alleged by a crude Marxism or a narrow sociology of knowledge. Such a claim, the author affirms, has in practice "brutalized political awareness," instead of making "for a moderation of political argument."[68]

The preceding passages are indicative of the nondoctrinaire thrust of the essays; but the author is more explicit in other contexts. In discussing the process of objectification, O'Neill describes "sociological anarchism" as "the dangerous possibility which derives from understanding alienation as a phenomenon resulting purely and simply from the institutional organization (externalization) of human behavior." At another point he defends intersubjective discourse against "certain highly subjectivist and solipsistic postures as well as political ideologies which invade classrooms and conferences and threaten to turn the modern mind into an armed camp—a result which, as Camus has remarked, would separate us from the Greeks." In reviewing Gouldner's proposal for a "reflexive sociology," O'Neill finds the formulation overly ambitious, "a quest for transcendence rejecting the conventional sociological celebration, embracing action and responsibility." For his own part, he asserts, "There can never be any question of the transcendence of sociology: it is given with my relation to the world and others around me without flight beyond this touch or talk. Socially, our universals lie between heaven and earth, in the toss of the clown, not on the tightrope of pompous metaphysical generalities but in the face-evident relations between myself, others, and the world around me." The social life-world, in his view, is anything but a chaos or a restless adventure. Rather, "in the ordinary course of life we take others at face-value and expect to be sustained" in the same manner: "There is a common-sense experience of the world and society as that which precedes us and survives us in which the simple sense of tradition and posterity is cultivated." The essay on Gouldner carefully shields contemporary ethnomethodology against sociological perspectives which depict concrete reality as a flimsy veil of appearances masking a realm of freedom and unlimited possibilities. "The possibilitarian," he notes, "is potentially a crackbrain, a dreamer, a fool, and a god who like Musil's man without qualities risks the possibilities of reality in the reality of possibility. But we cannot be above society or outside of it *and* part of it by means of a simple schizophrenic copulation or momentary inspiration."[69]

Probably, the author's intent is best revealed in his attempt to formulate an alternative version of reflexive or critical sociology. In contrast to Gouldner's "defiantly romantic" posture, O'Neill stresses the need for a "limited reflexivity" and for a more careful attention to social institutions. "Social science knowledge," he writes, "needs to be grounded in a limited but authentic reflexivity through which it recognizes its ties to individual values and community interests, notwithstanding its attempts to avoid bias and ideology." To accomplish this aim, reflection must be seen not only as embedded in social life but as itself endowed with an institutional dimension. By viewing "reflexivity as institution rather than as transcendental constitution," we gain a vantage point which, "instead of resting upon a transcendental subjectivity, is given in a field of presence and coexistence which situates reflexivity and truth as sedimentation and search." Far from being an a priori basis, reflexivity from this perspective appears as "a task which we take up in order to achieve self-improvisation, as well as the acquisition of a tradition or style of thought which is the recovery of original auspices opened in the past." The notion of "critique" which emerges from these considerations is "one which is grounded in a contextual environment which lies open horizontally to the corpus of social science knowledge rather than through any transcendental reflection." In contrast to Husserl and much of past philosophy, O'Neill maintains that "universality and truth" are not "an intrinsic property of the idea," but rather "an acquisition continuously established and reestablished in a community and tradition of knowledge called for and responded to by individuals in specific historical situations." As a corollary, the targets of human awareness are not abstractions, but "cultural objects"—"the vestiges of embodied beings" who "have opened up for us the hearth of culture and institutions which it is our first duty to tender." The critical act, in any case, implies a "declaration of membership in a continuing philosophical, literary, or scientific community"; the severance of these ties "would be the consequence of an absolute knowledge and ultimate nihilism." So understood, criticism is "close to Camus's conception of rebellion and order under the sun. Criticism reflects an aspiration to order under the auspices of the things that are present and of our fellow men, under a limit which is reflexively the recognition of solidarity and a rule of memory as an antidote to revolutionary absurdity."[70]

Although impressive as a corrective to militancy, O'Neill's antidote unfortunately is not free of hazards and questionable side-effects. While shunning the temptation of apodicticity, his argument—at points—risks muffling or compressing critical discourse from the opposite direction. The appeal to a "cosmic order," for example, hardly encourages a clarification of practical standards of conduct in relation to contemplation. More important, the stress on common-sense opinion occasionally tends to submerge knowledge entirely in social and historical contingency. Human speech or discourse, he notes at one point, "has no absolute goal of rational clarification, of disbelief, and rejection of prejudice," but "seeks just as well acceptance, or the understanding of what was already our belief, our native prejudice. This is the circle of language in which we dwell—the hermeneutic circle—which is not broken even when all come to understand our motives, our past experience." Although language, in Heidegger's terms, may be the "house" of man, it is not simply a dark cell, but endowed with luminous transparency. Human understanding, it seems to me, is not merely an indifferent mélange of knowledge and ignorance, a conglomeration of "clarification" and "prejudice"; nor does the "multiplicity" of meanings necessarily entail "a babel of tongues." Human cognition may be circular in the sense that an effort to understand always presupposes some prior understanding; but this does not mean that understanding cannot grow and that there is no hope of discriminating between levels of insight, between truth and falsehood. The "hermeneutic circle" in this sense is not so much a hopeless cycle as a porous spiral pointing beyond itself.[71] By stressing the opacity of concrete experience O'Neill's perspective occasionally approximates (but does not merge with) Gurvitch's "empirical dialectic." When moving in this direction, his presentation, in my view, is not entirely faithful to the legacy of Merleau-Ponty, who wrote: "What we propose here, and oppose to the search for the essence, is not the return to the immediate, the coincidence, the effective fusion with the existent" which "would nullify our questions and even reprehend our language."[72] Sociology, against this background, cannot entirely be identified with a "skin trade"—at least as long as color of skin is a powerful barrier in human discourse.

The present chapter has traversed a broad terrain: After presenting a condensed historical retrospective it delineated the contours of Paci's work, in order finally to compare his perspective with recent developments in sociology and social thought. However, the question animating these various explorations has been the same from the beginning: What is the character of phenomenology and of its relationship to Marxism? Now, at the end, we find that this question is far from resolved. Actually, we encountered a variety of responses and interpretations which do not seem readily compatible; but perhaps the situation is not hopeless. As the historical overview indicated, phenomenology during our century has tended to move from absolute evidence to a more subdued and critical posture open to intersubjective scrutiny and reciprocal correction; a similar development can be detected in neo-Marxist thought. These trends may furnish a direction signal for our question; they definitely provide a connecting link between the examined writers. Paci's study is replete with passages affirming the need for open-ended inquiry and the continued reexamination of convictions; however, this thrust tends to be blurred and side-tracked by his reliance on apodictic evidence. Both Piccone and O'Neill are committed to a critical Marxism and invoke the assistance of phenomenology in formulating this outlook; but both ultimately stop short of their goal, by retreating either into intuitive certainty or common-sense belief. In every instance, the incongruity seems to derive from the role assigned to phenomenology and from its somewhat indiscriminate fusion with Marxist thought. As it appears to me, there are hazards both in equating phenomenology with an apodictic "first philosophy" and in limiting it to conjecture without appeal. Perhaps, as long as it is tied to intuitive evidence, phenomenology cannot really be expected to be self-critical in a comprehensive and Socratic sense—

although it can certainly be critical by insisting on the constant renewal of intuitive insight and by being aware of its own limitations.

Such a result need not be damaging to phenomenology, nor
should it imply a disparagement of its significance for human thought.
If knowledge and wisdom are to be neither an esoteric privilege nor
a memorized formula, learning has to proceed on the basis of evidence
gained "in the first person," of what makes sense to the individual involved. In an age weary of philosopher-kings, when mankind seems
intent on coming of age, truth has to be the result of personal acquisition, of the slow transformation of habits and idiosyncrasies—just as
standards of conduct are not moral unless freely adopted. What the
suggested view does entail, however, is the need to reconsider the relationship of phenomenology to Marxism or to any perspective laying
claim to philosophical relevance and validity. The various formulations of this relationship encountered in the preceding pages do not
appear to me entirely adequate or persuasive. Least acceptable seems
to me the notion—one not actually asserted but merely intimated in
some passages—that phenomenology and Marxism might complement
each other by focusing respectively on subjective and objective dimensions. Such a division of labor would entirely prevent genuine contact;
if spheres of concern were so rigidly segregated, no amount of surgery
could transplant ingredients of one perspective into the other. Equally
unconvincing, in my estimate, is Sartre's differentiation between "philosophy" and "ideology." If, as he insists, a primary task of existential
phenomenology is to recover the critical impulse in Marxism, I do not
see how this endeavor can be termed "ideological" while the label of
"philosophy" is accorded to a stagnant orthodoxy. Another suggestion
contained in Sartre's argument is that the distinction between phenomenology and Marxism might follow the demarcation line between singular experience and general propositions; however, as far as I can see,
any type of knowledge involves some relationship of particulars and
universals. A related view—suggested by Paci and elaborated more
fully by Piccone—holds that phenomenology concentrates on a special
problem, the function of the sciences, to which Marxism offers the
more general solution. On these premises the relationship emerges as
a territorial dispute whose settlement hinges on the accident of prior
occupation. The situation is not improved if—as in the case of the early
Marcuse—roles are reversed and existential phenomenology is depicted
as general philosophy and Marxism as concrete application.

Perhaps the notion of a critical learning process can assist us at
this point. What I wish to suggest for consideration is the possibility
that phenomenology and Marxist theory might be related like "philol-

ogy" and "philosophy," as these terms were used by Giambattista Vico. In his *New Science*, Vico delineates the respective preoccupations as follows: "Philosophy contemplates reason, whence comes knowledge of the true; philology observes that of which human choice is author, whence comes consciousness of the certain. In its second part this axiom comprises among philologians all the grammarians, historians, and critics who concern themselves with the study of the languages and deeds of people." This same axiom, he continues, "shows the partial failure both of the philosophers who did not test their reasoning by appeal to the authority of the philologians, and likewise of the philologians in not taking care to give their authority the sanction of truth by appeal to the reasoning of the philosophers." A resort to these terms should not seem far-fetched from a Marxist perspective. At least one leading Marxist in our century has invoked Vico's distinction as a vital key to the understanding of social life. "If the concept of structure is approached speculatively," Gramsci wrote, "it certainly becomes a 'hidden god.' Therefore, it should not be conceived speculatively but historically, as the whole fabric of social relations in which real men move and operate, as the whole of objective conditions which can and must be studied with the methods of 'philology' and not of speculation, as something 'certain' that may also be 'true' but which must first of all be studied in its 'certainty' in order to be studied as 'truth.' "[73]

Actually, the combination of philology and philosophy may be not only compatible with but crucial and indispensable to Marxism. This would be so if we accept Merleau-Ponty's suggestion that Marxism is peculiarly lodged at the threshold of truth: "The mood of Lukács and, we believe, of Marxism as a whole is the conviction to be not in the possession but on the threshold of truth—a truth which is at the same time very close, being adumbrated by the entire past and the entire present, and in the infinite distance of a future waiting to be implemented."[74]

PART THREE
Marxism and Critical Theory

8. History and Class Consciousness: Lukács' Theory of Social Change

THE REPUBLICATION OF *Geschichte und Klassenbewusstsein* (History and Class Consciousness) as part of Georg Lukács' collected works came in the midst of widespread ferment and unrest in Western academic and intellectual life—a circumstance most propitious to its reception. The new German edition was followed, three years later, by the first complete English translation of the work. One can safely assert that, at least among Western social scientists and social theorists, intensive preoccupation with Lukács' arguments dates essentially from these two publications.[1]

The long odyssey of Lukács' book has been almost as intriguing as its content. First published in the early twenties of this century, *Geschichte und Klassenbewusstsein* immediately incurred the wrath of the Soviet hierarchy—dedicated to a "scientific" materialism devoid of dialectical vestiges—and has been largely suppressed by official communist doctrine. At the same time, the original German edition was quickly exhausted and became almost inaccessible in Western countries—a circumstance which provided an alibi for scholarly neglect. Yet, while officially silenced or shunned on both sides of the cold war, the study was by no means without impact and soon acquired the stature of one of the important underground documents of the period. To complicate matters, Lukács himself turned into a rentless critic of his product, thereby contributing to its underground existence. His severe denunciations of the book during his Moscow exile—while hardly persuasive to his enemies—were a source of considerable dismay and confusion to his friends. Over two decades ago, in a protest directed at Merleau-Ponty, Lukács dismissed his product as a book "forgotten for good reason."[2] As his preface to the new edition suggests, the harshness of this judgment seems to have somewhat mellowed in the meantime. Against this background the study assumes some of the traits of a prodigal son whose errings, mingled with his profuse talents and virtues, are at last perceived as part of a learning process.

There is a more immediate incentive for a renewed preoccupation with Lukács' study. Western social science today is increasingly shifting its attention from statics to dynamics, from the problem of stability to questions of social change and development—questions which are at the very heart of Lukács' work. In Western social science, the shift in attention seems to be motivated by a variety of reasons. To some extent, the concern with development is simply an outgrowth or consequence of scientific method, of the pervasive emphasis in contemporary behavioral disciplines on explanation and prediction in accordance with the canons of positive science. Nevertheless, methodology has hardly been the only impulse behind the recent turn to dynamics. Evidence of domestic unrest in Western countries was bound to perturb even the most carefully guarded academic retreats. At the same time, the "revolution of rising expectations"—the spectacle of the emergence of societies previously in the shadow of history—projected the problem of social development on a global scale. Whatever the reasons or motivations, contemporary social science has devoted considerable efforts to the scrutiny of change and to the formulation of frameworks and theories designed to explain and anticipate the development of societies. Despite their impressive analytical refinement, however, one can legitimately query whether these theories are suitable instruments for grasping the process of social transformation and innovation or whether they remain satisfied with projecting the present (perhaps a technologically perfected present) into the future.[3] The following pages are predicated, at least in part, on the assumption that a comparison or juxtaposition of current sociological approaches with Lukács' study can help to elucidate this question.

I. Some Current Theories of Social Change

Contemporary social science exhibits a great variety of conceptual frameworks and analytical approaches; the same diversity prevails in the study of social change. A comprehensive survey of available alternatives is clearly beyond the scope of the present essay. Fortunately, brevity in this matter is facilitated by the dominant position of one type of analysis: structural-functional and neo-evolutionary theory. In

the following I shall focus on this theoretical outlook, chiefly as expounded by Talcott Parsons. For purposes of contrast, versions of psychological or individualistic theory will also receive brief attention,
versions which have been formulated in explicit opposition to the dominant framework. Despite their apparent antagonism, it will be shown
that these perspectives are not necessarily incompatible.

Among its adherents, structural-functional theory has sometimes
received conflicting and ambiguous interpretations. According to
Ernest Nagel, however, a functional model can be defined as a special
kind of deterministic system: a system with added safeguards to maintain its equilibrium or stability.[4] Viewed in this manner, structural-
functionalism clearly is based on natural science analogies and endowed with a built-in teleology; the question which emerges here—and
will recur subsequently—is whether such analogies are conducive to
an explanation and anticipation of social change (the term taken as
denoting the appearance of significantly "new" social phenomena).
Structural-functional theory has frequently been accused of being
static and unable to account for social processes; the accusation probably has been overworked. Talcott Parsons at one time observed that
"there is a certain falsity in the dilemma between 'static' and 'dynamic'
emphases" and that a good theory should be applicable to both aspects.[5] This view, of course, was already shared by Comte and Spencer
who distinguished between "social statics" and "social dynamics" in the
broader field of positive or scientific sociology.

In some of his early writings, Parsons provided hints of a theory
of change by stipulating clusters of "pattern variables" corresponding
to different stages of social development. In this conception, traditional
society was characterized by particularism, ascription, diffuseness, and
affectivity, while modern society was seen as tending toward univer-
salism, achievement, specificity, and affective neutrality. It should be
obvious that these terms constituted an elaboration on well-known
dichotomies of historical sociology, especially those of Spencer, Toennies, and Durkheim. To a significant extent, however, the pattern
variables were merely descriptive terms labeling different historical
types of society, without indicating how social development moves
from one stage or pattern to another. In order to remedy this defect,
Parsons subsequently attacked the problem of change more directly
by developing various theoretical constructs, especially the "differentiation model" of change. In formulating this model, Parsons stipulated
that its focus was on the "process of structural differentiation and the
concomitant development of patterns and mechanisms which integrate
the differentiated parts." The model was designed to provide an ex-

planation not only of alterations within a stable system or state of equilibrium, but also of processes leading to structural change, that is, to the breakdown of one system and the establishment of a "new and different" system.[6] For present purposes, the general character of "change" stipulated in the theory requires brief attention. According to Parsons, a social system is composed of a structure with stable properties and of processes which make "something happen" and impel change; the separation of stable and dynamic elements is claimed to be dictated by "orderly procedure in scientific analysis." The stable properties either withstand or collapse under the impact of the dynamic factors (or elements of disturbance), whose material content and origin is assumed as given and not further explored.[7] The separation of stable and dynamic factors is highlighted in the explanation of "structural" change. Given the character of the functional model as a deterministic mechanism with inherent equilibrium tendencies, the properties of successive states are either contained in the original system—in which case it is difficult to speak of structural change in any meaningful sense; or successive states are assumed to reveal "new" properties—in which case there is a gulf (a *hiatus irrationalis*) between the stages of social development.

Apparently in response to this dilemma, Parsons somewhat later tried to bridge the gulf between social systems, by stipulating "evolutionary universals" as connecting links. His contribution in this respect is only one illustration among many others of the rebirth of evolutionary thinking in our time.[8] This rebirth, to be sure, is not simply a revival of nineteenth-century evolutionism, which is frequently denounced as naive and simplistic. In the place of simple linear progress, neo-evolutionary theory stresses multilinear development; instead of one-sided causality, it emphasizes multifactor explanation. Nevertheless, to justify its claim of coherent development, the new approach still has to rely on basic, overall trends and tendencies, on a "hidden hand" guiding the direction of change. In Parsons' case, the evolutionary framework applies not only to society but aims at explaining "human ways in direct continuity with the sub-human." As he writes, an evolutionary universal is "a complex of structures and associated processes, the development of which so increases the long-run adaptive capacity of living systems in a given class that only systems that develop the complex can attain certain higher levels of general adaptive capacity."[9] This statement, of course, shows great affinity to Spencer's theory of natural selection; however, Parsons makes the gentle modification that "lower" systems of social development are not necessarily condemned to extinction. Among the "universals" in the evolution of society, Parsons lists the development of social stratification from kinship ascription to vertical differentiation, the rise of bureaucratic organization, the emergence of money and a market economy, a universalistic legal system, and the principle of democratic association; clearly, most of these elements can be linked with his earlier pattern variables and with the differentiation model. In all these formulations, social change is conceived in terms of physical or naturalistic analogies, either in the form of an equilibrium mechanism or of a quasi-biological evolution.

As previously indicated, psychological and individualistic theories of social change are frequently advanced as substitutes for naturalistic models. A prominent ingredient in many of these theories is the complaint that naturalistic formulas cannot account for the emergence of new features in social structures. Coupled with this complaint is the assumption that structural change has to be attributed to spontaneous and somewhat abnormal (if not random) sources; typically, these sources are identified with extraordinary individuals or clusters of individuals. Richard LaPiere, a strong defender of this view, maintains "that changes that occur within a society are asocial; that they are not in any sense a product of the society per se," and that "the forces that make for social change are, if the organic analogy be pursued, abnormal—a violation of the normal process by which the social system is transmitted from generation to generation of members."[10] One difficulty with this position is that it may lead to a simple abdication of explanation. More importantly, however, the reliance on "asocial" or extrasocial factors alone is hardly able to weaken the dominance of naturalistic analogies; the intervention of "abnormal," undetermined factors regularly presupposes the "normal" operation of laws of nature. The individual subject, conceived as an "asocial" (or socially unrelated) agent, is likewise bound to encounter society as a complex of preordained relationships. In LaPiere's case, the abnormal factors of change include a great variety of "innovators"—ranging from religious and spiritual to secular and scientific leaders—while in David McClelland's model, the chief source of change and innovation is the modern entrepreneur.[11]

II. Lukács and the Dynamics of Change

The essays which compose Lukács' *Geschichte und Klassenbewusstsein* deal with a variety of topics, but all are connected and find their focus in a conception of social and human development.[12] This conception is elaborated in constant critical confrontation with other theories of society and social change—some of which bear a striking resemblance to contemporary doctrines.

The principal theory which Lukács critically explores is the naturalistic approach to social phenomena, that is, the assumption that society and social change are governed by natural "laws" in the same manner as mechanical or physical bodies.[13] The use of natural science analogies seems to furnish to social inquiry the qualities of rigor and precision; for limited purposes these qualities are clearly valuable. However, as Lukács points out, their exclusive application obscures and obliterates some of the key aspects of society, especially the aspect of social change. Natural science aims at capturing the unchanging and immutable properties of the empirical world; in Kant's terminology, "nature" signifies the empirical universe from the perspective of permanent and general laws. Natural science as a system does not admit internal conflicts or tensions; if some particular propositions are in conflict, science tries to remove the contradiction through the formulation of more general and abstract principles. In such a system, change (understood as the emergence of "new" features) is bound to disappear. This does not mean, of course, that natural science is not concerned with processes in the empirical universe; however, the empirical world is specially prepared or purified for analysis. Change, in this analysis, means largely the reaction of empirical objects with relatively fixed and abstract properties to the impulse of other objects or forces with similarly fixed and abstract properties; in a simplified form, the entire operation resembles the spatial movement of billiard balls. As Lukács observes, it matters little in this context whether the movement is conceived in terms of a mechanical determinism or of a functional correlation.[14] The implication of this approach for social change is that historical development appears at best as the operation of abstract sociological "laws," after the fashion of Comtian and Spencerian doctrines. Sometimes, to enhance the appearance of change, the operation of these laws is depicted as the goal and culmination of human development; in this case, however, it is hardly intelligible why such laws went into effect in a certain historical period and were prevented from operating during the larger portion of history.

The question becomes less puzzling once the stipulated laws of society are seen in a less abstract light. As Lukács observes, the naturalistic treatment of society proceeds within a distinct social and historical context and has definite social and political implications. Just as natural science looks for permanent laws in organic and inorganic nature, so the naturalistic treatment of social phenomena tends to endow existing society with immutable or "eternal" properties. A procedure which seems innocuous in the study of nature (since man's predominance is not in question) thus assumes major political connotations in the study of society. According to Lukács, the naturalistic approach is favored by some "vulgar Marxists" or materialists (in their effort to separate the scientific laws of society from concrete human aspirations). The primary significance of the approach, however, resides in its appeal to "bourgeois" thinking, to the mentality prevalent in (Western) industrial societies. The scientific "laws" of society in this case correspond to the "forces of the market"; they also serve as "self-protection," as a defense mechanism of the social order and its mode of economic production.[15] In order to render social phenomena amenable to naturalistic treatment, the social fabric has to be broken down into separate empirical parts with relatively fixed or constant properties. The resultant parts are then considered as "hard" (immediately given) empirical data which can be scientifically manipulated and transformed into quantitative formulas. In Lukács' view, the affinity of "bourgeois" thinking to this kind of naturalism and scientism is by no means accidental. Modern industrial society and the market economy have the tendency of transforming social relationships into relations of things, a tendency which is aggravated by the growing specialization and isolation of roles in the economic and social process. In this situation, it must seem particularly "scientific" to pursue the tendency inherent in the social environment to its logical conclusion and to elevate it into a theoretical system; by contrast, dialectical thinking—which emphasizes the concrete interrelation of elements and pierces their mask of rigid factuality—is likely to appear as a mere flight of fancy.[16]

With the transformation of social phenomena into scientific formulas, the social order seems to be raised to the level of a completely transparent and rational system; this impression, however, is deceptive for several reasons. First of all, the scientific "system" is only an abstract, formal model and, as such, not fully or substantively intelligible. The "laws" stipulated by economists and social scientists have the inexorable, transcendental quality of divine precepts; their significance is as opaque to human understanding as the laws of the physical universe. In fact, as Lukács points out, a modern market economy could not operate if its laws were fully or substantively intelligible (since such understanding could lead to the domination of the market).[17] The main reason, however, for the deceptive character of the scientific formulas resides in the fact that the stipulated model is only apparently able to function on an abstract level: actually it remains dependent on concrete human factors and contingent historical constellations. In the economic sphere (assuming a classical or pure market system), this dependence is demonstrated by periodic crises and depressions; in social relations, the dependence manifests itself in wars, revolutions, or other forms of conflict. The dependence on social factors is merely concealed in each case behind the façade of abstract, self-perpetuating laws. This concealment, however, is not only deceptive; it is also inevitable since the laws of science are by no means able to absorb the richness of concrete reality. The world of concrete, individual reality sets a definite limit to the formulas of natural science. As Lukács observes, an inverse relationship can be detected between science and reality, especially social reality; the more abstract and formally rational the scientific system is conceived, the more deeply social reality lapses into the darkness of unintelligibility and irrationality.[18]

That concrete reality establishes a limit to natural science formulas has frequently been observed. Wilhelm Windelband and Heinrich Rickert made this observation the cornerstone of their elaboration of historical or "individualizing" disciplines, as distinguished from "generalizing" or natural sciences.[19] Without further modification, however, this distinction merely segregates from natural science an immense amount of arbitrary and accidental material. Several approaches may be used to subdue this material. One approach consists in depicting all the individual facets of the historical material with equal attention, from a purely aesthetic point of view; but apart from exceeding human capacity or endurance, this treatment leaves the arbitrary factuality of the material undisturbed. In Rickert's approach, the historical material was to be examined in its "value relationship," in its relevance to a framework of cultural values; however, these values were in turn treated as factually given and thus remained basically irrational and static. To overcome the mere factuality of the material— Lukács points out—recourse is frequently taken to subjective evaluation or individual intervention. A customary procedure is to impose a subjective interpretation or personal philosophy on historical events; but this procedure remains contemplative and does not reveal the dynamic movement in historical sequences. It is at this point that the individual is sometimes introduced as subject or agent into the historical process: "great individuals" or "innovators" are viewed as sources of major social change. The question arises, however, what such individuals can accomplish in a basically alien and preordained universe?

As Lukács observes, there are chiefly two types of activities which the individual may perform in his relations with the surrounding social and physical world. Individuals may try to utilize and exploit to their advantage the scientific "laws" of nature and society; this application may lead to considerable advances in economic production, industry, and technology. However, such production is not quite the same as action or *praxis*.[20] Man, in this producing or technical capacity, relies on the operation of abstract scientific "laws" (whose concrete subject matter remains arbitrary and accidental); he is still essentially the object rather than the subject or agent of the surrounding world. By contrast, action or *praxis* seeks to change and transform the world, in an effort to render the arbitrary factuality meaningful and humanly intelligible. Without a supporting or sympathetic principle in the factual world, however, even "great individuals" can at best confront this world with their will power or normative demands; the gulf between human aspirations and irrational factuality persists (if it does not actually widen). This circumstance is generally recognized in historical literature where the actions of "great individuals" are portrayed against the background of an irrational "mass" (subject to opaque, natural laws). To the extent that the world remains unresponsive or uncooperative, human aspirations tend to be elevated into abstract norms whose implementation is largely restricted to the internal moral reform of the individual. As Lukács writes, the conflict between "is" and "ought," the rigid dichotomy between external determinism and internal "freedom" is the hallmark or chief trait of "modern" industrial society.[21]

The problem then, in Lukács' view, is to find the "subject" or agent that is able to penetrate and transform the sphere of necessity, thus rendering the world transparent and intelligible. The search for this agent is the purpose of Marxism (or of the theory advanced by Lukács); to this extent, he writes, Marx took seriously the statement by Vico that only what man has created, man can properly understand.[22] As he points out, the core of Marxism resides in its methodological perspective, not in isolated factual assertions. This perspective receives its dynamic quality from the fact that it is confined neither to theoretical (or "scientific") contemplation nor to random practice; rather, it revolves around the synthesis of theory and practice, around the dialectical relationship of object and subject in the historical process.[23] In order to penetrate to this perspective, however, it becomes necessary to abandon the prevalent conception of society and history. In this conception, social conditions appear as objective facts, as "fetishistic" things which conceal their character as categories of human interaction; human relations appear as relations of things or objects. For the same reason, social change is viewed as a movement of objects. It thus becomes imperative to pierce the "cloak of eternity" (*Ewigkeitshülle*) and the "cloak of thing-quality" (*Dinghaftigkeits-*

hülle) of social conditions. The unmasking of these disguises makes it possible to recover the reality of human relationships and to reveal social life as the result of human action and interaction and of the principles inherent in such action. From this perspective, Lukács observes, the core of reality can be grasped as a social process, sustained by human activity; he cites in this context the statement of Marx and Engels that the "production and reproduction of real life" constitute the "lastly determining element in history."[24]

When viewed as aspects of human relationships, social "facts" begin to lose their rigidity and intransigence; social and economic conditions appear amenable to modification through the transformation of these relationships. The breakdown of the rigidity of isolated "facts" is accomplished chiefly through their incorporation in a broader frame of reference: by placing them into the context of the whole fabric or evolving synthesis of social relations. This synthesis is not synonymous with identity or numerical addition—terms which are static and devoid of dynamic movement; rather, the framework intended here is based on a time dimension: the dimension of the constantly expanding universe of human experience in history. The mere juxtaposition of fixed objects would at best produce external movement or spatial "interaction" of these objects; by contrast, the historical synthesis or "totality" of social relations changes the very character of objects as objects, transforms the form and substance of social facts and conditions. This transformation proceeds in minor degrees in a continuous manner, frequently unnoticed. However, major transformations of the basic structure of society require a subject or agent which is at the same time a dominant structural element of the "object" or social fabric to be transformed; such agents are the key groups of society or "social classes." The role performed by these groups reveals the dialectical quality of social development: through their action, social classes transform the objective conditions of the social fabric to which they belong; at the same time they redefine themselves and their position in society. Not all groups are equally destined to perform this role of transformation; some groups participate in the development only in a retarding, supporting or accelerating capacity. As Lukács observes, the role of major structural change belongs to those groups from whose perspective the entire fabric of society can be reorganized on the basis of a new principle, in a new synthesis.

The reliance on action and social agents does not signify the surrender of social development to arbitrary practice or random mutation. Although deflected, disrupted, and corrupted a thousand times, social development (as a human enterprise) follows its own inherent pattern:

the pattern of the growing emancipation and self-consciousness of man. Every step of social transformation involves an attempt to overcome the alien, congealed objectivity of the external world, to remold the crust of arbitrary factuality into an intelligible human relationship. However, the social enterprise may proceed in different conditions and at different levels of consciousness. In most premodern societies, for instance, the social fabric was still deeply permeated by elements of "nature"; the conditions of human life could thus not properly be conceived as social or interhuman relations. Modern industrial society, by manipulating and dominating nature, established the basis for a social conception of human life; however, the conditions of society were in turn elevated to an abstract, transcendental level, to the position of a "second nature." Industrial society therefore appears governed by invariant natural laws which are "based on the unconsciousness of the participants."[25] At the same time, industrial society has produced a social group whose energies are most thoroughly utilized by the "laws" of machines and the "laws" of the market: the working population. In becoming conscious of its own position, this group is able to gain consciousness of the entire social fabric, of its character as a human enterprise—which is a step toward the transformation of society. The task imposed upon this group, however, is by no means easy; it is a continuous challenge. Growing awareness does not simplify life, but increases the burden of responsibility. "The path of consciousness in the process of history," Lukács writes, "does not become smoother, but on the contrary more and more difficult and demanding."[26]

III. The Stages of Social Development

In exploring the process of social change, Lukács indicates certain major steps in the historical development of society. To some extent, these steps are comparable to the "stages" of historical sociology or to the evolutionary scheme of Parsons' "pattern variables." There are, however, important differences. First, social development in Lukács' conception does not terminate at the stage which, in most versions of historical sociology, constitutes the "modern" pole of the "traditional-modern" dichotomy. More important, the development of society is viewed not simply as a quantitative movement of objects (in accordance with naturalistic analogies) but as a qualitative transformation of social relationships through human action. In premodern (or pre-industrial) society, social relations were still intimately linked with the conditions and processes of nature. Kinship and family bonds pre-

vailed, while human activity centered on the cultivation of the soil or
the manufacturing of individual products (in artisans' shops). The social fabric at this stage was still fairly homogeneous and balanced; at
the same time, however, due to the absence or embryonic form of division of labor, society retained a relatively incoherent or unorganized
character. The political, economic, and religious aspects of society were
blended and mixed, with the result that social structures and institutions remained undifferentiated and functionally diffuse. An important
corollary of this situation was that natural conditions and distinctions
were directly translated into legal forms, a process which led to the
proliferation of particularistic norms and to the growth of a social
hierarchy of orders and estates, each with distinct (frequently hereditary) privileges.[27] As Lukács observes, the prevalence of these conditions made it virtually impossible to conceive the social fabric as a
product of human interaction.

The beginning of the modern age saw far-flung explorations and
the accumulation of precious metals under mercantilist auspices.
Through these policies and the accumulation of wealth in private
hands, the foundations were laid for a modern market economy and
for modern advances in industry and technology. The emergence of
the market economy, coupled with industrialization, heralded the decline of the influence of natural conditions and the growing mastery of
man over nature. One effect of this change was the obliteration of
internal legal barriers in society, especially of the hierarchical arrangement of estates and hereditary privileges. The removal of "ascribed"
status positions encouraged a freer competition among individuals for
wealth, social prestige, and power—a competition guided by "achievement" motivation (to use Parsons' terminology). With competition and
a growing division of labor, the social fabric tended to become more
heterogeneous. To some extent, this development was manifested in the
differentiation (for limited purposes) of the economic, political, and religious aspects of society and in the increased functional "specificity"
of social structures and institutions. At the same time, the decline of
natural barriers and the growth of economic enterprise had the result
that, for the first time, social relations could be conceived, at least potentially, as the product of human action and interaction; the full
realization of this possibility, however, was obstructed by the prevailing mode of production. The carrier or agent of the described transformation was the "bourgeoisie"—a group chiefly composed of owners
of capital, entrepreneurs, and managers. From the perspective of this
group, social relations are indeed linked with human enterprise and
conscious motivation; but this linkage applies only to isolated parts, not

to the entire fabric of society. Economic production at this stage seems determined by the interests of individual entrepreneurs; this determination, however, is only apparent, for the individual entrepreneur is in turn controlled by the laws of supply and demand, by the impersonal, self-regulating "forces of the market." These forces or laws are "universalistic" in character (to use again Parsons' terminology), in the sense that they tend to obliterate all internal divisions and even external boundaries of society; they are also abstract and opaque to full human understanding. An attempt to raise these forces to the level of consciousness would actually run counter to the interests of dominant social groups, since such an attempt might lead to changes in the mode of production.[28] While thus having broken the bonds of nature, modern society has established a formidable new barrier to social change: the forces of the market have become the "second nature" of society.

The dominant influence of economic laws, their character as "second nature," is illustrated in the exchange of commodities and the structure of commodity relationships. In the modern market economy, the exchange of commodities has become the central form of social transaction, replacing the earlier exchange of goods through direct barter.[29] The term "second nature" in this context refers to the aspect that a relationship between human beings is conceived as a transaction of commodities and thus invested with a "phantom objectivity," subject to the forces of the market.[30] Human activity itself is increasingly transformed into a commodity, governed by the immutable "natural laws" of society. This transformation can be described as "reification," that is, the subjugation of human activity and human consciousness to the realm of things. According to Lukács, industrial society has an inherent tendency to pursue the process of reification to its ultimate limits. In this process, the traditional qualitative unity of work experience is progressively divided and specialized into partial operations whose performance can be quantitatively calculated and predicted. Commodities can be appraised and compared on the basis of the measurable work operations required for their production. The calculation of work performance can be pursued into the most minute, even psychological, details; in fact, modern Taylorism has carried the mechanization of labor into the mental and emotional participation of the worker (thus "reifying" his internal life). The refinement of calculation may be viewed as a progress toward rationality; however, the rationality involved is of a strictly abstract and formal character. While the partial operations of production are more and more precisely calculated and controlled, the interrelation of all these operations is secured only by quantitative formulas and devoid of substantive rationality or intelligibility. Moreover, the concrete differences of human performance are increasingly neglected or suppressed; in the words of Lukács, the human qualities of the worker tend to become "mere sources of error."[31] Man thus is transformed into a mechanized part of a mechanical system governed by immutable laws. In order to be able to obey the laws of the system, man has to assume a more and more contemplative or "theoretical" attitude. In a fully "theoretical" universe, however, the time dimension of human action or practice disappears; the immutable laws of the past govern the present and the future. As Lukács observes in a striking formulation: "Time is leveled into the dimension of space."[32]

The process of reification is by no means restricted to the economic sphere; it penetrates into all aspects of society and even into the various branches of "social science." This development is clearly visible in the modern state and its administrative services; in the words of Max Weber, the functioning of the state apparatus tends to be guided by the same principles on the basis of which "the expected output of a machine is calculated." Modern bureaucracy is a complex of specialized operations, designed to enhance the measurement and prediction of administrative performance; the principles of Taylorism are applied to regulate the details of psychological reaction and even to control moral conduct.[33] The same development can be seen in the various branches of science, including the social sciences. Every modern science, Lukács observes, tends to become a formal system of partial operations governed by relevant laws. However, the limit of the explanatory capacity of these systems resides in the formal character of their rationality. Concrete reality becomes increasingly elusive; in Kant's terminology, the real world is relegated to the realm of the "thing-in-itself," outside the grasp of science. Among social sciences, economics was perhaps the first to combine its propositions into a rigorous formal model. Economic transactions are treated as a system of quantitative operations governed by abstract laws; the social basis of these operations tends to be disregarded. Modern legal science or jurisprudence shows a similar tendency; while the formal procedures of law are linked in a rigorous analytical system, the social content and origin of laws are considered as "meta-juridicial."[34] Lukács' examples could be supplemented, of course, by reference to more recent trends in social science, especially the emergence of "systems analysis" and "cybernetics" in such disciplines as political science and sociology.

In a revealing excursion into the "antinomies of bourgeois thought," Lukács traces the relationship between modern philosophy and the development of modern society. As he points out, modern philosophy is characterized by the attempt to comprehend the world as a product of man, as a result of human capacities. This purpose is clearly illustrated in modern "rationalism," defined as a theoretical system which tries to assimilate the intelligible side of the universe of phenomena. In the early stage of "dogmatic" rationalism, the entire universe appeared dissolved in the formulas of human reason; however, this dogmatism was soon countered by a profound skepsis or distrust in the capacity of reason to digest empirical factuality. As Lukács writes, every rationalism, as a theoretical (or contemplative) system, is bound to encounter the barrier of irrationality in the factual world; the philosophical problem is how to overcome this barrier. Modern science tries to incorporate the world into a *mathesis universalis,* a system of abstract, quantitative categories. However, in order to accomplish this goal, empirical facts have to be specially prepared and purified; as in early rationalism, the real world disappears behind the *materia intelligibilis.*[35] German philosophy of the classical (idealist) period took a different approach: while not abandoning the quest of reason, it refused to disregard or ignore the irrational character of the factual world. In Kant's terminology, the realm beyond the grasp of reason was designated as "thing-in-itself"—a term which referred both to the material content of intellectual forms and to the concrete synthesis of knowledge. In order to breach the barrier of the "thing-in-itself," German philosophy turned to the search for the subject or agent capable of transforming factual reality. In Kant's *Critique of Practical Reason,* this agent was identified with the moral self-determination of the individual. However, the reliance on isolated individual action was unable to bridge the gulf between external determinism and human aspiration; the tension between form and content was not relieved. The situation was hardly remedied by a philosophical concentration on art and aesthetic creation; to be able to transform the world, individual creativity had to be expanded to romantic proportions. In its later phase, classical German philosophy turned toward history, that is, the concrete time dimension in which social action and interaction takes place; however, the agent of historical change remained hidden in transcendental categories (such as Hegel's "world spirit").

As Lukács suggests, German philosophy of the classical period offered important guideposts; but its quest had to be pursued in a more concrete social context. The transformation of factual reality requires a subject or agent which forms part of the same reality; according to Lukács, such an agent is the "proletariat" or working class. The "proletariat" is able to change the objective social world because it is itself this object (or a major structural element of this objective world). The emergence of the working population is not an abnormal or mysterious occurrence; like the "bourgeoisie," the working class is an outgrowth of industrialization. For both groups, the objective conditions of society and the process of reification are initially the same. However, while the industrialist can remain satisfied with his lot, the worker is compelled to transcend existing conditions if he wishes to achieve any degree of autonomy and self-determination. Although reification applies equally to both groups, the industrialist is able to find compensation or escape in positions of power and prestige or in industrial expansion. For the worker, by contrast, reification signifies his subjugation as a person, his transformation into a commodity governed by the "forces of the market." The task of transcending these forces is arduous and complex. The "proletariat" is by no means endowed with a ready-made consciousness of its destiny. As Lukács writes, the assumption of an immediately given group psychology is a myth; the consciousness of the working class emerges from its latent potentiality only through a constant struggle with immediately given conditions.[36] The first step in this struggle results only in the "self-consciousness of a commodity." But since this commodity is a human being, consciousness turns into a practical force: a force capable of transforming the object of perception.

The emancipation of the working class thus involves a dialectical relationship: By changing the objective structure of society, this class removes the prevalent conditions of domination; by the same act, however, the proletariat removes the conditions of its own existence as a class (and thereby the conditions of all "classes," at least in the narrow, conventional sense). The same process also reveals the close connection between theory and *praxis* in social change. The emancipation of the "proletariat" cannot merely rely on arbitrary or random activity; rather the disengagement from existing conditions is effected through their incorporation into the broader synthesis of social development. However, a theoretical awareness of social developments alone is insufficient for emancipation; social change—viewed as the emergence of "new" social structures—requires the free, creative intervention of social groups. The action of the "proletariat," in any event, is not merely the implementation or continuation of mechanical laws. By themselves, the "natural laws" of society would never produce emancipation. The end of "bourgeois" domination is therefore not inevitable, only possible. In Toynbee's terminology, the objective conditions of bourgeois (or industrial) society present a possibility, a "challenge"; the "response" is up to the proletariat. What is necessary to meet the challenge is a creative act, a conscious step into the "reign of freedom."[37]

One further aspect should probably be mentioned: by denying the inevitable or automatic character of social development, Lukács' theory raises the issue of moral justification of human action. If social change depends on the creative commitment of man, there must be the possibility of choice; choice, however, requires principles or standards of conduct. These principles, according to Lukács, cannot be found in abstract whims or utopian postulates imposed upon an alien, indifferent world. Rather, the goals of human aspiration and the standards of conduct arise in a concrete social context and are intimately linked with social development. The linkage of morals and society, however, is possible only because society itself is a human enterprise and its development is guided not by alien laws, but by human standards or values:[38] the values of the growing self-realization and self-awareness of man. From this perspective, it seems permissible to regard Lukács' theory as a form of humanism. One should add, however, that there are different variants of humanism; Lukács himself is very careful to dissociate his views from several such variants. A humanism, for instance, which relies on the isolated individual as a measure of all things can have only limited social significance. In this conception, the gulf between "is" and "ought," between external constraint and human aspiration, persists; the pursuit of moral values remains a private pastime while social "change" is reduced to a mental "solution" of conflicts of reality. More generally, a humanism which turns man into a fixed, immutable object cannot account for historical change. Such a conception can only lead to a dogmatic relativism; but every relativism is relative to an absolute standard. If man is the measure of all things, this measure has to be applied to man himself. Dialectical thinking, thus, is not properly a form of relativism, since the absolute is incorporated into the historical process.[39] This process, Lukács adds, is "a constant struggle for higher levels of truth, higher levels of the self-knowledge of man."

More than half a century has passed since the first publication of Lukács' study. During this period, many changes have occurred in intellectual climate and in the structure of industrial societies. The influences and repercussions of *Geschichte und Klassenbewusstsein* have been complex and pervasive. Probably, its intellectual impact was strongest on existential phenomenology and versions of critical and structuralist Marxism and, more recently, on *praxis*-oriented trends in Eastern Europe.[40] Equally complex and pervasive have been the social and political transformations during intervening decades. Keynesian reforms and welfare policies have mitigated the harshness of economic competition and the blatant features of industrial exploitation. As a result of the "technological revolution," scientific standards have permeated management practices and the entire social fabric more deeply than ever. The same technological advances have altered the character of social stratification and social conflict. In Western societies, the terms "bourgeoisie" and "proletariat" are probably no longer fully descriptive of social reality, at least to the extent that they refer to monolithic groups. While there is abundant evidence of continued class antagonisms, social conflict seems to follow a more untidy and less dichotomous path. The prospect of a proletarian world revolution—seemingly imminent at the end of the First World War—has lost some of its luster and has been replaced by the more concrete, but also more cumbersome and ambiguous, process of the emergence of developing nations.

Experiences of this kind could not fail to affect some of the accents of Lukács' study and to reveal some of its limitations. As previously indicated, Lukács has been among the severest critics of his product; for many years he considered its defects entirely beyond remedy. In the preface to the new edition, the limitations of the book are detailed by its author with compelling lucidity. One of the shortcomings listed in this indictment is the incipient subjectivism of the study, a subjectivism manifested in its relative neglect of "nature" and of concrete economic processes. Neglect of nature would seem to encompass a somewhat disdainful treatment of scientific method and a disregard of the emancipatory tendencies inherent in natural science as well as in some phases of capitalist production. More important and more damaging in Lukács' view is the somewhat visionary and simplified treatment of class conflict and the comparative inattention to the mediating elements in the dialectical process. The preface is eloquent in castigating the portrayal of the proletariat as the identical "subject-object" of social development, and the apocalyptic role assigned to it in the dénouement of history. As a corollary of this utopian vision, class consciousness tends to remain on a somewhat abstract and speculative level.[41]

Such limitations and changes of perspective, however, hardly impair the basic thrust of Lukács' argument. As he reluctantly concedes in the new preface, his book may disclose some redeeming qualities to a critical and discriminating reader. An essay of tribute is not under the same constraints of modesty. One indisputable merit of the study consists in the demonstration of the close linkage between Marx and Hegel, an insight which preceded the discovery and publication of some of Marx's early manuscripts by almost a decade. In this context, the exploration of alienation was instrumental in reclaiming a sub-merged human dimension for Marxist analysis. A central aspect of the study, however, is Lukács' definition and defense of Marxism as a method rather than a compendium of fixed assertations. This concep-tion—with its focus on the evolving dialectic of thought and practice—still seems as relevant as it did at the time of the book's first appear-ance. Technological refinements and the progress of automation have tightened the net of "natural laws" spread over industrial society, cast-ing doubt on man's ability to remain master of his products. A similar dilemma prevails in the international arena. If we are to believe Gun-nar Myrdal, the development of underprivileged nations cannot be en-trusted simply to the mechanical operation of economic forces; only a determined effort to overrule the "laws" of the market can prevent the continued exploitation of these areas by the developed countries.[42]

The method recommended by Lukács also has relevance for con-temporary theories of social change. As has been shown, current so-ciological efforts to forecast social development are commonly predi-cated on the operation of the "natural laws" of science. These laws, however, encapsulate the unchanging, permanent structure of the em-pirical world; what we can predict on the basis of these laws is thus not properly the future, but a continuation of the present. In this re-spect, Lukács' study contains an alternative or at least a corrective: in-stead of forecasting the present he invites us to participate in shaping the future. This alternative cannot simply rely on the automatic opera-tion of natural laws; it requires a creative effort and commitment: a commitment to man's future, to a revival—as Lukács says—of the "buried man." Only such a commitment can transmute necessity and contribute to the building of a human universe governed, at least to some extent, by human purpose.

9. Reason and Emancipation: Notes on Habermas

THE CONTEMPORARY MALAISE IN Western societies has produced an array of diverse interpretations; a recurrent theme in such assessments, however, is the resort to psychopathological vocabulary: to symptoms of schizoid behavior, disorientation, and loss of coherence. The marvels of the technological era have not immediately been translated into corresponding levels of human well-being. While rigor and rational lucidity reap unprecedented triumphs in scientific inquiry, the domain of private and public action tends to be relegated either to the force of habit or to blind impulse and arbitrary bias. Divorced from the matrix of human purpose, science and technology seem to flood society with a knowledge which is not worth knowing while practical pursuits are adrift without intelligible standards. To some extent, science itself has been elevated into a public doctrine or creed—a transformation which, apart from perverting the tenets of scientific objectivity, camouflages and distorts the aims of public policy. One of the most trenchant analysts of contemporary ills is the German philosopher and sociologist Jürgen Habermas; his works are at the same time important guideposts on the road to recovery. A leading postwar representative of the renowned "Frankfurt School," Habermas documents the long-standing thrust of that school in the direction both of critical social analysis and the elucidation of social purpose.[1] In his writings, therapeutic and diagnostic efforts have always been combined. As he noted in one of his publications, "the danger of an exclusively technological civilization in which theory and practice are divorced" consists in the trend toward "schizophrenia and the segregation of people into two classes: social engineers and inmates of mental institutions."[2]

One of Habermas' central preoccupations has been to uncover the subterranean linkages between knowledge and human experience and purpose. In the pursuit of this quest, he was led to challenge the claims to supremacy advanced by positivist science and to explore alternative modes of intellectual inquiry deviating from the dominant, "nomological" type of explanation. His search, however, has not been limited to a mere survey of strategies of investigation and their varied manifestations. Advancing beyond the descriptive level he has tried to trace cognitive concerns to an underlying metaempirical structure of human awareness. As he has endeavored to show, the different types of knowledge proceed from and are guided by a general frame of reference, a categorial set of "cognitive interests." In delineating this categorial framework, Habermas reiterated and reformulated the basic questions which animated Kant's critiques of human understanding: What can I know? What shall I do? What may I hope for? However, in contrast to Kant's conception, Habermas' categorial frame does not reflect the solitude of a purified transcendental consciousness; while metaempirical and presupposed in concrete inquiries, the stipulated interests are enmeshed in an evolving life-world conceived both as a reproductive and a social learning process.

Habermas' writings are justly acclaimed for their incisiveness and lucid presentation of arguments. To be sure, in proportion to its impact, his work has also been surrounded by controversy and critical commentary. Not surprisingly, the most severe strictures have been formulated by followers of the positivist creed, including the adherents of a moderate or "critical" version of positivism.[3] A recapitulation of the details of this protracted controversy vastly exceeds the ambition of these pages. In a sense, all of Habermas' publications constitute an eloquent and sustained rejoinder to the positivist position. The present chapter is concerned with a more limited, but, it seems to me, by no means marginal issue. The discussion will concentrate on some critical comments or queries which have been articulated chiefly by the German philosopher Karl-Otto Apel and some of his associates. These comments, I would like to stress, proceed from a perspective quite congenial to that of Habermas and are by no means intended as an attack on his work; their aim, to a large extent, is to point to certain difficulties or ambiguities in Habermas' position and to offer suggestions for clarification and further development. In very general terms this internal critique or commentary focuses on the framework of noetic categories and especially on the notion of an "emancipatory interest." The central question raised in that context is whether, in postulating this type of interest, Habermas is not unwittingly encouraging or lending support to a kind of militant activism or ideological intransigence which is in contrast to his own philosophical perspective and political inclinations. The presentation will proceed in three steps or phases. The first segment tries to give a condensed overview or outline of Habermas' main theoretical argument. The second part delineates the thrust of the critical queries. In the last section I intend to comment on the main issues involved in this debate and also on the relevance of these issues to democratic theory and to the construction and operation of a democratic society.

I

The conception of different cognitive pursuits and of a framework of noetic competences emerged only slowly in Habermas' writings. Yet, in embryonic form rudiments of this conception were present from the beginning. In one of his first major publications, devoted to a critical examination of "public opinion," he noted that the progressive refinement of technological and managerial rationality tended to corrode or render obsolete the "public discussion" of practical political issues which had been a central premise of classical liberal doctrine; to the extent that public affairs were increasingly controlled by specialized elites wedded to technical efficiency, the role of the citizen was reduced to the acclamation of alternative administrative teams—just as, economically, he functioned as passive consumer of the products provided by corporate industry.[4] Subsequently, in a volume entitled *Theory and Practice,* the contrast or contest between knowledge and practical orientations was projected against the broad canvas of historical development. As the study indicated, the relationship between theoretical knowledge and action was relatively harmonious and unproblematical in classical philosophy, in the sense that contemplation of the universe was assumed to disclose practical standards of conduct and to contribute to the formation of character. Only since the beginning of the modern era has knowledge become gradually emancipated from moral and political concerns; in proportion to the scientist's growing capacity for experimental replication and manipulation of physical processes, man tended to become the master rather than the pious disciple of nature. Drawing on Newtonian physics and Enlightenment precursors, nineteenth-century positivism proceeded to transfer the strategy of natural science to the social domain, thus laying the foundations for broad-scale social engineering. The sketched developments came fully to fruition in our own era when science and technology emerged as the chief sources of social and industrial productivity. The main intellectual result is the prevalence of a truncated and purely instrumental rationality, encouraging either the sway of a spurious scientific ideology or the rigid bifurcation of knowledge and decision.[5]

The essays contained in *Theory and Practice* were remarkable for their perceptive diagnosis of contemporary predicaments and their portrayal of historical sources and precedents; but suggestions for reorientation or reformulation remained sketchy and elusive. Even in the discussion of Marxist dialectics, scientific observation and theoretical analysis were only precariously linked with revolutionary action. The following years brought a series of new essays and monographs which, ranging broadly from the history of philosophy to the methodology of contemporary social sciences, offered significant clues regarding Habermas' emerging perspective. In an essay entitled "Labor and Interaction," Habermas argued that Hegel during his Jena period had developed an important but now largely neglected model of dialectical thinking. Departing from the Kantian premise of a pure transcendental consciousness, Hegel then as later held that human awareness was the result not of solitary inspiration, but of man's interchange with his environment and his fellow-men in an ongoing individual and social learning process. As he specified in his Jena lectures, however, this learning process was composed of a set of separate and distinct patterns of mediations: the patterns of language, labor and communicative interaction. Language established a first mediating linkage between individual reflection and the world of objects via symbolic representation. Through labor man entered into direct interchange with his environment, an interchange mediated through instruments designed to transform man's subjugation to the laws of nature into technical control. Communicative interaction, finally, revolved around the struggle for mutual recognition among contending individuals, the story of the disruption and restoration of moral bonds. Partially retained in the *Phenomenology of Mind*, this tripartite scheme of mediations was abandoned in Hegel's later works in favor of the idealist vision of the identity of spirit and nature. In Habermas' view, the complexity of the human learning process was simplified not only in absolute idealism but also in post-Hegelian and even Marxist philosophy; despite his differentiation between forces and relationships of production, Marx ultimately submerged communicative interaction in instrumental labor, thus inviting a positivist interpretation of his arguments.[6] At about the time of his Hegel paper, Habermas also wrote a lengthy monograph on methods and types of knowledge in the social sciences, juxtaposing for this purpose the strategy of the natural sciences to the tradition of hermeneutical and phenomenological inquiry. Apart from trying to show that both strategies were legitimate and important in the social sciences, the monograph hinted at the possibility of a dialectical combination by means of a reformulated psychoanalytical framework of investigation.[7]

The contours of Habermas' conception of the relationship between cognitive pursuits and human experience emerged more clearly in his inaugural address of 1965 at the University of Frankfurt, an address published under the title "Knowledge and Interest." The main thrust of the address was directed against the pretensions of a pure analysis or pure reflection entirely aloof from human concerns. Taking his point of departure from Husserl's observations on the "crisis of European sciences," Habermas argued that despite the cogency of Husserl's critical comments, the proposed phenomenological remedy was ambiguous and misleading. According to Habermas, Husserl was entirely correct in charging that positivist science neglected the premises of its own efforts and thus camouflaged its roots in a primordial life-world. However, his recommendation to recapture the virtues of traditional theory by means of phenomenological reflection tended to encourage a similar concealment—especially since phenomenological "reduction" aimed to purge consciousness of all substantive content. The therapeutic qualities of classical *theoria* were due not to the radical elimination of substantive human concerns, but rather to the fact that human purpose and standards had tacitly been projected on the contemplated universe. In the presence of such standards (and only in their presence), theory was able to perform a practical mission: the mission of purifying and liberating the individual from the bondage of blind passions perverting his will and thought alike. If the label "objectivist" applied to a perspective muffling or disregarding its essential human presuppositions, then traditional philosophy, not unlike modern science, was characterized by an incipient objectivism—an objectivism which Husserl seemed to embrace by sponsoring phenomenology as a practical therapy.

Drawing the lessons from this initial discussion, Habermas' address developed the outlines of a theory of knowledge which, preventing the pitfalls of an unreflected objectivism, aimed to explore the underpinnings of thought in a categorial frame of human experience. As he tried to show, it was possible to identify at least three basic "interests" operative in different types of knowledge: a *technical* interest animating the strategy of the strict empirical sciences; a *practical* interest reflected in historical and hermeneutical inquiry; and an *emancipatory* interest guiding the endeavors of "critically oriented" social sciences. The methodology of the empirical sciences revolved around the

formulation of hypothetical propositions linking observable phenomena, propositions which, following empirical experimentation or testing, serve to support law-like theorems endowed with explanatory and
predictive capacity. Contrary to the intimations of positivism, however,
the basic parameters of the nomological model were not themselves
derived from empirical observation, nor through purely logical deduction; rather, they were anchored in the pragmatic context of the success
and failure of experimental or instrumental operations. Accordingly, it
seemed legitimate to argue that the empirical sciences approach and
examine reality from an instrumental perspective, a perspective tutored
by the interest in the "technical control over objectified processes."
Turning to the hermeneutical disciplines, Habermas noted that they
concentrate on understanding of meaning instead of empirical observation; the testing of law-like propositions is replaced by the interpretation of texts. Paralleling the positivist misrepresentation of natural science strategies, historicism had misconstrued hermeneutical inquiry in
an objectivist direction, reducing the records of human history to relics
of a finished past. Actually—as Habermas insisted—hermeneutical understanding always presupposed the interpreter's perspective; interpretation implied a merger of horizons, an effort to grasp the meaning of
the past from the vantage point of its relevance and application to the
interpreter's situation. As a result, hermeneutics was guided by a practical interest: interest in the maintenance and expansion of the domain
of intersubjective understanding and interaction. To some extent, existing social sciences emulated the sketched methodological paradigms,
especially the paradigm of natural science; a unique kind of linkage,
however, emerged in the case of critical social analysis. Such analysis
proceeded from the distinction between invariant and inescapable laws
of nature and such social conditions which, though ideologically rigidi-
fied and seemingly permanent, were amenable to alteration or avoidance. In the latter case a properly designed "critique of ideology,"
patterned after the psychoanalytical model, was able to combine explanation and understanding: once accepted and assimilated by the victim of domination, explanations of law-like conditions could engender
a process of reflection which, in turn, could lead to reinterpretation and
practical reorientation. The categorial framework of this critical endeavor was constituted by self-reflection, a capacity which, due to its
liberating effect, could be said to be permeated by an emancipatory
interest.[8]

In the concluding portion of his address, Habermas presented a
cluster of five basic theses or postulates elucidating the relationship
between knowledge and interest. As he stressed, the stipulated types of

interests were not simply empirically variable endowments or pre-dilections. Far from being merely targets for empirical confirmation, they reflected the premises or conditions of the very possibility of cognitive pursuits. The perspectives of technical control, practical inter-action and emancipation delineated the metaempirical boundaries of possible human perception and cognition; as the first thesis stated, they were rooted in the natural structure and genesis of the human species. This statement, however, was in need of considerable qualification. The listed categorial interests reflected not only man's constitution as a biological creature, but also his physical deficiency, his perennial rift with his natural environment. The genesis of mankind was not merely a process of reproduction and adaptation, but a historical development predicated on social and cultural interaction. Apart from the drive for survival, the field of human experience also embraced conceptions of the "good life"; in the terms of the second thesis, knowledge both supported and transcended the aims of self-preservation. Revolving around a complex genesis, man's cognitive pursuits were not simply solitary excursions; despite their metaempirical or transcendental character, his categorial interests were enmeshed in a natural and social learning process. This process occurred in typical and distinct patterns of experience: in patterns of reproduction and instrumental adaptation; in patterns of socialization and cultural communication; and in the search for identity and self-determination. Cognitive interests—the third thesis proclaimed—were thus formed in the context of work, language, and domination. As Habermas added, the relationship between knowledge and categorial premises was not identical in the three instances. While in the case of adaptation and socialization the connection involved a series of mediations, the process of self-reflection witnessed a more intimate convergence. Only in this context was it feasible for thought to penetrate fully its own motivation. In the language of classical idealism, "reason" denoted both practice and awareness; rationality implied the will to be rational. On the level of self-reflection, pure contemplation merges with the postulate of autonomy and self-determination or—as the fourth thesis stated—knowledge and interest coincide. However, in application to concrete experience, this convergence was at best anticipatory, due to the persistent impact of social domination and repression. The assumption of an immediate congruence actually delayed its implementation by lending support to ideological distortion and deception. Only a critical theory which broke the spell of spurious bondage was able—according to the last thesis—to advance self-reflection along its historical path: the tortuous path of human maturation, of a mankind slowly coming of age.

The implications of Habermas' inaugural address were elaborated more fully and in a broader historical context in a book of the same (German) title which appeared in 1968; for present purposes it must suffice to delineate only some of the main highlights of the study. In line with the thrust of his address, *Knowledge and Human Interests* tried to uncover the philosophical and metaempirical premises of human cognition. Countering the positivist reduction of thought to scientific methodology, the study aimed to reconstruct "the prehistory of modern positivism" and, at the same time, to lay the foundations of a comprehensive theory of knowledge as a prelude and corollary to a theory of society. On a grand scale, a nonreductionist theory of knowledge—establishing the parameters of cognitive pursuits—had last been developed by Kant in his critiques of human understanding; in this case, the framework of possible knowledge was provided by an abstract and invariant consciousness and by the notion of a transcendental synthesis of perception. Hegel, especially in his *Phenomenology of Mind*, further radicalized the Kantian argument by exploring the source of transcendental consciousness, its embeddedness in an individual and historical learning process. By assuming an identity of nature and spirit, however, Hegel in the end transgressed the limits of phenomenological experience; his identification of speculative philosophy with true knowledge had the paradoxical effect of undermining critical reflection on the premises of cognition. While departing from the assumptions of absolute idealism, Marx's conception ultimately pointed in a similar direction, at least on the level of his articulated methodology. Like Hegel, Marx implanted human experience in a concrete genesis; yet, apart from its materialist connotations, his view of this genesis retained significant Kantian and, especially, Fichtean impulses. Fichte had reinterpreted Kant's transcendental synthesis as a basic act of self-production; accepting this reformulation but transplanting it to the social domain, Marx construed social genesis as the continuous self-production of mankind through labor or instrumental activity. Labor, in this perspective, served not only as the mediating link between man as natural creature and his environment, but also as metaempirical frame or synthesis of experience. Marx's treatment of this frame, however, prevented broad methodological reflection. Although his substantive writings stressed the importance of human interaction and critical emancipation, his theoretical analysis restricted experience to the level of instrumental activity and technical control over nature—a focus which encouraged positivist reductionism.

As propagated by Comte and his followers, positivism aimed to purge thought of all metaempirical vestiges in an effort to vindicate the exclusive validity of strict science. Yet, despite stringent methodological prohibitions, the exorcised legacy continued to haunt the positivist fortress—in Comte's speculative philosophy of history as well as in Mach's ontological "theory of elements"; by rejecting the legitimacy of reflection, positivism condemned to apocryphal status arguments justifying its own enterprise. In the latter part of the nineteenth century, the positivist paradigm was transgressed, at least partially, along two fronts: in Peirce's pragmatist interpretation of science and in Dilthey's rejuvenation of hermeneutical inquiry. In examining the logic of scientific inquiry, Peirce discovered its parameters in the cumulative learning experience of a "community of investigators," an experience propelled by the success and failure of experimental or instrumental operations. Yet, when called to explain how singular experiences could be translated into general propositions, he tended to lapse into a linguistically disguised ontology, ascribing the source of validity to the world of objects rather than the framework of research. At about the same time, Dilthey explored the underpinnings of science in the dimension of the sociocultural life-world; while nature, in his view, could be explained only through the arsenal of artificial hypotheses and models, intersubjective experience required the hermeneutic reconstruction and understanding of meaning, an understanding relying on the dialectical interrelation of singular phenomena and general contexts. Like Peirce, however, Dilthey was not entirely true to the thrust of his argument; at crucial junctures he derived the cogency of interpretations from their correspondence to a quasi-ontological life process. Correcting the positivist shortcomings in both instances, Habermas argued that knowledge claims had to be traced to their metaempirical premises, to the level of basic cognitive orientations or "interests." In the case of strict science, the pursuit of knowledge was channeled by the parameters of instrumental activity, by the structural condition of a physically fragile species condemned to seek survival in an inhospitable natural environment. Guided by the cognitive interest in technical control over natural processes, the "community of investigators" implemented a strategy which permitted the transformation of singular experiments into universal propositions. The conduct of scientific research, however, presupposed an interactive network among the participants; this dimension constituted the metaempirical framework of hermeneutics. Prompted by the practical interest in the maintenance of intersubjective communication and understanding, hermeneutical interpretation permitted the integration of singular experiences into larger meaning patterns.[9]

In the remaining chapters, Habermas concentrated on the central theme of the study: the relationship between knowledge and experience, and especially on the notion of cognitive interests or competences. As he emphasized, these competences denoted neither pure transcendental categories nor mere empirical impulses or instincts. "Cognitive interests," he wrote, "mediate . . . the natural genesis of mankind with the logic of its cultural learning process; they are not meant to reduce this process to a naturalistic dimension. *Interests* I call those basic orientations which are rooted in certain fundamental conditions of the possible reproduction and self-constitution of mankind: namely, work and interaction." However, the domains of work and interaction, of technical and practical endeavors were not simply juxtaposed, but could ultimately be traced to a common source: the experience of human self-reflection. Only in the process of self-reflection was thought able to grasp completely its own premises. As Fichte in particular had noted, the pursuit of knowledge for its own sake merged on this level with the quest for practical autonomy; by virtue of an inherent "emancipatory interest," reason and the will to be rational coincided. The advancement of self-reflection against the background of unconscious or unintelligible constraints was the basic concern of Freudian psychoanalysis—despite occasional lapses of its founder into positivist or physicalist modes of argument. Proceeding beyond purposive interaction, Freud's "depth hermeneutics" aimed at the decoding not only of intended, but of systematically distorted meaning patterns. Toward this end, causal explanation was intimately linked with interpretation: the analysis of pathological symptoms served the therapeutic goal of deepened self-understanding and self-awareness. Transposed to the social arena, psychoanalysis provided a paradigm for critical social inquiry, an inquiry whose explanatory propositions sustained the emancipatory thrust against political exploitation and against the suppression or corruption of social discourse.[10]

II

Habermas' writings offer a broad target area for critical explorations and assessments, both from a purely philosophical and a political vantage point. One such exploration, initiated primarily by Professor Apel and some associates, is concerned with the conception of categorial interests and especially with the presumed convergence of reason and emancipatory purpose. According to these friendly critics, the convergence as articulated by Habermas is at least ambiguous and in need of clarification; carelessly interpreted, the conception might even invite political abuse in the form of blind activism and ideological militancy. Judging from the record of Habermas' political statements and performance, the danger alluded to by the commentators is not immediately evident. Actually, one of the chief complaints lodged against him by politically committed readers has been his apparent lack of ideological zeal and his reluctance to provide unambiguous direction signals for political action.[11] On the level of popular prepossessions, to be sure, the apprehension tends to strike a responsive cord: according to a widely shared belief—verging on an article of public faith—any flirtation with Hegelian or Marxist dialectics carries with it the danger of dogmatism and even the implication of sinister "totalitarian" designs.[12] Professor Apel is by no means a partisan of this creed. The subtlety and philosophical sensitivity of his writings entirely remove his arguments from the arena of political recriminations; moreover, his views on many crucial issues closely approximate, and even coincide with Habermas' position. Precisely because of their internal and non-polemical character, his critical comments deserve careful attention and scrutiny.

To a considerable extent, Apel's work and development have paralleled Habermas' philosophical endeavors. For a long time, he has been preoccupied with methodological and epistemological questions, and especially with the philosophical status of different types of inquiries and knowledge claims. In 1965, the year of Habermas' inaugural address, he published a lengthy monograph devoted to the contemporary status and significance of hermeneutical investigation, especially in light of the pervasive challenge posed by neopositivism and linguistic analysis.[13] A few years later, in an essay entitled "Science, Hermeneutics, and Critique of Ideology," Apel presented in programmatic form the sketch of a comprehensive theory of knowledge drafted from the perspective of a "philosophical anthropology." Designed as an alternative or counterproposal to the neopositivist "logic of science," the sketch renewed the Kantian query regarding the premises of possible knowledge; however, instead of an exclusive reliance on pure consciousness, the validity of cognitive pursuits was traced to the complex structure of human experience. As Apel tried to show, the formation and aggregation of knowledge in the various disciplines derived not simply from a transcendental synthesis, but from a more concrete encounter between researcher and the investigated natural or cultural world. This encounter or engagement constituted the basic framework, the "bodily a priori," of perception and cognition; moreover, depending on the character of the encounter, it was possible to identify and delineate the different cognitive interests underlying different brands of research—a delineation which was the main objective of the sketched "anthropology of knowledge."

In Apel's presentation, cognitive interests and types of encounter were not randomly variable; as the title of the essay suggested, he was chiefly concerned with three dimensions of inquiry—the same dimensions which are familiar from Habermas' writings. The strict empirical sciences, Apel held, clearly presupposed a concrete bodily encounter. The advances of physical science, for instance, were due not merely to the formulation of abstract models, but to the construction of an instrumental apparatus permitting the replication and measurement of natural processes; only by imposing this apparatus on the physical universe were scientists able to test propositions or—in Kant's phrase—"to compel nature to respond to their questions." Replication and experimentation, however, were corollaries of manipulation and technical control; like Habermas, Apel thus arrived at the stipulation of a "technical interest" as metaempirical premise of empirical science. This interest, the essay continued, was by no means autonomous or self-sufficient. Countering the pretensions of neopositivism and especially of the "unified science movement," Apel argued that scientific inquiry itself was inconceivable without the infrastructure of semiotic interpretation in a community of investigators—as Peirce had shown. To explore the dimension of communicative interaction, both at a given time and between generations in a historical perspective, was the task of hermeneutical inquiry, an inquiry guided by the "practical interest" in the maintenance of an intelligible and meaningful social life-world. The bodily engagement at this level was revealed in the embeddedness of interpretation in the matrix of ordinary language and symbolic expression. In the concluding portion of the essay, Apel pointed to the limitations of hermeneutics as a decoding device of the social life-world, limitations deriving chiefly from the pervasive impact of unintelligible natural forces and opaque social constraints. In order to penetrate and relieve this dark legacy, it was necessary to combine the strategies of scientific explanation and hermeneutical interpretation, after the model of psychoanalysis, so that the diagnosis of symptoms could produce the therapeutic effect of deepened self-understanding. Transferred to the social domain, this model animated the enterprise of a critical social science centering on a "critique of ideology." The bodily engagement as well as the guiding cognitive interest of this enterprise revolved around the psychosomatic self-diagnosis and auto-therapy of man—a quest aiming at the complete interpenetration of body and spirit, at the simultaneous "naturalization of man" and "humanization of nature."[14]

Judging from the preceding arguments, the views of the two authors seem to be in complete harmony, at least on the level of the theory or anthropology of knowledge. Yet, even in the discussed essay, it was possible to detect hints of a philosophical divergence: the notion of a "bodily a priori" suggested or entailed the alternative of a purely reflective cognition; the anthropological perspective was introduced to supplement and expand rather than to supplant the Kantian focus on transcendental synthesis.[15] The broader, especially political, implications of this divergence emerged more clearly in one of Apel's subsequent essays, devoted to a clarification of the question "Science as Emancipation?" The immediate concern of the essay was the contemporary controversy surrounding higher education in Germany (and elsewhere) and in particular the demand, raised by segments of the student movement, for a "political mandate" of the university. As Apel readily conceded, the effects of this controversy were on the whole salutary: especially to the extent that it encouraged renewed reflection on the premises and functions of knowledge and education. Actually, the larger portion of the essay was couched as a defense of the program and central intentions of "critical theory" as formulated by Habermas and the Frankfurt School. In Apel's view, the thrust of this program had to be viewed against the background of contemporary technological society and of the positivist glorification of "scientific method." In advanced industrial countries, science and technology had entered into an unprecedented liaison with economic and bureaucratic institutions; at the same time, the dominant positivist creed prevented exploration of the social and purposive matrix of science, thus promoting either a scientific monopoly along technocratic lines or a bifurcation between expertise and arbitrary political bias. The situation was aggravated by the infiltration of science into the social domain and by the vastly expanded potential of social engineering and control. In the face of these trends, the critical program sought to uncover the premises of science and other types of knowledge, as a prelude to a comprehensive human and social reorientation and emancipation.

Despite this sympathetic portrayal, however, Apel indicated that critical theory was in need of modification or at least specification. His reservations became evident when he turned from general historical considerations to the more concrete starting point of his essay. In a broad sense, he suggested, Habermas' categorial framework and even the notion of an "emancipatory interest" were quite tenable and legitimate; on this level it was not farfetched to argue that "reason" implied the "will to be rational" and that the will to be rational entailed the

practical commitment to establish a livable, non-repressive social community and to remove the barriers obstructing this goal.[16] However,
what was the relevance of this general perspective for emancipatory
social practice? Was it possible to translate the stipulated rational
"commitment" into a concrete program of political action? To illustrate
the dilemmas encountered in this context, Apel focused attention on
the issue of the political role or "mandate" of higher learning. Two
extreme positions, he observed, confronted each other on this issue.
According to the first position, science and knowledge in general were
entirely value-free and removed from practical commitments, while
politics was at best the private pastime of the individual scientist as
citizen. In the second conception—which, he intimated, derived its impulses to a considerable extent from critical theory and the Frankfurt
School—the distinction between knowledge and practical politics was
obliterated, with the result of a complete "politicization" of scholarly
disciplines and the university as a whole. Both alternatives, in Apel's
judgment, were undesirable and defective. Turning to Habermas' version of critical theory, he suggested that its main difficulty resided in
a certain contraction of the categorial framework, in the tendency to
collapse theoretical reflection and political practice under the aegis of
the stipulated emancipatory interest.

"Fichte to the contrary notwithstanding," Apel commented, "the
notion of an emancipatory interest which Habermas postulates as central for critical social inquiry and philosophy, does not lead at the apex
of reflection to a simple identity of knowledge and interest, reflection
and practical commitment. At least this cannot hold true for us finite
human beings, as long as commitment is defined as risky, politically
effective partisanship." Despite the juncture of reason and rational
purpose, he continued, "theoretical reflection and concrete, practical
commitment do not coincide, but rather diverge at the highest level of
philosophical speculation into polar opposites, within the range of the
emancipatory cognitive framework." Theoretical knowledge and reflection aimed at universal validity and consensus. While not entirely
divorced from human purpose, reflection of this kind embraced only
one dimension of the emancipatory interest: the portion characterized
by opposition to dogmas and spurious convictions and by an attitude
of sustained doubt treating every commitment as tentative and subject
to revision on an experimental basis. In Apel's view, it was this particular dimension from which, "despite all heuristic commitments, science
derives its legitimacy as science." To assume that this aspect could be
stretched to cover the opposite pole of the emancipatory interest—the
portion invoked by Marx in his demand that the world should not only

be examined but changed—amounted to an "idealistic illusion." The merger of knowledge and interest, envisaged by Habermas, had to be treated not as an accomplished feat, but at best as a "regulative principle" in the Kantian sense of the term: a pure signal for reason, but without concrete substantive connotations. Drawing the implications from these statements, Apel interpreted constitutional democracy as an attempt to transfer the rules of the game of a critical "community of investigators" from the scholarly realm to the domain of politics. The "political mandate," he concluded, could plausibly be construed as a plea not for the politicization of knowledge, but for the responsible participation of scientists in the formulation of educational policy, with the goal of securing the political conditions necessary for scholarly inquiry.[17]

Apel's reservations were formulated in cautious and highly tentative language. In somewhat stronger terms, his line of argument has been pursued and expanded by Dietrich Böhler, one of his students and associates (during his stay at Saarbrücken). In Böhler's judgment, the entire Frankfurt School has always been characterized by a certain doctrinaire flavor; despite important modifications and deviations, Habermas' work still showed traces of this legacy. In an essay entitled "Critical Reflections on Critical Theory," Böhler has tried to depict the central features of the "older" Frankfurt School, concentrating for this purpose on the writings of Max Horkheimer and especially his *Eclipse of Reason*. The "eclipse" referred to by Horkheimer was the progressive obfuscation and obliteration of moral and political standards induced by the rise of modern science and technology. Modern science, in his view, was animated by a purely "instrumental rationality": a truncated intelligence combining dazzling analytical and methodological rigor with substantive blindness or myopia. The accomplishments of our technological era conjured up the prospect of large-scale social engineering obtuse to human purpose. To counteract this danger, critical theory aimed principally at the restoration of "substantive rationality," a rationality embedded in objective historical conditions and yet pregnant with unimpeachable standards of conduct. The task of recovery, as envisaged by Horkheimer, entailed a dual effort: the effort of social analysis and a "critique of ideology," designed to unveil social distortions and pathologies; and, at the same time, concrete revolutionary activity striving to implement a "correct" society congruent with the dictates of substantive reason. As Böhler observed, Horkheimer's conception of a critical yet objective theory constituted basically a revival of traditional "precritical" philosophy. Moreover, the departure of his program from instrumental knowledge was less dramatic than pretended: what critical theory shared with a positivist "logic of science" was primarily the indulgence in monologue and the complete disregard of the dimension of intersubjective discourse and communication. The derivation of practical aims from monologues, however, was the emblem of dogmatism; the merger of reason and emancipation provided justification for revolutionary violence and political repression. "Substantive criteria of historically relevant conduct," Böhler argued, could be found only through commitment; they could not be "generally deduced or objectified."[18]

Up to this point, Habermas was not, or was only obliquely, involved in the discussion. However, in one of his later essays, "On the Question of the Emancipatory Interest and Its Social Implementation," Böhler proceeded to provide the connection: by arguing that, irrespective of his impressive hermeneutical insights, Habermas was still in many respects a pupil of Horkheimer's critical theory and its doctrine of "substantive rationality." While the portrayals of a technical-scientific and a practical-communicative dimension were valuable innovations, Horkheimer's heritage was revealed in the postulate of an "emancipatory interest" as foundation and final linkage of knowledge and purposive action. In Böhler's view, Habermas' lapse into the mystique of substantive reason derived chiefly from his excessive reliance on Fichtean speculation, especially on the tenet regarding the coincidence of reason with the will to be rational. Actually, formulated in these stark terms, the coincidence was elusive if not spurious. What reason or reflection, pushed to its ultimate recesses, disclosed was not so much a comprehensive human purpose as rather a "formal" or theoretical interest in emancipation: an interest in pure, undogmatic knowledge and enlightenment. The exploration of the universally valid implications of reason was the task of transcendental philosophy. In Kantian language, such exploration revealed the a priori structure of pure consciousness; this formulation, however, had to be amended once it was realized that knowledge and cognition were not solitary ventures but embedded in intersubjective language. Pure reflection thus uncovered not merely disjointed soliloquies, but the transcendental rules of communication, the framework of a metaempirical "language game"; according to Peirce and Apel, the a priori of individual consciousness had to be expanded into the a priori of the community of investigators. Yet, this modification of transcendental philosophy permitted no broad purposive inferences. The stipulated community was devoted only to the formal value of emancipation from ignorance and superstition, to the objective of successful communication per se.

Beyond this formal domain, reason offered only dim and insufficient guidance. From the a priori status of communication and the community of investigators it was, perhaps, possible to derive minimal standards for behavior among scholars and a limited responsibility for the maintenance of conditions auspicious to research. No further postulates, however, could validly be justified: not even the postulate of an "open society" conceived as an undistorted communications network of *all* citizens, and certainly not Habermas' vision of a mankind coming of age, of a society pursuing the "good life" in terms of nonrepressive mutual relations. To arrive at substantive standards of any kind, it was necessary to descend from pure reflection to the level of practical commitment, of the partisan identification with a chosen "project." Emancipation in a comprehensive sense thus implied at least two complementary conditions or phases: detachment through pure reflection and concrete, bodily engagement in a historical situation. According to Böhler, the latter phase provided inspiration for critical social inquiry propelled by a special "situational interest." This interest, however, was rooted not in reason or a universal structural a priori, but rather in subjective experience or commitment, in a concrete "decision." Whatever his intentions and personal preferences, Habermas' merger of reason and substantive purpose was prone to give support to partisan—in particular neo-Marxist—stratagems, possibly even to revolutionary terror and violence. By contrast, the segregation or juxtaposition of reflection and commitment promoted tolerance and the equal treatment of preferences—central pillars both of traditional higher education and of liberal democracy.[19]

III

The seriousness of the questions raised by the commentators hardly needs elaboration. If substantiated, the affiliation with or sponsorship of doctrinaire partisanship would affect not only the periphery of Habermas' work: given the incompatibility between rational discourse and dogmatism, even indirect encouragement of the latter would tend to damage the integrity of his philosophical argument. In the following I intend to deal mainly with three points. First: How persuasive are the critical comments on a philosophical level? Is the notion of an emancipatory interest indeed fraught with the mentioned dilemmas and difficulties and does the stipulated convergence of reason and practical purpose necessarily entail the apprehended danger? On this point I would like to argue that the queries formulated by the commentators are certainly helpful in bringing important issues into sharper focus; at the same time, it seems to me that Habermas' position is perhaps less ambiguous than supposed and that suggested alternative formulations are not entirely free of quandaries or immune from hazardous exegesis. Next: Assuming the inherent legitimacy of the merger of reason and emancipation, does Habermas vitiate its practical implementation by sponsoring doctrinaire and possibly repressive policies and arrangements? On this level, I find again little direct evidence in Habermas' publications—despite occasional clamorings by zealots to act on his behalf. If he is less than blameless in this respect, the reason seems to reside not so much in his actual recommendations as in a certain elusiveness of his arguments, in his reluctance to specify the implications of his insights in concrete, institutional terms. Finally, I would like to explore the question whether the issues discussed in this context contain some general lessons for political theory, especially with regard to liberalism and democracy.

Regarding the first and probably central question, I think it is only fair to stress initially some simple rules of due process: that critical strictures do not carry presumptive weight in their favor and that, unless corroborated by unmistakable acts of complicity, guilt by association is an inadmissible charge. On these points, I am convinced, the commentators would heartily agree. There is, to be sure, much circumstantial evidence surrounding Habermas' position, but it tends to be inconclusive if not contradictory. In some instances, doctrinaire militancy has claimed to derive its credentials entirely from his writings and "critical theory" in general. On the other hand, as previously mentioned, some of the most pointed published attacks have aimed their fire not at his ideological fervor but at his presumed malleability and political moderation. More recently, a reviewer of his work reached a conclusion diametrically opposed to the charge of dogmatism. As formulated by Habermas, the reviewer observed, "emancipation aims at making possible 'the free dialog,' which comes close to saying that the aim is left an *open* question." The "upshot" of this, according to the reviewer, was that Habermas' argument was "comprehensive in a purely formal sense" and actually stood in the "liberalist tradition": "Habermas' theory may hence be said to be a comprehensive liberalistic methodology."[20] Although this assessment, in my estimate, is excessive if not simply erroneous, it serves to cast doubt on the imputation of a narrow partisanship. Actually, such doubts are shared and expressed by our commentators themselves. Apel's essays in particular contain several qualifying remarks which further mollify his already subdued reservations. Thus, he readily concedes at one point that Habermas, like Marcuse, has turned his back on a dogmatic historicism, on the

notion of an invariant developmental pattern inherent in human history—thereby heeding Merleau-Ponty's plea for a *"Marxisme sans illusions, tout expérimental."* Böhler, in turn, softens the thrust of his observations by differentiating sharply between Habermas' personal outlook—his "liberal socialism"—and the potential implications of his philosophical position.[21]

Yet, is it plausible in this instance to assume such a divergence
between the individual and the philosopher? As it seems to me, the
apprehension of doctrinaire implications would be warranted only if
it could be shown that the categorial interests stipulated by Habermas
were linked with comprehensive, substantive directives of a partisan
character—directives whose compelling force was predicated on their
congruence with a presumed objective reality. His writings, however,
offer little or no support for such an undertaking; on the contrary, in
several passages Habermas severely castigates the pretensions of a full-
blown substantive rationality. As Apel acknowledges, he has little sympathy for historical ontologies after the fashion of Marxist orthodoxy.
In his inaugural address of 1965, he denounced the arrogance of a
philosophy of history which, on the basis of an alleged objective
knowledge of the universe, dispenses practical instructions in a dogmatic manner, thus prejudging the course of human development.
"A mystifying doctrine of history," he commented, "is only the reverse
side of a blind decisionism: a contemplatively misconstrued objectivism agrees only too well with a bureaucratically imposed partisanship."[22] A central target in the case of both commentators is Habermas'
presumed infatuation with Fichtean metaphysics. Although Fichte's
contribution to the formulation of cognitive interests cannot be
doubted, the criticism ignores or deemphasizes Habermas' important
deviations from his idealistic precursor. Far from treating the merger
of reason and emancipatory purpose as an accomplished feat or as
the result of a solitary act of awareness, Habermas stresses the embeddedness of self-reflection in the meanderings and dialectical mediations of a concrete learning process—a process, moreover, devoid of
Hegel's preordained teleology. "Fichte's transcendental act of self-
reflection," he writes, "is diffused and diffracted into the experience of
reflection. . . . The human learning process is neither like Fichte's absolute self-production nor like the movement of an absolute spirit." Construed as a learning process, the movement of self-reflection is not
simply propelled by the imperatives of a pure reason, but is conditioned
by the contingent factors of man's social and natural environment: by
the coordinates of interaction and technical control.[23]

While Habermas, in my estimate, thus resists the temptation of global prescriptions, he does not permit himself the opposite comfort of abstinence. Although reticent to embrace ontological panaceas, he does not abandon himself to an abstract formalism or to the simple notion of the equivalence of preferences. In delineating the postulate of an emancipatory interest, his work adumbrates a basic categorial structure of human awareness and experience. The assumption of such a categorial frame appears to me both legitimate and entirely necessary for intelligible human discourse. Michael Oakeshott may be quite correct, in a broad sense, when he says that "the conjunction of dreaming and ruling generates tyranny";[24] but the remedy can hardly be found in indifference. The chief defect of this alternative is that is disavowed by elementary, everyday experience. Simply by being alive, we do not display indifference toward our own condition, nor toward human life in general. To pretend neutrality on this level—to assume the air of theoretical detachment—is an imposture. Habermas, by tracing cognitive efforts to an infrastructure of primordial interests, merely seems to acknowledge the circumstance that life is not the result of logical deduction. In fact, his entire categorial conception seems to be linked to this humble origin. For, life is not merely a fact, but an act of affirmation; in the words of Albert Camus, "to breathe is to judge."[25] By his mere existence, man demonstrates his intent to live: to live in the face of the human and natural environment he finds. Human awareness or reason transforms this propensity into a conscious design. The sheer effort of survival imposes on man the task to observe and analyze his environment as accurately as possible: a task which disposes him against ignorance and spurious beliefs. His human environment, however, presents him with an even greater challenge: the challenge to find standards of conduct which are mutually intelligible and acceptable. As soon as man faces his fellow creatures, the effort of survival is thus transmuted into the quest for the "good life."

In numerous passages, Habermas explores the intimate connection between survival and the "good life"; the postulate of an emancipatory interest, from this vantage point, appears to attest to the primordial linkage of reason and human purpose.[26] Speaking more loosely, one might say that human experience seems to be structured or designed in the direction of truth, goodness and, if one wishes, happiness. However, this statement, to my understanding, does not entail any immediate program of action. In effect, the central issue of politics—both on a theoretical and a practical level—appears to me to reside in the reconciliation of unity and diversity, in the simultaneous recognition of a common purpose or thrust and of the divergence of concrete interpretations. The two elements are mutually interdependent and the elimination of one detrimentally affects the other. Böhler suggests that a removal or bracketing of the purposive thrust—expressed in Habermas' emancipatory interest—would enhance intersubjective tolerance and the quality of public discourse; but I do not see how this can happen. Without a dimly perceived frame of reference, I fail to see how meaningful discourse is possible, how people can have anything to say to each other; social relations on such a premise seem to degenerate into emotive gestures or simply a series of soliloquies. Seen from this perspective, the heart of politics—I believe—lies in the question of what it makes *sense* to say under given circumstances. To be sure, some statements may make more sense than others. Also circumstances vary and conditions are not necessarily perceived in the same manner by all concerned: different segments of society, placed at different status levels, may sensibly wish to say different things. Yet, while "sense" seems to presuppose a context of meaning, this circumstance does not necessarily prejudge the outcome of the argument. Contrary to Böhler's intimation, the assumption of a purposive context does not inevitably support sectarian left-wing designs, to the exclusion of "conservative" views. If, as Oakeshott argues, the chief trait of a conservative disposition is the propensity to cherish familiar relationships for their own sake, rather than for the sake of success or profit, then it would seem to make sense in many instances to cultivate such an attitude; this is true at least as long as friendship and sincere fellowship are seen as desirable ingredients of the "good life." Moreover, one might even find it sensible in the face of proposed social changes to place the burden of proof on the would-be innovator, to show that expected improvements outweigh likely disadvantages.[27] All this, I think, can sensibly be maintained—even without abandoning reason in favor of ritual or habit.

As I have indicated previously, I not only find Habermas' thoughts on this point tenable and less equivocal than assumed, I also consider some of the suggested counterformulations fraught with quandaries and vulnerable to precarious interpretations or misinterpretations. Probably the chief remedy or corrective proposed by the commentators aims at the segregation of the emancipatory interest into its theoretical and practical components, at a more tidy distinction between reflection and concrete commitment. On a common-sense level and within a circumscribed range of discourse and experience, this distinction is unobjectionable—and does not seem to be controverted by Habermas' position. To the extent that his writings were insufficiently explicit or emphatic on the point, his commentators can be said to have made an important contribution to philosophical candor and circumspection. If erected into a full-fledged dichotomy, however, the differentiation becomes dubious and problematical. First of all, it requires no effort to show that such a dichotomy is at odds with a dialectical frame of thinking—a frame to which both reviewers seem to be firmly attached. At one point, in commenting on the postulate of an "open society," Apel notes that dialectical thought always has to pursue abstract principles to the level of concrete social experience, thus mediating between transcendental and empirical considerations. However, in strictly segregating contemplation from concrete engagement, the reflective from the bodily a priori, his arguments almost seem to hark back to a Cartesian mind-body dualism. On occasion, the statements of both writers resemble or at least approximate the neo-Kantian or neopositivist bifurcation of knowledge and choice—a position which they otherwise deplore. In Böhler's plea for the divorce of theory from situational "decision" the affinity can hardly be overlooked. One defect of this bifurcation is that it conjures up the very dogmatism which the commentators so urgently (and so legitimately) seek to avoid. For, in the absence of rational parameters or standards, how can commitments or decisions be made otherwise than blindly or dogmatically?[28] The bifurcation, however, is deficient not only because of its tendency to reduce choice to impulse, but also because of its mystifying effect on reflection. In line with his notion of a bodily encounter, Apel tends to conceive of practical commitment in terms of a "risky, politically effective partisanship"; in doing so, he intimates that contemplation—the adoption of a theoretical attitude—is somehow exempt from the constraints of practical choice and responsibility. This view is at best puzzling. Clearly, abstention from choice is itself a kind of choice; omission and commission are both types of activities and commitments—beset with the same risks and liabilities. The "excentric position" of human consciousness—a term invoked by both writers—denotes not so much a place of refuge for the theoretically oriented as a source of restlessness, an emblem of man's incongruence with his natural environment.[29] Viewed in this manner, reflection provides protection against the complacency of dogmatism, but only insufficient insulation from the exigencies of concrete experience.

Another corollary of the segregation of reflection and commitment is the tendency to erect a social barrier: the barrier between the knowledgeable and the untutored segments of society. This corollary, to be sure, is only distantly foreshadowed in the commentators' essays and would hardly be condoned as an actual consequence. Yet, in the case of both writers, reason seems to disclose standards or guidelines chiefly for learned inquiry and for the operation of a scholarly community.

Apel, it is true, stresses on several occasions the potentially unlimited character of the "community of investigators," the circumstance that *all* human beings are potential participants in the quest for knowledge and enlightenment. With regard to hermeneutical inquiry, he emphatically rejects the notion of a narrow clique of experts, pointing to the need for communicative interaction between the scholar and his audience; in the same context, he asserts the inescapability of purposive concerns, of questions concerning ultimate normative standards. However, when turning to the "universal" implications of reason or reflection, his perspective seems to narrow and to focus exclusively on a community of intellectuals and scientists, a community sustained only by a "minimal" ethics aiming at the destruction of dogmas and at the removal of obstacles hampering scholarly investigation.[30] The social differentiation emerges more explicitly in Böhler's argument. In his view, reason provides sanctions only for an investigating community of researchers, sanctions which contain minimal clues for conduct among practitioners and for the maintenance of the research enterprise. As he makes clear, however, the investigating fraternity is by no means coextensive with the larger community of *all* citizens; he even suggests that the prerequisites of scholarly interaction may be fulfilled—and the standards of reason satisfied—in the midst of widespread social repression and exploitation.[31] This suggestion is disturbing and could easily encourage misanthropic interpretations. Clearly in a world plagued by hunger and turmoil on a global scale, the identification of reason and scholarship can have little appeal—except to academicians. Against the affectations of the learned it seems imperative to return rationality into the common patrimony of mankind; once this is done, however, reason can no longer shun the universal predicaments of survival and the good life.

The endorsement of Habermas' general philosophical perspective does not necessarily or inevitably carry over to questions of concrete implementation. Although his notion of categorial interests—as I have tried to argue—properly embraces both reflection and practical purpose, his views on implementation may fall short of his insights, bending the broad injunctions of reason in the direction of sectarian partisanship. As it seems to me, the central issue on this level is the conception of a critical social science, a "critique of ideology" patterned after the model of Freudian psychoanalysis. Does this conception not entail an unduly intimate merger of knowledge and prescription, of diagnosis and therapy—a merger oblivious to the contingencies and complex mediations of concrete experience? Are we here not indeed engulfed in Fichtean metaphysics: in the instantaneous blending of reflection and self-creation? Moreover, is it possible to transfer the doctor-patient relationship from psychiatry to the social domain without encouraging intellectual presumptuousness and possibly the formation of another elite of experts? Again, as on previous occasions, I consider it important to stress that there is no presumptive rule militating against Habermas' views. Although embroiled in complex problems, the notion of a critical social inquiry is not necessarily, without further demonstration, vitiated by the abuses to which it may give rise. On the whole, Habermas' writings relating to the issue do not testify to abusive intent. In his interpretation, the Freudian model implies not so much the transfer or imposition of knowledge, but rather a complex dialogue between analyst and patient, a dialogue in which only the patient's acceptance of a diagnosis can have the emancipating effect of deepened self-awareness. The mutual relationship, he notes, is thus not technical but practical in character, and as such embedded in the contingencies of practical experience: apart from aiming at the relief of concretely identifiable pathologies, therapeutic efforts are experimental and never assured of success. In several of his essays, Habermas has explored the relationship between technical expertise and practical goals in a broader social and political context; none of these writings betrays a noticeable propensity to ignore the contingencies and mediations intervening between thought and action. A similar impression can be gained from his essays on student protest and the reform of higher education.[32]

Yet, the cited evidence is perhaps not entirely sufficient to obviate the abuse of intellectual elitism or paternalism; the writings to which I have referred are, by and large, more of a descriptive or critical than of a constructive character. Generally speaking, if Habermas' views on this point are not entirely satisfactory or convincing, the defect stems from omission rather than from explicit instructions, from a certain elusiveness of his argument rather than from concrete assertions. In his presentation, the notion of a critical social inquiry is more suggestive than instructive; given the importance of the category in Habermas' work, the reader is likely to sense a degree of impatience.[33] Perhaps it may be helpful at this point to resort to a conception which David Kettler has explored: that of a "politics of counsel." "The conception of a counselor," he observes, "is by no means identical with that of the 'expert,' who presumably makes available instrumental knowledge which can effectively implement any value specified by his principal. But neither is it (or need it be) a dishonest way of presenting the Mandarin or the Platonic philosopher-king." Kettler proceeds to specify some key elements of a relevant "code of etiquette": that the counselor gives advice rather than commands, that the form of his advice will be reasoned argument and explication, that its content will be mainly an interpretive statement of the situation together with tentative projections, and that the occasion of the advice should be appropriate to his relationship to the issues at hand. The entire argument, I should add, is developed with specific reference to the role of the intellectual in modern society and especially in the context of the contemporary university.[34] Relying on the notion of a politics of counsel, it might be possible to supply the concept of a critical social science with concrete and unobjectionable connotations. On the same basis, it should also be feasible to move beyond the alternatives which Apel has listed, regarding the relationship of higher learning to politics: those of abstinence, complete politicization, or the modest involvement of scientists in procuring the amenities for research. In an age of mass education when science and knowledge in general have advanced to key factors of social productivity, higher education is challenged to perform a more complex function: that of a "microcosm" or small-scale replica of society, a replica in which social pathologies together with proposed diagnoses and therapies are subjected to vigorous and sustained scrutiny and discourse.

By way of conclusion—to return from a pragmatic to a more general or theoretical level—I would simply want to raise, or rather allude to, a question which seems to emerge from the preceding discussion. The question is this: Is it possible to associate distinct political doctrines with particular conceptions regarding the relationship between theory and practice, reflection and concrete commitment? Or is it perhaps even possible to derive major political doctrines from, and explain them in terms of, a limited set of such conceptions? I do not propose to resolve this question here, nor do I pretend that I could do it justice; but perhaps it bears investigation. Some hints or direction signals for such an inquiry emerge, I believe, from the sketched exchanges. In some of the commentators' statements, the segregation of reason and commitment serves, or at least has the tendency, to buttress the vision of a completely "open society," a doctrine of a broadly liberal vintage. In Habermas' argument, on the other hand, dialectical thinking sustains the conception of a free or open community channeled in the direction of social justice and equity. Perhaps it is legitimate to assume that liberalism has always been characterized by a series of dichotomies: the dichotomies of state and society, reason and passion, reflection and experience. However, while at its inception liberalism may still have been pregnant with moral purpose, its contemporary representatives seem to have distilled reason into a procedural rule, an abstract formalism: a formalism which is implicit in the notion of a purely theoretical community of investigators. Against this background, it seems possible to delineate at least two types or models of democratic regimes: a "formal" democracy which, operating under a "rule of law" transformed into ritual, relegates social practice to habit or arbitrary compulsion; and a "real" democracy which, though following agreed-upon procedures, tries continually to correct the abuses of privilege and private ambition. As it seems to me (and probably to all participants in the foregoing discussion), the latter type is preferable not only for its pragmatic advantages, but also for its greater intellectual frankness and modesty. In the first type, reflection assumes the detached air of a transcendental spectator, purveying the human condition from the perspective of an accomplished destiny; in the second, reason is a participant in the human enterprise, illuminating—however dimly—the struggles of a journeying mankind, a mankind still underway.

10. Critical Epistemology Criticized

THAT BOOKS HAVE THEIR FATE is a familiar dictum; what is less frequently noted is that translations may have their own. Just as the original was part of an ongoing discourse in its native habitat, the translation enters a new realm of discussion and will find its significance measured by the new context. If, by chance, the two discourses were initially analogous or synchronized, new developments can easily disrupt this momentary convergence and prepare the way for divergent destinies. Habermas' book, *Erkenntnis und Interesse,* illustrates these observations. The first German edition of 1968 appeared at the height of student demonstrations and widespread intellectual ferment both in Europe and America, a ferment nurtured predominantly by the so-called "New Left" movement. Its translation, under the title *Knowledge and Human Interests,* was published at a time when this movement was beginning to wane and when, especially in Germany, unorthodox exuberance and experimentation were progressively eclipsed by sterner and more conventional forms of argumentation. Perhaps, the broad impact of the book in the New World suggests not only a general cultural difference but also a modified outcome of the student rebellion.[1]

Viewed from a long-range perspective, the fascination of Habermas' work derives not merely from a temporary effervescence, but from its contribution to the compendium of post-Marxist or neo-Marxist literature. As has often been observed, Marxist thought has traditionally been deficient chiefly in two dimensions: those of ethics and of epistemology or the theory of knowledge. What orthodox writings expounded in the epistemological domain was at best suggestive if it was not completely mired in paradox: the paradox of a "mirror view" of

246

mental receptivity juxtaposed to the postulate of revolutionary élan and creativity. *Knowledge and Human Interests* seeks to remedy this dilemma by formulating its arguments on a level which is both informed by, and competitive with, current philosophical articulations of the theme. Habermas' study, however, is prompted by a stronger motivation than the desire to fill a gap: it also seeks to illuminate the course of human liberation by rescuing it from the vicissitudes of arbitrary bias or partisan preference. Such an endeavor seems particularly urgent in a situation where the march of history, including the "class struggle," does no longer proceed like an automatic clockwork, and certainly not in accordance with a mechanical stimulus-response formula. Against this background, Habermas' explorations in the theory of knowledge can legitimately be viewed—as the Preface asserts—as a prelude or prolegomenon to an intelligible theory of society.[2]

Since its first publication, *Knowledge and Human Interests* has been the target of a great number of reviews and evaluations, ranging from mild appraisals to harsh denunciations. Its author has not been insensitive to these repercussions. Partly in response to his critics, partly (one can assume) as a result of independent further reflection, Habermas in the meantime has reformulated his perspective—occasionally sharpening its contours, occasionally shifting its philosophical accents. In an introductory essay written for a new edition of *Theory and Practice*, he has sketched a synopsis of the multifaceted development of his views, including recent reformulations or amendments; entitled "Some Difficulties in the Attempt to Link Theory and Praxis," the essay portrays his writings on knowledge and public opinion, on social science methodology, and on philosophical epistemology as different avenues or approaches on the path toward a critical sociology and social theory.[3] As Habermas recognizes, his writings and in particular his epistemological endeavors, have given rise to numerous objections— among which he considers three lines of argument particularly significant: first, objections relating to the character and status of "cognitive interests"; second, queries addressed to the postulated coincidence of knowledge and emancipatory interest in the process of self-reflection; and third, arguments relating to the conduct and organization of political action and to the transfer of the psychoanalytic model to the social domain. In view of the complexity of the issues involved, I consider it advantageous to use Habermas' enumeration as a guide through the maze of reviews. In the following I shall thus examine critical assessments by arranging them, at least in part, under the three mentioned headings. By way of conclusion I shall draw attention to additional evaluations and polemical attacks not mentioned by Habermas, in an

effort to lead theoretical discussions back to the dimension of contemporary political practice.

The major innovation or shift in emphasis which emerges in the
introductory essay and equally affects the three central objections, consists in a certian loosening of the linkage between knowledge and interest, between the validity of knowledge claims, on the one hand, and
the genesis as well as application of knowledge, on the other. This
loosening is effected primarily through the introduction of the notion of
"discourse" and its differentiation from everyday practice or experience. In Habermas' definition, discourses are efforts to provide reasons
or justifications for any kind of knowledge claims. While in everyday
experience cognitive assertions or intersubjective norms tend to be
naively accepted or taken for granted, discourses involve a virtual suspension of belief in the interest of thorough investigation and interrogation; in Habermas' words, they "demand a virtualization of the constraints of every-day reality, with the aim of deactivating any motivation except the willingness to cooperate in the search for knowledge
and of segregating validity from the genesis of cognition." As he adds,
discourses in a sense imply a phenomenological "reduction" of existence to potentiality: "in Husserl's terminology we bracket the general
thesis (of reality)."[4] Only by means of this virtualization is it possible
to arrive at a rational consensus—that is, to vindicate the truth of assertions in a manner which can be freely assented to by all participants
of the search. At the same time, only the model of a free consensus provides the standard against which the truthfulness of participants, their
commitment to the quest for truth, can properly be assessed.

I

The stipulation of a framework of "cognitive interests" is clearly
a central, if not the central, feature of Habermas' epistemological perspective; small wonder that it should have attracted a major share of
critical comments. Measured by its significance in the context of the
study, one can hardly deny that the formulation of the cognitive structure in *Knowledge and Human Interests* remained somewhat sketchy
and elusive. "The notion of 'interest,'" one reads there, "is not meant
to suggest a naturalistic reduction of transcendental-logical categories
to empirical ones; rather, it seeks precisely to prevent such reduction.
Cognitive interests mediate the natural genesis of mankind with the
logic of its cultural learning process." A little further one finds the
statement that "cognitive interest" is a "peculiar category which con-

forms as little to the distinction between empirical and transcendental or factual and symbolic categories as to the dichotomy between motivation and cognition. For knowledge is neither a mere instrument of an organism's adaptation to a changing environment nor the act of a purified consciousness, of a contemplation entirely removed from the context of life."[5] One may puzzle at this point how the framework of interests can both transcend and reflect the natural genesis and cultural history of mankind. What seems to emerge from the citation in any event is that the delineated framework points in the direction of a "philosophical anthropology," a view seeking to lodge the different types and variable content of knowledge in a "depth structure" of human experience. In this manner, epistemology assumes the connotations of an "anthropology of knowledge."[6]

The conception of "cognitive interests" has been challenged primarily from two sides, although not with equal subtlety and perserverance. On the one hand, some writers have charged that Habermas' presentation manifests the very shortcoming which he castigates as the basic defect of positivism: that of an unreflected empiricism or naturalism. On the other hand, the cognitive framework has been attacked as baseless speculation and as a transgression of the limits of empirical knowledge. As one can readily gather, the first indictment derives from idealist premises or from a religiously toned metaphysics, while the second emanates from the positivist camp. The charge of speculative exuberance has been articulated chiefly by Hans Albert, partisan of a moderate or "critical" version of positivism. In his *Plea for a Critical Rationalism* Albert portrayed the doctrines of the Frankfurt School, including Habermas' cognitive framework, as an example of the persisting lure of theological thinking, of a philosophical argument suffused with the spurious pretense of revealed knowledge. Among the most objectionable features of such doctrines he stressed the bias against empirical science and the predilection for a hermeneutical interpretation of history. Two basic traits, he noted, characterize theoretical orientations of this kind: "the strong emphasis on history as a domain pregnant with meaning and, related to this, the pronounced antinaturalism in ontological and methodological matters, that is to say, the rejection of the notion that man be treated as a 'mere' natural creature, as part of living nature, and simultaneously the refusal to accept the application of natural science methods in all areas of knowledge."[7]

The accusation of empiricist or naturalistic leanings has been raised with greater or lesser skill by a number of writers. Arguing from the basis of precritical philosophy and metaphysics, Günter Rohrmoser has assailed Habermas for his presumed lapse into a myopic empiricism and historical relativism. In *The Misery of Critical Theory* Habermas' writings appear as an updated version of the basic outlook of the Frankfurt School—in particular, its transformation of dialectical thinking into abstract negation. "Critical theory" which in the case of Adorno and Marcuse already had shrunk into the dichotomy between a corrupt social reality and the empty postulate of revolutionary action, is continued by Habermas in the further emaciated form of a critique of ideology or critical sociology. In contrast to the dialectical legacy of Marx, Habermas' perspective is said to incorporate the demand that "critique renounce any ontological and thus any metaphysical premise."[8] Rohrmoser is not oblivious to the fact that Habermas does not fully share Adorno's or Marcuse's intense aversion against scientific methodology or empirical social science. Although propelled by the aim of instrumental control over natural processes, empirical science in his scheme fulfills a far from negligible task: he "acknowledges the capacity of analytical social science to resolve competently the question of whether or not the objective conditions of revolution prevail in a given society." In Rohrmoser's view, however, Habermas' attitude toward science involves not so much an amendment as a deterioration of critical theory; the recognition of science merely implies a more intimate embrace by the tentacles of empiricism and historical relativism. As a result of this embrace, Rohrmoser notes, Marxist theory is reinterpreted and transformed into a "theory of history animated by a practical intent but subject to empirical test and verification."[9]

Instead of being remedied, the empiricist bent is merely reinforced at those points where Habermas' outlook transgresses the limits of the scientific paradigm. Rohrmoser realizes that Habermas treats hermeneutical understanding as a counterpoise and corrective to scientific inquiry; he even concedes that, in stipulating the model of a free and unimpeded dialogue, Habermas adumbrates a normative standard of political interaction, a standard reminiscent of "a concept of politics deriving from the Greek polis." However, apart from being patterned after the customs of academic communities, dialogue in Habermas' presentation is not fully competent to dissolve distorted communication or social repression and thus needs to be supplemented by critical reflection and emancipatory practice. At this juncture, the basic dilemma of his theory is said to come into view: in his inability to differentiate legitimate from illegitimate practice and, in general, to distinguish between valid arguments and arbitrary impulses. According to Rohrmoser, Habermas' entire epistemological framework is nothing but a masked and stylized doctrine of natural instincts; far from exuding a transcendental aura, the different "cognitive interests" as well as their structural correlation are grounded in contingent empirical reality. What the cognitive scheme thus accomplishes is at best a reproduction of the factual constellations of contemporary society. The dismal consequences of this empiricism are particularly evident in the case of emancipatory action. Since emancipatory interest is nothing but the impulse of the discontented, society can with equal legitimacy assert an interest in maintaining the status quo; the conflict can only be resolved through a resort to force. "Both types of interest," Rohrmoser writes, "have the ontological status of purely contingent facts. As it appears, ontology—exiled by Habermas in his de-mythologization of Marx—cannot so readily be expelled as the Frankfurt School imagined. The destruction of philosophy in the form of metaphysics and ontology has as a consequence that a theory aiming to support emancipatory-critical practice can find its justification only in a contingent factual interest." The misery of critical theory, he concludes, derives ultimately from this rejection of traditional philosophy, a rejection resulting in "the loss of the idea of truth"; with the loss of this legacy, political practice is bound to degenerate into a struggle of competing programs and ideologies. Only faith in God and a religious rejuvenation can reactivate moral conscience and lead to the restoration of a "valid theory of truth."[10]

In a somewhat more careful and subtle manner the charge of an unreflected empiricism is advanced by Michael Theunissen in his *Society and History*, a study proceeding from the perspective of a religiously colored idealism. In contrast to Rohrmoser, Theunissen avows his general agreement with the basic intent or program of "critical theory"; as he tries to show, however, the actual implementation of the program by Horkheimer and Habermas falls short of its goal and at crucial junctures degenerates into naturalistic bias or into the dualism of nature and human subjectivity. The basic thrust of the Frankfurt School was originally delineated, although not fully developed, by the young Horkheimer in his famous essay on "Traditional and Critical Theory," an essay opposing passive contemplation to a perspective incorporating both theory and practice, subject and object in an ongoing historical process.[11] Despite misleading statements of its founder, critical theory—according to Theunissen—diverges only partially from classical Greek thought, mainly by shifting the central accent from natural ontology to historical reflection. Actually, critical and classical theory remain linked by subterranean similarities: especially by their philosophical autonomy—the lacking subservience to extraneous, instrumental purposes—and their orientation toward an untarnished vision of the "good life." What, in Theunissen's view, critical theory primarily opposes or rejects is an objectivist outlook such as has been sponsored by the rise of modern science, an outlook which transforms nature into an external target of theoretical analysis and technical designs. While, in its chief inspiration, critical theory thus constitutes a translation of classical thought, characterized by universal contemplation, into the medium of a universal philosophy of history, the execution of this intent falls prey to a naturalistic and basically anti-historical objectivism.

The source of this lapse, Theunissen notes, consists in general terms in an excessive reliance on human subjectivity, an overindulgence which is offset by the resort to a naturalistic counterpoise. The overindulgence manifests itself in the tendency, present among all members of the Frankfurt School, to ascribe the synthetic functions of Kant's "transcendental consciousness" to empirical subjects or to the human species, after the fashion of the Young or Left Hegelian movement. In the early writings of Horkheimer, synthetic capabilities of this kind were assigned to the projected socialist society, and the means of implementation were discovered in human labor; however, labor had as an objective human domination over natural processes and thus the reduction of nature to an external object of exploitation. Subsequently, Horkheimer grew increasingly weary of his initial vision, mainly due to insight into its counterproductive results: technical designs presupposed obedience to nature's laws and control over nature thus implied nature's control over man. Progressively, therefore, he abandoned the nightmare of domination in favor of a gentler "reconciliation" of man with nature; yet, however cogent his pleas, such reconciliation meant acceptance of a naturalistic ontology alien to historical experience. While trying to avoid these pitfalls, Habermas in Theunissen's view ultimately steers in the same direction. As he observes, Habermas departs from Horkheimer primarily by means of two correctives: by juxtaposing communicative interaction to the domain of instrumental labor; and by lodging both orientations in a transcendental framework of cognitive interests. According to Theunissen, however, the transcendental turn itself betrays a naturalistic bias: the appeal to transcendental categories reveals nature as a factual contingency. Moreover, portrayed as invariant structures, the stipulated cognitive orientations disclose a naturalistic or, in any event, nonhistorical character. In the end, the transcendental capacities of cognition are bestowed on the empirical human species—an example of Left Hegelian predilections. Even in the process of self-reflection, Theunissen discovers the naturalistic specter: imitating Fichte, Habermas allegedly collapses the historical distance between critical awareness and practical implementation.

Recapitulating his findings, Theunissen, by way of conclusion, re-assesses the basic quandary of the Frankfurt theorists; the quandary is now defined in terms of a tension between Hegel and Marx and, more specifically in terms of a post-Hegelian or materialistic deviation from the essentially Hegelian conception of a universal historical philosophy. From Marxist or materialistic sources the Frankfurt theorists derive both the notion of an external nature juxtaposed to history and, what is perhaps more striking, the vision of human society as the productive motor and constitutive agent of historical development. Both legacies, naturalism and social self-production, are correlated and mutually reinforcing; the latter aspect in particular implies a rejection of the Hegelian standard of an "absolute objectivity" in history and its replacement by empirical contingency and historical relativism. While Hegel still recognized two types or levels of dialectical thinking, critical theory restricts itself to the exploration of subject-object relations, neglecting the movements of the "absolute spirit"—a neglect which stands in stark contrast to the claim of critical theory to offer valid knowledge about society. Such a claim, Theunissen observes, is untenable on the level of empirical contingency to which critical theory in its actual execution clings. If at all, it can be sustained only by a return to the "absolute" dimension of Hegelian dialectics, a dimension which—in Theunissen's view—preserves and rearticulates "the patrimony of Christian theology." To the extent that critical theory appeals to this patrimony and especially to the "Christian doctrine of freedom," he affirms, "one can legitimately assume that philosophy of history proceeds not only from theological origins, but continues to be possible only as theology."[12]

Similar arguments, although with less pronounced theological connotations, can be found in an essay by Rüdiger Bubner entitled "What is Critical Theory?" Bubner takes his departure from the notion of "interest" which, as he correctly asserts, occupies an important place in Marxist and especially in critical theory and which continues to exert its influence in Habermas' cognitive framework. To Bubner, this notion appears profoundly ambiguous. On the one hand, the term refers to empirically contingent and idiosyncratic impulses and motivations; on the other, the concept is invoked by Frankfurt theorists as a critical standard segregating valid claims and aspirations from spurious and ideologically corrupted views. Together with Theunissen, Bubner regards this confusion as manifestation of a typically Young Hegelian bias: of the merger of absolute principles with empirical reality and the assignment of quasi-transcendental tasks to contingent social agents. From the time of Horkheimer's early writings, he notes, critical theory has insisted on presenting a true and valid account of historical developments—after the fashion of Young Hegelian self-confidence which had been castigated by Marx in his *Holy Family*. At the same time, Frankfurt theorists have refused to accept in its entirety either Hegel's dialectical philosophy or Marx's naturalistic doctrine, preferring instead the perspective of an open or "unfinished dialectic" enmeshing reflection in the meanderings of concrete empirical experience. As a result of these simultaneous predilections, critical theory is characterized by "a peculiar ambivalence between dogmatic certitude and hypothetical openness," between a priori convictions and factual contingency. The basic source of this ambivalence cannot be in doubt: it resides in a certain distrust of speculative thought, in the unwillingness to expose critical premises to comprehensive philosophical reflection.

According to Bubner, the shortcomings of the Frankfurt School are readily apparent in Habermas' epistemological writings. In the synoptic sketch of his framework, contained in his inaugural address of 1965, Habermas built his argument specifically on Horkheimer's dichotomy of traditional and critical theory;[13] unaccountably, Husserl was treated as representative of the first type, although his later writings pointed at least obliquely in the direction of a broad philosophical reflection on the linkage between knowledge and its experiential parameters (*Lebenswelt*). By contrast, Habermas' framework—apart from blandly asserting this linkage— is marred by its indiscriminate terminology: while interests regularly denote empirical or naturalistic leanings which require critical exposure, "cognitive interests" are elevated to the level of a priori certitude and thus at least partially shielded against further theoretical inquiry. The curtailment of reflection is also noticeable in Habermas' treatment of language and communicative interaction, in the sense that dialogue is viewed both as empirical social condition and as standard of valid cognition. With particular force, the same defect emerges in his relationship to the Hegelian legacy. In tracing the fortunes and misfortunes of reflection— Bubner notes again correctly—"Knowledge and Interest" follows the pattern of Hegel's *Phenomenology of Mind*; yet, Habermas at numerous points expresses his disenchantment with Hegel's later "system," criticizing the preoccupation with "absolute spirit" as a withdrawal from the domain of possible human experience. According to Bubner, however, Hegel's *Phenomenology* is merely preparatory and derives its justification solely from the later system, since only absolute reflection can provide a yardstick for the critique of experience and the validity of knowledge; the removal of this yardstick, on the other hand, can only result in a "decapitated phenomenology" and a myopic empiricism.[14]

The importance of the sketched critical thrust can hardly be questioned. Perhaps it is possible to neglect details of the argument; thus, Theunissen's charge of "dogmatism" can probably be discounted, given his strong reliance on theology. Undeniably, however, the critics have highlighted a twilight zone of critical theory. By combining an "unfinished dialectic" with claims of a priori knowledge, critical theory has invited the challenge of Hegelians—or other champions of universal systems—either to defend its a priori claims on the level of pure theory or to accept the stricture of contingent empiricism. In a sense, the ambivalence arises already from the chosen label: by adopting the term "critical theory," the Frankfurt School suggested that its endeavors are both competitive with traditional philosophy on a theoretical level and at the same time "critical" of purely theoretical or contemplative postures. To this extent, Theunissen's quandary is not self-inflicted when he queries whether Frankfurt theorists are opposed to all traditional thought or merely seek to buttress universal reflection against the onslaught of positivist science. Probably the Frankfurt School would have been well advised from the beginning to adopt a more modest stance and acknowledge more frankly the degree to which, at least with regard to social matters, its ambitions stand on the ground of "practical thought."[15] At this point one may also find reason to regret the long-standing opposition of critical theory to Husserl's phenomenological legacy—and, more specifically, the peculiar insulation of contemporary German from French thought. Clearly the notion of an "unfinished dialectic" parallels Merleau-Ponty's preference for a dialectic under open horizons, for a *"Marxisme sans illusions, tout expérimental."* Yet the writings of the Frankfurt School do not betray a notable receptiveness or sensitivity for Merleau-Ponty's practical phenomenology.

Habermas' response to his critics, in the mentioned "introductory essay," shows signs of a cautious rapprochement. Broadly speaking, the response involves a relaxation of the knowledge-interest nexus, effected chiefly through a resort to the mediating function of "discourse." As previously indicated, Habermas himself suggests a certain affinity between the notion of discourse and Husserl's *epoché*; in effect his elaborations on the concept are strongly reminiscent of the phenomenological effort to gain insight by unsettling the grip of immediate impressions. Taking his cues from Bubner's comments on language and communication, Habermas concedes the need to differentiate more clearly between empirical interaction and the validation of knowledge claims; his previous writings, he notes, had explored the linkage of knowledge and interest without sufficiently clarifying the distinction

"between communications which remain directly subject to the constraints of action, and discourses which transcend such constraints."
The claim to objectivity presupposes "a virtualization of the pressure of
experience and decision," a transformation which alone "permits a discursive testing of hypothetical propositions and thus the emergence of
valid knowledge"; as a result, true and well-founded insights can never
be derived immediately "from the imperatives of practical life." Virtualization of the knowledge-interest nexus, however, does not imply
its complete obliteration; in Habermas' view, cognitive endeavors remain embedded, however loosely, in different contexts of experience
and practice. These contexts link the genesis of a particular type of
knowledge with its possible application and even affect the relevant
mode of validation. "Cognitive interests"—and especially the most
"deeply rooted" technical and practical interests—are shorthand labels
for such linkages: they "maintain a latent practical relevance of cognition," across and underneath the mediations of discourse—but they do
not nullify the distinction between spurious and valid knowledge.
Cognitive interests thus indicate general strategies of human orientations which are guided and corrected by discursive validation.

     These remarks, to be sure, do not entirely settle all queries. One
may note, for instance, that the term "discourse" seems to be more
intimately related to the domain of communicative interaction than to
the more stylized procedures of scientific method. Terminological quandaries also beset the basic cognitive framework. Habermas notes (I
think correctly) that, on this level of argumentation, some dichotomies
of traditional philosophy, especially the dichotomy between empirical
"contingency" and a priori "necessity," become blurred and elusive.
The designation of the cognitive map thus presents difficulties which
are not accidental or idiosyncratic. The introductory essay assigns to
the technical and practical interests a "quasi-transcendental status" or a
place hovering between strict transcendence and concrete experience.
To the extent, Habermas writes, that these interests are derived from
the "logic of investigation" in the natural and human sciences, they can
claim transcendental status; however, when viewed as part of the
"natural genesis" of mankind, they acquire empirical connotations. In
the latter respect, the essay expects some helpful pointers from a reconsideration and reassessment of "evolutionary" theory.[16] Probably, the
entire discussion could gain additional corroboration from a closer inspection of the phenomenology of perception and of developments in
contemporary "philosophical anthropology." On the empirical level,
some attention should perhaps also be paid to psychological investigations of the relationship of motivation and cognition.[17]

II

The second critical argument focuses on the dimension of self-reflection and the postulated convergence of knowledge and "emancipatory interest." In a sense the argument is merely a corollary and extension of the first objection relating to the character of the epistemological framework. To Theunissen, the emancipatory interest is evidence of the excessive indulgence of critical theory in human subjectivity—a subjectivity, moreover, which merely conceals a latent naturalism. Bubner views the same interest as a particularly telling illustration of Young Hegelianism: of the tendency to collapse transcendental categories with empirical motivations. The assumed convergence of cognition and emancipatory aspiration, of reason and the will to be rational, short-changes philosophical reflection in favor of an immediate practical application of unexamined principles. Contrary to Habermas' allegations, Bubner adds, such a convergence was never a part of idealistic philosophy which rather culminated in the exploration of pure theory or "absolute spirit." As he concedes, theory of this type was only distantly or precariously related to practical experience; but only pure reflection can prepare the ground for adequate practice.

In greater detail and from a different vantage point, the emancipatory thrust of self-reflection has been examined by Karl-Otto Apel and Dietrich Böhler. Since I have reviewed their comments in the preceding chapter I can be brief at this point.[18] In contrast to the idealistic critics whose central aim is to preserve pure consciousness from contamination, the arguments of Apel and Böhler are prompted primarily by the objective to shield the domain of practical action against the pretense of absolute knowledge; moreover, broadly sympathetic to the thrust of critical theory, their views are advanced not so much as objections than as amendments to Habermas' perspective. Apel's essay, "Science as Emancipation?", devoted to an investigation of the public role of higher learning, demonstrates his far-reaching agreement with the central intentions of critical theory. As he points out, these intentions have to be viewed in the context of contemporary technological society and the almost exclusive dominance of "scientific method," a situation aggravated by the growing infiltration of science into the social domain and the resulting danger of social engineering. Faced with these trends, the critical program seeks to uncover the purposive matrix of science and other types of knowledge, as a prelude to an adequate social theory and political practice. The point at which, in Apel's view, the program becomes dubious is where general vistas are immediately joined with practical directives. Habermas' notion of an "emancipatory interest" inherent in self-reflection seems to suggest such a merger. However, is it possible or legitimate to translate a general commitment to rationality into a concrete strategy of political action?

The hazards of such an undertaking, Apel notes, are evident in the controversy surrounding the role of higher education. Reacting to the positivist paean on value-free scientific knowledge entirely devoid of purposive parameters, critical theory has the tendency to lapse into the opposite extreme and to encourage a complete "politicization" of scholarly inquiry and of the university as a whole. To some extent, this tendency is abetted by Habermas' concept of self-reflection with its contraction of the linkage between knowledge and interest. To obviate the dangers implicit in such contraction, Apel counsels a sharper differentiation between the various layers of the critical program, especially between reflection and concrete, possibly risky, political involvement. Despite the broad nexus of reason and rational purpose, he writes, "theoretical reflection and concrete, practical commitment do not coincide, but rather diverge at the highest level of philosophical speculation into polar opposites, within the range of the emancipatory cognitive framework." Properly speaking reflection supports only one type of emancipation: the liberation from dogma and spurious convictions; the assumption, by contrast, that such emancipation has immediate political repercussions is an "idealistic illusion." Liberation from social oppression, and political change in general, presuppose active participation in practical political life—a participation which is exposed to the ambiguities of concrete situations and lacks the comfort of a priori certitude. As Apel concludes, the juncture of reason and commitment, envisaged by Habermas, thus cannot be treated as an accomplished feat, but at best as a "regulative principle" in the Kantian sense of the term: a pure signal for reason but without substantive connotations.[19]

Apel's comments have been pursued and reinforced by Dietrich Böhler, especially in his essay "On the Question of the Emancipatory Interest and Its Social Implementation." According to Böhler, critical theory as originally outlined by Horkheimer was still intimately linked with pre-critical philosophy, especially through its devotion to a "substantive rationality" merging theoretical analysis with practical injunctions. Despite his turn to hermeneutics, Habermas' epistemology preserves traces of this legacy—and nowhere more clearly than in the notion of an "emancipatory interest" linking knowledge and purposive action. Together with Apel Böhler perceives danger in the presumed

coincidence of reason with the will to be rational; perhaps more vig-
orously than the former, he insists on a sharp segregation of the supposed ingredients of self-reflection. What reason, pursued to its ultimate recesses, reveals is not so much a comprehensive strategy as a
"formal" or theoretical interest in emancipation: an interest in enlightenment and undogmatic knowledge. Even when transferred from individual consciousness to a "community of investigators," reflection
vouches at best for a liberation from ignorance and for the objective of
successful communication; beyond this formal range, however, its counsel is muffled and obscure. To arrive at substantive standards for concrete activity, Böhler affirms, it is necessary to move from pure reflection to the level of practical commitment, of the partisan identification with a chosen "project." Such identification derives its justification
not from universal a priori principles, but rather from subjective involvement in a concrete context, from a personal choice or "decision."
Emancipation in a comprehensive sense thus implies at least two complementary conditions: detachment through reflection and concrete,
bodily engagement in a historical situation.[20]

In light of these comments and reservations, Habermas has rephrased his position in regard to self-reflection and emancipation;
whether this reformulation involves a change of perspective or merely
an elaboration of previous views can remain an open question at this
point.[21] His "introductory essay" presents a somewhat more complex
picture of the relationship between cognition and emancipatory aspirations. Just as one can differentiate between "discourses" and immediate
action contexts, Habermas notes, it is desirable to discriminate within
the process of reflection and self-knowledge: primarily by distinguishing
between "self-reflection" and rational or theoretical "reconstruction."
While "self-reflection" in the narrow sense of the term seeks to retrace
the contorted path of individual experience and development, rational
"reconstruction" uncovers deeply rooted regulatory mechanisms which
every individual requires in order to engage in cognitive endeavors of
any type. Self-reflection thus focuses on the intricate matrix of personal
awareness, including the impact of ideological orientation and social
domination; reconstruction, by contrast, discloses anonymous sets of
rules—such as logical or linguistic rules—which, in theory, can be generally or universally mastered and obeyed. The two categories, however, are separated not only by the dimensions of individual uniqueness
and generality, but also by their different practical implications. By
rendering transparent previously hidden or mangled layers of experience, self-reflection is able to produce a personal catharsis and transformation of character, an emancipation from the domination of past

constraints; reconstruction, on the other hand, by explicating impicitly followed depth mechanisms may lead to a broadening of the range of theoretical knowledge, but without normally changing practical conduct.

In comparison with discourses, self-reflection according to Habermas accomplishes both more and less. Attached to individual learning experiences, self-reflection cannot aspire to validate interactive norms or scientific procedures in the same manner as discursive endeavors. In the context of therapeutic exchanges, moreover, the partners initially are far from occupying the symmetric relationship presupposed in discourses; rather, symmetry and equality are only the result of successful therapy. On the other hand, self-reflection surpasses discourses in one important respect. Precisely due to its intimate linkage with practical experience, the successful pursuit of self-awareness can lead to a situation which satisfies not only the standard of valid truth, but also the condition of personal veracity or truthfulness. This circumstance is again illustrated in the therapeutic context, in the patient's acceptance of a proposed interpretation. "The correct interpretation," Habermas writes, "renders possible the truthfulness of the patient in regard to those statements through which previously he deceived both himself and (possibly) others." In contrast to self-reflection, rational reconstructions can be viewed as discourses, although discourses of a special kind. While ordinary discourses seek to validate propositions relating to the objective or intersubjective world—practical norms or scientific theorems—reconstruction involves a reflective return to the premises of discourses and of thought in general. To this extent, reconstructive cognition has always claimed the status of a "pure" theoretical knowledge; under such rubrics as logics, epistemology, and theory of language, this type of knowledge continues to form the nucleus of philosophical inquiry. Although relatively autonomous, however, reconstruction is not entirely removed from self-reflection: only through reliance on reconstructed depth rules can self-reflection gain theoretical contours. Reconstruction thus maintains at least an indirect and oblique nexus with emancipatory aspirations, aspirations which are immediately operative in the process of self-reflection.[22]

III

The third critical query concerns the implications of the assumed knowledge-interest linkage for practical political life and, in particular, the legitimacy of the transfer of psychoanalysis to the domain of critical social theory and practice. Basically, queries of this kind can arise from two different—although not always clearly demarcated—perspectives: either from concern over a contemplative stifling of practical initiative or from apprehensions regarding a militant exploitation of theoretical doctrines. The two attitudes can be readily discerned with respect to the psychoanalytic model: on the one hand, utilization of the model in the social arena can be denounced as an effort to defuse or emasculate social conflicts; on the other hand, adoption of the doctor-patient formula conjures up the danger of large-scale manipulation at the hand of self-appointed therapists. In our time the hazards of the latter alternative seem particularly pronounced; given the contemporary refinement of techniques of social domination, the prospect of psychic control and mental torture is far from imaginary. Perils of this type were by no means ignored by the founders of the psychoanalytic movement; in his *Civilization and Its Discontents* Freud counseled against rash or careless applications of his findings to the social arena. "I would not say," he wrote, "that an attempt of this kind to carry psychoanalysis over to the cultural community was absurd or doomed to be fruitless. But we should have to be very cautious and not forget that, after all, we are only dealing with analogies and that it is dangerous, not only with men but also with concepts, to tear them from the sphere in which they have originated and been evolved." Apart from the difficulty of defining standards of social normalcy, Freud noted particularly the dilemma of implementation: "And as regards the therapeutic application of our knowledge, what would be the use of the most correct analysis of social neuroses, since no one possesses authority to impose such a therapy upon the group?"[23]

The argument that Habermas has been insufficiently careful in specifying the practical implications of his outlook is a recurrent theme in critical reviews.[24] To some extent, the argument is implicit in the sketched comments on self-reflection. In voicing reservations regarding the coincidence of reason and the will to be rational, Apel seems concerned, at least in part, about the possibility of a militant abuse of rational injunctions. Likewise, in stressing the limitations and ambiguities of situational commitment, Böhler seeks to obviate the snare of doctrinaire intransigence. From the vantage point of a flexible "New Left" strategy, Oskar Negt has focused on the elusiveness of Habermas' posture. In a collection of essays entitled *Politics as Protest,* Habermas is taken to task for his reluctance to consider seriously the dilemmas of practical political involvement. Arguing in favor of a "decentralized activity" bypassing the pitfalls of merely theoretical enlightenment or unreflected activism, Negt is particularly distressed by Habermas' silence on questions of tactics and concrete organization. Habermas, he notes, may have properly chided the "New Left" for its occasionally flamboyant or erratic behavior; yet, instead of offering viable alternative strategies, he has preferred to withdraw into the sphere of detached contemplation: either by offering analyses of the structure of post-industrial society, or by reiterating traditional formulas of Marxist strategy. Such withdrawal, however, flies into the face of Habermas' own practical intentions; the reiteration of traditional formulas, in particular, conflicts with the thrust of an unfinished dialectic. Unable to bridge the gulf between theory and practice, Habermas thus vacillates between the two: since he fails to draw "the political consequences inherent in an emancipatory cognitive interest," Negt concludes, he is confined to a "prepolitical stance of objective partisanship"—a stance which, confronted with concrete political challenges, easily lapses into arbitrary personal preference.[25]

With regard to the social application of psychoanalysis, the danger of a manipulative abuse has been stressed primarily by Hans-Georg Gadamer. Proceeding from the context of an existential hermeneutics— a hermeneutics attentive to the constraints of particular historical and social situations—Gadamer sees in the use of psychoanalysis an overextension of the range of reason and self-reflection. As he observes, the therapeutic relationship presupposes a common orientation of doctor and patient, a mutual readiness to participate in the task of joint self-reflection. Such a common perspective, however, may precisely be lacking in the social arena. "In the case of psychoanalysis," Gadamer writes, "the patient's suffering and desire to be cured provide the basis for the therapeutic efforts of the doctor who, relying on his authority and not without pressure, attempts to uncover repressed motivations; implied in this relationship is a voluntary subordination of one to the other. In social life, by contrast, reciprocal resistance between opponents is the common practice of all participants." Serious or irreconcilable conflicts between social and political groups are not simply the result of distorted communication, of a temporary disruption of mutual comprehension; rather, they are grounded "in the difference of concrete interests and the discrepancy of experiences." To assume a therapeutic posture in this context betrays a considerable measure of doctrinaire arrogance: the charge that opponents are mentally incompetent or deranged implies a "monopoly of mental rectitude"—a claim which can be viewed as "a special case of derangement." Communicative interaction and mutual understanding between groups presuppose a framework of social solidarity; this framework, however, cannot in turn be derived from communicative exchanges. Regularly, the construction of social solidarity requires concrete political involvement and activity, including the use of the "gentle force" of inducement and persuasion.[26]

In appealing to the force of inducement, Gadamer joins ranks with another critical reviewer, Hans Joachim Giegel, whose arguments, it is true, are prompted by different motivations. While the former is mainly alarmed by the danger of doctrinaire pretense, Giegel fears primarily the paralyzing effects of psychoanalysis on revolutionary militancy. Together with Gadamer, he stresses the common purposive context of the therapeutic relationship. Psychoanalytic therapy, he asserts, is "a type of social interaction in which the assertion of one partner (the doctor) regarding the communicative incompetence of the other (the patient) can be communicatively justified at the end of a process which coincides neither with pure dialogue nor with merely external compulsion." Such a purposive context, however, is regularly absent in social conflicts and especially in revolutionary situations. Although class antagonisms may be described as "systematic disruption of dialogical exchanges," the conflicting groups are not linked by a social consensus. In Giegel's view, "revolutionary struggle is by no means a psychoanalytic treatment writ large." The distinction resides in the different character of interactions. While in psychoanalytic therapy both partners are committed to the liberation from psychic constraints, dominant classes view the liberation of the oppressed typically as a threat to their power; under these circumstances, appeals to a therapeutic consensus merely serve to buttress further the prevailing stratification. A determined pursuit of emancipatory aspirations on the part of the oppressed thus permits only one strategy: "without regard to the will or thought of the ruling class to dismantle those institutional structures which maintain its position." In supporting this strategy, incidentally, Giegel departs from existential hermeneutics also in another respect. Contrary to Gadamer, he regards psychoanalysis less as an overextension than as a curtailment of rational reflection. In transcending the therapeutic linkage, class conflict is not merely propelled by contingent factors but sanctioned by objective standards: standards ultimately deriving from the "emancipatory development of the species."[27]

Habermas' "introductory essay" goes a long way toward meeting the objections of his critics, especially objections arising from the peril of manipulative exploitation. As he recognizes, regular therapeutic relations are protected against abuse by a variety of professional and pragmatic safeguards which are not immediately present in the social domain. To compensate for this deficiency he considers it important to distinguish between at least two types of social application: a therapeutic application in the proper sense of the term and a broader theoretical use for purposes of general explanation. As long as society is held together by a minimal consensus, therapeutic efforts can be directed at the removal of inequities and the restoration of a general sense of legitimacy. In a polarized society, however, in which classes are diametrically opposed, therapy can prevail, if at all, only within camps, between the leadership of an organized group and its mass constituency. In this situation, the psychoanalytic model has at best indirect relevance for society as a whole: by providing a series of theoretical propositions and hypothetical explanations. Such indirect usage, Habermas notes, involves an "objectivistic" restriction of psychoanalysis, but a restriction which is not necessarily illegitimate. Which of the main types of social application is pertinent cannot be predetermined, but depends on prevailing circumstances.[28] In every instance of social antagonism, political leaders have to choose broadly between the strategy of therapeutic interaction and that of stark confrontation. Only in the first case can the leaders' claims and proposals be fully justified and tested: by being freely accepted by all members of society. Even under conditions of direct confrontation, however, the therapeutic model does not completely lose its significance. First of all, the nexus of instruction and acceptance tends to prevail between the leadership and its immediate constituency. More importantly, even an "objectivistic" application to society as a whole is not exempt from the therapeutic test: hypothetical propositions obtain legitimacy in the end only through the anticipation of a general consensus.

Going beyond the confines of the psychoanalytic analogy and drawing again on the mediating function of "discourse," Habermas in the remainder of the essay comments on questions of political conduct and organization, especially as they affect the relationship of theory and praxis. As he observes, clarification of these questions is particularly urgent in our time due to the far-going erosion of social consensus and political legitimacy, an erosion resulting from large-scale industrialization and the effects of class stratification. In this situation, two main tendencies have emerged: on the one hand, a positivist disregard of the issues of legitimacy as such; on the other, an effort to reconstruct society by means of comprehensive political doctrines and centrally controlled party organizations. The question remains, however, how partisan directives can be reconciled with the goal of popular participation and emancipation. According to Habermas, advancement toward this goal presupposes a differentiation between at least three levels of political endeavors: the formulation of social theories; the therapeutic application of such theories for purposes of endorsement and justification; and finally, the domain of appropriate strategies and concrete tactical maneuvers. The first level aims at valid or true propositions, the second at self-knowledge and the experience of truthfulness, the third at prudent decisions; validation requires the possibility of theoretical discourses, self-reflection the conduct of therapeutic exchanges, and commitment the process of practical discursive interaction. An attempt to collapse the three levels is bound to be detrimental to each; a political organization which purports to satisfy all three tasks simultaneously is liable to fulfill none properly. This indiscriminate merger of theory and practice perverts both reflection and practical involvement: "There cannot be a theory which, from the start, insures its potential targets or victims of a historical mission."[29]

The preceding discussion has concentrated on three main lines of critical inquiry and exploration, lines which Habermas himself has recognized as productive and revealing. To be sure, the outlined comments and reservations are far from exhausting the entire range of critical assessments or attacks. Almost without exception, the discussed arguments proceed on a level of attentive exegesis at which sustained mutual interrogation and reciprocal critique are feasible. In the case of several other reviews, however, this feasibility is doubtful; substituting polemical confrontation for interrogation they either hover at the borderline or move resolutely outside the confines of "discourse" (in Habermas' sense of the term). Actually, the number of such reviews seems to be on the increase; not restricted in their appeal to narrow academic circles, they may also be more representative of prevailing sectional or factional attitudes. As previously noted, the translation of Habermas' book coincides with a general decline of the "New Left" movement and, at least in West Germany, with a pronounced strengthening of more orthodox or doctrinaire political postures. Since Habermas' perspective is markedly at odds with these trends, he seems predestined to receive his share of factional vituperation. At this point a few illustrations, originating both from conservative and communist sources, must suffice.

To strict conservatives, of course, Habermas and the entire Frankfurt School have always been anathema; faced with the School's preoccupation with social criticism and dialectical negation,[30] some have tended to salvage the "positive" features of the world by a resort to realist if not positivist postures. In an essay entitled "Interest and Objectivity," Nikolaus Lobkowicz defends objective reality by relying on a perspective which curiously manages to blend Thomistic and positivist ingredients. Against Habermas' linkage of knowledge and interests, Lobkowicz initially invokes the Thomistic dictum that philosophy should aim not at mere opinion but valid truth. In the light of objective insight, Habermas' study appears to his critic as a "thoroughly German product"—more specifically, a product of that "peculiar tradition" of thought which "from Fichte over Hegel and the Young Hegelians" leads to the young Marx, Heidegger, and the Frankfurt School. Habermas' predilection for historical hermeneutics is said to be characteristic of "Hegelians of all kinds"; with Hegel he also shares the ambition to achieve "a comprehensive critical justification of all conditions of possible knowledge"—a claim, however, which is "non-sensical." The "patient positivist" in any case, analyzing such claims, will soon discover that the presumed standard of reflection denotes a lack of precise criteria and "the entire dialectical method merely a license for arbitrary speculation." Habermas' notion of "interest" is castigated primarily for its ambivalence, its merger of empirical and transcendental connotations: while its empirical aspect requires and awaits the test of positive science, its transcendental significance is simply obscure. According to the critic, this dilemma derives from Habermas' misconception both of scientific procedure and theoretical reflection. Although conceding that Habermas' "operationalist" interpretation converges largely with the view of leading contemporary philosophers of science, Lobkowicz chides him for not being "up to date" on positivist theory, citing as authority one less known writer. Regarding reflection, Lobkowicz finds Habermas' stress on self-knowledge and therapeutic reminiscence entirely obnoxious. "It requires little experience to know," he writes, "that people are apt to recognize themselves in the most hair-raising nonsense"—including philosophical "interpretations" denigrating an objective "belief in things."[31]

From the opposite side of the political spectrum, Habermas is also accused of ignoring objective reality: this time the objective conditions of capitalist production with its monopolistic and imperialistic tendencies. In a symposium held in Frankfurt on the occasion of Lenin's centennial anniversary, the entire Frankfurt School was subjected to searching scrutiny "in the light of Marxism." In his contribution to the conference, Erich Hahn attacks as presumptuous Habermas' claim to have corrected Marxism on the basis of recent developments; far from "improving" on orthodox doctrine, he notes, Habermas' arguments are marred by a pronounced "idealistic" bias which impedes a correct comprehension both of historical materialism and of objective social and economic conditions. One of Habermas' central misconceptions is said to consist in his juxtaposition of "labor" and "interaction" and in the notion that, focusing on purely instrumental labor aiming at control over nature, Marx was unable to grasp the dimension of historical and social experience. This notion, in Hahn's view, ignores Marx's stress on the dialectical linkage of "forces" and "relations of production" and his insistence that labor is always an essentially social and historical process. What Habermas accomplishes is merely a dualistic segregation of nature and "ideas," of a "deeconomized history" and an "ahistorical economy," in place of Marx's materialistic-monistic conception according to which "men, in one and the same process of material activity, produce and reproduce the forces and the relations of production." Marx's "unique discovery" resided precisely in the endeavor to explain "the objective character, the materially determined content and necessary condition of original social relations" on the basis of the developmental state of productive forces.[32] The effect of Habermas' idealistic and subjectivistic bias emerges also in his epistemological framework and especially in his predilection for Freud. Instead of concentrating on social reality, Habermas' epistemology reveals universal "cognitive interests" transcending class barriers; in a similar way, the focus on Freud replaces class struggle by general psychological tensions and pathologies. Against the danger of such obfuscation, Hahn urges a "clear, class-based orientation—an orientation which requires a sustained effort to grasp the tenets of Marxism-Leninism."[33]

Similar arguments, but presented in a more elaborate (and sometimes more subtle) manner, can be found in a study by Jürgen Ritsert and Claus Rolshausen entitled *The Conservativism of Critical Theory*. According to the authors, Habermas' views are basically indebted to an idealistic "action theory," while the central categories of historical materialism are either neglected or only rhetorically invoked; preference for intersubjective dialogue and disdain for economic class analysis, however, are emblems of a conservative sociological outlook. In contrast to other social theories, Marxism is not merely a heuristic model or "paradigm" useful for academic inquiry, but maintains a close contact with objective reality and concrete social experience, particularly through the mediating impact of "class consciousness." From this vantage point scientific "revolutions" or changes of paradigms appear intimately linked with the conditions of class struggle; by embracing instead an interactionist framework, Habermas withdraws from this arena into the antinomies of contingent motivations and normative regulations which are the hallmark of "bourgeois" social thought. Apart from other detrimental consequences, action theory transforms the antagonism between labor and capital into a diffuse competition of interests, while political control is seen as a "generalized medium" of regulation and tension management rather than as the expression of class domination. The obfuscation of class rule is enhanced by Habermas' bifurcation of work and interactive communication. Together with Hahn, the authors assume that Marx successfully grounded "symbolic interaction" in the process of economic production—although they concede that "elements of the superstructure" may influence the material economic foundations. The bifurcation of industrialization and distorted communication, by contrast, constitutes an idealistic camouflage which "departs from the confines of political economy in favor of the reconstruction of an apparent class consciousness, without exploring the materialistic nexus between social reality and consciousness." The same camouflage is evident in Habermas' epistemological and cognitive scheme, particularly in the concepts of emancipation and self-reflection. Emancipation, the authors note, appears more as the removal of communication barriers than as a dismantling of concrete domination; liberation thus evaporates into a symbolic exercise, social criticism into a "critique of ideology." Translated into the vocabulary of psychoanalysis, social conflict is reduced to a process of reciprocal self-reflection, class struggle to "large-scale psychotherapy."[34]

It would not be very difficult to multiply examples pointing in the same direction, but little would be gained in the process.[35] There are indications that these examples are merely part of a broader pattern of intellectual developments, a pattern disclosing a considerable hardening of ideological fronts in comparison with the flexibility and unorthodox zest characteristic of the student movement. Despite the current flurry of diplomatic overtures, the experimental outlook fostered by this movement and encouraged by Frankfurt theorists seems in process of succumbing again to the rigid constraints of bloc politics. Although not without ideological roots, Habermas' writings illustrate the search for persuasive new propositions and tenable practical commitments; a central part of this search is the endeavor to rediscover the sinews of democratic legitimacy, under the debris of partisan recriminations. There is a chance that the translations of his writings will encounter an environment more conducive to this endeavor; clearly the student rebellion should be able to produce alternative outcomes apart from a return to doctrinaire certitude and partisan soliloquies. Perhaps due to a longer tradition of openness, the New World may prove more hospitable to the notion of an "unfinished dialectic." While not shirking human responsibility for social conditions, such a dialectic remains alert to the hazards and ambiguities of all social undertakings, to the fact that politics is not so much a puzzle to be solved by technical blueprints but a continuous practical challenge. Equally removed from self-assurance and despair, this view involves that political experience, in Merleau-Ponty's words, is "no longer a laboratory test but a trial of life." The notion of an open dialectic is also compatible with the lessons of psychoanalysis. According to one of Freud's favorite expressions, "one must learn to bear some portion of uncertainty."[36]

11. Toward a Critical Reconstruction of Ethics and Politics

As HAS BEEN FREQUENTLY NOTED, our age is marked by a peculiar mixture of progress and despair. The scientific revolution has produced a "knowledge explosion" of unheard-of proportions; this advance, however, is not matched by a corresponding clarification of standards of conduct. Actually, an inverse relationship can be detected between knowledge and purpose: to the extent that science has sharpened and perfected the instruments of rational analysis, our aptitude for practical moral reasoning seems to have progressively atrophied. Although not of recent origin, the dilemma has acquired an unsettling dimension in our time. While contemporary technology provides the means both for alleviating suffering on a large scale and for engineering a nuclear holocaust, the criteria for making the choice appear hopelessly confused or obscure.[1] The dilemma presents itself with particular acuteness in Western industrial societies. In fact, the conflict between knowledge and purposive action can be viewed as the touchstone of "pluralistic liberalism"—a regime marked by the juxtaposition of scientific objectivity and subjective whim, abstract rules and private fancy. Both socio-economic and philosophical developments in our century have conspired to intensify the antinomies endemic in the liberal-pluralist model. In the words of one observer, the "incongruity of contemporary thought" consists in the fact that at the very time when moral issues such as war and racial segregation confront people with dramatic vehemence, "ethical skepticism is more influential, probably, than it has ever been."[2]

Although adequate as a rough approximation, the preceding diagnosis is over-simplified in a number of ways. First of all, the sway of ethical relativism has not been uncontested; on the contrary, the challenge of moral confusion has engendered a widespread willingness to embrace unshakable convictions. Certainly no shortage of comprehensive world views and social panaceas has plagued our century. In countering the threat of relativism, absolute doctrines of all kinds have promised quick relief from moral anguish and intellectual uncertainty. Prominent among them have been orthodox Marxism, speculative intuitionism, and traditional natural-law teachings—not to mention naturalistic and racial conceptions. Science and technology themselves have occasionally functioned as social ideologies by suggesting an equal competence to resolve both empirical and purposive issues. Despite their apparent antagonism, there is an underlying affinity between relativist and absolutist perspectives. Protagonists of absolute views have been notoriously impatient with opponents and have shown little inclination to justify their tenets by convincing or plausible arguments; typically, their endeavors have been consumed with preaching to the faithful. By projecting toward nonbelievers the posture of idiosyncratic creeds, absolutist claims thus have tended to compound and corroborate the prevailing ethical fragmentation.

The initial assessment, however, is simplified in another, more significant respect. Evidence mounts that the field of purposive action is no longer monopolized today either by agnostics or missionaries. Without fanfare, sustained efforts have been under way for some time to rescue moral and political argument from the stranglehold of dogma and subjective whim. The impulse of this orientation can be described as "critical" in a broad sense: apart from scrutinizing prevailing doctrines or theoretical positions, the ambition of its supporters is to provide a critical account of their own undertaking in order to lay a tenable foundation for moral discourse. Above all, attention is focused not only at the normative level strictly speaking, but also at "metaethical" concerns: the goal is not simply (or not primarily) to articulate moral injunctions, but to clarify the manner in which normative judgments can be justified. In the present chapter I wish to discuss a recent (and, in my view, particularly instructive) initiative pointing in this direction: an approach originating in, or at least loosely affiliated with the Frankfurt School.[3] The involvement of Frankfurt theorists in the domain of normative reconstruction is hardly surprising or fortuitous; committed since its inception to the standard of a "critical theory," the school was bound to be drawn, sooner or later, into the debate concerning the critical justification of norms. In the following presentation I shall try to delineate this particular initiative in successive steps. In order to provide a background for the issues at stake, an attempt is made first of all to sketch a panorama or historical overview of recent developments in the field of ethical theory. The subsequent section outlines the perspective of critical theory by focusing on the arguments of Karl-Otto Apel, a philosopher presently active at the University of Frankfurt and broadly sympathetic to the critical program inaugurated by Max Horkheimer and Theodor W. Adorno.

I

Contemporary ethical theory is a multi-layered enterprise, marked by considerable complexity. A major distinction commonly made is between "normative" ethics and "metaethical" theory, between the formulation of standards of moral and political conduct and inquiry into the character or meaning of ethical propositions and the possibility of their justification.

In our century, philosophical interest has primarily (although not exclusively) been concentrated on metaethical issues; customarily two major perspectives are distinguished in this domain: "cognitivism" and "noncognitivism." According to the former position, moral statements are informative assertions about the world or states of affairs and thus can be shown (or claimed) to be either true or false; according to the second view, by contrast, such statements are devoid of informative content, thus lack cognitive status and have no relationship to truth or falsehood. Complexity does not end with this bifurcation but extends into the opposing camps. Although the delineation of noncognitivism arouses little dispute, opinions and nomenclature differ with regard to the proper ordering of cognitivist schools. While some writers use labels like "objectivism" and "subjectivism," others prefer to talk about "naturalism," "nonnaturalism" and "supernaturalism." In his *Moral Principles in Political Philosophy*, Felix Oppenheim expounds a classification of cognitivism which is instructive and sufficiently detailed for present purposes. He distinguishes first of all between "naturalists" and "intuitionists": the former holding that ethical propositions are subject to the verification procedures of empirical science; the latter ascribing to ethical terms special "nonnatural" properties amenable to non-empirical inspection. He further differentiates among intuitionists on the basis of whether ethical knowledge is claimed to be derived from moral, religious, or rational insights; naturalists, in turn, are said to rely either on empirical generalizations, teleological notions or descriptive definitions applied to empirical facts—with "subjectivism" or the thesis that goodness designates the empirical preferences of a group being the major type in the last category. Oppenheim also clarifies the place of natural-law theories in his scheme: by asserting that normative principles are inherent in the basic order of nature, such theories either alternately or simultaneously assume intuitionist and naturalist postures.[4]

Clearly, the preceding divisions and labels are neither comprehensive nor timeless. To a large extent, the sketched arrangement reflects the imprint of logical positivism, with its stress on the dichotomies of logical analysis and empirical research, factual assertions and "value" judgments. With the exception of intuitionists, advocates of both cognitivism and noncognitivism can readily agree on the same positivist paradigm: while to the former normative statements are factual and hence demonstrable, the latter view the same statements as nondemonstrable precisely because they are not factual. Little imagination is required to see that the two positions do not necessarily exhaust available alternatives, for, one can ask, might moral statements not be amenable to rational justification without having the cognitive status of informative propositions? Actually, over a variety of paths, philosophical inquiries during recent decades have been moving precisely in this direction; by means of a more attentive and critical scrutiny of normative sentences, philosophers of different backgrounds have progressively uncovered the autonomy and special character of moral discourse. At least in this domain it is possible to detect a gradual rapprochement of Anglo-American and Continental European schools of thought; proceeding from vastly different, perhaps opposite intellectual traditions, trends in both areas point toward a revival of the classical dimension of "practical" thought, in contradistinction to theoretical analysis and technical implementation.[5] Grossly simplified, the difference between the two backgrounds can be described as that between skepsis and absolutism: while the Anglo-American scene has been dominated by noncognitivists and cognitive naturalists, Continental thought has been prolific in the articulation of broadly intuitive vistas. As previously indicated, the two outlooks are not entirely incompatible; rephrasing the affinity, one might say that both tend to neglect intersubjective relations. While absolute intuitionists rely on personal evidence or introspection, positivists base their case either on subjective exclamations or on solitary scientific experiments. To this extent, the recovery of practical reasoning signifies the strengthening of intersubjective dialogue in lieu of cognitivist or noncognitivist soliloquies.

In order to illustrate the mentioned rapprochement, I shall first trace developments on the Anglo-American side and then turn to the European context. Wittgenstein's *Tractatus Logico-Philosophicus* may serve as an appropriate starting point since the book was widely regarded as the Bible of early logical positivism. Reducing meaningful statements to syllogisms or factual assertions, the author affirmed at the time that "there can be no ethical propositions." Literally interpreted, the dictum imposed a virtual ban on moral theorizing; one should note, however, that the ban did not necessarily coincide with ethical relativism. At least in Wittgenstein's case, the injunction seemed to reflect a "negative ethics" and even "negative theology"—a determination to shield ultimate standards from the profanity of ordinary discourse.[6] Few of his followers and sympathizers preserved Wittgenstein's moral rigor, his peculiar blend of skepsis and absolutism; all, however, accepted one important tenet implicit in the *Tractatus* and similar writings of the period: the distinction between logical and empirical statements and, correspondingly, between "object language" and analytical "metalanguage." Consistently applied to the moral domain, the distinction was translated into the dichotomy between normative ethics and metaethics—the former concerned with the promulgation of particular standards, the latter dedicated to precise and ethically neutral analysis of normative statements. On the level of metaethical inquiry, positivists bent on breaking Wittgenstein's silence were able to adopt a variety of formulations, without abandoning the basic premise of the *Tractatus*. Some, like Alfred Ayer, maintained that moral phrases were purely emotive and noncognitive exercises expressing the feelings or sentiments of the speaker; others attributed to them the significance of imperatives or commands designed to influence the behavior of listeners. Theorists unwilling to embrace either emotive or imperativist doctrines (or a combination of the two) were compelled to demonstrate that normative statements were reducible to empirical assertions; attempts of this kind led to different versions of cognitive naturalism—primarily to claims that moral phrases were factual reports on the psychological attitudes or interests of an individual or statistical generalizations of widely held dispositions.[7]

Doctrines of this type, at least in undiluted form, no longer find much acclaim among Anglo-American philosophers; during the postwar period, the rigidity of logical positivism has progressively given way to a more subtle scrutiny of the nuances of moral discourse. To a large extent, the change was due to the labors of the "ordinary language" movement, with its center in the Oxford School. Curiously, Wittgenstein—this time his later work—played again an important role in the reorientation. "If language is to be a means of communication," his *Philosophical Investigations* observe, "there must be agreement not only in definitions, but also (queer as this may sound) in judgments."[8] Linguistic analysts have made significant strides toward a more critical assessment of ethics; above all their inquiries restored the dimension of justification to moral discourse. Emulating Wittgenstein's explication of "language games" and of their relationship to social life styles, Oxford theorists have been careful in delineating the ways in which moral terms are used in everyday situations; instead of clinging to a set of preconceived categories, they explored the different shades of meaning which words or phrases assume in varying contexts. In this process, their endeavors disclosed the autonomous status enjoyed by normative statements in many instances, a status not simply convertible into that of factual claims or verbal exclamations; they also revealed the role played by rational argument in attempts to justify moral judgments. Despite its contributions, however, the Oxford program was not free of shortcomings or ambiguities. Continuing the legacy of logical positivism, many theorists maintained the bifurcation of normative standards and neutral analysis or at least failed to reexamine the relationship in the light of their own new assumptions. More important, in discussing the issue of justification, their writings frequently left it unclear whether moral reasoning meant simply the kind actually employed in a given community or whether it was thought to be endowed with intrinsic validity.

The ambivalent character of the ordinary language approach can readily be discerned in two of the pioneering studies in the field of morals: Stephen Toulmin's *Reason in Ethics* and Kurt Baier's *The Moral Point of View*. The two studies constituted a decisive advance over the narrow formulas of the preceding era; departing from the positivist classification of statements, both authors emphasized the aspect of practical reasoning and deliberation in moral discourse. Toulmin's book launched a broadside attack on three traditional metaethical perspectives: intuitionism, psychological subjectivism, and the imperative approach; in a similar manner Baier denounced both cognitivist and noncognitivist theories of the past for misrepresenting the actual thrust of moral arguments. In lieu of the criticized doctrines, Toulmin's study alerted the reader to the complexity of everyday dialogue and especially to the "logic of moral reasoning," while Baier explored what kinds of arguments could function as "good reasons" in support of normative judgments. Similarities of this kind, however, cannot conceal an underlying divergence. Toulmin's basic ambition was to show how moral discourse is commonly conducted and what sort of reasoning is normally employed by participants in this context; as he stated in the concluding section, his aim was chiefly to provide "a descriptive account of the function of ethical concepts." Moreover, his inquiry was largely limited to moral questions arising within a given moral tradi-

tion or within the confines of accepted community standards. Once the
focus was shifted outside this domain, from particular actions to social
practices at large, the criterion of choice in his view had to be largely
"a private one"—unless recourse was taken to the "fecundity" or beneficial results of the choice, such as its conduciveness to reduced suffering. In this respect at least, his presentation tended to slip back into
the positivist fact-value scheme and, more broadly, into the liberal-
pluralist paradigm. The thrust of Baier's study pointed in a different
direction: his intention was not merely to portray actual discourse but
to show the intrinsic validity of moral claims—although his discussion
was probably not always commensurate with this task. "The very
raison d'être of a morality," he noted at one point, "is to yield reasons
which overrule the reasons of self-interest in those cases when everyone's following self-interest would be harmful to everyone. Hence
moral reasons are superior to all others."[9]

The indicated divergence between the two studies foreshadowed
a broader controversy which was only beginning to emerge at the
time and which since then has gained a central place in metaethical
discussions: the controversy between "descriptivism" and "prescriptivism." Dedicated to the investigation of ordinary discourse, Oxford
theorists in preponderant numbers have concluded that the chief and
perhaps only task of philosophical analysis is to provide a descriptive
account of various language games, including the mode of moral reasoning; convictions of this type have fostered a widely shared outlook
of linguistic empiricism (or quasi-empiricism) concerned with portraying the broad range of moral experience.[10] Normative statements from
this perspective are always part of an ongoing social process, a context
which imposes severe limitations on arbitrary individual choice, thus
greatly diminishing the relevance of the positivist fact-value dichotomy. Writers of this persuasion differ in regard to specific formulations
and especially in their assessment of the fact-value issue. According to
some, normative statements can always be reduced to factual assertions—provided the relevant "facts" are properly defined. Thus, in John
R. Searle's view, moral questions normally arise within the confines of
"institutional facts" from which standards of conduct can typically be
derived. According to others, norms are so deeply enmeshed in actual
social experience that the segregation of facts and values becomes a
hopeless task. In this manner, relying on the late Wittgenstein, Peter
Winch has been led to argue that a social group is essentially a moral
community. Similarly, Geoffrey J. Warnock has tried to show that, despite the diversity of individual preferences, the social context furnishes criteria for what a person can "understandably" claim or want.

In a study entitled *Moral Reasoning*, R. W. Beardsmore in turn has defended the proposition that, to be intelligible, judgments purporting to be moral have to invoke a "range of concepts" normally or traditionally related to virtue or vice. Most descriptivists, one should add, tend to concur on the intricate linkage of moral beliefs and human wants or needs (although there is dispute as to which of the elements can claim priority).[11]

As many critics have pointed out, the simplicity of the descriptive approach is in many respects deceptive. First of all, the appeal to customary practices notoriously breaks down in case of competing practices or where communal standards are obscure. Thus, Searle concedes the intervention of arbitrary choice at least in the establishment of "institutional facts" or in case of conflicting obligations. Similarly, Alasdair MacIntyre, noting the progressive disintegration of traditional rules, admits that "each of us therefore has to choose both with whom we wish to be morally bound and by what ends, rules, and virtues we wish to be guided"—although, in his view, "our social past determines that each of us has some vocabulary with which to frame and to make his choice." Moreover, on the assumption of self-contained language games, description seems to be a more complex task than Oxford theorists pretend. As Ernest Gellner and others have argued, the accounts of moral reasoning offered by leading representatives are themselves imbued with peculiar Anglo-Saxon mores, especially with the idiom of Oxford academics.[12] Above all, even granting neutrality, the descriptive enterprise seems to presuppose an effort of philosophical detachment—a step not covered by the parameters of everyday discourse. For these and other reasons, descriptivism has for some time been under attack from a perspective which insists on the decisional element in moral choice and on the basic discrepancy between factual and evaluational statements. According to Richard M. Hare, the leading spokesman of this perspective, moral arguments are characterized by "three most important" traits: first, although commonly invoking factual support, they involve a prescriptive judgment; second, they are distinguished from simple commands by their claim to universal validity; last, moral thinking is amenable to rational elucidation, mainly because consistency can obtain not only in syllogisms or between factual assertions, but also between prescriptive judgments. On this view, moral beliefs may be contingently related to, but cannot be derived from factual wants or interests.[13]

There can be little doubt that Hare's writings have greatly enlivened moral philosophy in our time. Nevertheless, some points in his argument are ambiguous or in need of clarification. First of all, the aspiration of moral judgments to universal validity seems to imply chiefly the need for formal rules—a requirement which presumably can be satisfied by a variety of substantive standards (provided each standard meets the test of consistency). More crucially, not only the choice of particular norms but the adoption of the moral perspective itself, including Hare's metaethical scheme, appears to depend on a prior choice or commitment (although this point is either glossed over or treated as self-evident). To bring these latent decisional features out into the open is one of the central ambitions of Karl R. Popper and his school of "critical rationalism." According to Popper and his followers, linguistic analysis has produced a novel situation which is not fully appreciated by descriptivists: once attention is focused on ongoing language games, descriptive accounts become submerged in the same context of discourse, thus losing their claim to independent analytical status. If the analytical goal is to be preserved, descriptivism has to be sacrificed since every portrayal of normative statements presupposes a prior delineation of the "moral" domain. In either case, one of the last strongholds of logical positivism—the juxtaposition of normative standards and metaethical neutrality—is bound to crumble or at least be seriously weakened. Pursuing this line of argument Hans Albert, a Continental exponent of the school, has advocated adoption of a plurality of analytical approaches paralleling the pluralism of normative standards. Metaethical theories, in his view, perform a purely heuristic function comparable to the role of hypothetical models in scientific inquiry; both types of frameworks are explanatory schemes inspired by a particular outlook and guided by the choice of criteria of relevance. Precisely because of their nonneutral character, such frameworks encourage critical evaluation and comparison; submitted as tentative proposals, moreover, they are subject to revision in the light of further experience. As Albert adds, even the adoption of the critical-rationalistic perspective presupposes a commitment or "decision" in favor of rationality—a commitment which cannot further be justified by rational argument, except to those willing to take the same step.[14]

As the last statement indicates, Popper's decisionism implies a definite curtailment of the range of rational discussion; despite the critique of logical positivism, the basic positivist dilemma seems to return on a new level: in the conflict between choice and factual experience. It is against the competing backgrounds of descriptivism and decisionism that one has to view a new approach recently formulated by a group of philosophers centered at Erlangen. The approach is particularly significant in the present context since it constitutes, in a sense, a meeting ground between Anglo-American and Continental developments; it also provides an important impulse to the arguments of Frankfurt theorists. Paul Lorenzen, the leading representative of the group, seems peculiarly predestined for such rapprochement, having taught at both American and German universities. Deviating from linguistic empiricism as well as prescriptive formalism, Lorenzen in *Normative Logic and Ethics* attempts a critical "reconstruction" of ordinary, including moral, language; by placing himself within the context of everyday discourse and by dissecting and reassembling sentence patterns, he seeks to lay a tenable foundation of logical reasoning and of practical philosophy broadly conceived.[15] Of course, his endeavor conflicts with both cognitivist and noncognitivist postures. While emotivism muffles rational clarification, cognitivist doctrines typically restrict the significance of normative statements. Although important aspects of moral discourse are amenable to the true-false criterion, practical philosophy deals not only with theoretical "truth" or even primarily with it but rather "with the justification of norms." Moral argument, in Lorenzen's view, does not occur in a vacuum; rather, it proceeds within the confines of already accepted norms and social customs. The central task of moral philosophy, therefore, is to elucidate the basis of normative standards and the reasons for their acceptance.

Such an effort cannot be entirely a descriptive enterprise since description might simply mirror "uncritically accepted fashions or traditions, including the tradition of natural language." Every act of reasoning, whether of the theoretical or the practical-moral variety, implies an attempt to overcome subjective bias or short-sightedness—an attempt which does not involve a leap into absolute knowledge but simply a reduction of idiosyncratic delusions.[16] Translating this implicit thrust into explicit normative language, Lorenzen stipulates the "transcendence of subjectivity" or the aim of "transsubjectivity" as the first basic principle or "supernorm" of moral experience. As he explains, transsubjectivity in this context "is not a fact, but it is not a postulate either"; rather, it is "simply a term characterizing that activity in which we are always already involved if we begin to reason at all." To a considerable degree, the mentioned supernorm resembles Kant's "categorical imperative" and Hare's universal rule by establishing primarily a formal standard for evaluating conduct. Like Hare's rule, Lorenzen's principle is not simply derived from human wants; instead, it is meant as a general benchmark for the assessment of such wants. However, to arrive at a choice in concrete situations, formal ethics has to be supplemented by a substantive criterion permitting the differentiation between legitimate (or justifiable) and illegitimate claims. In order to find such a criterion, Lorenzen proposes inquiry into the genesis of given interests, an inquiry aiming not so much at the deduction of individual instances from abstract laws as at an "understanding" of the background and cultural meaning of human wants. Expressed in normative terms, the "moral principle" of transsubjectivity needs to be corroborated by a second supernorm: a "cultural principle" enjoining the genetic or "dialectical" reconstruction of prevailing standards and aspirations. Genetic exploration of this type is not designed merely to satisfy historical curiosity; rather, like hermeneutical exegesis, it contributes to the growth of moral insight and sensitivity. Regarding the justification of the supernorms themselves, Lorenzen adds that they are "not arbitrary" stipulations but "the only principles which make 'reasonable' decisions possible"—although, at another point, he avows his inability "to 'justify' these principles, since the term 'justification' makes sense only after one has accepted such principles."[17]

Turning now to the Continental European context, I shall try to indicate developments pointing in the direction of a similarly critical clarification. Broadly speaking, Continental thought has been characterized in our century by a strong bent toward speculative vistas and encompassing world-views; this statement, to be sure, has to be qualified immediately by the reminder that this bent has neither enjoyed complete predominance in Europe nor is it entirely absent from the Anglo-American scene. The major perspectives I wish to review briefly are the natural-law doctrine, phenomenology, and Marxism. While Marxism, at least in its "orthodox" version, can be described as a type of cognitive naturalism, and while phenomenology is wedded to intuitive evidence, the first position by and large constitutes a merger of intuitive and naturalistic ingredients. Among the three positions, natural-law theory has probably been least flexible or least willing to face counter-arguments; frequently linked with theological teachings, its tenets have largely been immune from critical scrutiny. While claiming to possess valid truth, proponents have been reluctant to engage in the task of justification.[18] Especially in its theological versions, natural-law thinking has tended to transform ethical rules into divine commandments—a position criticized already in Plato's *Eutyphro*. The same result, however, can obtain even in the absence of religious overtones; where classical writers are invoked as rigid authorities, their views are liable to be transformed into semidivine pronouncements.[19] Nevertheless, there are signs that intellectual self-enclosure is no longer the order of the day. Changes in religious climate have produced a weariness of ponderous dogmas. More important, religious natural-law advocates have come to be receptive to contemporary empirical findings, while the philosophical turn to practical questions has encouraged a more attentive reconsideration of the Aristotelian legacy.[20]

Intuitionism in the strict sense is linked in our time primarily with the Continental phenomenological movement—although subdued types of intuitive arguments have also been formulated elsewhere.[21] While the founder of modern phenomenology, Edmund Husserl, preferred to concentrate attention on the act of evaluation, some of his early followers proceeded from this modest level to the construction of a scheme of substantive ethics grounded in intuitive experience. Probably the most ambitious effort in this direction was undertaken by Max Scheler whose writings defended the possibility of a direct, nonrational perception of absolute values or norms; moral standards in his view were objective "essences" accessible to the "higher reaches of emotional life." A similar outlook, but with an even greater stress on apodictic insight, was articulated by Nicolai Hartmann who portrayed values as "objects of emotional intuition."[22] In the meantime, the attractiveness of such schemes has greatly declined, even among phenomenologists. Under the influence of Husserl's later focus on the "life-world," phenomenological inquiry has increasingly turned to an exploration of the social or intersubjective parameters of experience; to this extent, simple intuition has tended to give way to "hermeneutical" endeavors—interpretive efforts to decode the meaning both of historical texts and dialogical exchanges. Moreover, the legacy of "bracketing"—a method designed to suspend the supposed reality of findings—has encouraged a more critical approach to claims of immediate personal evidence. To some extent, parallel developments are noticeable in regard to Heidegger's existential phenomenology—provided the synthesis of contemplation and existential experience peculiar to his outlook is explicated in the direction of an intersubjective praxis transcending technological domination and manipulation.[23]

The effects of these trends in the moral domain have been intriguing although by no means uniform. Particularly significant for present purposes are contemporary elaborations of a phenomenological or hermeneutical ethics. Once the interpreter is seen as participant in an ongoing dialogue both with past generations and with his contemporaries and once it is realized that this dialogue is animated, at least partially, by a moral purpose, hermeneutics can readily be associated with the heritage of practical philosophy. The implications of this affiliation, however, are not free of ambiguity. Given the embeddedness of human experience in a social life-world permeated by moral values, it is possible to find the interpreter's task chiefly in the portrayal and elucidation of inherited or prevailing community standards; to this extent, recent investigations have fostered the emergence of a descriptive phenomenology or hermeneutics roughly comparable to linguistic empiricism.[24] This outcome, to be sure, is far from unchallenged. On the opposite end of the ethical spectrum, some existentialist writers have advocated a theory of free human choice completely oblivious to surrounding circumstances. Drawing on decisionist features in Heidegger's *Being and Time,* Jean-Paul Sartre in some of his early writings expounded a doctrine of virtually blind, individual commitment—although his stress on activism seemed to be nurtured by a concealed apodictic vision. Actually, even prior to his turn to Marxism, Sartre's arguments were scarcely an endorsement of pure emotivism. At least to the extent that the individual was always supposed to choose "for mankind," the stress on commitment carried overtones of a universal prescriptivism. Perhaps, by combining this universal element with the notions of authenticity and "bad faith," it is possible to lay a broader basis for existentialist ethics.[25] However this may be, it seems fair to say that the relationship between descriptive and prescriptive trends remains a significant and unresolved issue in contemporary phenomenology and hermeneutics.

Despite impressive obstacles, recent Marxist thought has been characterized by considerable ferment and experimentation. As is well known, orthodox Marxism has always been averse to ethical considerations—not entirely without reason since the appeal to general principles easily serves as a screen camouflaging particular interests and ambitions. In a society marked by gross disparities of status and opportunities, the pretense of a common moral bond heaps insult together with injury on the disfavored. Nevertheless, the neglect of ethics carries a price: the danger that human aspirations are sacrificed to a precharted historical process (and, indirectly, to a party elite); moreover, the denigration of reflection in favor of material infrastructures jeopardizes Marxism's own claim to general validity. A leading exponent of the orthodox position was Leon Trotsky; denouncing theories of a "classless" morality as "bourgeois" maneuvers, he persistently stressed class struggle and proletarian victory as prerequisites for moral discourse. To a large extent his views were the outgrowth of a controversy occupying Marxist intellectuals around the turn of the century—a controversy which, under the label "Kant versus cant," pitted absolute imperatives against partisan expediency. Trotsky's outlook has left its imprint on official communist hierarchies and party strategists; it also continues to permeate neo-orthodox arguments in our time.[26] Yet, orthodoxy is far from uncontested in the Marxist camp. Both in Western and Eastern

Europe, materialistic naturalism has been challenged by a renewed concern with standards of human conduct. Leading among insurgent positions are existentialist (or quasi-existentialist) assertions of human choice, together with explorations of a prescriptive metaethics.[27] As a result of these initiatives, Marxist thinking not surprisingly has become preoccupied both with the issue of justification and with the problem of linking prescriptive norms with material conditions. It is precisely at this point that Frankfurt theorists enter the debate with the intent of contributing to a critical reconstruction of ethics and politics.

II

Although committed since its inception to the program of a "critical" theory, the Frankfurt School has long been reticent to delve into the scrutiny of normative questions. In a sense, this delay reflects the slow maturation of the adopted perspective. While trenchant in dissecting opposing views, Frankfurt theorists only gradually assumed the burden of critically assessing their own premises. Yet, at least incipiently, the thrust of the school's outlook was always critical in a comprehensive manner. From the beginning, its posture implied a rejection of positivistic Marxism, with its tendency to submerge human action in a historical development governed by inscrutable laws. More broadly, the school's program was in conflict with all types of cognitivist schemes pretending to deduce human goals from a natural or intuited set of conditions. By highlighting the tension or incongruity between individual choice and society or the world at large, adherents of the program seemed predestined to enter into a critical review of purposive issues. Efforts in this direction are particularly prominent in the writings of Jürgen Habermas. In one of his initial publications, the "public" domain of modern social life was portrayed as an arena of practical discourse devoted to the clarification of common purposes—a domain increasingly threatened in advanced industrial societies by managerial manipulation. In a similar vein, his *Theory and Practice* presented a broad historical overview of the progressive disintegration of practical argument under the onslaught of scientific and technological rationality. Delineating the pervasive effects of positivism, the study attacked both cognitivist and noncognitivist ethical doctrines: the former represented by attempts to deduce standards of action from scientific analysis, the latter by the abdication of reason in favor of blind commitments. More recently, Habermas has attempted to outline standards of social conduct by means of a critical reconstruction of inter-subjective communication and through the elaboration of a complex theory of nonrepressive discourse and "ideal speech" situations—situations depending on the development of the "communicative competence" of all participants.[28]

In the present context I would like to discuss briefly parallel arguments which have been advanced by Karl-Otto Apel, a philosopher whose thinking broadly concurs with the Frankfurt perspective. Apel's outlook, it is true, is not tied to any particular school, but has been shaped by a great variety of intellectual currents; in fact, one of his distinctive traits is his thorough familiarity with both Continental and Anglo-American trends. In numerous essays, Apel has explored the Continental legacy of dialectical and existential thought as represented chiefly by Hegel, Marx, and Heidegger; the development of linguistic philosophy from logical positivism over Wittgenstein to ordinary language analysis; and the open as well as subterranean linkages between these vantage points. One of his most notable and widely heralded accomplishments has been a German edition of Peirce's writings, published with lengthy introductory comments disclosing the relevance of Peirce's thought for contemporary epistemology and philosophy of science.[29] Given this background, it is hardly surprising that Apel should participate in current efforts aiming at a critical re-examination of ethics and politics—efforts which, as previously noted, can be viewed as a major bridge between Continental and Anglo-American philosophical traditions.

Although his views on normative issues can be gleaned from several of his publications, I wish to concentrate for present purposes mainly on his essay entitled "The Apriori of Communication and the Foundation of Ethics."[30] The essay starts from the glaring discrepancy endemic to our age of "scientific revolution": the discrepancy between the urgent need for moral standards to harness man's growing technological prowess and the inability of scientific rationality to provide such standards. On the one hand, the effects of a rampant technology have long ceased to be of merely local concern. While unchecked industrial expansion increasingly erodes man's ecological habitat, military exploitation of technological advances threatens human survival on a global scale. The knowledge explosion of our time is not matched, on the other hand, by a comparable growth of moral sensitivity: although prolific in discoveries and analytical insights, scientific research tends to be mute on questions of purpose. In the normative domain, the contemporary dilemma has given rise primarily to two conflicting responses: "absolutist" doctrines offering full-fledged world-views for practical guidance, and "relativist" perspectives abandoning moral issues to private choice. Among the former, Apel concentrates chiefly on orthodox Marxist thought. As he recognizes, Marxism has particular significance in our time because of its vision of a global society sustained by unconstrained moral agents. In orthodox Communist teachings, however, the road toward this goal is usually depicted as a preordained destiny amenable to scientific calculation, with the result that normative questions are submerged in a comprehensive explanatory scheme supposedly congruent with objective reality. This pretense of a scientific teleology is countered, at the opposite end of the spectrum, by the relativist posture of "pluralist liberalism," with its simultaneous insistence on scientific neutrality and arbitrary individual commitment. According to Apel, science and commitment in this outlook are not so much antithetical as complementary; the much-belabored antagonism between logical positivism and voluntaristic existentialism emerges against this background as a simple division of labor. In a long-range historical perspective, the division can be viewed as present-day adaptation of the traditional dichotomy of state and society, public and private domains; the two elements, however, are no longer of equal weight. Given the predominance of science and technology, private choice is increasingly transformed into an insignificant mental reservation—with the consequence that the distance between liberal and Communist models is progressively reduced.

The aim of the essay is to chart a path between these models, a path avoiding the pitfalls of both dogmatism and private whim. In approaching this aim, Apel discusses two major strategies or lines of argument: the strategies of linguistic or phenomenological descriptivism and of critical reconstruction. As he tries to show, the first strategy—despite the cogency of some of its central premises—cannot provide a sufficient account of normative discourse and thus needs to be corrected or at least supplemented by the second approach. Descriptivism in its various forms challenges one of the main pillars of the liberal-pluralist model: the distinction between facts and values, between normative and empirical statements. In the view of both hermeneutics and ordinary language theory, normative aspirations form an intrinsic part of the life-world of everyday experience, a life-world which inevitably slips through the liberal bifurcation. This outlook, Apel notes, is based on a crucial philosophical premise or insight: the premise of the "a priori of communication," of the embeddedness of all human thought in language and ordinary discourse. The premise, he adds, has distinct ramifications in such disciplines as the humanities and the social sciences; given their preoccupation with a subject matter permeated by moral concerns, inquiry in these disciplines requires to a large extent understanding of intentional conduct and an involvement of the observer in the investigated life-world. The notion of the communicative a priori stands in sharp contrast to all "monological" or solipsistic types of investigation according to which knowledge is the result of isolated observation and analysis. In the same manner, the thesis conflicts with the rigid segregation between natural and artificial languages, and especially between normative theory and neutral meta-ethics—a segregation championed tenaciously by logical positivism. Even Popper and his followers do not seem to be fully attentive to the implications of the thesis; although stressing the normative presuppositions of theoretical constructs, "critical rationalism" ascribes the selection of approaches to independent individual judgment removed from communicative bonds.

According to Apel, however, the significance of the sketched thesis needs to be carefully assessed. As he observes, the conception of the communicative a priori is valid only if language is viewed as a broad, "quasi-transcendental" matrix of thought and communication is seen as an open-ended process amenable to critical, normative evaluation. Difficulties arise when transcendental parameters are replaced by contingent boundaries and where language patterns are congealed into an insurpassable ontological framework. Instead of relying on normative premises, everyday discourse in this case appears as the sole standard of moral conduct. Such congealment, in Apel's view, can be detected primarily in linguistic descriptivism or empiricism. As initiated by Wittgenstein, ordinary language analysis regularly concentrates on the description of ongoing "language games" which are simultaneously conceived as "life-forms"—without exploring the communicative relationship between observer and investigated practices. Treated as self-enclosed factual domains, language games in this perspective are exempt from critical scrutiny. A similar bent toward self-enclosure is noticeable in descriptive phenomenology and hermeneutics. Where the decoding of meaning is seen as a contingent historical event or experience, the "hermeneutic circle" readily turns into a confining maze and moral judgment into a synonym for habit. Against empirical shortcuts of this type, Apel insists on the transcendental horizons of hermeneutics; ordinary language, he writes, "is insurmountable only in the sense that it constitutes the vehicle—the only available vehicle—for anticipating and implementing the normative goal of consensus."[31]

Several reasons are cited by Apel to corroborate his opposition to descriptivism. First of all, the focus on ordinary language as a self-sufficient dimension neglects the impact of extralinguistic factors on the human life-world. Together with Habermas, Apel notes the modifications and deformations of communicative interaction produced by socio-economic infrastructures and political domination. In our time, technology exerts a particularly pervasive influence on everyday life patterns, an influence which cannot easily be reconciled with customary discourse; in fact, the moral dilemma of our time derives largely from the excess of analytical capacities over the prevailing reservoir of moral sensitivity. At least equally important is another objection which relates to the core of moral discourse: by restricting argument to everyday communication, descriptivism short-circuits or contracts the justification of norms. An effort to justify standards, Apel argues, presupposes at least the tentative distinction between empirical and evaluative statements and the treatment of established norms as factual claims in need of rational support. The task of rational scrutiny requires a detachment or critical distance of the observer from prevailing practices, a detachment akin to the phenomenological "bracketing" of reality. By means of such disengagement, the observer is able to assume an attitude of temporary "neutrality" toward norms and thus to undertake an unbiased assessment of competing arguments. This goal of critical assessment furnishes a limited warrant for independent metaethical discourse. In Apel's words: "The thesis of metaethical neutrality derives its validity ultimately from this purpose. Its significance thus resides not in the endeavor of analytical philosophy to abandon normative ethics, but rather in the radicalization of the philosophical demand for an undogmatic justification of standards."[32] Contrary to a Cartesian or even Husserlian method of detachment, however, the scrutiny proposed by Apel is not a solitary venture. Implicit in this proposal is the challenge to discover criteria of critical judgment without relinquishing the matrix of intersubjective communication.

To meet this challenge is the ambition of critical reconstruction. As Apel indicates, this line of argument has several advantages over the descriptive approach. By starting from the transcendental parameters of communication, the strategy is able to show not only that moral judgments are one possible type of statement among others, but that they are presupposed in any kind of discourse, including logical or scientific propositions. The judgments or standards presupposed in this sense are not simply willful stipulations or hypothetical assumptions—as Popper contends. Moral norms are not equivalent to theoretical constructs in scientific explanation, constructs which can be accepted or rejected in accordance with criteria of heuristic utility and expediency. If it is true that every inquiry or proposition relies on language, the sense or meaning of a proposition cannot be articulated or defended without recourse to an intersubjective communicative fabric with implicit moral standards. In Apel's terms, "the logical validity of arguments cannot be tested without the premise of a community of investigators, who are willing and able to engage in intersubjective discourse and the formation of consensus." This premise, however, is not merely a factual condition but a normative yardstick. The scrutiny and validation of statements in such a community cannot proceed without "the reciprocal recognition of all participants as equal partners in the discussion," that is, without their recognition as moral agents equally committed to the search for truth and both able to justify their arguments and entitled to receive justifications in return. Mental reservations and play-acting in this situation are of no avail, since communication is a permanent and open-ended process comprising both present and future generations. As Apel adds, the communicative a priori can be illustrated by resort to the theory of "speech acts," and especially to the relationship between "propositional" and "performative" portions of discourse. According to this theory, propositions are not simply isolated factual statements, but are always accompanied at least implicitly by performative communications—communications making moral claims on participants. By pretending to be defensible, individual statements—even monologues—place themselves into a dialogical framework: "Every factual proposition aspiring to validation or justification thus presupposes in its pragmatic depth structure a performative context."[33]

While the preceding considerations are able to undermine scientific self-sufficiency, they do not yet provide an adequate basis for ethics; the task is not only to show the importance of norms but to give a theoretical account of moral discourse. According to Apel, the task is hopeless if theoretical explication is identified with logical deduction (since such deduction would presuppose logical standards); rather, giving an account can only mean an effort to gain insight into the foundations of human thought by reconstructing the a priori conditions of discourse and argument. Applied to the moral domain, the strategy requires the attempt to recover the normative premises implicit in ongoing interactions. Reconstruction in this area discloses first of all that communicative interaction—and every purposive conduct or act of life—is always already involved in an intersubjective and morally significant dimension of meaning. This involvement is not a matter of choice or individual preference. Contrary to the allegations of Popper and his followers, the adoption of the "criticist frame" of rational argument does not depend ultimately on private decision or an "act of faith"—since it is the only alternative which makes sense. As Apel argues, thinking and intelligibly choosing are impossible apart from the matrix of intersubjective discourse; every action or decision purporting to be intelligible testifies to an underlying framework of rational argument and reciprocal understanding. Irrationalism, therefore, is not a viable or plausible alternative because it cannot sensibly be articulated or defended: "The adoption of the 'criticist frame' in a philosophical discussion is not an irrational act of faith, but rather the only possible decision congruent semantically and pragmatically with the ongoing language game." From this perspective Apel is able not only to counter Popper's decisionism but also to correct Lorenzen's ambivalence regarding the basis of normative discourse. Intersubjective meaning, he notes, is not a contingent assumption depending on empirical conditions, but rather a transcendental premise of argument; as long as discourse is supposed to make sense, "the moral standard implicit in argument can be termed unconditional or categorical."[34]

By virtue of its categorical character, the mentioned standard in Apel's view also escapes the "naturalistic fallacy" or the charge that norms are derived from the fact of communicative interaction. This charge, he concedes, is a cogent rejoinder to contractual or consensual theories basing moral obligation on the contingent circumstance of social acceptance. Although contracts require free reciprocal agreement, the binding quality of such agreement presupposes tenable moral criteria. In contrast to the tenets of contractualism, the consensus uncovered by critical reflection belongs to the transcendental horizons of human thought and thus to the parameters permitting the recognition and validation of empirical facts themselves. Moreover, as premise of moral discourse, the transcendental framework reveals a normative rather than merely cognitive connotation by delineating the purposive thrust of human conduct. These considerations, according to Apel, permit the inference that the communicative a priori has the character not of an empirical fact but of a Kantian "fact of reason"—although Kant did not fully elucidate this notion. Translated into the idiom of contemporary philosophy, he suggests, the Kantian concept can be viewed as a synonym for critical reconstruction: a strategy involving the patient retracing of everyday practices with the aim of uncovering their premises and of dissolving contingency in rational insight. Reconstruction discloses that every individual engaging in discourse or purposive action implicitly subscribes to the moral code of intersubjective respect and understanding. Explication of the code, to be sure, does not insure its actual implementation or observance since rational insight needs to be corroborated by an act of will; moreover, concrete situations require complex interpretations of the code and possibly hazardous commitments. Yet, the basic thrust of the communicative standard cannot sensibly be denied. Although an individual may choose to ignore the standard in his behavior, he cannot articulate his neglect—without severing his ties with the human species.

By way of conclusion, Apel sketches some of the practical implications of his perspective, especially for a period of scientific revolution. As he reiterates, the communicative a priori involves as basic norm the postulate of the reciprocal justification of individual claims; according to this principle of "transsubjectivity," moral claims are not simply derived from human wants, but wants are entitled to recognition provided they can be justified in intersubjective discourse. The practical implications of the standard are due chiefly to its dialectical character. Mutual recognition, he stresses, is not merely an abstract or formal postulate divorced from concrete experience and devoid of substantive content; nor does the demand for justification sanction an elusive "ethic of conviction" in contrast to an "ethic of responsibility." The peculiarity of communication consists rather in the circumstance that it points simultaneously to two levels of discourse: to ongoing interactions in a given society and to a context of ideal consensus and understanding. This combination of real and ideal levels—in which the norm is always presupposed in actual encounters—involves not so much a contradiction as a dialectical tension and conflict: a tension which cannot logically be dissolved but has to be faced and sustained as a challenge in the "unfinished dialectic" of history. In Apel's view, this challenge can be differentiated into at least two major long-range tasks or regulative guideposts: the tasks of protecting the life-chances of the human species and of promoting consensus on a global scale. Given man's growing technological mastery over nature, the survival of the species can no longer be taken for granted and requires complex precautions; at the same time, although a necessary precondition of all endeavors, life makes sense only if guided by the purpose of ideal understanding. From the perspective of the communicative a priori, therefore, self-preservation needs to be joined with moral emancipation, survival with the striving for the "good life." Moral emancipation and consensus, however, are impossible without the progressive removal of communicative distortions and deformations or, in Marxist terms, without the dismantling of class barriers and other impediments to intersubjective discourse.

III

As one can gather from Apel's concluding remarks, ethics is intimately linked with politics, moral conduct with social and political arrangements. Against this background, the preceding discussion is bound to have ramifications in political theory and even political science. These ramifications, it is true, will not readily blend with prevailing professional preferences. If one were to believe the leading journal of the discipline, political scientists are still chiefly preoccupied with the battle between cognitivism and noncognitivism.[35] Yet, there are signs that these battle lines are in the process of eroding and of being replaced by different and more subtle concerns. In an essay entitled "The Moral Foundation of Political Obligation," John Chapman pointed to the distinction between descriptive and prescriptive-rationalist positions, the former being exemplified chiefly by Sir Isaiah Berlin, the latter by John Rawls. Linguistic and phenomenological empiricism, he observes, supports the conclusion that human experience is "morally structured"—a conclusion reflected in Berlin's "vision of the 'fundamental moral categories' of human nature" and in his attempt to trace moral standards to their "empirical origins" in human needs. As he adds, however, descriptivism may not be entirely satisfactory since an approach solely guided by observed practices and the "prevailing sense of justice" may be "insufficiently egalitarian" and ignore the "positive and prospective dimension" of political obligation. This defect is corrected by Rawls's "categorical rationalism," with its stress on freely accepted standards of justice and its "Rousseauan drift toward greater equality"; but in Chapman's view, the advantage is marred by drawbacks, especially by the bent to impose "a monistic solution to the problem of political obligation" in contrast to Berlin's empirical pluralism. Political deliberation, he suspects, involves "more balancing, and balancing of a different type, than seems consistent with Rawls's metaethical postulate." His observations finally lead him to the recognition of a dual metaethical legacy, "one seeking precision in the standards of rationality and impartiality, the other more flexible, grounded in our persisting moral attributes, tensions among which are reflected in the complexity of evaluative language."[36]

The preceding pages are not far removed from these considerations. As it seems to me, the perspective of critical reconstruction can be readily correlated with the two legacies noted by Chapman—although it tends to reformulate their relationship. Due to its dialectical thrust, reconstructionism seeks to uncover rational standards within the confines of human discourse and experience, but without submerging norms in contingent reality. Reason, from this vantage point, is not so much the stern task-master as the patient tutor of human conduct— a tutor attentive to the complex fabric of human inclinations without catering to spurious whims. In connecting real and ideal levels of discourse, self-preservation with the vision of the "good life," reconstructionism tackles an important dilemma which has long baffled moral thought: the bifurcation between form and content, between abstract imperatives and concrete human interests. This dilemma has recently surfaced again as a major philosophical concern, a concern not limited to any particular theoretical orientation. In the context of the Frankfurt School, the preoccupation can be traced at least in part to Marxist impulses; from a Marxist or socialist vantage point, the chief vice of classical economics has always been its disregard of actual conditions and its readiness to sacrifice human needs to abstract rules. Contemporary liberal and rationalist thinkers, on the other hand, are by no means unaware of this complaint. While focusing on the acceptance of general rules, Rawls finds it important—and not merely for purposes of expediency—to balance rational postulates with human interests, the requirements of justice with considerations of utility. In a similar manner, Baier acknowledges the desirability that rules should "command the highest possible respect and voluntary obedience" in society: "A rational way of achieving this is to give them a content such that it is in the interest of everyone alike that they should be followed."[37]

Critical reconstruction, in my view, also eludes another quandary mentioned by Chapman: the quandary of endorsing either a haphazard pluralism or a "monistic solution." Without lapsing into randomness or relativism, reconstructionism strongly opposes absolute vistas—especially cognitive doctrines claiming to derive moral standards from the natural universe. As Merleau-Ponty had noted, such doctrines tend to be not only dogmatic but idolatrous—by invoking the testimony of "a God who would be only the guarantor of the natural order, who would consecrate not only all the world's goodness but all the world's evil as well, who would justify slavery, injustice, the tears of children, the agony of the innocent by sacred necessity, who would finally sacrifice man to the cosmos as 'the absurd Emperor of the world.'" Without disclaiming the legitimate aspirations of reason, critical thought is suspicious of the indiscriminate merger of knowledge and practical conduct; as both Habermas and Apel emphasize, concrete actions always require a complex mediation of normative standards and particular conditions. In an age marked by heavily armed ideological camps and an unprece-

dented technological potential of destruction, the combination of tolerance and moral conviction may well hold the key both to human survival and to viable interactions on a global scale. In pursuing this goal,
critical reconstruction steers a course between two alternatives delineated by Merleau-Ponty: a "politics of common sense" preoccupied
with everyday issues, and a "politics of reason" proposing total solutions to historical and social issues. As he wrote, "the experience of the
last half century has been this: the presumed modesty of common sense
evades the problem of overall purpose as little as the self-confident outlook of reason the dilemma of circumstances."[38]

Notes

Introduction

1. The notion and need of such a "revival" have been articulated especially by Dante Germino in *Beyond Ideology: The Revival of Political Theory* (New York: Harper & Row, 1967). According to Germino, incipient signs of such a revival could be found chiefly in the works of Eric Voegelin and Leo Strauss. For a critical appraisal of the Straussian posture in terms of "metaphysical realism" or "ontological determinism" see Hwa Yol Jung, "Leo Strauss' Conception of Political Philosophy: A Critique," *The Review of Politics*, 29 (1967), 492–517.

2. For some literature on the relationship between phenomenology and Marxism see Barry Smart, *Sociology, Phenomenology and Marxian Analysis* (London: Routledge & Kegan Paul, 1976); and William L. McBride, "Marxism and Phenomenology," *Journal of the British Society for Phenomenology*, 6 (1975), 13–22. The similarities and divergencies between existential phenomenology and Habermas' version of critical theory are explored in some detail in my "Einleitung" and "Epilog" in *Materialien zu Habermas' "Erkenntnis und Interesse"* (Frankfurt–Main: Suhrkamp, 1974), pp. 10–21, 418–432.

3. See, e.g., Max Horkheimer, "Traditional and Critical Theory," in his *Critical Theory: Selected Essays*, trans. Matthew J. O'Connell et al. (New York: Herder & Herder, 1972), pp. 188–243. Regarding the Frankfurt School see Martin Jay, *The Dialectical Imagination: A History of the Frankfurt School and the Institute of Social Research, 1923-1950* (Boston: Little, Brown & Co., 1973); Trent Schroyer, *The Critique of Domination: The Origins and Development of Critical Theory* (New York: Braziller, 1973); Phil Slater, *Origin and Significance of the Frankfurt School: A Marxist Perspective* (London: Routledge & Kegan Paul, 1977); and regarding Georg Lukács his *History and Class Consciousness: Studies in Marxist Dialectics*, trans. Rodney Livingstone (Cambridge, Mass.: MIT Press, 1971), esp. p. 1.

4. For a comprehensive review of Habermas' writings see Thomas McCarthy, *The Critical Theory of Jürgen Habermas* (Cambridge, Mass.: MIT Press, 1978); Apel's major work is his *Transformation der Philosophie*, 2 vols. (Frankfurt–Main: Suhrkamp, 1973). Regarding the latter see my review

"Sinnerlebnis und Geltungsreflexion: Apels Transformation der Philosophie," *Philosophische Rundschau*, 25 (1978), 1–42.

5. Maurice Merleau-Ponty, *In Praise of Philosophy*, trans. John Wild and James M. Edie (Evanston, Ill.: Northwestern University Press, 1963), pp. 4–5, 38, 58. Commenting on Husserl, he noted at another point: "The philosopher, as the unpublished works declare, is a perpetual beginner, which means that he takes for granted nothing that men, learned or otherwise, believe they know." *Phenomenology of Perception*, trans. Colin Smith (New York: Humanities Press, 1962), p. xiv. Regarding his general philosophy see esp. Garth Gillan, ed., *The Horizons of the Flesh: Critical Perspectives on the Thought of Merleau-Ponty* (Carbondale, Ill.: Southern Illinois University Press, 1973); Samuel B. Mallin, *Merleau-Ponty's Philosophy* (New Haven, Conn.: Yale University Press, 1979); and, regarding his political thought, Barry Cooper, *Merleau-Ponty and Marxism: From Terror to Reform* (Toronto: University of Toronto Press, 1979).

6. See *In Praise of Philosophy*, pp. 46, 63; Paul Ricoeur, *History and Truth*, trans. Charles A. Kelbley (Evanston, Ill.: Northwestern University Press, 1965), p. 12.

7. Karsten Harries, "Martin Heidegger: The Search for Meaning," in *Existential Philosophers: Kierkegaard to Merleau-Ponty*, ed. George A. Schrader, Jr. (New York: McGraw-Hill, 1967), pp. 171, 185. See also Helmut Fahrenbach, "Heidegger und das Problem einer 'philosophischen' Anthropologie," in *Durchblicke: Martin Heidegger zum 80. Geburtstag* (Frankfurt–Main: Klostermann, 1970), pp. 97–131.

8. Heidegger, *An Introduction to Metaphysics*, trans. Ralph Manheim (New Haven, Conn.: Yale University Press, 1959), pp. 29–30. As Richard E. Palmer comments: "Questioning, then, is a way that man contends with and draws being into showing itself. It bridges the ontological difference between being and the being of beings." *Hermeneutics: Interpretation Theory in Schleiermacher, Dilthey, Heidegger, and Gadamer* (Evanston, Ill.: Northwestern University Press, 1969), p. 150.

9. See *In Praise of Philosophy*, p. 44; and *Sense and Non-Sense*, trans. Hubert L. and Patricia A. Dreyfus (Evanston, Ill.: Northwestern University Press, 1964), pp. 66 ("Hegel's Existentialism") and 72 ("The Battle over Existentialism"). At another point he observed that man is "like an open notebook in which we do not yet know what will be written"; *The Primacy of Perception and Other Essays*, ed. James M. Edie (Evanston, Ill.: Northwestern University Press, 1964), p. 6. See also Paul Ricoeur, "The Antinomy of Human Reality and the Problem of Philosophical Anthropology," in *Readings in Existential Phenomenology*, ed. Nathaniel M. Lawrence and Daniel O'Connor (Englewood Cliffs, N.J.: Prentice-Hall, 1967), pp. 390–402.

10. Hwa Yol Jung, "The Radical Humanization of Politics: Maurice Merleau-Ponty's Philosophy of Politics," *Archiv für Rechts-und Sozialphilosophie*, 53 (May 1967), 239.

11. See Lukács, *History and Class Consciousness*, pp. 186–190.

12. Ernst Bloch, *Das Prinzip Hoffnung*, 3 vols. (Frankfurt–Main: Suhrkamp, 1959), 1:4, 225, 327; *Subjekt-Objekt: Erläuterungen zu Hegel* (Frankfurt–Main: Suhrkamp, 1962), p. 471. Cf. also David Gross, "Ernst Bloch: The Dialectics of Hope," in *The Unknown Dimension: European Marxism Since Lenin*, ed. Dick Howard and Karl E. Klare (New York: Basic Books,

1972), pp. 107–130, and Pierre Furter, "Utopia and Marxism according to Bloch," *Philosophy Today,* 14 (Winter 1970), 236–249.

13. Habermas, "Anthropologie," in *Fischer-Lexikon: Philosophie,* ed. Alwin Diemer and Ivo Frenzel (Frankfurt–Main: Fischer, 1958), pp. 19, 21, 32–33. See in this context also Martin Jay, "The Frankfurt School's Critique of Marxist Humanism," *Social Research,* 39 (Summer 1972), 285–305; and Christian K. Lenhardt, "Rise and Fall of Transcendental Anthropology," *Philosophy of the Social Sciences,* 2 (September 1972), 231–246.

14. See Edmund Husserl, *Experience and Judgment: Investigations in a Genealogy of Logic,* ed. Ludwig Landgrebe, trans. James S. Churchill and Karl Ameriks (Evanston, Ill.: Northwestern University Press, 1973), pp. xxi–xxii ("Translator's Introduction").

15. See Heidegger, *Being and Time,* trans. John Macquarrie and Edward Robinson (New York: Harper & Row, 1962), esp. sections 41–42; Max Scheler, *Die Wissensformen und die Gesellschaft* (1926), 2nd ed. (Bern and Munich: Francke Verlag, 1960), pp. 60–69, 200–211. Regarding Heidegger's triad, I am indebted to Theodore Kisiel's essay "Habermas' Purge of Pure Theory: Critical Theory without Ontology?" *Human Studies,* 1 (1978), 167–183.

16. See Merleau-Ponty, *Phenomenology of Perception,* pp. viii–ix, xiii, xv; also "The Primacy of Perception and Its Philosophical Consequences," in *The Primacy of Perception and Other Essays,* pp. 13, 16–17, 19, 21.

17. Merleau-Ponty, "The Philosopher and Sociology," in *Signs,* trans. Richard C. McCleary (Evanston, Ill.: Northwestern University Press, 1964), pp. 99, 101–102, 110. As he added (p. 98): "We need neither tear down the behavioral sciences to lay the foundations of philosophy, nor tear down philosophy to lay the foundations of behavioral sciences. Every science secretes an ontology; every ontology anticipates a body of knowledge."

18. Merleau-Ponty, "Phenomenology and Psychoanalysis: Preface to Hesnard's L'Oeuvre de Freud," in *The Essential Writings of Merleau-Ponty,* ed. Alden I. Fisher (New York: Harcourt, Brace & World, 1969), pp. 81, 84–86.

19. See Ricoeur, "Ethics and Culture: Habermas and Gadamer in Dialogue," *Philosophy Today,* 17 (Summer 1973), 163; also "The Model of the Text: Meaningful Action Considered as a Text," *Social Research,* 38 (Autumn 1971), 529–562, and *Freud and Philosophy: An Essay on Interpretation* (New Haven, Conn.: Yale University Press, 1970).

20. Merleau-Ponty, "The Battle over Existentialism," in *Sense and Non-Sense,* p. 77; "The Primacy of Perception," in *The Primacy of Perception and Other Essays,* p. 25; *Humanism and Terror,* trans. John O'Neill (Boston: Beacon Press, 1969), p. xiv.

1. Political Science and the "Two Cultures"

1. Jacques Barzun, *Science: The Glorious Entertainment* (New York: Harper & Row, 1964), p. 12; Edward H. Carr, *What Is History?* (New York: Knopf, 1962), p. 110; see also Viscount Hailsham, *Science and Politics* (London: Faber & Faber, 1963), p. 33.

2. C. P. Snow, *The Two Cultures: And a Second Look* (New York: Mentor Books, 1964), pp. 63–64. The Rede Lecture was orginally presented at

Cambridge University in 1959.

3. Norbert Wiener, *The Human Use of Human Beings* (Garden City, N.Y.: Doubleday, 1954), pp. 179–181.

4. See David R. Derge, "B.S. and P.S.: An Enquiry into the Recent Science–Anti-Science Battle," Indiana Academy of the Social Sciences, *Proceedings*, 1962, n.s. 7:93; James W. Prothro, "The Nonsense Fight Over Scientific Method: A Plea for Peace," *Journal of Politics*, 18 (1956), 565–570. On the "third culture" theme see esp. Sanford A. Lakoff, "The Third Culture: Science in Social Thought," in *Knowledge and Power*, ed. Lakoff (New York: Free Press, 1966), pp. 1–61; George E. G. Catlin, *Political and Sociological Theory and Its Applications* (Ann Arbor: University of Michigan Press, 1964), pp. 85–104.

5. See Robert Flint, *Philosophy as Scientia Scientiarum and A History of Classifications of the Sciences* (Edinburgh and London: W. Blackwood, 1904), p. 70.

6. The division of practical philosophy into ethics, economics, and politics seems to have been developed by the Peripatetic School; see Hans Maier, "Die Lehre der Politik an den deutschen Universitäten," in *Wissenschaftliche Politik*, ed. Dieter Oberndörfer (Freiburg: Verlag Rombach, 1962), p. 65, n. 16.

7. Flint, p. 86. Against this background, David Easton's statement that "by the eighteenth century . . . we can already disinguish what came to be called natural philosophy from moral philosophy" remains enigmatic; see his *A Framework for Political Analysis* (Englewood Cliffs, N.J.: Prentice-Hall, 1965), p. 11.

8. On the interchangeable use of these terms from the Renaissance to the Enlightenment period see Robert McRae, *The Problem of the Unity of the Sciences: Bacon to Kant* (Toronto: University of Toronto Press, 1961), p. ix, n. 6.

9. Ibid., p. 44. On the development of Bacon's classification scheme see also Henry E. Bliss, *The Organization of Knowledge and the System of the Sciences* (New York: Holt, 1929), pp. 316–320.

10. Locke's scheme is found in the last chapter of his *Essay Concerning Human Understanding*; for comments and especially for Leibniz' criticism see Flint, pp. 122–124, McRae, pp. 83–84. There is no room here to explore the social context of the intellectual developments I have sketched, especially of the rise of "theoretical" knowledge; it must suffice to point to the contemporaneous emergence of a modern market economy governed by a (supposedly) neutral mechanism of economic and social laws.

11. Cf. Flint, p. 142; McRae, pp. 107 ff.

12. According to Mill, the distinction between the two fields resided only on an elementary level in their subject matter, the one being concerned "with the human mind, the other with all things whatever except the mind." But, he added, in the "higher regions" this distinction becomes ambiguous: "Take the science of politics, for instance, or that of law: who will say that these are physical sciences? And yet is it not obvious that they are conversant fully as much with matter as with mind?" *John Stuart Mill's Philosophy of Scientific Method*, ed. Ernest Nagel (New York: Hafner, 1950), p. 414.

13. Flint, pp. 175–178; Bliss, pp. 341–345.

14. Charles W. Shields, *The Order of the Sciences, an Essay on the Phil-*

osophical Classification and Organization of Human Knowledge (New York: Scribner's, 1882).

15. Wilhelm Dilthey, *Gesammelte Schriften,* 5th ed. (Stuttgart: Teubner, 1962), 1:12, 7:148, 5:144. Cf. Joseph Meurers, *Wilhelm Diltheys Gedankenwelt und die Naturwissenschaft* (Berlin: Junker & Dünnhaupt, 1936).

16. Wilhelm Wundt, "Über die Einteilung der Wissenschaften" (1889), *Kleine Schriften* (Leipzig: Engelmann, 1921), 3:32; also *Logik der Exakten Wissenschaften,* 3rd ed. (Stuttgart: F. Enke, 1907), 2:90.

17. Wilhelm Windelband, "Geschichte und Naturwissenschaft" (1894), *Präludien,* 5th ed. (Tübingen: J. C. B. Mohr, 1915), 2:144.

18. Heinrich Rickert, *Die Grenzen der naturwissenschaftlichen Begriffsbildung,* 3rd and 4th ed. (Tübingen: J. C. B. Mohr, 1921); *Kulturwissenschaft und Naturwissenschaft,* 2nd ed. (Tübingen: J. C. B. Mohr, 1910). Compare Don Martindale, *The Nature and Types of Sociological Theory* (Boston: Houghton Mifflin, 1960), pp. 18, 222–223, 377–379; also my essay, "Heinrich Rickert und die amerikanische Sozialwissenschaft," *Der Staat,* 5 (1966), 17–46.

19. See Martin Heidegger, *Being and Time,* trans. John Macquarrie and Edward Robinson (New York: Harper & Row, 1962), sections 41–42; Max Scheler, *Die Wissensformen und die Gesellschaft* (Leipzig: Neue Geist-Verlag, 1926).

20. See Max Horkheimer, "Traditional and Critical Theory," in his *Critical Theory: Selected Essays,* trans. Matthew J. O'Connell et al. (New York: Herder & Herder, 1972), pp. 188–243; Jürgen Habermas, *Knowledge and Human Interests,* trans. Jeremy J. Shapiro (Boston: Beacon Press, 1971); Karl-Otto Apel, "Szientistik, Hermeneutik, Ideologie-Kritik: Entwurf einer Wissenschaftslehre in erkenntnisanthropologischer Sicht," in his *Transformation der Philosophie* (Frankfurt: Suhrkamp, 1973), 2:96–127.

21. Cf. Bernard Crick, *The American Science of Politics, Its Origins and Conditions* (Berkeley and Los Angeles: University of California Press, 1959); Robert A. Dahl, "The Behavioral Approach in Political Science: Epitaph for a Monument to a Successful Protest," *American Political Science Review,* 55 (1961), 763–772.

22. Eric Voegelin, *The New Science of Politics* (Chicago: University of Chicago Press, 1952), pp. 1–2, 4–6, 11, 13.

23. F. A. Hayek, *The Counter-Revolution of Science: Studies on the Abuse of Reason* (New York: Free Press, 1964), pp. 33, 35; for comments cf. Ernest Nagel, "Logic of Science," in *Logic Without Metaphysics* (Glencoe, Ill.: Free Press, 1956), p. 364.

24. Peter Winch, *The Idea of a Social Science, and Its Relation to Philosophy* (London: Routledge & Kegan Paul, 1958), p. 123.

25. Michael Oakeshott, *Rationalism in Politics and Other Essays* (New York: Basic Books, 1962), pp. 10–11, 112, 123–124, 129–130.

26. Wilhelm Hennis, *Politik und praktische Philosophie, Eine Studie zur Rekonstruktion der politischen Wissenschaft* (Neuwied and Berlin: Luchterhand, 1963), p. 35. Cf. also Dieter Oberndörfer, "Politik als praktische Wissenschaft," in *Wissenschaftliche Politik,* pp. 9–58; and Bernard Crick, *In Defence of Politics* (Baltimore: Penguin Books, 1964).

27. See Christian Bay, "Thoughts on the Purposes of Political Science Education," in George J. Graham, Jr., and George N. Carey, eds., *The Post-*

Behavioral Era: Perspectives on Political Science (New York: David McKay, 1972), pp. 89–91; Peter Bachrach, *The Theory of Democratic Elitism: A Critique* (Boston: Little, Brown & Co., 1967), pp. 6–7, 99–100. Cf. also Herbert Reid, "American Social Science in the Politics of Time and the Crisis of Technocorporate Society: Toward a Critical Phenomenology," *Politics and Society*, 3 (1973), pp. 201–243.

28. Apart from the previously mentioned Frankfurt theorists, this sketch is indebted to the following sources: Mulford Q. Sibley, "The Limitations of Behavioralism," in James C. Charlesworth, ed., *The Limits of Behavioralism in Political Science* (Philadelphia: The American Academy of Political and Social Science, 1962), pp. 68–93, esp. pp. 86–88; Eric Weil, "Philosophie politique, théorie politique," *Revue française de science politique*, 11 (1961), pp. 267–294; Maurice Merleau-Ponty, *Signs* (Evanston, Ill.: Northwestern University Press, 1964), pp. 98–113. Cf. also Dolf Sternberger, *Begriff des Politischen* (Frankfurt: Insel-Verlag, 1961); Arnold Bergstraesser, "Die Stellung der Politik unter den Wissenschaften," *Freiburger Dies Universitatis*, 6 (1957–1958), pp. 85–95; Carl J. Friedrich, "Grundsätzliches zur Geschichte der Wissenschaft von der Politik," *Zeitschrift für Politik*, NF, 1 (1954), 325–336.

2. Empirical Political Theory and the Image of Man

1. See, for example, Ralph Linton, *The Study of Man, An Introduction* (New York: Appleton-Century, 1936); Lynn T. White, ed., *Frontiers of Knowledge in the Study of Man* (New York: Harper & Row, 1956); Michael Polanyi, *The Study of Man* (Chicago: University of Chicago Press, 1963); also the chapters "The Root Is Man" and "The Goal Is Man" in Heinz Eulau, *The Behavioral Persuasion in Politics* (New York: Random House, 1963), pp. 3–11, 133–137.

2. On empirical theory, frameworks and approaches, see Alan C. Isaak, *Scope and Methods of Political Science* (Homewood, Ill.: Dorsey Press, 1969), pp. 135–160; Oran R. Young, *Systems of Political Science* (Englewood Cliffs, N.J.: Prentice Hall, 1968), pp. 8–12, 95–102; Eugene J. Meehan, *Contemporary Political Thought, A Critical Study* (Homewood, Ill.: Dorsey Press, 1967), pp. 23–26, and *The Theory and Method of Political Analysis* (Homewood, Ill.: Dorsey Press, 1965), pp. 130–163; Fred M. Frohock, *The Nature of Political Inquiry* (Homewood, Ill.: Dorsey Press, 1967), pp. 4–13; Gordon J. DiRenzo, ed., *Concepts, Theory and Explanation in the Behavioral Sciences* (New York: Random House, 1966), pp. 239–259; Vernon Van Dyke, *Political Science, A Philosophical Analysis* (Stanford: Stanford University Press, 1960), pp. 89–109. Some current scientific theories are actually axiomatic or "normative" (in a formal sense) rather than empirical; on this distinction see Jürgen Habermas, "Zur Logik der Sozialwissenschaften," *Philosophische Rundschau*, Beiheft 5 (Tübingen: J. C. B. Mohr, 1967), pp. 49–58.

3. Maurice Duverger, *The Idea of Politics* (Indianapolis: Bobbs-Merrill, 1966), p. xii.

4. See Ralf Dahrendorf, *Class and Class Conflict in Industrial Society* (Stanford: Stanford University Press, 1959), p. 159 (integration theory versus coercion or conflict theory); Irving L. Horowitz, "Consensus, Conflict and

Cooperation: A Sociological Inventory," *Social Forces*, 41 (1962), 177–188; John Horton, "Order and Conflict Theories of Social Problems as Competing Ideologies," *American Journal of Sociology*, 71 (1966), 701–713; Bert N. Adams, "Coercion and Consensus Theories: Some Unresolved Issues," ibid., pp. 714–717; Robert Cole, "Structural-Functional Theory, the Dialectic, and Social Change," *The Sociological Quarterly*, 7 (1966), 48 (dialectical versus integration models).

5. A fourth alternative might be found in the combination of a system focus with a conflict perspective; however, except on a subsystem level, the combination is difficult to conceive and little developed in the literature.

6. Morton A. Kaplan, "Systems Theory," in James C. Charlesworth, ed., *Contemporary Political Analysis* (New York: Free Press, 1967), p. 150. See also his "Systems Theory and Political Science," *Social Research*, 35 (1968), 30–47; Peter Nettl, "The Concept of System in Political Science," *Political Studies*, 14 (1966), 305–338; Ludwig von Bertalanffy, "General System Theory," *General Systems*, 1 (1956), 1–10; A. Hall and R. Fagen, "Definition of a System," ibid., 18–28.

7. Burkhart Holzner, "The Concept of 'Integration' in Sociological Theory," *The Sociological Quarterly*, 8 (1967), 53.

8. Young, p. 14; see also his "The Impact of General Systems Theory on Political Science," *General Systems*, 9 (1964), 239–255.

9. Thus, the heartbeat might be assigned the function of producing heart sounds; see Carl G. Hempel, "The Logic of Functional Analysis," in Llewellyn Gross, ed., *Symposium on Sociological Theory* (Evanston, Ill.: Row, Peterson, 1959), p. 279.

10. Marion J. Levy, Jr., "Some Aspects of 'Structural-Functional' Analysis and Political Science," in Roland Young, ed. *Approaches to the Study of Politics* (Evanston, Ill.: Northwestern University Press, 1958), p. 53. According to a slightly different formulation, structural functional analysis (as distinguished from eclectic and empirical functionalism) involves "first, an emphasis on the whole system as the unit of analysis; second, postulation of particular functions as requisite to the maintenance of the whole system; third, concern to demonstrate the functional interdependence of diverse structures within the whole system." William Flanigan and Edwin Fogelman, "Functional Analysis," in Charlesworth, p. 76. See also Martin Landau, "On the Use of Functional Analysis in American Political Science," *Social Research*, 35 (1968), 48–75; A. James Gregor, "Political Science and the Uses of Functional Analysis," *American Political Science Review*, 62 (1968), 425–439.

11. Robert T. Holt, "A Proposed Structural-Functional Framework," in Charlesworth, pp. 86–107; Talcott Parsons, "Some Highlights of the General Theory of Action," in Roland Young, pp. 282–301; a similar scheme was used by William C. Mitchell in *The American Polity* (New York: Free Press, 1962) and "The Polity and Society: A Structural-Functional Analysis," *Midwest Journal of Political Science*, 2 (1958), 403–420. For other schemes see, for example, Marion J. Levy, Jr., *The Structure of Society* (Princeton, N.J.: Princeton University Press, 1952), pp. 149–197; Gabriel A. Almond and James S. Coleman, eds., *The Politics of the Developing Areas* (Princeton, N.J.: Princeton University Press, 1960), pp. 3–64; Almond, "A Developmental Approach to Political Systems," *World Politics*, 17 (1965), 183–214.

12. David Easton, *A Framework for Political Analysis* (Englewood Cliffs,

N.J.: Prentice-Hall, 1965), pp. 21, 50.

13. Easton, *A Systems Analysis of Political Life* (New York: Wiley, 1965), p. 17. See also his statement (p. 475) that "persistence and change of systems, or rather, persistence through change has seemed to be the most inclusive kind of question that one might ask about a political system."

14. Oran Young does not include cybernetics among system derivatives, mainly because of its emphasis on decision processes; but as Deutsch has indicated, cybernetic concepts may with certain adjustments be incorporated into structural functionalism. See Karl W. Deutsch, *The Nerves of Government, Models of Political Communication and Control* (New York: Free Press, 1963), p. 50.

15. Ibid., p. 80.

16. Deutsch, "Communication Models and Decision Systems," in Charlesworth, p. 278. For Deutsch's views on integration see also his *Nationalism and Social Communication* (New York: Wiley, 1953), pp. 70–74; *Political Community and the North Atlantic Area* (Princeton, N.J.: Princeton University Press, 1957), p. 5; and the chapters on "Communication Theory and Political Integration" and "Integration and the Social System: Implications of Functional Analysis," in Philip E. Jacob and James V. Toscano, eds., *The Integration of Political Communities* (Philadelphia: Lippincott, 1964), pp. 46–74, 179–208.

17. Norbert Wiener, *The Human Use of Human Beings, Cybernetics and Society* (Garden City, N.Y.: Doubleday, 1954), p. 27.

18. See, for example, Parsons, p. 291; Easton, *A Framework for Political Analysis*, pp. 36, 52; *A Systems Analysis of Political Life*, p. 380.

19. *The Nerves of Government*, pp. 94–95, 124. See also Oran Young's statement: "Various questions concerning patterns of control, power, and influence do not play an important part in input-output analysis. Most of the systemic approaches share this pattern of deemphasis to some extent since they focus on the operation of a system in fairly abstract terms rather than on the behavior patterns of human beings. To continue, input-output analysis has little to say about the politics of decline, disruption, and breakdown in political systems." *Systems of Political Science*, p. 45.

20. See Parsons, p. 283, and "Evolutionary Universals in Society," *American Sociological Review*, 29 (1964), 339–357; Easton, *A Farmework for Political Analysis*, p. 99; *A Systems Analysis of Political Life*, pp. 19–21, and "Limits of the Equilibrium Model in Social Research," *Behavioral Science*, 1 (1956), 96–104; Deutsch, *The Nerves of Government*, pp. 88–91, 248–254, and "Communication Models and Decision Systems," pp. 279–282, 293–297.

21. *Systems of Political Science*, pp. 5–8, 33–36, 44–48, 56–59.

22. *A Systems Analysis of Political Life*, p. 409, n. 6; Easton's main objection is to a "neo-Benthamite" or "utilitarian" conception of human behavior according to which individuals rationally calculate and pursue their interests. See also David Easton and Jack Dennis, "The Child's Acquisition of Regime Norms: Political Efficacy," *American Political Science Review*, 61 (1967), 25–38; Easton and Robert D. Hess, "The Child's Political World," *Midwest Journal of Political Science*, 6 (1962), 229–246.

23. *Systems of Political Science*, 47. See also Deutsch, "Communication Models and Decision Systems," p. 286.

24. Kaplan, "Systems Theory," p. 159.

25. Parsons, "Some Highlights of the General Theory of Action," pp. 288–291. As Mancur Olson, Jr., comments on Parsonian theory: "The central preconception of this type of theory is that people do what they are brought up to do. It holds in effect that the hand that rocks the cradle does indeed rule the world." See "The Relationship Between Economics and the Other Social Sciences: The Province of a 'Social Report,'" in Seymour M. Lipset, ed., *Politics and the Social Sciences* (New York: Oxford University Press, 1969), p. 146. See also Alfred L. Baldwin, "The Parsonian Theory of Personality," in Max Black, ed., *The Social Theories of Talcott Parsons* (Englewood Cliffs, N.J.: Prentice-Hall, 1961), pp. 153–190.

26. Ralf Dahrendorf, "Sociology and Human Nature," in *Essays in the Theory of Society* (Stanford: Stanford University Press, 1968), pp. 90–91.

27. Dahrendorf, "Homo Sociologicus," ibid., pp. 35–36, 56. More strongly than Parsons, Dahrendorf insists on the normative character of role expectations, on the fact that "social roles are a constraining force on the individual, whether he experiences them as an obstacle to his private wishes or a support that gives him security" (p. 38). Moreover, in contrast to some systemic writers, he argues that role expectations are established not so much by a nondescript "society," but by "reference groups," that is, groups "to which a person has a necessary relation" by virtue of his social positions (pp. 46, 49).

28. See Ralph E. Turner, "Role-Taking: Process versus Conformity," in Arnold M. Rose, ed., *Human Behavior and Social Processes* (Boston: Houghton Mifflin, 1962), pp. 20–38. On role theory see, for example, Heinrich Popitz, *Der Begriff der sozialen Rolle als Element der soziologischen Theorie* (Tübingen: J. C. B. Mohr, 1967); Bruce J. Biddle and Edwin J. Thomas, eds., *Role Theory, Concepts and Research* (New York: Wiley, 1966); Michael P. Banton, *Roles: An Introduction to the Study of Social Relations* (London: Tavistock Publications, 1965); Neal Gross, Ward S. Mason and Alexander W. McEachern, *Explorations in Role Analysis* (New York: Wiley, 1958).

29. Dennis H. Wrong, "Human Nature and the Perspective of Sociology," *Social Research*, 30 (1963), 304–306, and "The Oversocialized Conception of Man in Modern Sociology," *American Sociological Review*, 26 (1961), 184–185. Cf. also Paul F. Kress, "Self, System, and Significance: Reflections on Professor Easton's Political Science," *Ethics*, 77 (1966), 1–13.

30. Hans L. Zetterberg, "Compliant Actions," *Acta Sociologica*, 2 (1957), 189.

31. This reservation seems to apply primarily to the so-called "decision-making" framework; compare James N. Rosenau, "The Premises and Promises of Decision-Making Analysis," in Charlesworth, pp. 189–211.

32. William C. Mitchell, "The Shape of Political Theory to Come: From Political Sociology to Political Economy," in Lipset, ed., p. 105. (The paper was first presented at the 1967 Annual Meeting of the American Political Science Association.)

33. "More recent political sociology has followed the lead of Lipset, Parsons and Kornhauser in emphasizing consensus. In so doing they have furnished a potential linkage with the new political economy which I hope both schools will perceive and develop to their mutual benefit." Ibid., p. 106; cf. also his "The New Political Economy," *Social Research*, 35 (1968), 76–110.

34. James M. Buchanan and Gordon Tullock, *The Calculus of Consent*,

Logical Foundations of Constitutional Democracy (Ann Arbor, Mich.: University of Michigan Press, 1962). Mitchell describes this book as "perhaps the best single statement by economists of their version of the political system"; "The Shape of Political Theory to Come," p. 133, n. 13. For other examples of the political economy genre see, for example, Robert L. Curry and Lawrence Wade, *A Theory of Political Exchange: Economic Reasoning in Political Analysis* (Englewood Cliffs, N.J.: Prentice-Hall, 1968); Mancur Olson, Jr., *The Logic of Collective Action* (Cambridge, Mass.: Harvard University Press, 1965); James M. Buchanan, *Fiscal Theory and Political Economy* (Chapel Hill: University of North Carolina Press, 1960); Duncan Black, *The Theory of Committees and Elections* (Cambridge, Mass.: Harvard University Press, 1958); Anthony Downs, *An Economic Theory of Democracy* (New York: Harper & Row, 1957); Robert A. Dahl and Charles E. Lindblom, *Politics, Economics, and Welfare* (New York: Harper & Row, 1953); Kenneth Arrow, *Social Choice and Individual Values* (New York: Wiley, 1951); also George E. G. Catlin, *The Science and Method of Politics* (New York: Knopf, 1927).

35. *The Calculus of Consent*, pp. 11, 19. For a more direct attack on systemic approaches, especially structural functionalism, see John C. Harsanyi, "Rational-Choice Models of Political Behavior vs. Functionalist and Conformist Models," *World Politics*, 21 (1969), 513–538.

36. *The Calculus of Consent*, pp. 12, 26.

37. Ibid., pp. 3, 23–24, 33, 37, 171 ff. (on Pareto-optimality). As the authors add, however, their discussion does not mean "to suggest that in modern political process, as it operates, elements that are characteristic of the zero-sum game are wholly absent" (p. 344, n. 13). In another context (p. 266) they observe that "our conception of the political process, as such, is surely more congenial to those seeking 'sweetness and light,' 'peace' and all such good things than the conception usually implicit in political discourse. We view collective decision-making (collective action) as a form of human activity through which mutual gains are made possible. Thus, in our conception, collective activity, like market activity, is a genuinely *cooperative* endeavor in which *all* parties, conceptually, stand to gain." Cf. also James M. Buchanan, "An Individualistic Theory of Political Process," in David Easton, ed., *Varieties of Political Theory* (Englewood Cliffs, N.J.: Prentice-Hall, 1966), pp. 25–37; James G. March, "The Power of Power," ibid., pp. 39–70.

38. George C. Homans, *Social Behavior: Its Elementary Forms* (New York: Harcourt, Brace & World, 1961), pp. 2–3, 12–13; he thus combines the axiomatic, deductive approach of economic theory with the empirical bent of psychological behaviorism. For an earlier statement (containing a strong criticism of structural functionalism) see his "Human Behavior as Exchange," *American Journal of Sociology*, 63 (1958), 597–606.

39. *Social Behavior*, pp. 61, 68–70, 74–75. On his rule of distributive justice see W. G. Runciman, "Justice, Congruence and Professor Homans," *European Journal of Sociology*, 8 (1967), 115–128; C. Norman Alexander, Jr. and Richard L. Simpson, "Balance Theory and Distributive Justice," *Sociological Inquiry*, 34 (1964), 182–192.

40. *Social Behavior*, p. 57. As he adds, "while the exchange of rewards tends toward stability and continued interaction, the exchange of punishments tends toward instability and the eventual failure of interaction in

escape and avoidance: the pain experienced comes to outweigh the pleasure of revenge."

41. Peter M. Blau, *Exchange and Power in Social Life* (New York: Wiley, 1964), pp. 4, 91, 93–96, 104–105, 116. For his views on fair exchange and integration see pp. 151–160, 289–292; also his "Justice in Social Exchange," *Sociological Inquiry*, 34 (1964), 193–206, and "A Theory of Social Integration," *American Journal of Sociology*, 65 (1960), 545–556. Kenneth E. Boulding at one point differentiates between exchange systems with positive-sum properties, threat systems with zero-sum properties, and "love systems" characterized by consensus or merger of preference structures; "An Economist's View," *American Journal of Sociology*, 67 (1962), 460.

42. *The Calculus of Consent*, p. 9. As they add: "The essential difference between our 'economic' approach to political choice and that approach represented by the Bentley school lies in our attempt to examine the results of political activity in terms of simplified analytical models and, in this way, to suggest some of the implications of the theory that might be subjected to empirical testing." For a more critical appraisal of interest group theory see Charles E. Lindblom, *The Intelligence of Democracy* (New York: Free Press, 1965), 12–16; Olson, *The Logic of Collective Action*, pp. 111-131; Harsanyi, pp. 516–517.

43. See Arthur F. Bentley, *The Process of Government* (Evanston, Ill.: Principia Press of Illinois, 1949), p. 264; David B. Truman, *The Governmental Process* (New York: Knopf, 1951), pp. 510–516; also Bernard Crick, *The American Science of Politics, Its Origins and Conditions* (Berkeley: University of California Press, 1964), pp. 123–125.

44. Nelson W. Polsby, *Community Power and Political Theory* (New Haven, Conn.: Yale University Press, 1963), p. 118. See also Heinz Eulau's comment that, in *Who Governs?*, Robert A. Dahl created a "complex model of the democratic order in a competitive environment—a political system in which the politics of influence is not a zero-sum game, but a function of highly fragmented patterns of more or less direct influence, of reciprocal relations between leaders, sub-leaders and constituents, of shifting coalitions and bargaining between more or less overlapping networks of influentials who specialize in different issue areas." *American Political Science Review*, 56 (1962), 144.

45. Elmer E. Schattschneider, *The Semisovereign People* (New York: Holt, Rinehart & Winston, 1960), 35. See also William E. Connolly, ed., *The Bias of Pluralism* (New York: Atherton Press, 1969), pp. 3–34; Peter Bachrach, *The Theory of Democratic Elitism, A Critique* (Boston: Little, Brown, 1967), pp. 35–46; Olson, *The Logic of Collective Action*, pp. 126–130.

46. *The Calculus of Consent*, pp. 3–4, 14, 17.

47. *An Economic Theory of Democracy*, pp. 5, 7.

48. Ibid., pp. 4–5, 6, 11, 20, 24, 27–28, 295–297; *The Calculus of Consent*, pp. 4, 29, 33–34. Despite their emphasis on the calculus of loss and gain, Buchanan and Tullock sharply differentiate their behavioral assumption from models concentrating on political power and domination. While superficially the "power-maximizer" and the "utility-maximizer" may seem to be "country-cousins," the two approaches are said to be "different in a fundamental philosophical sense" (p. 23). For additional features of the political economist's model of man see Harsanyi, pp. 521–524.

49. *The Calculus of Consent*, p. 27. For other endorsements or adaptations of utilitarian philosophy see David Braybrooke and Charles E. Lindblom, *A Strategy of Decision* (New York: Free Press, 1963), pp. 203–223; Jan Narveson, *Morality and Utility* (Baltimore: Johns Hopkins University Press, 1966).

50. *Social Behavior*, p. 79. As he adds: "Let not a reader reject our argument out of hand because he does not care for its horrid profit-seeking implications. . . . It may ease his conscience to remember that if hedonists believe men take profits only in materialistic values, we are not hedonists here. So long as men's values are altruistic, they can take a profit in altruism too."

51. Ibid., p. 82; his reservations extend to the traditional postulate of utility maximization (p. 72). The deemphasis of rationality is shared by Blau, although in more cautious terms: "The only assumption made is that human beings choose between alternative potential associates or courses of action by evaluating the experiences or expected experiences with each in terms of a preference ranking and then selecting the best alternative. Irrational as well as rational behavior is governed by these considerations. . . . What is explicitly *not* assumed here is that men have complete information, that they have no social commitments restricting their alternatives, that their preferences are entirely consistent or remain constant, or that they pursue one specific ultimate goal to the exclusion of all others." *Exchange and Power in Social Life*, p. 18; for a more positive assessment of utility maximization see ibid., p. 96.

52. Homans, *Social Behavior*, pp. 5–6; Blau; *Exchange and Power in Social Life*, p. 104. On Homans compare Morton Deutsch and Robert M. Kraus, *Theories in Social Psychology* (New York: Basic Books, 1965), pp. 109–116; Helmut R. Wagner, "New Economic Man: Pigeons, Sentiments, and the Pay-Off," *Social Research*, 29 (1962), 239–242; Boulding, pp. 458–461.

53. Horowitz traces the ancestry of the conflict approach back to antiquity when he writes: "The roots of conflict theory reach back in time to Hobbes and the formation of the modern nation-state, Marsilius of Padua in the medieval world and Thrasymachus, Socrates and Plato in ancient Greek society." See "Consensus, Conflict and Cooperation," p. 179.

54. Robert A. Dahl, *Congress and Foreign Policy* (New York: Harcourt, Brace & World, 1950), p. 223; Francis D. Wormuth, "The Politics of George Catlin," *Western Political Quarterly*, 14 (1961), 811. See also Robert Presthus' comment: "However difficult it may be to develop a higher toleration for ambiguity on a national scale, criticism and conflict must again become fashionable." *The Organizational Society* (New York: Knopf, 1962), p. 294.

55. This statement, of course, requires qualification; for elements of a conflict perspective in political science literature compare, for example, Robert A. Dahl, *Pluralist Democracy in the United States: Conflict and Consent* (Chicago: University of Chicago Press, 1967); J. David Singer, "The Political Science of Human Conflict," in Elton B. McNeil, *The Nature of Human Conflict* (Englewood Cliffs, N.J.: Prentice-Hall, 1965), pp. 139–154; Robert E. Agger, Daniel Goldrich and Bert E. Swanson, *The Rulers and the Ruled* (New York: Wiley, 1964); Kalman H. Silvert, *The Conflict Society* (New York: American Universities Field Staff, 1961); Harold D. Lasswell and

Abraham Kaplan, *Power and Society, A Framework for Political Inquiry* (New Haven, Conn.: Yale University Press, 1950); Charles E. Merriam, *Political Power* (New York: McGraw-Hill, 1934).

56. William H. Riker, *The Theory of Political Coalitions* (New Haven, Conn.: Yale University Press, 1962), pp. 10–12, 21–22, 28–31. The passage acknowledging the positive-sum character of bargaining situations refers explicitly to the work of Buchanan and Tullock; on power see Riker's "A Test of the Adequacy of the Power Index," *Behavioral Science*, 4 (1959), 120–131. Cf. also William T. Bluhm, *Theories of the Political System: Classics of Political Thought and Modern Political Analysis* (Englewood Cliffs, N.J.: Prentice-Hall, 1965), pp. 290–299.

57. Dahrendorf, "Toward a Theory of Social Conflict," in Amitai and Eva Etzioni, eds., *Social Change* (New York: Basic Books, 1964), p. 98. In another context, he describes the work of Vilfredo Pareto, Gaetano Mosca, and Raymond Aron as "the proximate origin" of his thought; however, at least with regard to Pareto and Mosca, he notes a "crucial difference between elite theories and conflict theories." *Class and Class Conflict in Industrial Society*, pp. 194, 199.

58. However, Dahrendorf opposes the reduction of sociological explanation to psychological factors or individual behavior. See "Homo Sociologicus," pp. 24, 64; also *Class and Class Conflict in Industrial Society*, pp. 145–149.

59. Ibid., pp. 169–170.

60. See "Out of Utopia: Toward a Reorientation of Sociological Analysis," in *Essays in the Theory of Society*, pp. 108, 112, 114–117. As he added (p. 118): "There is nothing logically wrong with the term 'system.' It begins to give birth to undesirable consequences only when it is applied to total societies and is made the ultimate frame of reference of analysis."

61. "In Praise of Thrasymachus," ibid., p. 137. The thesis of systemic persistence is exemplified in David Easton's emphasis on the continuity and adaptive capacity of the German political system from the Imperial order over Weimer Republic and Nazi regime to the Bonn Republic. As Dahrendorf comments (p. 143): "What a miserable, indeed almost inhuman, way to describe the most dramatic changes in the composition and substance of Germany's political order." For a critical reference to Deutsch see ibid., p. 140.

62. "Market and Plan: Two Types of Rationality," ibid., pp. 219, 222–223, 225–226. As he adds (p. 226), the market "is but one of the many versions of the utopia of powerlessness, of which neither modern political theory nor modern political practice seems to tire." The market utopia may be more dynamic than consensus models; but the "notion of the market shares with other utopias the impossibility of accounting for the necessity, the direction, and indeed the origin of change." This assessment does not prevent Dahrendorf from coming down ultimately on the side of a "sociologically refined" market rationality.

63. Ibid., p. 227; "Toward a Theory of Social Conflict," pp. 103–109; *Class and Class Conflict in Industrial Society*, pp. 157–240. For additional sociological literature see Lewis Coser, *The Functions of Social Conflict* (Glencoe, Ill.: Free Press, 1956) and *Continuities in the Study of Social Conflict* (New York: Free Press, 1967); Irving L. Horowitz, *The New Sociology*

(New York: Oxford University Press, 1965), pp. 3–48; T. B. Bottomore, *Elites and Society* (New York: Basic Books, 1964); Barrington Moore, Jr., *Political Power and Social Theory* (Cambridge, Mass.: Harvard University Press, 1958); James S. Coleman, *Community Conflict* (Glencoe, Ill.: Free Press, 1957); C. Wright Mills, *The Power Elite* (New York: Oxford University Press, 1956).

64. See "Homo Sociologicus," p. 38; also "On the Origin of Inequality among Men," ibid., p. 167; and *Class and Class Conflict in Industrial Society*, pp. 177–178.

65. *The Theory of Political Coalitions*, p. 22.

66. Hans J. Morgenthau, *Scientific Man vs. Power Politics* (Chicago: University of Chicago Press, 1946), p. 9.

67. Philip Rieff, *Freud: The Mind of the Moralist* (Garden City, N.Y.: Doubleday, 1961), pp. 391–392; see also Edward C. Tolman, *Behavior and Psychological Man* (Berkeley: University of California Press, 1951).

68. Max Marc, "What Image of Man for Political Science?" *Western Political Quarterly*, 15 (1962), 593, 595–596. He quotes this passage from Sigmund Freud, *Civilization and Its Discontents* (London: Hogarth Press, 1953), p. 85: "The bit of truth behind all this is—one eagerly denied—that men are not gentle friendly creatures wishing for love, who simply defend themselves if they are attacked, but that a powerful measure of desire for aggression has to be reckoned with as part of their instinctual endowment. Homo homini lupus; who has the courage to dispute it in the face of all evidence in his own life and in history?"

69. Harold D. Lasswell, *Psychopathology and Politics* (Chicago: University of Chicago Press, 1930; new ed. with afterthoughts by the author; New York: Viking Press, 1960), p. 75. According to Lasswell, Spranger's power seeker was characterized primarily by "desire to control the motives of others; methods varying from violence to wheedling; and success in securing communal recognition" (p. 52).

70. Lasswell, *Power and Personality* (New York: W. W. Norton, 1948; new ed. New York: Viking Press, 1962), pp. 20–21, 37–41, 57. See also Gordon J. DiRenzo, *Personality, Power and Politics* (Notre Dame, Ind.: University of Notre Dame Press, 1967); Arnold A. Rogow and Harold D. Lasswell, *Power, Corruption, and Rectitude* (Englewood Cliffs, N.J.: Prentice-Hall, 1963); Robert A. Dahl, *Modern Political Analysis* (Englewood Cliffs, N.J.: Prentice-Hall, 1963), p. 67; Marc, pp. 600–601.

71. As Dahrendorf notes in "Homo Sociologicus," p. 44: "Society is the alienated persona of the individual, homo sociologicus a shadow that has escaped the man to return as his master." See also Julian N. Hartt, *The Lost Image of Man* (Baton Rouge: Louisiana State University Press, 1963); Fritz Pappenheim, *The Alienation of Modern Man* (New York: Monthly Review Press, 1959); Allen Wheelis, *The Quest for Identity* (New York: W. W. Norton, 1958); Maurice Natanson, "Alienation and Social Role," *Social Research*, 33 (1966), 375–388; Peter L. Berger, "Identity as a Problem in the Sociology of Knowledge," *European Journal of Sociology*, 7 (1966), 105–115; Carl J. Couch, "Self-Identification and Alienation," *The Sociological Quarterly*, 7 (1966), 255–264.

72. See, for example, Talcott Parsons and Edward A. Shils, eds., *Toward a General Theory of Action* (Cambridge, Mass.: Harvard University Press,

1951); Gordon Tullock, *A General Theory of Politics* (U. of Virginia, 1958, private circulation); George C. Homans, *The Nature of Social Science* (New York: Harcourt, Brace & World, 1967).

73. As Jürgen Habermas points out: "As soon as the attitude of objectivity is turned into an ideological affirmation, the difficulties of the methodologically unconscious individual distort themselves into the doubtful virtue of a scientistic creed." See "Knowledge and Interest," *Inquiry*, 9 (1966), 298; also *Knowledge and Human Interests*, trans. Jeremy J. Shapiro (Boston: Beacon Press, 1971), p. 315.

74. For a listing of some of the advantages of conflict theory see Horowitz, "Consensus, Conflict and Cooperation: A Sociological Inventory," pp. 184–185.

75. Olson, "The Relationship Between Economics and the Other Social Sciences," pp. 147, 160–161. On the Freudian concepts see Wrong, "The Oversocialized Conception of Man in Modern Sociology," pp. 186–187, and "Human Nature and the Perspective of Sociology," p. 315; Dahrendorf, "Homo Sociologicus," pp. 57, 75; also Harold D. Lasswell, "The Triple-Appeal Principle: A Contribution of Psychoanalysis to Political and Social Science," *American Journal of Sociology*, 37 (1932), 523–538. To some extent the three models can be viewed as axiomatic formalizations of the three approaches to political inquiry delineated in the preceding essay—with the systemic model corresponding to the "analytical," the exchange model to the "practical-hermeneutical," and the conflict model to the "critical-dialectical" perspective.

76. Robert Musil, *Der Mann ohne Eigenschaften* (Hamburg: Rowohlt, 1952), p. 35, quoted in Dahrendorf, "Homo Sociologicus," p. 74. See also Helmuth Plessner, *Die Stufen des Organischen und der Mensch*, 2nd ed. (Berlin: W. de Gruyter, 1964); Ruth Wylie, *The Self-Concept* (Lincoln: University of Nebraska Press, 1961); Anselm Strauss, *Mirrors and Masks* (Glencoe, Ill.: Free Press, 1959); Eduard Urbanek, "Roles, Masks and Characters," *Social Research*, 34 (1967), 529–562; Robert R. Ehman, "Two Basic Concepts of the Self," *International Philosophical Quarterly*, 5 (1965), 594–611; Gajo Petrović, "Man as Economic Animal and Man as Praxis," *Inquiry*, 6 (1963), 35–56; Richard A. Schermerhorn, "Man the Unfinished," *The Sociological Quarterly*, 4 (1963), 5–17.

3. Social Role and "Human Nature"

1. Helmuth Plessner was born on September 4, 1892 in Wiesbaden, Germany. After studying zoology and philosophy in Freiburg, Berlin, and Heidelberg, he began his academic career at the University of Cologne from 1920 to 1933. Following Hitler's takeover, Plessner emigrated to Holland, where he taught at the University of Groningen until 1951. In that year he accepted a call to Göttingen, where he remained until 1962; during the following year he taught at the New School for Social Research in New York. Since 1963 he has lived in Zürich, Switzerland.

2. In the words of Jürgen Habermas, philosophical anthropology "integrates and digests the findings of all those sciences which—like psychology, sociology, archeology or linguistics—deal with man and his works; but it is

not in turn a specialized discipline." Perched "between empiricism and theory," the task of philosophical anthropology is "to interpret scientific findings in a philosophical manner." See his article "Anthropologie" in Alwin Diemer and Ivo Frenzel, eds., *Fischer-Lexikon: Philosophie* (Frankfurt–Main: Fischer Verlag, 1958), pp. 18, 20.

3. See Max Scheler, *Die Stellung des Menschen im Kosmos* (Bern: Francke Verlag, 1927). See also Manfred S. Frings, *Max Scheler* (Pittsburgh: Duquesne University Press, 1965); and Wilfried Hartmann, "Max Scheler's Theory of Person," *Philosophy Today*, 12 (1969), 246–261.

4. On this point and on the relationship between structure and "essence" see Günter Dux, "Epilogue," in Helmuth Plessner, *Philosophische Anthropologie* (Frankfurt–Main: Fischer Verlag, 1970), pp. 262–263.

5. For Plessner's joint reliance on empiricism and philosophy and especially for the role of phenomenology in his work see Felix Hammer, *Die exzentrische Position des Menschen: Helmuth Plessners Philosophische Anthropologie* (Bonn: Bouvier Verlag, 1967), pp. 32–58, 141–152.

6. As Plessner comments at one point, man has neither a fixed ecological milieu nor is he a completely unrestrained agent; one should consider the possibility that "in the case of man ecological milieu and openness collide and are locked in a reciprocal relationship which cannot be stably adjusted." See "Über das Welt-Umweltverhältnis des Menschen," *Studium Generale*. 3 (1950), 117.

7. See Plessner, *Vom Anfang als Prinzip transzendentaler Wahrheit* (Heidelberg: C. Winter, 1917); *Krisis der transzendentalen Wahrheit im Anfang* (Heidelberg: C. Winter, 1918).

8. Plessner, *Die Einheit der Sinne; Grundlinien einer Ästhesiologie des Geistes* (Bonn: Bouvier Verlag, 1923).

9. Plessner, *Die Stufen des Organischen und der Mensch* (1928), 2nd ed., (Berlin: Walter de Gruyter, 1965), pp. 185–346. On man's "eccentric position" see Dux, pp. 289–309; Hammer, pp. 130–140, 153–188.

10. See in this context F. J. J. Buytendijk, *Mensch und Tier; Ein Beitrag zur vergleichenden Psychologie* (Hamburg: Rowohlt, 1958); Erwin W. Straus, *Phenomenological Psychology* (New York: Basic Books, 1966), esp. pp. 137–187; also Hans Jonas, *The Phenomenon of Life: Toward a Philosophical Biology* (New York: Dell, 1966), esp. pp. 135–156.

11. See Plessner, *Lachen und Weinen* (Bern: Francke Verlag, 1941); trans. James S. Churchill and Marjorie Grene under the title *Laughing and Crying: A Study of the Limits of Human Behavior* (Evanston, Ill.: Northwestern University Press, 1970). See also his essay "Das Lächeln" (1950), in *Philosophische Anthropologie*, pp. 173–186.

12. Plessner, *Conditio Humana* (1961; republished, Pfullingen: Neske Verlag, 1964), pp. 42, 45.

13. See ibid., p. 54; "Zur Frage der Vergleichbarkeit tierischen und menschlichen Verhaltens," in Plessner, *Diesseits der Utopie; Ausgewählte Beiträge zur Kultursoziologie* (Düsseldorf: Diederichs Verlag, 1966), pp. 184–186; "Unmenschlichkeit," ibid., pp. 223–224; and *Grenzen der Gemeinschaft, Eine Kritik des sozialen Radikalismus* (Bonn: Cohen Verlag, 1924), p. 26.

14. See "Das Problem der Öffentlichkeit und die Idee der Entfremdung," in *Diesseits der Utopie*, pp. 19–21; "Soziale Rolle und menschliche Natur,"

ibid., pp. 23–30, 34–35; and *Conditio Humana,* pp. 53–61.

15. See "Macht und menschliche Natur," in Plessner, *Zwischen Philosophie und Gesellschaft* (Bern: Francke Verlag, 1953), pp. 241–317, esp. pp. 243–244, 270–290; also "Die Emanzipation der Macht," in *Diesseits der Utopie,* pp. 190–209, trans. under the title "The Emancipation of Power," in *Social Research,* 31 (1964), 155–174. Regarding the inexhaustible character of human nature see the statement: "This boundlessness of the human being, anchored in his specific life structure though he may be, allows us to speak of the *homo absconditus,* the man who knows the limits of his boundlessness yet grasps himself as unfathomable. Open to himself and to the world, he recognizes his own concealment. . . . He can never discover himself completely in his actions—only his shadow which precedes him and remains behind him: an imprint, a clue to himself." "De Homine Abscondito," ibid., 36 (1969), 501, 503.

16. Karsten Harries, "Martin Heidegger: The Search for Meaning," in George A. Schrader, Jr., ed., *Existential Philosophers: Kierkegaard to Merleau-Ponty* (New York: McGraw-Hill, 1967), pp. 171, 185. See also J. Glenn Gray, "The New Image of Man in Martin Heidegger's Philosophy," in George L. Kline, ed., *European Philosophy Today* (Chicago: Quadrangle Books, 1965), pp. 31–60; and Helmut Fahrenbach, "Heidegger und das Problem einer 'philosophischen' Anthropologie," in *Durchblicke: Martin Heidegger zum 80. Geburtstag* (Frankfurt–Main: Klostermann, 1970), pp. 97–131.

17. Maurice Merleau-Ponty, "The Battle over Existentialism," in *Sense and Non-Sense,* trans. with preface by Hubert L. and Patricia A. Dreyfus (Evanston, Ill.: Northwestern University Press, 1964), pp. 73–76. See also David Carr, "Maurice Merleau-Ponty: Incarnate Consciousness," in Schrader, ed., pp. 369–429.

18. See Arnold Gehlen, *Der Mensch: Seine Natur und seine Stellung in der Welt* (1940), 8th ed. (Frankfurt–Main and Bonn: Athenäum Verlag, 1966), esp. pp. 9–85.

19. Gehlen, *Urmensch und Spätkultur* (Bonn: Athenäum Verlag, 1956), esp. pp. 9, 21, 233. Regarding modern subjectivism and the question of human freedom see also his *Die Seele im technischen Zeitalter* (1949; rev. ed., Hamburg: Rowohlt, 1957), and "Über die Geburt der Freiheit aus der Entfremdung," *Archiv für Rechts-und Sozialphilosophie,* 40 (1952–1953), 338–353. For a discussion of some of these writings, and Gehlen's approach in general, see Peter L. Berger and Hansfried Kellner, "Arnold Gehlen and the Theory of Institutions," *Social Research,* 32 (1965), 110–115.

20. Gehlen, *Moral und Hypermoral* (Frankfurt–Main: Metzner, 1969).

21. Cf. Wilbert E. Moore and Arnold S. Feldman, "Society as a Tension-Management System," in George Baker and Leonard S. Cotrell, Jr., eds., *Behavioral Science and Civil Defense,* Disaster Research Group, Study No. 16 (Washington, D.C.: National Academy of Sciences, National Research Council, 1962), pp. 93–115; Wilbert E. Moore, *Social Change* (Englewood Cliffs, N.J.: Prentice-Hall, 1963), pp. 10–11; David Easton, *A Systems Analysis of Political Life* (New York: Wiley, 1965), esp. pp. 57–69, 85–116. 247–266; and Karl W. Deutsch, *The Nerves of Government: Models of Political Communication and Control* (New York: Free Press, 1963), esp. pp. 110–127.

22. Talcott Parsons, "Some Highlights of the General Theory of Action," in Roland Young, ed., *Approaches to the Study of Politics* (Evanston, Ill.: Northwestern University Press, 1958), pp. 288–289. For a more strongly "institutional" focus see, e.g., Samuel P. Huntington, *Political Order in Changing Societies* (New Haven, Conn.: Yale University Press, 1968).

23. Plessner, *Conditio Humana*, pp. 42–46; "The Emancipation of Power," p. 158.

24. Habermas, "Anthropologie," pp. 28, 33.

25. See "Arnold Gehlen: Nachgeahmte Substantialität," in Habermas, *Philosophisch-politische Profile* (Frankfurt–Main: Suhrkamp, 1971), pp. 200–221. The relationship between Gehlen and Habermas is discussed by Wolf Lepenies in "Anthropologie und Gesellschaftskritik: Zur Kontroverse Gehlen-Habermas," in Lepenies and Helmut Nolte, *Kritik der Anthropologie* (Munich: Hanser Verlag, 1971), pp. 77–102; trans. under the title "Anthropology and Social Criticism: A View on the Controversy between Arnold Gehlen and Jürgen Habermas," in *The Human Context*, 3 (1971), 205–225. Lepenies finds in the treatise on ethics a subtle change in Gehlen's position: in lieu of the previous opposition between instinctual diffuseness and normative-institutional stabilization the study, in his view, bases normative standards directly on biological needs and dispositions.

26. Karl-Otto Apel, "Arnold Gehlens 'Philosophie der Institutionen,' " *Philosophische Rundschau*, 10 (1958), 1–21, esp. pp. 7–11, 18–19. For a detailed critique of Gehlen's writings, from a perspective akin to Apel's, see Dietrich Böhler, "Arnold Gehlen: Die Handlung," in Josef Speck, ed., *Probleme der grossen Denker*, vol. 2 (Göttingen: Vandenhoeck & Ruprecht, 1973).

27. See Robert Musil, *Der Mann ohne Eigenschaften* (Hamburg: Rowohlt, 1952); also John Helmer, "The Face of the Man Without Qualities," *Social Research*, 37 (1970), 547–574.

28. See Karl Jaspers, *Von der Wahrheit* (Munich: Piper, 1947), p. 83; also Richard F. Grabau, "Karl Jaspers: Communication through Transcendence," in Schrader, ed., pp. 109–160.

29. Frederick H. Heinemann, *Existentialism and the Modern Predicament* (New York: Harper & Row, 1958), pp. 60–61, 69–70, 82. Jean-Paul Sartre's critique in the *Search for a Method* seems excessively harsh—especially in view of his own fascination with abstract freedom during his earlier period. "Jaspers," he writes, "mute on Revelation, leads us back—through discontinuity, pluralism, and impotence—to the pure, formal subjectivity which is discovered and which discovers transcendence through its defeats." *Search for a Method*, trans. Hazel E. Barnes (New York: Knopf, 1963), p. 15.

30. Theodore Roszak, *The Making of a Counter Culture: Reflections on the Technocratic Society and Its Youth Opposition* (Garden City, N.Y.: Anchor Books, 1969), pp. 218–220, 227–230, 240.

31. Charles A. Reich, *The Greening of America* (New York: Random House, 1970), pp. 4, 18, 21–22, 67–70, 81, 129–130, 139–148, 225–228, 233, 255–256. The image of Protean man has left its imprint on contemporary social science. Among political theorists, Henry S. Kariel has been most eloquent in insisting on human malleability and the need for social and political improvisation; see, e.g., his *Open Systems: Arenas for Political Action* (Ithaca, Ill.: Peacock Publishers, 1969). Regarding the bent toward intro-

spection see Robert Hunter, *The Storming of the Mind: Inside the Consciousness Revolution* (Garden City, N.Y.: Doubleday, 1972), and Roger Poole, *Towards Deep Subjectivity* (New York: Harper & Row, 1972).

32. Plessner, *Diesseits der Utopie,* pp. 21, 32–34; Habermas, *Philosophisch-politische Profile,* pp. 218–220; and Maurice Natanson, "Alienation and Social Role," *Social Research,* 33 (1966), 383. For a critique of the Protean or "possibilitarian" conception of man see also John O'Neill, *Sociology as a Skin Trade: Essays Toward a Reflexive Sociology* (New York: Harper & Row, 1972), pp. 17, 217.

33. See Ralf Dahrendorf, "Homo Sociologicus: On the History, Significance and Limits of the Category of Social Role," in his *Essays on the Theory of Society* (Stanford: Stanford University Press, 1968), pp. 19–87; and "Sociology and Human Nature: A Postscript to Homo Sociologicus," ibid., 88–106. For a critical evaluation of his perspective see, e.g., Plessner, *Diesseits der Utopie,* p. 34; Habermas, *Theorie und Praxis: Sozialphilosophische Studien,* 4th rev. ed. (Frankfurt–Main: Suhrkamp, 1971), pp. 239–243; Judith Janoska-Bendl, "Probleme der Freiheit in der Rollenanalyse," *Kölner Zeitschrift für Soziologie und Sozialpsychologie,* 14 (1962), 459–475; and Peter Weingart, "Beyond Parsons? A Critique of Ralf Dahrendorf's Conflict Theory," *Social Forces,* 48 (1969), 91–105.

34. See in this context Carr's comment on Merleau-Ponty that "ambiguity is an expression not of absurdity but of dialectic. The necessarily unfulfilled intentions which hold between subject and object, subject and other subject, subject and itself are the conditions of the operative syntheses of which life is made." In Schrader, ed., p. 409.

35. Plessner, *Die Stufen des Organischen und der Mensch,* p. 26; "The Emancipation of Power," p. 158. Relying to some extent on Plessner, Hans Peter Dreitzel has examined the social and behavioral pathologies arising from the conflict of regulation and anomie; see *Die gesellschaftlichen Leiden und das Leiden an der Gesellschaft: Vorstudien zu einer Pathologie des Rollenverhaltens* (Stuttgart: F. Enke Verlag, 1968).

36. Regarding the older Frankfurt School see Max Horkheimer, "Bemerkungen zur philosophischen Anthropologie" (1935), in Alfred Schmidt, ed., *Kritische Theorie: Eine Dokumentation* (Frankfurt–Main: Fischer Verlag, 1968), 1: 200–227; Theodor W. Adorno, *Negative Dialektik* (Frankfurt–Main: Suhrkamp, 1966), p. 9; Ulrich Sonnemann, *Negative Anthropologie* (Hamburg: Rowohlt, 1969); and, for a very perceptive overview, Martin Jay, "The Frankfurt School's Critique of Marxist Humanism," *Social Research,* 39 (1972), 285–305. Concerning Habermas see, e.g., his *Knowledge and Human Interests* (Boston: Beacon Press, 1971) and his *Kultur und Kritik: Verstreute Aufsätze* (Frankfurt–Main: Suhrkamp, 1973), pp. 232–235; Christian K. Lenhardt, "Rise and Fall of Transcendental Anthropology," *Philosophy of the Social Sciences,* 2 (1972), 231–246; also, for a development of some of Habermas' views on role theory, Lothar Krappmann, *Soziologische Dimensionen der Identität* (Stuttgart: E. Klett Verlag, 1972). Among the various influences on Habermas' outlook one should mention in this context also Erich Rothacker whose philosophical anthropology (despite a stronger emphasis on cultural milieus) is broadly comparable to Plessner's work. Plessner's impact can be detected in several of Karl-Otto Apel's writings; e.g., in his "Wissenschaft als Emanzipation?" *Zeitschrift für allgemeine Wissen-*

schaftstheorie (Journal for General Philosophy of Science), 1 (1970), 193.

37. Plessner, "Der Weg der Soziologie in Deutschland" (1959), in *Diesseits der Utopie*, pp. 52–53.

4. Phenomenology and Social Science

1. David Easton, "The New Revolution in Political Science," *American Political Science Review*, 63 (1969), 1051. (The address was delivered at the annual meeting in September 1969).

2. Ibid., pp. 1053, 1057.

3. Wilhelm Dilthey, *Gesammelte Schriften*, 5th ed. (Stuttgart: Teubner, 1962), 7: 148. See also Joseph Meurers, *Wilhelm Diltheys Gedankenwelt und die Naturwissenschaft* (Berlin: Junker & Dünnhaupt, 1936), p. 36; Jürgen Habermas, *Erkenntnis und Interesse* (Frankfurt–Main: Suhrkamp, 1968), pp. 178–233, trans. Jeremy J. Shapiro as *Knowledge and Human Interests* (Boston: Beacon Press, 1971), pp. 140–186.

4. Heinrich Rickert, *Kulturwissenschaft und Naturwissenschaft* (1899), 2nd ed. (Tübingen: J. C. B. Mohr, 1910), trans. George Reisman as *Science and History* (Princeton, N.J.: Van Nostrandt, 1962). See also my essay "Heinrich Rickert und die amerikanische Sozialwissenschaft," *Der Staat*, 5 (1966), 17–46.

5. In the words of Helmuth Plessner: "The call 'to the things themselves,' away from theorizing, had an impact on the young generation of the time comparable to the impact which the demand of out-door painting must have exerted on the academicians of the mid-nineteenth century." *Diesseits der Utopie* (Düsseldorf–Cologne: Diederichs Verlag, 1966), p. 147.

6. The first volume of *Ideas* appeared in 1913, while the second and third volumes were published posthumously. On *Ideas I* and *Ideas II* see especially Paul Ricoeur, *Husserl: An Analysis of his Phenomenology*, trans. Edward G. Ballard and Lester E. Embree (Evanston, Ill.: Northwestern University Press, 1967), pp. 13–81.

7. The first alternative is intimated by Herbert Spiegelberg, *The Phenomenological Movement, A Historical Introduction*, 2nd ed. (The Hague: Martinus Nijhoff, 1969), 1: 161. For a divergent interpretation see Ricoeur, p. 12. On life-world cf. also Plessner, p. 158, n. 5; Aron Gurwitsch, "The Last Work of Edmund Husserl," *Philosophy and Phenomenological Research*, 17 (1957), 397.

8. "Since the first awakening of my philosophical consciousness the questions: 'What is Man? And what is his place in the universe of being?' have occupied me more deeply and more centrally than any other philosophical question." Max Scheler, *Die Stellung des Menschen im Kosmos* (1928), 4th ed. (Munich: Nymphenburger Verlagsanstalt, 1948), p. 9.

9. Cf. Manfred S. Frings, *Max Scheler* (Pittsburgh: Duquesne University Press, 1965); also Martin Buber, "The Philosophical Anthropology of Max Scheler," *Philosophy and Phenomenological Research*, 6 (1946), 307–321; Alfred Schutz, "Scheler's Theory of Intersubjectivity and the General Thesis of the Alter Ego," ibid., 2 (1942), 323–347, reprinted in *Collected Papers*, ed. Maurice Natanson, 2nd ed. (The Hague: Martinus Nijhoff, 1967), 1: 150–179.

10. His perspective is sharpened and refined in his essay "Zeit und Sein" (1962) in *L'endurance de la pensée: Pour saluer Jean Beaufret* (Paris: Plon, 1968), pp. 12–71; trans. Joan Stambaugh in *On Time and Being* (New York: Harper & Row, 1972), pp. 1–24. Cf. also Calvin O. Schrag, "Phenomenology, Ontology, and History in the Philosophy of Heidegger," *Revue internationale de philosophie*, 12 (1958), 117–132.

11. Cf. Ricoeur, "New Developments in Phenomenology in France: The Phenomenology of Language," *Social Research*, 34 (1967), 4.

12. Cf. Alfred Schutz, "Sartre's Theory of the Alter Ego," *Philosophy and Phenomenological Research*, 9 (1948), 181–199, reprinted in *Collected Papers*, 1: 180–203; also Maurice Natanson, "Jean-Paul Sartre's Philosophy of Freedom," *Social Research*, 19 (1952), 362–380, reprinted in his *Literature, Philosophy and the Social Sciences, Essays in Existentialism and Phenomenology* (The Hague: Martinus Nijhoff, 1962), pp. 62–75.

13. Cf. Arthur Lessing, "Marxist Existentialism," *Review of Metaphysics*, 20 (1967), 461–482; George Lichtheim, "Sartre, Marxism and History," *History and Theory*, 3 (1963), 222–246; also Lucien Goldmann, *Recherches dialectiques* (Paris: Gallimard, 1959); Leszek Kolakowski, "Responsibility and History," in his *Toward a Marxist Humanism: Essays on the Left Today* (New York: Grove Press, 1968), pp. 85–157.

14. On hermeneutics see especially Hans-Georg Gadamer, *Wahrheit und Methode*, 2nd ed. (Tübingen: J. C. B. Mohr, 1965), trans. under the title *Truth and Method* (New York: Seabury Press, 1975); Richard E. Palmer, *Hermeneutics: Interpretation Theory in Schleiermacher, Dilthey, Heidegger, and Gadamer* (Evanston, Ill.: Northwestern University Press, 1969); and Rüdiger Bubner, Konrad Cramer, and Reiner Wiehl, eds., *Hermeneutik und Dialektik*, 2 vols. (Tübingen, J. C. B. Mohr, 1970); on Wittgenstein, e.g., Thomas N. Munson, "Wittgenstein's Phenomenology," *Philosophy and Phenomenological Research*, 23 (1962), 37–50; on phenomenology of language, Ricoeur, "New Developments . . ." pp. 8–30, and Remy C. Kwant, *Phenomenology of Language* (Pittsburgh: Duquesne University Press, 1965).

15. Prominent illustrations of this interaction are Gestalt theory, experimental phenomenology of perception, and existential psychology. Simply for reasons of brevity, the present pages also neglect the discipline of economics. For some comments, particularly on Walter Eucken, see Anna-Teresa Tymieniecka, *Phenomenology and Science in Contemporary European Thought* (New York: Farrar, Straus & Cudahy, 1962), pp. 97–104; see also Friedrich A. Hayek, *The Counter-Revolution of Science* (Glencoe, Ill.: Free Press, 1955).

16. See Max Weber, " 'Objectivity' in Social Science and Social Policy" (1904), in Maurice Natanson, ed., *Philosophy of the Social Sciences: A Reader* (New York: Random House, 1963), p. 382.

17. In addition to interpretive understanding, however, Weber also referred to scientific validation, envisaging even the possibility of a "correspondence" between understanding and demonstration—a balanced view rarely attained in later social science. See Guenther Roth and Claus Wittich, eds., *Economy and Society, An Outline of Interpretive Sociology* (New York: Bedminster Press, 1968), 1: 4–22.

18. On Reinach see Spiegelberg, 1: 195–205; Tymieniecka, pp. 90–97.

19. See Edward A. Tiryakian, "Existential Phenomenology and the Socio-

logical Tradition," *American Sociological Review*, 30 (1965), 680. Cf. also Rudolph H. Weingartner, *Experience and Culture* (Middletown, Conn.: Wesleyan University Press, 1962).

20. See Alfred Vierkandt, *Gesellschaftslehre*, 2nd ed. (Stuttgart: F. Enke, 1928), pp. v, 4–7, 19–20, 23–24, 105–107, 161–167, 208–224. On Vierkandt cf. also Tymieniecka, pp. 87–88; Don Martindale, *The Nature and Types of Sociological Theory* (Boston: Houghton Mifflin, 1960), pp. 268–273; Nicholas S. Timasheff, *Sociological Theory, Its Nature and Growth*, rev. ed. (New York: Random House, 1957), pp. 267–268; Theodore Abel, *Systematic Sociology in Germany* (New York: Columbia University Press, 1929), pp. 59–79.

21. In Martindale's words: "The sociological character of forms of knowledge (of thought, intuition, and cognition) is unquestionable, according to Scheler. Nevertheless, neither the content nor the objective validity of knowledge is determined by social structures. Knowledge *per se* consists of a realm of essences." *Sociological Theory*, p. 275. Cf. also Howard Becker and Helmut O. Dahlke, "Max Scheler's Sociology of Knowledge," *Philosophy and Phenomenological Research*, 2 (1942), 309–322.

22. See Helmuth Plessner, *Die Stufen des Organischen und der Mensch, Einleitung in die philosophische Anthropologie* (1928), 2nd ed. (Berlin: Walter de Gruyter, 1965), in particular pp. vii–xiv for comments on his relations to Scheler and Heidegger; also *Laughing and Crying, A Study of the Limits of Human Behavior*, trans. James S. Churchill and Marjorie Grene (Evanston, Ill.: Northwestern University Press, 1970); *Conditio Humana* (Pfullingen: Neske Verlag, 1964), and "De Homine Abscondito," *Social Research*, 36 (1969), 497–509.

23. Karl Mannheim, "Competition as a Cultural Phenomenon" (1928), in Paul Kecskemeti, ed., *Essays on the Sociology of Knowledge* (New York: Oxford University Press, 1952), p. 194. Cf. also David Kettler, "Sociology of Knowledge and Moral Philosophy: The Place of Traditional Problems in the Formation of Mannheim's Thought," *Political Science Quarterly*, 82 (1967), 400.

24. Cf. Maurice Natanson, "Knowledge and Alienation: Some Remarks on Mannheim's Sociology of Knowledge," in *Literature, Philosophy and the Social Sciences*, pp. 167–171; Robert K. Merton, "Karl Mannheim and the Sociology of Knowledge," in *Social Theory and Social Structure*, rev. ed. (Glencoe, Ill.: Free Press, 1957), pp. 489–508; Leopold Rosenmayr, "Max Scheler, Karl Mannheim und die Zukunft der Wissenssoziologie," in Alphons Silbermann, ed., *Militanter Humanismus, Von den Aufgaben der modernen Soziologie* (Frankfurt: Fischer Verlag, 1966), pp. 200–231.

25. See Alfred Schutz, *The Phenomenology of the Social World*, trans. George Walsh and Frederick Lehnert (Evanston, Ill.: Northwestern University Press, 1967), pp. 11–12, 43–44, 59–61, 88, 97, 144–146, 163–194, 202–214, 240.

26. See Schutz's comments in "Husserl's Importance for the Social Sciences" (1959), in *Collected Papers*, 1: 149; also "Concept and Theory Formation in the Social Sciences" (1953), ibid., p. 57; "On Multiple Realities" (1945), ibid., p. 228. See also his *Reflections on the Problem of Relevance*, ed. Richard M. Zaner (New Haven and London: Yale University Press, 1970); and Aron Gurvitsch, "The Common-Sense World as Social Reality:

A Discourse on Alfred Schutz," *Social Research*, 29 (1962), 50–72.

27. Cf. Maurice Natanson, "Phenomenology and Typification: A Study in the Philosophy of Alfred Schutz," *Social Research*, 37 (1970), 1–22, and "Alfred Schutz on Social Reality and Social Science," ibid., 35 (1968), 217–244; also Robert Bierstedt, "The Common Sense World of Alfred Schutz," ibid., vol. 30 (1963), 116–121; and Richard M. Zaner, "Theory of Intersubjectivity: Alfred Schutz," ibid., 28 (1961), 71–93.

28. The relationship is explored in Maurice Natanson, *The Social Dynamics of George H. Mead* (Washington, D.C.: Public Affairs Press, 1956); see also Herbert Blumer, "Sociological Implications of the Thought of George Herbert Mead," *American Journal of Sociology*, 71 (1966), pp. 535–544.

29. See Aaron V. Cicourel, *Method and Measurement in Sociology* (Glencoe, Ill.: Free Press, 1964), esp. p. 14; also his *The Social Organization of Juvenile Justice* (New York: Wiley, 1968) and *Cognitive Sociology* (New York: Free Press, 1974).

30. George Psathas, "Ethnomethods and Phenomenology," *Social Research*, 35 (1968), 509. See Harold Garfinkel, *Studies in Ethnomethodology* (Englewood Cliffs, N.J.: Prentice-Hall, 1967); and for critical comments "Review Symposium on *Studies in Ethnomethodology*," *American Sociological Review*, 33 (1968), 122–130. Cf. also Hans P. Dreitzel, ed., *Recent Sociology No. 2: Patterns of Communicative Behavior* (New York: Macmillan, 1970); Richard J. Hill and Kathleen S. Crittenden, eds., *Proceedings of the Purdue Symposium on Ethnomethodology* (Lafayette, Ind.: Purdue University, 1968); Norman K. Denzin, "Symbolic Interactionism and Ethnomethodology: A Proposed Synthesis," *American Sociological Review*, 34 (1969), 922–934.

31. Peter L. Berger and Thomas Luckmann, *The Social Construction of Reality, A Treatise in the Sociology of Knowledge* (Garden City, N.Y.: Anchor Books, 1967), pp. 3, 14–15, 18, 61, 187.

32. Jean-Paul Sartre, *Search for a Method*, trans. Hazel E. Barnes (New York: Alfred A. Knopf, 1963), pp. 51–52, 133–135, 152–159; Leszek Kolakowski, "Ist der verstehende Marxismus möglich?" in Frank Benseler, ed., *Festschrift zum achtzigsten Geburtstag von Georg Lukács* (Neuwied and Berlin: Luchterhand, 1965), pp. 270–286.

33. See Georges Gurvitch, *Dialectique et Sociologie* (Paris: Flammarion, 1962); Phillip Bosserman, *Dialectical Sociology: An Analysis of the Sociology of Georges Gurvitch* (Boston: P. Sargent, 1968); for his earlier work see Martindale, pp. 276–278; Timasheff, pp. 268–271. Cf. also Stephan Strasser, *The Idea of Dialogal Phenomenology* (Pittsburgh: Duquesne University Press, 1969) and *Phenomenology and the Human Sciences* (Pittsburgh: Duquesne University Press, 1963), esp. pp. 245–259.

34. See Peter Winch, *The Idea of a Social Science, and Its Relation to Philosophy* (London: Routledge & Kegan Paul, 1958); also Arnold Levison, "Knowledge and Society," *Inquiry*, 9 (1966), 75–93; Karl-Otto Apel, "Die Entfaltung der 'sprachanalytischen' Philosophie und das Problem der 'Geisteswissenschaften,'" *Philosophisches Jahrbuch*, 72 (1965), 239–289.

35. See Anselm L. Strauss, *Mirrors and Masks, The Search for Identity* (Glencoe, Ill.: Free Press, 1959); Erving Goffman, *Stigma, Notes on the Management of Spoiled Identity* (Englewood Cliffs, N.J.: Prentice-Hall, 1963); Arthur C. Danto, *Analytical Philosophy of History* (Cambridge: Uni-

versity Press, 1965).

36. Cf. John G. Gunnell, "Reduction, Explanation, and Social Scientific Inquiry," *American Political Science Review*, 63 (1969), 1233–1246.

37. On typifications and typologies see Carl G. Hempel, "Typological Methods in the Social Sciences," in Natanson, ed., *Philosophy of the Social Sciences*, pp. 210–230. Cf. also Hempel's *Aspects of Scientific Explanation* (New York: Free Press, 1965), and John C. McKinney, *Constructive Typology and Social Theory* (New York: Appleton-Century-Crofts, 1966).

38. Cf. John G. Gunnell, "Social Science and Political Reality: The Problem of Explanation," *Social Research*, 35 (1968), 177; also James W. van Evra, "Understanding in the Social Sciences," *Inquiry*, 12 (1969), 347–349; Murray L. Wax, "On Misunderstanding *Verstehen*: A Reply to Abel," *Sociology and Social Research*, 51 (1967), 323–333; William Tucker, "Max Weber's *Verstehen*," *Sociological Quarterly*, 6 (1965), 156–165; Abraham Kaplan, *The Conduct of Inquiry* (San Francisco: Chandler Publ. Co.,1964), p. 32; Fred R. Dallmayr and Thomas A. McCarthy, eds., *Understanding and Social Inquiry* (Notre Dame, Ind.: University of Notre Dame Press, 1977), pp. 19–100.

39. Ernest Nagel, "Problems of Concept and Theory Formation in the Social Sciences," in Natanson, ed., *Philosophy of the Social Sciences*, pp. 189–209; Alfred Schutz, "Concept and Theory Formation in the Social Sciences," ibid., pp. 239, 245; Gunnell, "Social Science . . ." p. 187.

40. Strasser, *Phenomenology and the Human Sciences*, pp. 295–302.

41. Jürgen Habermas, "Zur Logik der Sozialwissenschaften," *Philosophische Rundschau*, Beiheft 5 (Tübingen: J. C. B. Mohr, 1967), pp. 118–124, 134–144, 172–180.

42. "Phenomenology and the Sciences of Man," in James M. Edie, ed., *The Primacy of Perception, and Other Essays* (Evanston, Ill.: Northwestern University Press, 1964), p. 44. See also his statement in "The Philosopher and Sociology": "We need neither tear down the behavioral sciences to lay the foundations of philosophy, nor tear down philosophy to lay the foundations of the behavioral sciences." *Signs*, trans. Richard C. McCleary (Evanston, Ill.: Northwestern University Press, 1964), p. 98.

5. Hobbes and Existentialism

1. Jürgen Habermas, *Theorie and Praxis* (Neuwied: Luchterhand, 1963), 32–46; Crawford B. Macpherson, *The Political Theory of Possessive Individualism: Hobbes to Locke* (Oxford: Clarendon Press, 1962), pp. 9–106, and "Hobbes's Bourgeois Man," in *Hobbes Studies*, ed. Keith C. Brown (Oxford: Blackwell, 1965), pp. 169–183.

2. As is well known, Camus frequently objected to the existentialist (or to any other) label, but his objection derived largely from a presumed coincidence of existentialism with a leap into faith or an escape into transcendental meaning, e.g., Albert Camus, *The Myth of Sisyphus, and Other Essays*, trans. Justin O'Brien (New York: Alfred A. Knopf, 1955), pp. 24–31.

3. Maurice Merleau-Ponty, "Hegel's Existentialism," in *Sense and Non-Sense*, trans. with preface by Hubert L. and Patricia A. Dreyfus (Evanston, Ill.: Northwestern University Press, 1964), p. 70. On the theme of alienation

see, e.g., Frederick H. Heinemann, *Existentialism and the Modern Predicament* (New York: Harper Torchbooks, 1958), pp. 9–13.

4. See Leo Strauss, *The Political Philosophy of Hobbes* (Phoenix ed.; Chicago: University of Chicago Press, 1963), p. 9; also my essay, "Strauss and the 'Moral Basis' of Thomas Hobbes," *Archiv für Rechts- und Sozialphilosophie*, 52 (Spring 1966), 25–63.

5. Thomas Hobbes, *Elements of Law*, pt. I, ch. 7, art. 3, 4, 5; ch. 9, art. 21 (comparison of human life with a "race").

6. Thomas Hobbes, *De Cive*, pt. I, ch. 1, art. 2; Thomas Hobbes, *Leviathan*, pt. I, chs. 2, 3, 5. Compare also these passages in a letter to the Marquis of Newcastle: "The passions of man's mind, except only one, may be observed all in other living creatures. They have desires of all sorts, love, hatred, fear, hope, anger, pity, emulation, and the like: only curiosity, which is the desire to know the causes of things, I never saw sign in any other living creature but in man. . . . And therefore as in the cognitive faculties reason, so in the motive curiosity, are the marks that part the bounds of man's nature from that of beasts." *English Works*, ed. Sir William Molesworth, 11 vols. (London: J. Bohn, 1839–1845), 7: 467.

7. *Leviathan*, pt. I, chs. 11, 13 (Hobbes phrases the argument somewhat differently, e.g., by using the term "glory" instead of resentment); also *De Cive*, pt. I, ch. 1, art. 6: "But the most frequent reason why men desire to hurt each other, arises hence, that many men at the same time have an appetite to the same thing; which yet very often they can neither enjoy in common, nor yet divide it; whence it follows that the strongest must have it and who is strongest must be decided by the sword."

8. Camus, *The Myth of Sisyphus*, pp. 5, 46, 61; also Albert Camus, *The Rebel*, trans. A. Bower (New York: Vintage Books, 1956), pp. 11, 248.

9. Merleau-Ponty, "Hegel's Existentialism," pp. 66–68. See also John F. Bannan, *The Philosophy of Merleau-Ponty* (New York: Harcourt, Brace & World, 1967), p. 86.

10. Jean-Paul Sartre, *Being and Nothingness*, trans. with introduction by Hazel E. Barnes (New York: Philosophical Library, 1956), p. xxxi; at another point she adds (p. xxviii): "With Sartre, to destroy all desire would be to destroy the for-itself—not in the nothingness of Nirvana but absolutely. A satisfied for-itself would no longer be a for-itself. The for-itself is desire; that is, it is the nihilating project toward a being which it can never have or be but which as an end gives the for-itself its meaning." For Sartre's statements see ibid., pp. 24–25; Jean-Paul Sartre, *Nausea*, trans. Lloyd Alexander (Norfolk, Conn.: New Directions, 1949), p. 172; Jean-Paul Sartre, *The Transcendence of the Ego*, trans. with introduction by F. Williams and R. Kirkpatrick (New York: Noonday Press, 1957), p. 100.

11. Jean-Paul Sartre, *Search for a Method*, trans. under this title by Hazel E. Barnes (New York: Alfred A. Knopf, 1963), pp. 150–151.

12. Sartre, *Being and Nothingness*, pp. 364, 410.

13. Jean-Paul Sartre, *Critique de la raison dialectique* (Paris Gallimard, 1960), pp. 204, 206, 208; Wilfrid Desan, *The Marxism of Jean-Paul Sartre* (Garden City, N.Y.: Doubleday, 1965), pp. 91-94.

14. Compare A. E. Taylor, "The Ethical Doctrine of Hobbes," and Stuart M. Brown, Jr., "The Taylor Thesis: Some Objections," in *Hobbes Studies*, pp. 35–55, 57–71; Strauss, *Hobbes*, p. 8ff.; Howard Warrender, *The Politi-*

cal Philosophy of Hobbes (Oxford: Clarendon Press, 1957), pp. 93, 213, and his "Hobbes's Conception of Morality," *Rivista Critica di Storia della Filosofia*, Fall 1962, pp. 435–450. Reviewing the two alternatives, Michael Oakeshott has advanced a "third" solution, tracing all obligation to the command of a legitimate authority—a solution that bypasses rather than answers the question of a precivil, moral obligation; "The Moral Life in the Writings of Thomas Hobbes," in *Rationalism in Politics and Other Essays* (London: Methuen, 1962), pp. 248–300. Cf. also his "Introduction" to *Leviathan* (Oxford: Blackwell, 1946), pp. lviii–lxi.

15. *Elements of Law*, pt. I, ch. 14, art. 6, 7.

16. "The state of hostility and war being such, as thereby nature itself is destroyed and men kill one another . . . he therefore that desires to live in such a state as is the state of liberty and right of all to all, contradicts himself. For every man by natural necessity desires his own good, to which this state is contrary." Ibid., pt. I, ch. 14, art. 12.

17. Ibid., pt. I, ch. 15, art. 1. Macpherson argues that Hobbes derives moral obligation from the fact of existence; Macpherson, *Possessive Individualism*, pp. 81–87. Perhaps it would be more accurate to say that, at this level at least, fact and value merge because life is both a fact and an affirmation.

18. "By right reason in the natural state of men, I understand not, as many do, an infallible faculty, but the act of reasoning, that is, the peculiar and true ratiocination of every man concerning those actions of his which may either rebound to the damage or benefit of his neighbours." *De Cive*, pt. I, ch. 2, art. 1, note; see also *Leviathan*, pt. I, ch. 5.

19. "They therefore who could not agree concerning a present, do agree concerning a future good, which indeed is a work of reason; for things present are obvious to the sense, things to come to our reason only. Reason declaring peace to be good, it follows by the same reason, that all the necessary means to peace be good also. . . . The law therefore, in the means to peace, commands also good manners, or the practice of virtue: and therefore it is called moral." *De Cive*, pt. I, ch. 3, art. 31.

20. "And thus much for the ill condition, which man by mere nature is actually placed in, though with a possibility to come out of it, consisting partly in the passions, partly in his reason. The passions that encline men to peace are fear of death, desire of such things as are necessary to commodious living, and a hope by their industry to obtain them. And reason suggests convenient articles of peace, upon which men may be drawn to agreement." *Leviathan*, pt. I, ch. 13.

21. "But if any man pretend somewhat to tend necessarily to his preservation, which yet he himself does not confidently believe so, he may offend against the laws of nature." *De Cive*, pt. I, ch. 1, art. 10, note; see also ch. 3, art. 27, 30; *Leviathan*, pt. I, ch. 15.

22. Camus, *The Myth of Sisyphus*, pp. 16, 40, 46, 49, 50. The close linkage of fact and value at this level is evident in Camus's statements (pp. 40, 45) that "once and for all, value judgments are discarded here in favor of factual judgments" and that "revolt gives life its value. Spread out over the whole length of a life, it restores its majesty to that life." See also Edward T. Gargan, "Revolution and *Morale* in the Formative Thought of Albert Camus," *Review of Politics*, 25 (October 1963), 483–496.

23. The continued merger of fact and value can be gleaned from his statements that "the transition from facts to rights is manifest . . . in rebellion" and that rebellion is "contradictory in its content because, in wanting to uphold life, it excludes all value judgments, when to live is, in itself, a value judgment. To breathe is to judge." However, while still critical of transcendent or "absolute values," Camus now argued that "revolution, in order to be creative, cannot do without either a moral or metaphysical rule to balance the insanity of history." Camus, *The Rebel*, pp. 8, 15, 21, 251.

24. "If injustice is bad for the rebel, it is not because it contradicts an eternal idea of justice, but because it perpetuates the silent hostility that separates the oppressor from the oppressed. It kills the small part of existence that can be realized on this earth through the mutual understanding of men. In the same way, since the man who lies shuts himself off from other men, falsehood is therefore proscribed and, on a slightly lower level, murder and violence, which impose definitive silence." Ibid., p. 283; see also pp. 6, 285.

25. Ibid., p. 100. As he adds (p. 101): "The rebel does not ask for life, but for reasons for living. He rejects the consequences implied by death. . . . To fight against death amounts to claiming that life has a meaning, to fighting for order and for unity." Cf. also Richard H. Cox, "Ideology, History and Political Philosophy: Camus' *L'Homme Révolté*," *Social Research*, 32 (Spring 1965), 71–97; Fred H. Willhoite, Jr., "Albert Camus' Politics of Rebellion," *Western Political Quarterly*, 14 (June 1961), 400–414; Terry Hoy, "Albert Camus: The Nature of Political Rebellion," ibid., 13 (September 1960), 573–580; Richard Wollheim, "The Political Philosophy of Existentialism," *Cambridge Journal*, 7 (October 1953), 3–19.

26. Merleau-Ponty, "Man, the Hero," in *Sense and Non-Sense*, pp. 183, 185.

27. His observations on this point resembled to some extent Camus's arguments against absolute affirmation. See Maurice Merleau-Ponty, *Humanisme et terreur* (Paris: Gallimard, 1947), pp. 25, 40; also Bannan, *Merleau-Ponty*, pp. 200–205.

28. Merleau-Ponty, "Hegel's Existentialism," p. 67. As he adds (p. 69): "Learning the truth about death and struggle is the long maturation process by which history overcomes its contradictions and fulfills the promise of humanity—present in the consciousness of death and in the struggle with the other—in the living relationship among men." Cf. Maurice Merleau-Ponty, *The Structure of Behavior*, trans. Alden L. Fisher (Boston: Beacon Press, 1963), p. 223.

29. See Marjorie Grene, "Authenticity: An Existential Value," *Ethics*, 62 (July 1952), 266–274.

30. "The spirit of seriousness has two characteristics: it considers values as transcendent givens independent of human subjectivity, and it transfer the quality of 'desirable' from the ontological structure of things to their simple material constitution. . . . Man pursues being blindly by hiding from himself the free project which is his pursuit. He makes himself such that he is *waited for* by all the tasks placed along his way. Objects are mute demands, and he is nothing in himself but the passive obedience to these demands." Sartre, *Being and Nothingness*, p. 626.

31. Ibid., p. xxxv. Cf. Frederick A. Olafson, *Principles and Persons, An Ethical Interpretation of Existentialism* (Baltimore: Johns Hopkins Univer-

sity Press, 1967).

32. Commonwealth or sovereignty by acquisition "differs from sovereignty by institution only in this, that men who choose their sovereign do it for fear of one another and not of him whom they institute: but in this case they subject themselves to him they are afraid of. In both cases they do it for fear: which is to be noted by them that hold all such covenants, as proceed from fear of death or violence, void; which if it were true, no man in any kind of commonwealth could be obliged to obedience." *Leviathan,* pt. II, ch. 20.

33. *De Cive,* pt. I, ch. 2, art. 9; pt. II, ch. 8, art. 3.

34. *Leviathan,* pt. II, ch. 17; also *Elements of Law,* pt. I, ch. 19, art. 6, pt. II, ch. 1, art. 6; *De Cive,* pt. II, ch. 5, art. 1, 4.

35. *Leviathan,* pt. II, ch. 17; *De Cive,* pt. II, ch. 6, art. 1; *Elements of Law,* pt. I, ch. 19, art. 4; on the possibility of cementing social relations through "oath" see *Leviathan,* pt. I, ch. 14; *De Cive,* pt. I, ch. 2, art. 20–22; *Elements of Law,* pt. I, ch. 15, art. 15–17.

36. *Leviathan,* pt. II, ch. 17; *De Cive,* pt. II, ch. 5, art. 7, 9; *Elements of Law,* pt. I, ch. 19, art. 7, 8.

37. Camus, *The Rebel,* 19, 22, 250, 284, 294.

38. Merleau-Ponty, "Hegel's Existentialism," p. 68.

39. Maurice Merleau-Ponty, "A Note on Machiavelli," in *Signs,* trans. with introduction by Richard C. McCleary (Evanston, Ill.: Northwestern University Press, 1964), pp. 211, 212, 215, 219. As he concludes (p. 223), the widespread repudiation of Machiavelli assumes from this vantage point "a disturbing significance: it is the decision not to know the tasks of a true humanism. There is a way of repudiating Machiavelli which is Machiavellian: it is the pious dodge of those who turn their eyes and ours toward the heaven of principles in order to turn them away from what they are doing. And there is a way of praising Machiavelli which is just the opposite of Machiavellianism, since it honors in his works a contribution to political clarity." See also Hwa Yol Jung, "The Radical Humanization of Politics: Maurice Merleau-Ponty's Philosophy of Politics," *Archiv für Rechts-und Sozialphilosophie,* 53 (Summer 1967), 233–256.

40. Sartre, *Being and Nothingness,* pp. 361–364, 408–409.

41. Sartre, *Critique,* pp. 307, 377, 395, 440, 453, 520, 527, 580ff.; Desan, *Jean-Paul Sartre,* pp. 109, 122–183. Cf. Mary Warnock, *The Philosophy of Sartre* (London: Hutchinson, 1965), pp. 173–175; Arthur Lessing, "Marxist Existentialism," *Review of Metaphysics,* 20 (March 1967), 461–482; Howard R. Burkle, "Jean-Paul Sartre: Social Freedom in *Critique de la raison dialectique,*" ibid., 19 (June 1966), 742–757; Edouard Morot-Sir, "Sartre's *Critique of Dialectical Reason,*" *Journal of the History of Ideas,* 22 (October-December 1961), 573–581.

42. *Leviathan,* pt. II, chs. 17, 24, 29, 30; *De Cive,* pt. II, ch. 6, art. 3; ch. 12, art. 1–11; ch. 13, art. 12. The above is not meant to deny that Hobbes's argument ultimately points in the direction of a dynamic conception of politics, as has been noted by R. C. Collingwood: "According to Hobbes . . . a body politic is a dialectical thing, a Heraclitean world in which at any given time there is a negative element." *The New Leviathan* (Oxford: Clarendon Press, 1942), p. 183. Similarly, Dennis H. Wrong writes that "the whole tenor of his thought is to see the war of all against all and

Leviathan dialectically, as coexisting and interacting opposites." See "The Oversocialized Conception of Man in Modern Sociology," *American Sociological Review*, 26 (April 1961), 185; also Peter Cornelius Mayer-Tasch, *Thomas Hobbes und das Widerstandsrecht* (Tübingen: Mohr, 1967).

43. Sartre, *Critique*, pp. 509, 521, 573, 609; Desan, *Jean-Paul Sartre*, pp. 158, 162-165, 174-181.

44. Merleau-Ponty, "Man and Adversity," in *Signs*, p. 239; "Author's Preface," in *Sense and Non-Sense*, p. 5.

6. Hermeneutics and Historicism

1. See Giorgio Tagliacozzo and Hayden V. White, eds., *Giambattista Vico: An International Symposium* (Baltimore: Johns Hopkins University Press, 1969); and Giorgio Tagliacozzo and Donald P. Verene, eds., *Giambattista Vico's Science of Humanity* (Baltimore: Johns Hopkins University Press, 1976).

2. See especially Norwood R. Hanson, *Patterns of Discovery* (Cambridge: Cambridge University Press, 1958); Thomas S. Kuhn, *The Structure of Scientific Revolutions* (Chicago: University of Chicago Press, 1962); also, for a comparison of Anglo-Saxon and Continental trends, Theodore Kisiel, "Zu einer Hermeneutik naturwissenschaftlicher Forschung," *Zeitschrift für allgemeine Wissenschaftstheorie* (Journal for General Philosophy of Science), 2 (1971), 195-221.

3. See, e.g., Leo Strauss, *Natural Right and History* (Chicago: University of Chicago Press, 1953), ch. 1; Eugene F. Miller, "Positivism, Historicism, and Political Inquiry," *American Political Science Review*, 66 (1972), 796-817. For a response to some of Strauss' arguments see "Supplement I: Hermeneutics and Historicism," in Hans-Georg Gadamer, *Truth and Method* (New York: Seabury Press, 1975), pp. 460-491.

4. Similarly, while insisting (against Weber) on the need for value judgments as a premise for all types of inquiry, he tends to proceed immediately to the stipulation of absolute standards—a stipulation claiming a degree of objective neutrality comparable to value-free scientific propositions. See, e.g., Strauss, *Natural Right and History*, ch. 2; *What is Political Philosophy? And Other Essays* (Glencoe, Ill.: Free Press, 1959); for a more recent statement cf. his "Philosophy as Rigorous Science and Political Philosophy," *Interpretation*, 2 (1971), 1-9.

5. Peter Winch, *The Idea of a Social Science, and Its Relation to Philosophy* (London: Routledge & Kegan Paul, 1958), pp. 11-12, 15, 40.

6. Ibid., pp. 25, 29, 57, 100. Commenting on logical propositions, Winch noted at another point (p. 126) that "it is only from their roots in this actual flesh-and-blood intercourse that those formal systems draw such life as they have; for the whole idea of a logical relation is only possible by virtue of the sort of agreement between men and their actions which is discussed by Wittgenstein in the *Philosophical Investigations*. . . . It will seem less strange that social relations should be like logical relations between propositions once it is seen that logical relations between propositions themselves depend on social relations between men."

7. Ibid., pp. 30, 63. As he added (p. 32): "Establishing a standard is not

an activity which it makes sense to ascribe to any individual in complete isolation from other individuals. For it is contact with other individuals which alone makes possible the external check on one's actions which is inseparable from an established standard."

8. Ibid., pp. 15–16, 84–85, 87, 110.

9. Ibid., pp. 3, 23, 47, 71–72, 104, 109, 112–113, 118–119, 123.

10. See Peter Winch, "Mr. Louch's Idea of a Social Science," *Inquiry*, 7 (1964), 202–208. The essay is primarily a rejoinder to A. R. Louch's "The Very Idea of a Social Science," ibid., 6 (1963), 273–286. On a broader basis, the charge of an idealist bias was advanced by Ernest Gellner in "The New Idealism—Cause and Meaning in the Social Sciences," in Imre Lakatos and Alan Musgrave, eds., *Problems in the Philosophy of Science* (Amsterdam: North-Holland Publishing Co., 1968), pp. 377–406. The issues raised in the exchange between Louch and Winch were further pursued by Arnold Levison, "Knowledge and Society," *Inquiry*, 9 (1966), 132–146; and Stuart Silvers, "On Our Knowledge of the Social World," ibid., 10 (1967), 96–97.

11. *The Idea of a Social Science*, pp. 84, 100, 107–108; for a direct attack on Popper see ibid., pp. 127–128. The challenge to scientific progress and objectivity was noted, among others, by Gellner, pp. 381–406; see also A. K. Saran, "A Wittgensteinian Sociology?" *Ethics*, 75 (1965), 195–200.

12. *The Idea of a Social Science*, p. 103. As he added (p. 102), "the philosopher will in particular be alert to deflate the pretensions of any form of enquiry to enshrine the essence of intelligibility as such, to possess the key to reality. For connected with the realization that intelligibility takes many and varied forms is the realization that reality has no key."

13. See Winch, "Nature and Convention," *Proceedings of the Aristotelian Society*, n.s. 60 (1959–60), 235–238, 240–242, 250–252; Giambattista Vico, *The New Science*, trans. by Thomas C. Bergin and Max H. Fisch, paragraph 161 (New York: Anchor Books, 1961), p. 25.

14. See Winch, "Understanding a Primitive Society," *American Philosophical Quarterly*, 1 (1964), 308–309, 321–324. The relevant passages in Vico's treatise read: "Now since the world of nations has been made by men, let us see in what institutions men agree and always have agreed. . . . We observe that all nations, barbarous as well as civilized, though separately founded because remote from each other in time and space, keep these three human customs: all have some religion, all contract solemn marriages, all bury their dead. And in no nation, however savage and crude, are any human actions performed with more elaborate ceremonies and more sacred solemnity than the rites of religion, marriage, and burial. For by the axiom that 'uniform ideas, born among peoples unknown to each other, must have a common ground of truth,' it must have been dictated to all nations that from these institutions humanity began among them all, and therefore they must be most devoutly guarded by them all, so that the world should not again become a bestial wilderness. For this reason we have taken these three eternal and universal customs as the first principles of this Science." *The New Science*, paragraphs 332–333, p. 53. For another example of Vico's influence on ordinary language philosophy see Stephen Toulmin, *Human Understanding*, vol. 1 (Princeton, N.J.: Princeton University Press, 1972), p. 23.

15. In Winch's words, the task of social inquiry was to bring the inherent sense of an alien culture (S) into "relation with our own conception of intel-

ligibility . . . we are seeking a way of looking at things which goes beyond our previous way in that it has in some way taken account of and incorporated the other way that members of S have of looking at things." See "Understanding a Primitive Society," pp. 310, 316–317, 321.

16. Ibid., pp. 310, 313, 319. A purely conceptual interpretation of the "limiting notions" gains support from Winch's formalistic assessment of universal "rationality" (p. 318). His reluctance to compare and evaluate religious life-forms was aptly criticized by Kai Nielsen when he wrote: "Without a participant's understanding of God-talk, we could not raise the question of the reality of God, but with it, this is perfectly possible and perfectly intelligible." "Wittgensteinian Fideism," *Philosophy*, 42 (1967), 208. For other recent criticisms of Winch's essay, originating chiefly from Popperian premises (with an insistence that experimental science furnishes the criteria of cross-cultural evaluation) see, e.g., I. C. Jarvie, "Understanding and Explanation in Sociology and Social Anthropology," in Robert Borger and Frank Cioffi, eds., *Explanation in the Behavioral Sciences* (Cambridge: Cambridge University Press, 1970), pp. 231–248; also I. C. Jarvie and J. Agassi, "The Problem of the Rationality of Magic," in Bryan R. Wilson, ed., *Rationality* (Evanston, Ill.: Harper & Row, 1970), pp. 172–193; and Hugo Meynell, "Truth, Witchcraft and Professor Winch," *Heythrop Journal*, 13 (1972), 162–172.

17. See, e.g., Thomas N. Munson, "Wittgenstein's Phenomenology," *Philosophy and Phenomenological Research*, 23 (1962), 37–50; Herbert Spiegelberg, "The Puzzle of Ludwig Wittgenstein's Phänomenologie (1929–?)," *American Philosophical Quarterly*, 5 (1968), 244–256. For a broader comparison of the two philosophical contexts see Cornelis A. van Peursen, *Phenomenology and Analytical Philosophy* (Pittsburgh: Duquesne University Press, 1972), and Gerard Radnitzky, *Contemporary Schools of Metascience*, 2nd rev. ed. (Göteberg: Akademiförlaget, 1970).

18. For detailed comparisons between Anglo-Saxon and Continental thought, with a focus on Wittgenstein, see his essays "Wittgenstein und Heidegger: Die Frage nach dem Sinn von Sein und der Sinnlosigkeitsverdacht gegen alle Metaphysik" and "Wittgenstein und das Problem des hermeneutischen Verstehens," in Karl-Otto Apel, *Transformation der Philosophie* (Frankfurt–Main: Suhrkamp, 1973), 1: 225–275, and 335–377.

19. Apel, "Die Entfaltung der 'sprachanalytischen' Philosophie and das Problem der 'Geisteswissenschaften'," ibid., 2: 83.

20. Ibid., pp. 89, 91, 93, 95. A translation of the essay under the title "Analytic Philosophy of Language and the 'Geisteswissenschaften'" appeared in *Foundations of Language*, supp. series No. 4 (Dordrecht: Reidel, 1967).

21. Apel, "Die Kommunikationsgemeinschaft als transzendentale Voraussetzung der Sozialwissenschaften," in *Transformation der Philosophie*, 2: 253–255. As he noted (p. 260): "The ideological confusion of ideal conditions with social reality—a confusion characterizing the idealistic outlook of the 'Geisteswissenschaften' in the 19th century—merges here with a perspective of relativism according to which history is devoid of any regulative principle pointing toward its possible transcendence. I would use in this case the label 'idealistic fallacy,' as a counterpart to the 'naturalistic fallacy' implicit in the positivist reduction of intelligible conduct to scientifically explicable

conditions. At the same time I would propose to interpret the nexus of ordinary language, action, expression and world view inherent in Wittgenstein's 'language games' or 'life-forms' as a dialectical unity or synthesis which does not preclude conflict between its various elements."

22. Ibid., pp. 255–259, 262, n. 85. In a recent rejoinder to a critic, Winch hints at least broadly at the distinction between a "demystifying" and a "restorative" hermeneutics when he writes: "It is easy to point out, as Jarvie does, obvious advantages in tackling, e.g., disease by the methods of Western medicine rather than by the methods of Zande magic. It is also easy to overlook the good things that may be lost in such a transition; though again, of course, I do not claim that the losses must outweigh the gains." See "Comment," in Borger and Cioffi, eds., *Explanation in the Behavioral Sciences*, p. 258. For the distinction between the two types of hermeneutics see especially Paul Ricoeur, *Freud and Philosophy: An Essay on Interpretation*, trans. Denis Savage (New Haven, Conn.: Yale University Press, 1970), pp. 3–56.

23. "Although devoid of immediate impact," he wrote, "Vico's inauguration of a 'transcendental philology' (the aim of his 'New Science') is classical evidence for the rise of later transcendental hermeneutics out of the merger of humanist philology and Christian 'logos'-speculation." See Apel, *Die Idee der Sprache in der Tradition des Humanismus von Dante bis Vico*, Archiv für Begriffsgeschichte, vol. 8 (Bonn: Bouvier Verlag, 1963), pp. 20, 29, 83, 141.

24. Ibid., pp. 321–332, 338–344, 374–378.

25. See ibid., pp. 20, 52–62, 153–155. By contrast, the tradition of nominalistic empiricism was sketched from Occam over Bacon, Hobbes, Locke and Berkeley to John Stuart Mill, while the rationalist conception of a "*mathesis universalis*" was traced over Bernouilli, Lambert, Condillac, and Frege to Russell's and Whitehead's *Principia Mathematica;* see ibid., pp. 68–70.

26. See Apel, "Der philosophische Wahrheitsbegriff als Voraussetzung einer inhaltlich orientierten Sprachwissenschaft" and "Sprache und Wahrheit in der gegenwärtigen Situation der Philosophie," in *Transformation der Philosophie*, 1: 106–137 (esp. 126–130) and 138–166 (esp. 163–166). See also W. B. Macomber, *The Anatomy of Disillusion: Martin Heidegger's Notion of Truth* (Evanston, Ill.: Northwestern University Press, 1967), and Ernst Tugendhat, *Der Wahrheitsbegriff bei Husserl und Heidegger*, 2nd ed. (Berlin: Walter de Gruyter, 1970).

27. See Apel, "Einleitung: Transformation der Philosophie," in *Transformation der Philosophie*, 1: 9–76, esp. 35–52. A similar trend (but perhaps aiming at a more thorough separation) is noticeable in some of Jürgen Habermas' writings; e.g., his "Einleitung zur Neuausgabe," in *Theorie and Praxis*, 4th rev. ed. (Frankfurt–Main: Suhrkamp, 1971), pp. 9–47; and his "Wahrheitstheorien," in *Festschrift für Walter Schulz* (Pfullingen: Neske Verlag, 1973). In his monograph on humanism Apel interpreted the relationship between "philology" and "philosophy" quasi-dialectically in the sense of a "hermeneutical circle," pointing to Vico's statement: "These philological proofs enable us to see in fact the institutions we have meditated in idea as touching this world of nations. . . . Thus it is that with the help of the preceding philosophical proofs, the philological proofs both confirm their own

authority by reason and at the same time confirm reason by their authority."
See Apel, *Die Idee der Sprache*, p. 336; Vico, *The New Science*, paragraph
359, p. 65.

28. Paul Ricoeur, *History and Truth*, trans. Charles A. Kelbley (Evanston,
Ill.: Northwestern University Press, 1965), pp. 42, 50–51, 54–55, 282–283.
See also Maurice Merleau-Ponty's comments: "The concept of history in its
most profound sense does not shut the thinking subject up in a point of
space and time; he can seem to be thus contained only to a way of thinking
which is itself capable of going outside all time and place in order to see
him in his time and place. . . . Since we are all hemmed in by history, it is up
to us to understand that whatever truth we may have is to be gotten not in
spite of but through our historical inherence. Superficially considered, our
inherence destroys all truth; considered radically, it founds a new idea of
truth." "The Philosopher and Sociology," in *Signs*, trans. Richard C. Mc-
Cleary (Evanston, Ill.: Northwestern University Press, 1964), p. 109.

7. Phenomenology and Marxism

1. Enzo Paci, *The Function of the Sciences and the Meaning of Man*,
trans. James E. Hansen and Paul Piccone (Evanston, Ill.: Northwestern
University Press, 1972); originally published as *Funzione delle Scienze e
Significato dell' Uomo* (Milan: Il Saggiatore, 1963).

2. In the words of one observer: "It has seldom been remarked that nearly
all of Marx's theoretical works were called, or subtitled, 'A Critique. . . .' "
See Dick Howard, "On Marx's Critical Theory," *Telos*, No. 6 (Fall 1970), p.
224.

3. See *Karl Marx: Selected Writings in Sociology and Social Philosophy*,
ed. T. B. Bottomore and Maximilien Rubel (New York: McGraw-Hill, 1964),
pp. 74 (from *German Ideology*) and 232–233 (from *The Holy Family*). For
an extensive review of the doctrinaire elements in Marxist thought see
Dietrich Böhler, *Metakritik der Marxschen Ideologiekritik* (Frankfurt–Main:
Suhrkamp, 1971).

4. "Phenomenological philosophy," Richard M. Zaner writes, "is most
accurately conceived as criticism now firmly established on its own sound
foundations." Critical inquiry in this sense, he adds, "is the rigorous science
of presuppositions: of beginnings, origins, or foundations. It is this reflexive
character of critical dialogue, grounded both in the things being examined
and in the dialogic responsibility to others mutually engaged in the quest,
which uniquely characterizes the discipline of criticism." See *The Way of
Phenomenology: Criticism as a Philosophical Discipline* (New York: Pegasus,
1970), pp. xii, 207.

5. In the words of Dorian Cairns: "No opinion is to be accepted as philosophical knowledge unless it is seen to be adequately established by observation of what is seen as itself given 'in person.' Any belief seen to be
incompatible with what is seen to be itself given is to be rejected." "An
Approach to Phenomenology," in Marvin Farber, ed., *Philosophical Essays
in Memory of Edmund Husserl* (New York: Greenwood Press, 1968), p. 4.

6. Edmund Husserl, *The Crisis of European Sciences and Transcendental
Phenomenology*, trans. David Carr (Evanston, Ill.: Northwestern University

Press, 1970), p. 283; also *Die Krisis der europäischen Wissenschaften und die transzendentale Phänomenologie,* ed. Walter Biemel (The Hague: Martinus Nijhoff, 1962), pp. 506–507.

7. Compare Andrew Arato, "Lukács' Path to Marxism," *Telos,* No. 7 (Spring 1971), pp. 128–136; also G. H. R. Parkinson, "Introduction," in Parkinson, *Georg Lukács: The Man, His Work and His Ideas* (New York: Vintage Books, 1970), pp. 1–33. For Lukács' own account of his intellectual development see, e.g., "Mein Weg zu Marx" (1933) with "Postscriptum" (1957) in Georg Lukács, *Schriften zur Ideologie und Politik,* ed. Peter Ludz (Neuwied: Luchterhand, 1967), pp. 323–329, 646–657; and his Preface to *Geschichte und Klassenbewusstsein, Werke,* vol. 2 (Neuwied: Luchterhand, 1968), pp. 11–41, trans. Rodney Livingstone as *History and Class Consciousness* (Cambridge, Mass.: MIT Press, 1971), pp. ix–xxxiv.

8. This merger, Goldmann adds, implied both a progressive and regressive step on the part of Lukács: progressive in that he subjected Dilthey's intuition to rigorous phenomenological description; regressive in that he abandoned historical experience for Husserl's inspection of transtemporal essence. See "Zu Georg Lukács: Die Theorie des Romans," in Goldmann, *Dialektische Untersuchungen* (Neuwied: Luchterhand, 1966), pp. 287–289.

9. See "Gibt es eine marxistische Soziologie?" ibid., p. 229.

10. "Assuming, though not conceding," he writes, "that recent research had clearly proved as substantively incorrect each and every individual assertion of Marx, a serious 'orthodox' Marxist could acknowledge all these new findings without hesitation and reject all of Marx's particular theses—without having to abandon for a moment his Marxist orthodoxy. Orthodox Marxism, thus, does not mean the blind acceptance of the results of Marx's inquiry, nor a 'belief' in this or that thesis, nor the interpretation of a 'holy' text. Orthodoxy in regard to Marxism refers exclusively to *method."* Lukács, *Geschichte und Klassenbewusstsein,* p. 171, *History and Class Consciousness,* p. 1.

11. The concrete political consequences of the above defects have been noted by several writers. "As soon as Lukács (following Marx) posits a *universal* class, an absolute class (the essence of society)," James Miller comments, "he is in trouble in so far as he fails to ground this (ideal) class in the particular, concrete lives whose actual consciousness and intersubjective experiences, as well as praxis, (potentially) comprehend it. Once the carrier of proletarian true consciousness becomes the party, the danger becomes even greater; and when the party announces its monopoly on true class-consciousness, the dialectic of equivocation turns into its opposite, reification: the subject-object of history becomes the object of a false subject, the historical falsity of which was announced by each peasant murdered by Stalin in the name of socialist 'reason.'" See "Marxism and Subjectivity: Remarks on Georg Lukács and Existential Phenomenology," *Telos,* No. 6 (Fall 1970), pp. 179–180.

12. In both writings, Husserl is depicted as chiefly or exclusively concerned with "formal-logical" problems; however, his method is said to be entirely congruent with subsequent elaborations by other phenomenologists and existentialists (especially Scheler and Heidegger). See Lukács, *Existentialisme ou Marxisme?* (Paris: Editions Nagel, 1948), pp. 57, 74–84; *Die Zerstörung der Vernunft* (1st ed., 1954); 2nd ed., *Werke,* vol. 9 (Neuwied:

Luchterhand, 1960), pp. 16, 378–379, 415–458, 722–723.

13. Lukács, *Ontologie des gesellschaftlichen Seins, Werke,* vols. 13–14 (Neuwied: Luchterhand, forthcoming). To some extent, the treatise still corroborates Maurice Merleau-Ponty's judgment: "Lukács' story is that of a philosopher who believed it possible to encompass realism within the dialectic and the thing itself in the thought of the thing. The blade eventually wears through the sheath, and ultimately neither the philosopher nor the ruling power remains satisfied." See "Pravda," in *Adventures of the Dialectic,* trans. Joseph Bien (Evanston, Ill.: Northwestern University Press, 1973), pp. 71–72 (translation slightly altered).

14. Mihály Vajda, "Marxism, Existentialism, Phenomenology: A Dialogue," *Telos,* No. 7 (Spring 1971), pp. 3–29. The participants in the discussion are Louis, an orthodox Marxist-Leninist; Andras, a flexible Marxist close to Lukács' position but open to other perspectives; Pietro, a Husserlian phenomenologist; and Erich, a somewhat cynical and individualistic existentialist (strongly influenced by Heidegger). The dialogue is full of revealing exchanges and suggestive observations.

15. Gajo Petrović, *Marx in the Mid-Twentieth Century* (Garden City, N.Y.: Anchor Books, 1967), p. 17. See also Petrović, ed., *Revolutionäre Praxis: Yugoslavischer Marxismus der Gegenwart* (Freiburg: Rombach, 1969).

16. "Dialectic means critical thinking which aims to grasp 'the thing itself' and queries systematically how such grasping of reality is possible." See Karel Kosík, *Die Dialektik des Konkreten* (Frankfurt–Main: Suhrkamp, 1967), p. 15, and p. 16, n. 5 (for a specific reference to Husserl's phenomenology). Cf. also "Introduction to Karel Kosík," *Telos,* No. 2 (Fall 1968), pp. 19–20.

17. In Gramsci's words: "The concept of 'objective' in metaphysical materialism seems to mean an objectivity which exists even without man. . . . We know reality only in relation to man, and since man is historically evolving, knowledge and reality are a becoming; and even objectivity is a becoming." *Il Materialismo Storico e la Filosofia di Benedetto Croce* (Turin: Einaudi, 1948), pp. 142–143. See also Antonio Labriola, *Essays on the Materialist Conception of History,* trans. Charles H. Kerr (1903), (New York: Monthly Review Press, 1966).

18. On these points see Andrea Calzolari, "Structure and Superstructure in Gramsci," *Telos,* No. 3 (Spring 1969), pp. 33–42.

19. See Tran Duc Thao, "Marxisme et Phénoménologie," *La Revue internationale,* No. 2 (1946); also *Phénoménologie et Matérialisme dialectique* (Paris: Minh-Tan, 1951). For a review of these studies and some of his later writings see Silvia Federici, "Viet Cong Philosophy: Tran Duc Thao," *Telos,* No. 6 (Fall 1970), pp. 104–117.

20. Sartre, "Materialism and Revolution," in William Barret and Henry D. Aiken, eds., *Philosophy in the Twentieth Century,* vol. 2 (New York: Random House, 1962), pp. 387–429. The doctrinaire features were corroborated in the domain of practical politics by Sartre's strong endorsement at the time of the policies of the Communist Party.

21. See Sartre, "Marxism and Existentialism," in *Search for a Method,* trans. Hazel E. Barnes (New York: Knopf, 1963), pp. 26–30. Sartre's formulation of an existentialist Marxism has given rise to a large bulk of both sup-

portive and critical literature. Cf., e.g., Raymond Aron, *Marxism and the Existentialists* (New York: Simon & Schuster, 1970); George Novack, ed., *Existentialism versus Marxism: Conflicting Views on Humanism* (New York: Delta Books, 1966); Walter Odajnyk, *Marxism and Existentialism* (Garden City, N.Y.: Anchor Books, 1965); Arthur Lessing, "Marxist Existentialism," *Review of Metaphysics*, 20 (1967), 461–482.

22. At another point he added: "This concrete thinking, which Marx calls 'critique' to distinguish it from speculative philosophy, is what others propound under the name of 'existential philosophy.' " See *Sense and Non-Sense*, trans. Hubert L. and Patricia A. Dreyfus (Evanston, Ill.: Northwestern University Press, 1964), pp. 72, 79–81, 133. See also his critical comments on Communist policies (pp. 153–171); and his differentiation between Husserl's "oldest formulas: the philosophy of essences, philosophy as a strict or absolute science, consciousness as a transcendental and constituting activity" and some more recent accents: "the point of departure as a 'dialectical situation,' philosophy as 'infinite mediation or dialogue' " (pp. 134–135).

23. Merleau-Ponty, *Adventures of the Dialectic*, pp. 7, 29, 57, 206–207, 226, 230–231. For the relationship between philosophy and politics see also his comments written in 1960: "One thing that is certain at the outset is that there has been a political mania among philosophers which has not produced good politics or good philosophy. . . . Instead of combining their virtues, philosophy and politics exchanged their vices: practice became tricky and thought superstitious." "Introduction" to *Signs*, trans. Richard C. McCleary (Evanston, Ill.: Northwestern University Press, 1964), p. 6.

24. Merleau-Ponty, *The Visible and the Invisible*, ed. Claude Lefort, trans. Alphonso Lingis (Evanston, Ill.: Northwestern University Press, 1968), p. 103.

25. Marcuse, "Contributions to a Phenomenology of Historical Materialism," *Telos*, No. 4 (Fall 1969), pp. 5–11, 14–16, 21–22, 26, 29–30, 33. (The essay appeared first under the title "Beiträge zu einer Phänomenologie des historischen Materialismus" in *Philosophische Hefte*, No. 1, July, 1928, pp. 45–68.) While stressing the validity of universal historical principles, Marcuse acknowledged the "ambiguity" of historical details due to the "multiplicity of meanings" inherent in concrete contexts. For this concession he is taken to task by Mitchell Franklin in "The Irony of the Beautiful Soul of Marcuse," *Telos*, No. 6 (Fall 1970), pp. 3–35. For a review of "Contributions" together with related writings of the early Marcuse see Alfred Schmidt, "Existential-Ontologie und historischer Materialismus bei Herbert Marcuse," in Jürgen Habermas, ed., *Antworten auf Herbert Marcuse* (Frankfurt–Main: Suhrkamp, 1968), pp. 17–49.

26. Theodor W. Adorno, *Zur Metakritik der Erkenntnistheorie* (Stuttgart: Kohlhammer, 1956); *Jargon der Eigentlichkeit* (Frankfurt–Main: Suhrkamp, 1964). For later references of Marcuse to phenomenology see, e.g., "The Concept of Essence" (1936) in *Negations: Essays in Critical Theory* (Boston: Beacon Press, 1969), pp. 43–87 (where he criticized the phenomenological inspection of essences as purely receptive and contemplative, but without abandoning the apodictic thrust); also *One-Dimensional Man* (Boston: Beacon Press, 1964), pp. 162–166; and "On Science and Phenomenology," in Robert S. Cohen and Marx W. Wartofsky, eds., *Boston Studies in the Philosophy of Science*, vol. 2 (New York: Humanities Press, 1965), pp. 279–290.

27. Jürgen Habermas, *Theorie und Praxis* (Neuwied: Luchterhand, 1963), pp. 299–306, 329–335; "Erkenntnis und Interesse" (1965), in *Technik und Wissenschaft als "Ideologie"* (Frankfurt–Main: Suhrkamp, 1968), pp. 146–168. For a critique of phenomenological applications in social science (Alfred Schutz, Aaron Cicourel, Harold Garfinkel, Erving Goffman) see "Zur Logik der Sozialwissenschaften" (1967), in Habermas, *Zur Logik der Sozialwissenschaften; Materialien* (Frankfurt–Main: Suhrkamp, 1970), pp. 188–220.

28. See Habermas, *Erkenntnis und Interesse* (Frankfurt–Main: Suhrkamp, 1968), pp. 239–244; trans. under the title *Knowledge and Human Interests* by Jeremy J. Shapiro (Boston: Beacon Press, 1971), pp. 194–198; also "Einleitung" to *Theorie und Praxis*, 4th rev. ed. (Frankfurt–Main: Suhrkamp, 1971), pp. 9–47; and "Vorbereitende Bemerkungen zu einer Theorie der kommunikativen Kompetenz," in Habermas and Niklas Luhmann, *Theorie der Gesellschaft oder Sozialtechnologie—Was leistet die Systemforschung?* (Frankfurt–Main: Suhrkamp, 1971), pp. 101–141.

29. As professor of philosophy at the University of Milan, Paci was the leading member of a circle of "Left Husserlians" or phenomenological Marxists in Italy. Among his other works see *Tempo e Relazione* (Turin: Taylor, 1954); *Dall' Esistenzialismo al Relazionismo* (Messina–Florence: G. d'Anna, 1957); *Tempo e Verità nella Fenomenologia di Husserl* (Bari: Laterza, 1961). For a perspective similar to his see Pier Aldo Rovatti, "A Phenomenological Analysis of Marxism: The Return to the Subject and to the Dialectic of the Totality," *Telos*, No. 5 (Spring 1970), pp. 160–173.

30. At another point Paci observes: "Essentially, since truth as the meaningful direction of being can never be possessed, intentionality is infinite and its goal unreachable. The goal has always been, is, and always will be present as a demand in the world; but it is not the world. It is the meaning of truth that is inexhaustible in the world. The inexhaustible demand is such that the movement is perennial and the becoming immortal." See *Function of the Sciences*, pp. 59–60, 71, 78, 202–203, 251.

31. Ibid., pp. 81, 187, 230.

32. Ibid., pp. 318, 345, 443. See also the statement (p. 360): "It is certainly not technological and scientific success that differentiates socialism from neo-capitalism. If the problem is only practical and technological, and praxis itself is reduced to technology in both the socialist and the capitalist camp, it becomes increasingly difficult to distinguish the neo-capitalism that proclaims the abundance of goods as its goal from the empirico-pragmatic Marxism which merely seeks to replicate the same abundance."

33. "In the phenomenological sense," Paci adds, "beginning from the subject means beginning from that nucleus of truth which, although minimal, the subject contains precisely because he is a subject who departs from the evidence of what he directly experiences in the first person." Turning to Marxism he notes: "By returning to the subject and his operations, I can discover that appearances are abstractions that have become real and have transformed workers into abstractions, while actually the worker is the concrete man. . . . Therefore, the original concreteness from which Marx in fact departs, is the subject." See ibid., pp. 6, 240, 340, 346, 352, 415.

34. The arbitrary character of the reliance on "subjectivity" can be gleaned from the following statement: "The ego as a man—as a real man of

flesh and blood who contains the world and yet constitutes it, and who contains the past and yet founds it, the individual ego born from intersubjectivity and yet constitutive of intersubjectivity—this ego is the real precategorial foundation of phenomenology." The same impression can be gained from the critique of the dualism between objective and subjective reality as a "construction" which phenomenology should overcome. See ibid., pp. 129, 221, 235, 262, 284, 347.

35. Ibid., pp. 66–67, 172, 216, 295, 297, 352.

36. Cf. also these statements: "The true being of the world is its progressive self-revelation as truth, as phenomenon. Phenomenology discovers that *the world has being insofar as it has a meaning,* to the extent that the truth inhering in it is discovered and becomes the aim and intentional meaning of human life. . . . Since being is meaning, the being of the world is constituted in subjectivity. Transcendental consciousness (subjectivity), as the being of the world that is constituted in consciousness, is not the acceptance of the pregiven being (which is not true being). Rather it is the active constitution of meaning: forming subjectivity." See ibid., pp. 63–64, 68–69, 131, 353.

37. Ibid., pp. 35, 85, 91–93, 96, 253, 334–336.

38. If this is so, he adds, then "inert matter is *subjective* in its own way. Materialism is not a substantialism extraneous to the subject: I am the world, the whole world." For a more subdued and plausible formulation compare his comment that, in Marxism, "matter and structure are vindicated in order to negate the dualism imposed by bourgeois society which divides the *soul* from the *body,* the *res cogitans* from the *res extensa,* just as the feudal world reduced the serf to pure *res extensa,* reserving the soul to the *otium* of the lord. The aim of Marxist materialism is to vindicate the whole man, the concrete monad, or simply, *man,* if we do not thereby reduce him naturalistically, as Feuerbach does." See ibid., pp. 132, 161, 172, 175, 218–219, 294–295, 398.

39. Easily one of the most puzzling comments of the study reads: "Therefore, in terms of a coherent Marxism, the dialectic of nature must be nonnaturalistic and it must not be a dialectic of history." See ibid., pp. 72, 106, 279, 290–291, 299, 301, 318, 336, 367, 444.

40. "The problems of Hegelianism and the Hegelian Left," he notes at another point, "live their hidden and unrecognized life within the turbulent elaboration of Husserlian phenomenology." Ibid., pp. 248, 281–283. See also his essay, "Anthropology, Dialectics, and Phenomenology in Hegel," *Radical America,* 4 (September–October 1971), 33–53.

41. "To be so, in flesh and blood," he notes, "is to be transcendental, like all other egos. . . . Thus, it is clear that when I speak of the transcendental ego in the Husserlian sense I am speaking of my singularity in the first person." He also acknowledges the Fichtean overtones of this view: "Fichte's individual ego contains transcendental self-consciousness." *Function of the Sciences,* pp. 21, 34, 93–95, 100, 140.

42. See Merleau-Ponty, *Signs,* p. 33; Paci, *Function of the Sciences,* pp. 6, 8, 10. Compare also Paci's statement (p. 435): "Capital is the abstract first person who acts as if he were concrete against man's authentic and unmasked experience of himself, others, and the world in the first person."

43. Paci, *Function of the Sciences,* pp. 6–7, 28, 44. The above, it is true should be compared with the statement (p. 269): "This does not mean that

the final meaning is there, or that it is innate in man, and that, as such, it tries to express itself as much as possible."

44. Ibid., p. 373. As Goldmann indicates, the concept of an immanent, evolutionary teleology was strongly cherished both by Social Darwinists and Darwinian Marxists; Goldmann, *Dialektische Untersuchungen*, p. 219. Apart from the vision of a scientific history, Merleau-Ponty points to the opposite alternative of permanent unrest, deriving from the incongruence between internal impulse and external conditions; see *Adventures of the Dialectic*, pp. 221–222.
267.

45. "What is reasserted," he adds elsewhere, "is the fact that the species and mankind's *telos* lives in the individual. Furthermore the individual can negate the negation of the life of the species through revolutionary praxis." Paci's statements on these issues, it is true, are by no means unequivocal. Thus, in regard to concrete political involvement he writes at one point: "Given all these modalities, my actions can very well result in something I did not want, or at any rate, result in something very different from what I intended. Here we rediscover the theme of ambiguity." On class struggle through dialectical negation he comments: "How this inversion is going to take place cannot be defined a priori, nor can it be left to an abstract revolutionary will or to a revolution for the sake of revolution. Furthermore, the model of one inversion cannot be applied to another situation, except for the gravest situations which are common to all men." See *Function of the Sciences*, pp. 36–37, 264, 271, 296, 327, 330, 397, 438; also pp. 182, 289–290, 353–355 (on needs).

46. See also the statement: "The criterion of truth becomes the precategorial and subjective foundation which can clarify in the diverse philosophies the way in which the foundation has been pursued and forgotten, ignored and prepared, investigated or occluded, and negated or distorted in theoretical or intellectualistic constructions." Ibid., pp. 8, 53–54, 107–108, 238–239, 242, 321, 348.

47. As he adds: "Here, *science* has a *new* meaning. It is no longer the verification of an objectivity in itself. Rather, it is the consciousness of praxis, its intentional direction, the positive meaning of truth, and the effort of actualizing this meaning in the *epoché* of the mundane, i.e., in the *epoché* of a truth coinciding with the given." See ibid., pp. 47, 52, 75, 282, 381, 445.

48. See, e.g., the statement: "The surveyor who uses idealized figures to measure the field that has now become an exact figure, or that has been divided into exact figures, already exists in the *Lebenswelt* and in its spatio-temporal causal nexuses. These nexuses are given to him before the idealization as figures which are not yet exact but susceptible to idealization. The field is not exactly divided into perfect squares. By surveying and measuring its surfaces, I perform the operations that lead me to squares that 'correspond' to the field." See ibid., 58–59, 96–98, 209, 417; and for comments on the correspondence theory, including Lenin's formulations, pp. 332–333.

49. Thus, the previous quote referring to the "evidence of the will" is part of a comment on Husserl's statement (in *Krisis*, pp. 485–486): "Every purpose, in particular that which intentionally implies a multiplicity of mediations, requires a recurring consideration, a recurrence as a renewal."

See *Function of the Sciences*, pp. 232–233, 235–238, 243–244, 264–265, 276–278.

50. For the comments on Marx see ibid., pp. 371–372, 381, 407–409, 413–415; on Lukács, pp. 331–333, 336–340; on Labriola and Gramsci, pp. 305–316, 342; on Sartre, pp. 297, 347–370; on Merleau-Ponty, pp. 95, 251–252, 283, 325–326, 328–329, 346.

51. Norman Birnbaum, *Toward a Critical Sociology* (New York: Oxford University Press, 1971), pp. 94–129, 234, 367–392; Alvin W. Gouldner, *The Coming Crisis of Western Sociology* (New York: Basic Books, 1970), pp. 157–163, 390, 481–512.

52. See, e.g., Georges Gurvitch, *Dialectique et sociologie* (Paris: Flammarion, 1962); *The Spectrum of Social Time* (Dordrecht: Reidel, 1964); also Phillip Bosserman, *Dialectical Sociology, An Analysis of the Sociology of Georges Gurvitch* (Boston: Beacon Press, 1968); Marcel Rioux, "Critical versus Aseptic Sociology," *Berkeley Journal of Sociology*, 15 (1970), 33–47.

53. See *Function of the Sciences*, pp. xix–xxvii ("Translators' Introduction" by James E. Hansen and Paul Piccone); also p. 454.

54. As he adds: "If oppression is first and foremost a function of sex, race, etc., and only after considerable Marxist theoretical mediation becomes a function of the proletarianization process produced by the bourgeois mode of production, then it does not make much sense to retain the old class analysis, which is mediated, but it becomes necessary to scrap the entire approach." See Piccone, "Phenomenological Marxism," *Telos*, No. 9 (Fall 1971), pp. 3–6, 23, 27, 29.

55. Compare also the statement: "Far from being a passive process, perception itself is a form of labor: the very process of perception exhibits the structure of labor. It involves the preconceptual apprehension of reality, the sorting out of concepts needed to abstract certain crucial features of that reality, and the conceptualizing of these features of reality deemed relevant, i.e., determined as essential in relation to some *telos* itself given to us as need in the *Lebenswelt*." Ibid., pp. 6, 12–13, 15–17, 24–25, 30–31. For the relationship of consciousness and labor see also his "The Problem of Consciousness," *Telos*, No. 5 (Spring 1970), pp. 178–187.

56. "Phenomenological Marxism," pp. 19, 23–26. Similar arguments can be found in another article by Piccone entitled "Reading the Crisis," *Telos*, No. 8 (Summer 1971), pp. 121–129. Regarding the proposal for a coalition of underprivileged groups—coupled, however, with the plea for a flexible strategy—see also his "Students' Protest, Class-Structure, and Ideology," *Telos*, No. 3 (Spring 1969), pp. 106–122.

57. "In reaction to the mechanistic Marxism of the Second International," he writes, Lukács "sought to dialectically articulate a dynamic Marxism free of the metaphysical shackles of scientism and positivism. He did this by vindicating the Hegelian heritage of Marxism and uncompromisingly approaching every problem in terms of totality. His whole effort, however, was fundamentally vitiated by objective idealism, since it did not deal with the concrete realities of the time but instead substituted for them a set of highly articulate categories lifted out *tout court* from Marx's works." See Piccone, "Phenomenological Marxism," p. 8; also his "Lukács' *History and Class-Consciousness* Half a Century Later," *Telos*, No. 4 (Fall 1969), pp. 95–112.

58. "Phenomenological Marxism," pp. 4, 10–11, 14–15. At one point (p.

12, n. 24) the essay suggests that the difference between Sartre and Husserl is one between an egocentric and an intersubjective outlook; but the inter-subjective character is not fully explicated. In another context existentialism is described as "a pessimistic expression of cultural bankruptcy which tells the European petty bourgeois to accept his *Angst* as a state of being and which seeks to eternalize the bankruptcy as an unsurpassable, uneliminable metaphysical dimension"; see "Reading the Crisis," p. 123. In regard to Marcuse cf. also Piccone and Alex Delfini, "Marcuse's Heideggerian Marxism," *Telos*, No. 6 (Fall 1970), pp. 36–46.

59. "Phenomenological Marxism," p. 25. The reference is to Alfred Schutz, *Collected Papers*, vol. 1, ed. Maurice Natanson (The Hague: Martinus Nijhoff, 1962).

60. See Piccone, "Dialectical Logic Today," *Telos*, No. 2 (Fall 1968), pp. 45, 65–66.

61. See John O'Neill, *Perception, Expression, and History: The Social Phenomenology of Maurice Merleau-Ponty* (Evanston, Ill.: Northwestern University Press, 1970); among his translations see Merleau-Ponty, *Themes from the Lectures at the Collège de France, 1952-1960* (Evanston, Ill.: Northwestern University Press, 1970), and *Humanism and Terror: An Essay on the Communist Problem* (Boston: Beacon Press, 1969).

62. There are overtones of class antagonism in the focus on skin trades: "The vast symbiosis of social life is naturally represented as a body in which the spiritual functions are relieved for prayer and thought through the excremental services of the lower orders. In this scheme of things, the skin trades have been traditionally low-caste, their services being required in order to keep the higher castes free from bodily impurities and thus holy." See John O'Neill, *Sociology as a Skin Trade, Essays Towards a Reflexive Sociology* (London: Heinemann, 1972), pp. xi, 5–8.

63. As he writes: "In calling sociology a skin trade I want to restore its symbiotic connections with the body-politic and to situate it in relation to the exchange of organic needs and the utopian celebration of libidinal community which surpasses all understanding." Ibid., pp. 10, 116–117, 119, 120–121, 129.

64. "It is this Hegelian legacy," he observes, "which is the treasure of Marxist critical theory. I hold Hegel in this regard for the reason that it was he who took over Hobbes's vision of man's bodily organization and its competitive felicity and built its capacities of reason, fear, and speech into a covenant with the whole of humanity and not just a convenient article of peace in an essentially unstable social order." Ibid., pp. 238, 261.

65. Contrary to the widespread allegation that Hegel collapsed objectification and alienation, O'Neill maintains that Hegel and Marx were in accord in the differentiation of the two processes; see ibid., pp. 77, 118, 128–131, 156–159, 161, 168. For differences between Hegel and Marx see pp. 114–115, 193–194.

66. What tends to be overlooked, he notes at another point, is "that the claim to truth is a call to the freedom of the other and is inseparable from its dialogic constitution. That is why we read and think and talk and argue—not endlessly but because of the inexhaustible depth and variety of human culture to which we are always latecomers." Ibid., pp. xxi, 232, 234, 262.

67. On this basis, he criticizes Habermas for presenting communicative

interaction as a supplementary dimension to instrumental labor—but without disclosing where and how Marx explicated the dimension sufficiently in both an epistemological and a practical sense. See ibid., pp. 243, 247, 249, 259.

68. Ibid., pp. 118, 160, 162, 226, 243.

69. More generally, he detects "a naive dogmatism underlying the liberal social science conception of understanding which still draws upon the rationalist tradition of Enlightenment unmasking. But there is nothing behind the face of the man who speaks, beyond what else he has to say or how he keeps his silences." In regard to ethnomethodology compare this comment: "So far from putting commonsense knowledge of social structures up for grabs, Garfinkel's experiments are intended to show that our mundane experience of the self and its definition of the situation is given to us through the same set of typifications, role-conceptions, and course-of-action patterns which are the convenience of anyone." See ibid., pp. 132, 173–175, 217–219, 222, 236.

70. Ibid., pp. 224, 226, 230–234.

71. O'Neill himself seems to suggest such a view when he writes that "there is no privileged standpoint from which either Marx himself or ourselves as interpreters could see or fail to see what he had in mind, except as the production of its sense within this same hermeneutic circle and the conjuncture of meaning and facticity which makes it impossible for us to foreclose upon its sense." Ibid., pp. 236, 239, 254, 262. On the question to what extent hermeneutics is self-enclosed or self-sufficient see Habermas, "Der Universalitätsanspruch der Hermeneutik," in Karl-Otto Apel et al., *Hermeneutik und Ideologiekritik* (Frankfurt–Main: Suhrkamp, 1971), pp. 120–159; also Hans-Georg Gadamer, "Rhetorik, Hermeneutik und Ideologiekritik," ibid., pp. 57–82.

72. *The Visible and the Invisible*, pp. 121–122. "This has been the experience of the last half century," he comments in another context: "the supposed modesty of common sense is as little able to escape the problem of the meaning of the whole as the self-confident anticipation of reason the dilemma of circumstances." *Adventures of the Dialectic*, p. 6 (translation slightly altered).

73. Vico, *The New Science*, Book 1, Section 2, Axiom X (Garden City, N.Y.: Anchor Books, 1961), p. 21; Gramsci, *Il Materialismo Storico*, p. 191.

74. *Adventures of the Dialectic*, p. 53.

8. History and Class Consciousness

1. See Georg Lukács, *Geschichte und Klassenbewusstsein, Studien über marxistische Dialektik*, in *Georg Lukács Werke*, vol. 2; *Frühschriften II* (Neuwied and Berlin: Luchterhand, 1968); *History and Class Consciousness, Studies in Marxist Dialectics*, trans. Rodney Livingstone (Cambridge, Mass.: MIT Press, 1971). The first German edition was published by Malik Verlag, Berlin, 1923. Subsequent page references will be to the new edition, with numbers in parentheses indicating the pages in the English translation. Excerpts from *Geschichte und Klassenbewusstsein* appeared, e.g., in Iring Fetscher, *Der Marxismus, Seine Geschichte in Dokumenten*, vol. 1 (Munich: R. Piper, 1963), and Peter Ludz, ed., *Georg Lukács: Schriften zur Ideologie*

und Politik (Neuwied and Berlin: Luchterhand, 1967).

2. See Morris Watnick, "Relativism and Class Consciousness: Georg Lukács," in Leopold Labedz, ed., *Revisionism* (New York: Praeger, 1962), p. 152; also his "Georg Lukács: An Intellectual Biography," in *Soviet Survey*, Nos. 23–25 and 27 (1958–1959). For a very perceptive account of Lukács' intellectual background and the general significance of his work compare Albert W. Levi, *Humanism and Politics* (Bloomington: Indiana University Press, 1969), pp. 418–438; as he adds in a note (p. 485, n. 30): "Neither in West Germany nor in Budapest (where I searched all the bookstores, old and new, in the spring of 1965) have I been able to secure a copy of *Geschichte und Klassenbewusstsein . . .*, nor has the book ever been translated into English." (He used the French translation by K. Axelos and J. Bois, *Histoire et conscience de classe*, Paris: Editions de Minuit, 1968.)

3. For the distinction between forecasts of historical change and scientific projections or predictions, see Karl R. Popper, *The Poverty of Historicism* (London: Routledge & Kegan Paul, 1957); Mulford Q. Sibley, 'The Limitations of Behavioralism," in James C. Charlesworth, ed., *The Limits of Behavioralism in Political Science* (Philadelphia: American Academy of Political and Social Science, 1962), pp. 83–86. Compare also Bertrand de Jouvenel, *The Art of Conjecture* (New York: Basic Books, 1967) and Henry S. Kariel, "Expanding the Political Present," *American Political Science Review*, 63 (1969), 768–776.

4. Ernest Nagel, "A Formalization of Functionalism," in *Logic Without Metaphysics* (Glencoe, Ill.: Free Press, 1956), pp. 253–256; also Francesca Cancian, "Functional Analysis of Change," *American Sociological Review*, 25 (1960), 818–826.

5. Talcott Parsons, *The Social System* (Glencoe, Ill.: Free Press, 1951), p. 535.

6. Talcott Parsons, "Some Considerations on the Theory of Social Change," *Rural Sociology*, 26 (1961), 219–239; reprinted in Amitai Etzioni and Eva Etzioni, *Social Change* (New York: Basic Books, 1964), pp. 83–97, at pp. 83, 85.

7. In addition, the social system is viewed as embedded in a "cultural" framework and as operating on concrete individual "personalities"—factors which are again assumed as given; ibid., p. 88.

8. See, e.g., M. D. Sahlins and E. R. Service, *Evolution and Culture* (Ann Arbor: University of Michigan Press, 1960); also Herbert R. Barringer, George I. Blanksten, and Raymond W. Mack, *Social Change in Developing Areas: A Reinterpretation of Evolutionary Theory* (Cambridge, Mass.: Schenkman, 1965).

9. Talcott Parsons, "Evolutionary Universals in Society," *American Sociological Review*, 29 (1964), 340.

10. Richard T. LaPiere, *Social Change* (New York: McGraw-Hill, 1965), pp. 38–39. For a criticism of this view see, e.g., Ralf Dahrendorf, *Class and Class Conflict in Industrial Society* (Stanford: Stanford University Press, 1959), p. 123.

11. David C. McClelland, *The Achieving Society* (Princeton, N.J.: Van Nostrand, 1961).

12. One difficulty in presenting Lukács' theory of social change results from the fact that his study is a collection of essays dealing with diverse

topics, e.g., "What is Orthodox Marxism?" "Rosa Luxemburg as Marxist," "Class Consciousness," "Reification and the Consciousness of the Proletariat," "Legality and Illegality," and others. For present purposes his theory had to be gleaned from passages in different contexts.

13. Lukács, p. 174 (4).

14. Ibid., pp. 185 (13), 326 (144).

15. Ibid., pp. 204–205 (32).

16. Ibid., p. 177 (6).

17. Ibid., p. 278 (102).

18. Ibid., p. 280 (104).

19. For comments on Rickert see ibid., pp. 298 (120), 333–334 (150–151). Compare in this context also Sartre's statement: "Whether the scientist be Newton, Archimedes, Laplace or Einstein, he studies not the concrete totality, but the general and abstract conditions of the universe. Not the *particular* event which catches and absorbs into itself light, heat and life and which we call the 'glistening of the sun through leaves on a summer's day,' but light in general, heat phenomena, the general conditions of life. There is never any question of examining *this particular* refraction through *this particular* piece of glass which has its history and which, from a certain point of view, is regarded as the concrete synthesis of the universe, but the conditions of possibility of refraction *in general.*" Jean-Paul Sartre, "Materialism and Revolution," in William Barrett and Henry D. Aiken, eds., *Philosophy in the Twentieth Century* (New York: Random House, 1962), vol. 2, p. 395.

20. Lukács, p. 211 (38–39); for the distinction between production and *praxis* see especially pp. 310–312 (131–133). The distinction between production (labor) and action or interaction is explored, e.g., in Hannah Arendt, *The Human Condition* (Chicago: University of Chicago Press, 1958), pp. 119–223, and Jürgen Habermas, *Technik und Wissenschaft als "Ideologie"* (Frankfurt–Main Suhrkamp, 1969), pp. 9–103.

21. Lukács, pp. 344 (160–161), 384–385 (196–197).

22. Ibid., p. 288 (112).

23. Ibid., pp. 184 (12), 199 (27). Watnick's article (cited *supra*, note 2) is silent on this central aspect of Lukács' theory. Habermas, by contrast, criticizes Lukács for obfuscating the practical component by his emphasis on theoretical "class consciousness," and conversely for neglecting the "truth of a theory" by his stress on the practical imperatives of the class struggle; see *Theorie und Praxis* (Neuwied and Berlin: Luchterhand, 1963), pp. 286–287, and *Theory and Practice*, trans. John Viertel (Boston: Beacon Press, 1973), pp. 34–35.

24. Lukács, pp. 186–187 (14–15), 191 (18). See also his statement that "becoming is the truth of being," p. 366 (181).

25. Ibid., pp. 192–193 (19–20), 227 (54).

26. Ibid., p. 197 (23–24).

27. Ibid., pp. 228–229 (55–56), 406 (230). Cf. S. N. Eisenstadt, "Social Change, Differentiation and Evolution," *American Sociological Review*, 29 (1964), 375–386. One may also recall in this context Sir Henry Maine's theory of the progress from *jus sanguinis* to *jus soli* or Max Weber's theory of the transition from personal to territorial laws.

28. Lukács, pp. 238–239 (63–64).

29. Cf. Cycil S. Belshaw, *Traditional Exchange and Modern Markets*

(Englewood Cliffs, N.J.: Prentice-Hall, 1965).

30. Lukács, pp. 257–258 (83–84).

31. Ibid., p. 263 (89). One should realize that this statement was written before the development of the modern computer.

32. Ibid., p. 264 (90). Cf. Max Heirich, "The Use of Time in the Study of Social Change," *American Sociological Review*, 29 (1964), 386–397.

33. One might recall in this context Sartre's statement that recent American behaviorism is a manifestation of "the philosophy of Taylorism"; op. cit., p. 420.

34. Lukács at this point cites Kelsen's dictum that the genesis of laws is the "mystery" of jurisprudence, pp. 284–285 (108). Recent "jurimetrics" tends to substitute a formal model of behavior for the formal analysis of legal imperatives.

35. Ibid., pp. 295–298 (117–120).

36. Ibid., p. 358 (173–174); also pp. 248–249 (72–73).

37. Ibid., pp. 482–490 (305–314).

38. More recently, Kolakowski has rejected the relevance of abstract historical laws for moral conduct; he agrees, however, that moral conduct is embedded in society and in social development. See Leszek Kolakowski, "Responsibility and History," in his *Toward a Marxist Humanism* (New York: Grove Press, 1968), pp. 85–157; also George L. Kline, "Leszek Kolakowski and the Revision of Marxism," in Kline, ed., *European Philosophy Today* (Chicago: Quadrangle Books, 1965), pp. 133–163; and Gerschom K. Freyer, "Morality and The Historical Process," *Science and Society*, 28 (1964), 409–431.

39. Lukács, pp. 373–375 (187–189). From this perspective, the title of Watnick's essay, "Relativism and Class Consciousness: Georg Lukács," appears very ill-chosen (see *supra*, note 2). On humanism compare Sartre's statement: "Class-consciousness demands a new humanism, above and beyond the rational organization of the community; it is an alienated freedom which has taken freedom as its end" (op. cit., p. 422). See also Sartre's *L'Existentialisme est un humanisme* (Paris: Nagel, 1946); Erich Fromm, ed., *Socialist Humanism, An International Symposium* (Garden City, N.Y.: Doubleday, 1965); and György Markus, "Marxist Humanism," *Science and Society*, 30 (1966), 275–287.

40. Compare especially Maurice Merleau-Ponty, *Les aventures de la dialectique* (Paris: Gallimard, 1955), chap. 2; Sartre, "Materialism and Revolution," pp. 387–429 and his *Search for a Method* (New York: Knopf, 1963); Lucien Goldmann, *Recherches dialectiques* (Paris: Gallimard, 1959); and, concerning the *praxis*-group, Gajo Petrović, ed., *Revolutionäre Praxis* (Freiburg: Rombach, 1969) and Mihailo Marković, *Dialektik der Praxis* (Frankfurt–Main: Suhrkamp, 1968). Lukács has been highly critical of some of the trends claiming affinity to his work, notably in *Existentialisme ou marxisme* (Paris: Nagel, 1948). For signs of a renewed preoccupation with Lukács in the West see, e.g., *supra*, note 2; G. H. R. Parkinson, ed., *Georg Lukács: The Man, His Work and His Ideas* (New York: Random House, 1970); David Kettler, *Marxismus und Kultur, Mannheim und Lukács in den ungarischen Revolutionen 1918/19* (Neuwied and Berlin: Luchterhand, 1967); Victor Zitta, *Georg Lukács' Marxism: Alienation, Dialectics, Revolution* (The Hague: M. Nijhoff, 1964) and the literature cited there, pp. 1–5.

41. See "Vorwort," pp. 18–29 (xvi–xxvii), especially p. 25 (xxiii): "The proletariat as identical subject-object of the real history of mankind is thus not a materialistic concretization, able to overcome idealistic speculations, but rather a super-Hegelian construction which in its bold transcendence of reality tries to surpass the master himself." Other aspects of the study criticized by Lukács are the excessive stress on dialectical "totality" as compared with economic factors and industrial production, the tendency to transform alienation into an eternal "condition humaine," and the cursory dismissal of the mirror theory of knowledge.

42. As John Strachey paraphrases Myrdal's argument: When a class of citizens, a region or a country "has fallen markedly behind, a complex of interacting factors tends to push it still farther back and to widen the gap between it and the successful classes, regions or countries. Then only the most vigorous and sustained intervention, designed to overrule and reverse the natural 'laws' of the market, can effect an improvement in the lot of the disfavoured." *The End of Empire* (New York: Praeger, 1964), p. 11. See also Gunnar Myrdal, *An International Economy* (New York: Harper, 1956); idem, *Economic Theory and Under-Developed Regions* (London: Duckworth, 1957); idem, *Rich Lands and Poor* (New York: Harper, 1957).

9. Reason and Emancipation

1. Aside from Habermas, the "Frankfurt School" is identified primarily with the work of Theodor W. Adorno, Max Horkheimer, and Herbert Marcuse. See, e.g., Albrecht Wellmer, *Critical Theory of Society*, trans. John Cumming (New York: Herder and Herder, 1971); Trent Schroyer, *The Critique of Domination* (New York: George Braziller, 1973); and Martin Jay, *The Dialectical Imagination: A History of the Frankfurt School and of the Institute of Social Research, 1923–1950* (Boston: Little, Brown, 1973).

2. Jürgen Habermas, *Theorie und Praxis: Sozialphilosophische Studien* (Neuwied and Berlin: Luchterhand, 1963; 2nd ed., 1967), p. 257; trans. John Viertel under the title *Theory and Practice* (Boston: Beacon Press, 1973), p. 282.

3. The main spokesmen of this critical version are Karl R. Popper and Hans Albert. See Theodor W. Adorno et al., *Der Positivismusstreit in der deutschen Soziologie* (Neuwied and Berlin: Luchterhand, 1969); also Hans Albert, *Traktat über kritische Vernunft* (Tübingen: J. C. B. Mohr, 1968). Even Guttorm Flöistad's otherwise perceptive review is not entirely devoid of positivist overtones, at least to the extent that different noetic competences are treated as interacting "substructures," conceivably amenable to systems analysis; see "Social Concepts of Action: Notes on Habermas's Proposal for a Social Theory of Knowledge," *Inquiry*, 13 (1970), 175–198.

4. *Strukturwandel der Öffentlichkeit, Untersuchungen zu einer Kategorie der bürgerlichen Gesellschaft* (Neuwied and Berlin: Luchterhand, 1962).

5. See *Theorie und Praxis*, esp. pp. 231–257 ("Dogmatismus, Vernunft und Entscheidung"); *Theory and Practice*, pp. 253–282; also my review in *Archiv für Rechts—und Sozialphilosophie*, 54 (1968), 435–445.

6. As he added: "Today when efforts are afoot to reconstruct the communicative patterns of indigenous (quasi-natural) interactions after the

model of technically progressive systems of instrumental behavior, we have every reason to keep the two elements strictly apart. . . . The *liberation from hunger and toil* does not necessarily coincide with the *liberation from domination and oppression*, for there is no automatic developmental connection between labor and interaction." See "Arbeit und Interaktion: Bemerkungen zu Hegel's Jenenser 'Philosophie des Geistes' " (1967), in *Technik und Wissenschaft als "Ideologie"* (Frankfurt–Main: Suhrkamp, 1968), p. 46; for an English version see *Theory and Practice*, p. 169.

7. "Zur Logik der Sozialwissenschaften," *Philosophische Rundschau*, Beiheft 5 (Tübingen: J. C. B. Mohr, 1967), esp. ch. 3, pp. 95 ff.

8. "Erkenntnis und Interesse," in *Technik und Wissenschaft als "Ideologie,"* pp. 146–168; for an English version see *Knowledge and Human Interests*, trans. Jeremy J. Shapiro (Boston: Beacon Press, 1971), pp. 301–317. For an elaboration of the different types of inquiry and their underlying interests see Trent Schroyer, "Toward a Critical Theory for Advanced Industrial Society," in Hans Peter Dreitzel, ed., *Recent Sociology No. 2* (New York: Macmillan, 1970), pp. 210–234, esp. pp. 220–228; also his "The Tradition of Critical Theory," *Critical Anthropology*, 1 (1970), 23–43, esp. pp. 36–39, and "Marx and Habermas," *Continuum*, 8 (1970), 52–64. Compare also Kurt Jürgen Huch, "Interest in Emancipation," ibid., pp. 27–39; and Gerard Radnitzky, *Contemporary Schools of Metascience*, 2nd ed. (Göteborg: Akademiförlaget, 1970).

9. Habermas, *Erkenntnis und Interesse* (Frankfurt–Main: Suhrkamp, 1968), esp. pp. 166, 171–173, 176, 195, 221–222.

10. Ibid., pp. 242–243, 244, 256, 260–262, 266, 279–280, 286, 312, 328, 331, 336, 341, 349–351. More recently Habermas has developed a linguistic framework for the semantic analysis of distorted communication, postulating for this purpose the notion of a "communicative competence" (in place of Chomsky's "linguistic competence"); see "Toward a Theory of Communicative Competence," in Dreitzel, pp. 115–148, also reprinted in two parts in *Inquiry*, 13 (1970), 205–218, 360–375.

11. See, e.g., *Die Linke antwortet Jürgen Habermas* (Frankfurt–Main: Europäische Verlagsanstalt, 1968).

12. For a typical statement reflecting this belief see, e.g., Bertrand Russell's comments on Hegel: "It follows from his metaphysic that true liberty consists in obedience to an arbitrary authority, that free speech is an evil, that absolute monarchy is good, that the Prussian state was the best existing at the time when he wrote, that war is good, and that an international organization for the peaceful settlement of disputes would be a misfortune. . . . It is obvious that an autocratic system, such as that advocated by Hegel or by Marx's present-day disciples, is only theoretically justifiable on a basis of unquestioned dogma." "Philosophy and Politics" (1947), in Robert E. Egner and Lester E. Dennon, eds., *The Basic Writings of Bertrand Russell* (New York: Simon & Schuster, 1961), pp. 461–462.

13. Karl-Otto Apel, "Die Entfaltung der 'sprachanalytischen' Philosophie und das Problem der 'Geisteswissenschaften,' " *Philosophisches Jahrbuch der Görresgesellschaft*, 72 (1965), 239–289; translated under the title "Analytic Philosophy of Language and the 'Geisteswissenschaften,' " in *Foundations of Language*, Suppl. Series, vol. 5 (Dordrecht: Reidel, 1967). His concern with linguistic analysis and, more broadly, with the philosophy of language is re-

flected, e.g., in his essays "Wittgenstein und das Problem des hermeneuti-
schen Verstehens," *Zeitschrift für Theologie und Kirche*, 63 (1966), 49–87;
"Sprache und Wahrheit in der gegenwärtigen Situation der Philosophie,"
Philosophische Rundschau, 7 (1959), 161–184; and in his monograph "Die
Idee der Sprache in der Tradition des Humanismus von Dante bis Vico,"
Archiv für Begriffsgeschichte, vol. 8 (Bonn: Bouvier, 1963).

14. "Szientifik, Hermeneutik, Ideologie-Kritik: Entwurf einer Wissenschaftslehre in erkenntnisanthropologischer Sicht," *Man and World*, 1 (1968),
37–63. Apel's close familiarity with Peirce is evident from his edition of the
latter's works; see *Charles S. Peirce, Schriften*, 2 vols. (Frankfurt–Main:
Suhrkamp, 1967 and 1970).

15. "On the whole," the essay stated, "the bodily apriori of cognition
stands in a complementary relationship to the apriori of consciousness; that
means, both conditions of possible knowledge necessarily supplement each
other in the formation of knowledge. In the actual process of cognition, however, either the bodily or the reflective apriori takes precedence: 'knowledge
through reflection' and 'knowledge through engagement' separate into polar
opposites." See "Szientifik, Hermeneutik, Ideologie-Kritik," p. 40.

16. "Wissenschaft als Emanzipation? Eine Auseinandersetzung mit der
Wissenschaftskonzeption der 'Kritischen Theorie,'" *Zeitschrift für allgemeine
Wissenschaftstheorie* (Journal for General Philosophy of Science), 1 (1970),
191.

17. Ibid., pp. 193–195. Compare in this context his essay "Reflexion und
materielle Praxis: Zur erkenntnisanthropologischen Begründung der Dialektik zwischen Hegel und Marx," *Hegelstudien*, Beiheft 1 (1969), pp. 151–
166; also Richard McKeon, "Mankind: The Relation of Reason to Action,"
Ethics, 74 (1964), 174–185.

18. Dietrich Böhler, "'Kritische Theorie'—Kritisch reflektiert," *Archiv für
Rechts- und Sozialphilosophie*, 56 (1970), 511–525, esp. pp. 513–514, 522.
The essay relied chiefly on Max Horkheimer's *Eclipse of Reason* (New York:
Oxford University Press, 1947), recently translated by Alfred Schmidt and
incorporated in Horkheimer, *Zur Kritik der instrumentellen Vernunft* (Frank-
furt: Fischer Verlag, 1967); also on a series of essays (published between
1932 and 1941) assembled in the collection *Kritische Theorie*, 2 vols.
(Frankfurt–Main: Suhrkamp, 1968).

19. Böhler, "Zum Problem des 'emanzipatorischen Interesses' und seiner
gesellschaftlichen Wahrnehmung," *Man and World*, 3 (1970), 26–53, esp.
pp. 27–38. Regarding a minimal ethics among scientists see also Robert K.
Merton, "Science and Democratic Social Structure," in *Social Theory and
Social Structure*, rev. and enlarged ed. (Glencoe, Ill.: Free Press, 1957), pp.
550–561.

20. Flöistad, pp. 183–184. As he added (p. 183), Habermas' liberalism
was attested by his independent treatment of the Marxian superstructure:
"To regard the practical-interest level as a level *sui generis*, as do Habermas
and Kapp, places these writers clearly in a liberalist tradition. Now this tradition has undergone a remarkable development. From being in the main a
source of substantial, normative theory, stating and recommending specific
values (e.g., Hobbes's theory of natural rights and religious values), it has, to
a large extent, been turned into a critical methodology (e.g., Popper's social
theory). Habermas (despite his alleged 'origin' in Marxism) and Kapp both

fit well into this development." Flöistad's reference is to K. William Kapp, *Toward a Science of Man in Society* (The Hague: Martinus Nijhoff, 1961).

21. Apel, "Wissenschaft als Emanzipation?" p. 178; Böhler, "Zum Problem . . .," p. 38.

22. Habermas, "Erkenntnis und Interesse," pp. 166–167.

23. *Erkenntnis und Interesse*, pp. 258–259.

24. Michael Oakeshott, "On Being Conservative," in *Rationalism and Politics, and Other Essays* (New York: Basic Books, 1962), p. 194.

25. Albert Camus, *The Rebel* (New York: Vintage Books, 1956), p. 16.

26. See, e.g., *Erkenntnis und Interesse*, p. 350.

27. Oakeshott, pp. 168–177. See Böhler's statement that "conservatives would be wrong from the start, since they act and think politically in contravention of the supreme emancipatory interest whose cognitive sanction they require for their arguments." "Zum Problem . . .," p. 28.

28. If, following Kant, rationality is allocated both to reflection and practice, the dilemma of the relationship between the two components arises—a dilemma which Fichte recognized when he wrote: "This question Kant forgot to ask himself; for, nowhere did he deal with the basis of *all* philosophy. Rather, in the *Critique of Pure Reason* he was only concerned with theoretical philosophy in which the categorical imperative has no place, while the *Critique of Practical Reason* concentrated on practical thought, a domain solely preoccupied with substantive content and leaving no room for the investigation of the type of the underlying consciousness." J. G. Fichte, "Zweite Einleitung in die Wissenschaftslehre," in Fritz Medicus, ed., *Ausgewählte Werke* (Hamburg: Felix Meiner, 1962), 3: 56; see also Habermas, *Erkenntnis und Interesse*, p. 256.

29. The notion of man's "excentric position" in the universe derives from Helmuth Plessner. Cf. Apel, "Wissenschaft als Emanzipation?" p. 193; Böhler, "Zum Problem . . .," p. 35.

30. Apel, "Wissenschaft als Emanzipation?" pp. 188–195.

31. Böhler, "Zum Problem . . .," pp. 33–34, also p. 52, n. 24.

32. Some of these essays are collected in *Toward a Rational Society: Student Protest, Science, and Politics* (Boston: Beacon Press, 1970). See also his *Protestbewegung und Hochschulreform* (Frankfurt–Main: Suhrkamp, 1969). For the comments on the Freudian model see *Erkenntnis und Interesse*, pp. 282, 302, 344–345.

33. Flöistad probably overstates the case when he complains about Habermas' "total neglect of theory-application," claiming that "one cannot even find an instance of the kind of detailed criticism of social institutions, etc., for which the theory is supposed to be a comprehensive methodological framework." "Social Concepts of Action," p. 196. To a considerable extent, Apel's critique also seems to derive from concern with questions of concrete application and implementation; "Wissenschaft als Emanzipation?" pp. 186, 192.

34. David Kettler, "The Vocation of Radical Intellectuals," *Politics and Society*, 1 (1970), 23–49, esp. 44–48. As he notes (p. 46), "adequate radical theory must be able to comprehend complexities, ambiguities, a multilayered reality. The contrary view derives from a failure to distinguish between the categorical judgments embodied in action, and the critical assessment which reviews, interprets, and evaluates such judgments on the basis of as adequate a theory as may be available at any time." See also his "Polit-

ical Science and Political Rationality," in David Spitz, ed., *Political Theory and Social Change* (New York: Atherton Press, 1967), pp. 59–89; and Brian Fay, *Social Theory and Political Practice* (London: Allen & Unwin, 1975).

10. Critical Epistemology Criticized

1. Jürgen Habermas, *Erkenntnis und Interesse* (Frankfurt–Main: Suhrkamp, 1968); *Knowledge and Human Interests*, trans. Jeremy J. Shapiro (Boston: Beacon Press, 1971).

2. For condensed presentations of the main arguments in *Knowledge and Human Interests* see Trent Schroyer, "Toward a Critical Theory for an Advanced Industrial Society," in Hans Peter Dreitzel, ed., *Recent Sociology No. 2* (New York: Macmillan, 1970), pp. 210–234; Kurt Jürgen Huch, "Interesse an Emanzipation," *Neue Rundschau*, 80 (1969), 534–548; also my "Reason and Emancipation: Notes on Habermas," *Man and World*, 5 (1972), 79–109 (chapter 9 above).

3. "Einleitung zur Neuausgabe: Einige Schwierigkeiten beim Versuch, Theorie und Praxis zu vermitteln," newly revised and expanded edition of *Theorie und Praxis* (Frankfurt–Main: Suhrkamp, 1971); for an English version see *Theory and Practice*, trans. John Viertel (Boston: Beacon Press, 1973), pp. 1–40. Habermas' afterthoughts are further detailed in his "Nachwort (1973)" to *Erkenntnis und Interesse* (Frankfurt–Main: Suhrkamp, 1973), pp. 367–417; for an English version see "A Postscript to *Knowledge and Human Interests*," *Philosophy of the Social Sciences*, 3 (1975), 157–189.

4. "Einleitung zur Neuausgabe," p. 25.

5. As Habermas adds, the "interests" underlying cognition are "basic orientations which are rooted in certain fundamental conditions of the possible reproduction and self-constitution of mankind." See *Erkenntnis und Interesse*, pp. 241–243; *Knowledge and Human Interests*, pp. 196–197. The study differentiates three main types of interests: a "technical" interest founded on labor; a "practical" interest linked with communicative interaction; and an "emancipatory" interest anchored in self-reflection.

6. The term "anthropology of knowledge" is employed by Karl-Otto Apel in "Szientifik, Hermeneutik, Ideologie-Kritik: Entwurf einer Wissenschaftslehre in erkenntnisanthropologischer Sicht," *Man and World*, 1 (1968), 37–63; an expanded version appears in Apel et al., *Hermeneutik und Ideologiekritik* (Frankfurt–Main: Suhrkamp, 1971), pp. 7–44.

7. Hans Albert, *Plädoyer für kritischen Rationalismus* (Munich: Piper, 1971), pp. 54–55.

8. Günter Rohrmoser, *Das Elend der kritischen Theorie*, 2nd ed. (Freiburg: Rombach, 1970), p. 89.

9. Ibid., pp. 90, 92. The same aspect is explored in greater detail by Harald Pilot, "Jürgen Habermas' empirisch falsifizierbare Geschichtsphilosophie," in Theodor W. Adorno et al., *Der Positivismusstreit in der deutschen Soziologie*, 3rd ed. (Neuwied and Berlin: Luchterhand, 1971), pp. 307–334.

10. Rohrmoser, pp. 96–97, 99, 101–104.

11. Max Horkheimer, "Traditionelle und kritische Theorie," *Zeitschrift*

für Sozialforschung, 6 (1937), 245–292; reprinted in Horkheimer, *Kritische Theorie*, ed. by Alfred Schmidt, vol. 2 (Frankfurt–Main: S. Fischer, 1968), pp. 137–191, trans. Matthew J. O'Connell et al. as *Critical Theory: Selected Essays* (New York: Herder and Herder, 1972), pp. 188–243.

12. Michael Teunissen, *Gesellschaft und Geschichte* (Berlin: Walter de Gruyter, 1969), pp. 8–11, 14, 17, 20–26, 28–30, 32, 39–40; see also his *Hegel's Philosophie des absoluten Geistes als theologisch-politischer Traktat* (Berlin: Walter de Gruyter, 1971).

13. The reference is to "Erkenntnis und Interesse," in Habermas, *Technik und Wissenschaft als "Ideologie"* (Frankfurt–Main: Suhrkamp, 1968), pp. 146–168; a translation of the essay appears as an appendix in *Knowledge and Human Interests*, pp. 301–317.

14. Rüdiger Bubner, "Was ist kritische Theorie?" in *Philosophische Rundschau*, 16 (1969), 213–249, esp. pp. 216–219, 225–227, 232–233, 239–241; also reprinted in Apel, *Hermeneutik und Ideologiekritik*, pp. 160–209. See also his "Problemgeschichte und systematischer Sinn einer Phänomenologie," *Hegelstudien*, 5 (1969).

15. The linkage between Habermas' epistemological perspective and practical philosophy is noted by Guttorm Flöistadt, "Social Concepts of Action: Notes on Habermas' Proposal for a Social Theory of Action," *Inquiry*, 13 (1970), 175–198.

16. For Habermas' comments see "Einleitung zur Neuausgabe," pp. 15–16, 26–28; also p. 46, n. 31.

17. See, e.g., Helmuth Plessner, *Philosophische Anthropologie* (Frankfurt–Main: Fischer, 1970), esp. pp. 253–316 (epilogue by Günter Dux); also M. Merleau-Ponty, *Phenomenology of Perception*, trans. Colin Smith (London: Routledge & Kegan Paul, 1962); Robert R. Blake and Glenn V. Ramsey, eds., *Perception, An Approach to Personality* (New York: Ronald, 1951); George Klein, *Perception, Motives, and Personality* (New York: Knopf, 1970).

18. See "Reason and Emancipation" (*supra*, n. 2).

19. Karl-Otto Apel, "Wissenschaft als Emanzipation? Eine Auseinandersetzung mit der Wissenschaftskonzeption der 'kritischen Theorie,'" *Zeitschrift für allgemeine Wissenschaftstheorie* (Journal for General Philosophy of Science), 1 (1970), 173–195.

20. Dietrich Böhler, "Zum Problem des 'emanzipatorischen Interesses' und seiner gesellschaftlichen Wahrnehmung," *Man and World*, 3 (1970), 26–53. See also his *Metakritik der Marxschen Ideologiekritik* (Frankfurt–Main: Suhrkamp, 1971).

21. While from the vantage point I adopted in "Reason and Emancipation" the reformulation has more the character of an elaboration, others may tend to view it as a change of "paradigm."

22. Habermas, "Einleitung zur Neuausgabe," pp. 28–31. Responding to Apel's comments, Habermas concedes that "theoretical reflection," rephrased as rational reconstruction, is only indirectly linked with "emancipatory interest." On the other hand, self-reflection in his view is grounded not only in a particular situational commitment, but rather in a general motivation deriving from the "institutionalization of power" or social control; ibid., p. 47, n. 35.

23. Sigmund Freud, *Civilization and Its Discontents*, trans. and ed. James Strachey (New York: Norton, 1962), p. 91.

24. In somewhat harsh terms, Flöistadt complains about Habermas' "total neglect of theory-application," charging that "one cannot even find an instance of the kind of detailed criticism of social institutions, etc., for which the theory is supposed to be a comprehensive methodological framework." "Social Concepts of Action," p. 196.

25. Oskar Negt, "Revolution und Geschichte: Eine Kontroverse mit Jürgen Habermas," in *Politik als Protest* (Frankfurt–Main: Agit-buch-vertrieb, 1971), pp. 87–101, esp. pp. 96, 100.

26. Hans-Georg Gadamer, "Replik," in Apel et al., *Hermeneutik und Ideologiekritik*, pp. 283–317, esp. pp. 305–308; see also his "Rhetorik, Hermeneutik und Ideologiekritik," ibid., pp. 57–82.

27. Hans Joachim Giegel, "Reflexion und Emanzipation," ibid., pp. 244–282, esp. pp. 274–280. For a more subdued critique of the assumed relationship between psychoanalysis and practical emancipation see Bernhard Badura, "Ein neuer Primat der Interpretation? Zum Problem der Emanzipation bei Jürgen Habermas," *Soziale Welt*, 21 (1970–71), 321–329.

28. As Habermas suggests, broad therapeutic endeavors may be a more promising avenue of change in post-industrial societies than narrow partisanship. "These are empirical questions which cannot be prejudged," he adds. "Sensibly speaking, there cannot be a theory which enjoins militancy irrespective of circumstances. At best, we can discriminate between theories on the basis of whether or not, in their structure, they are conducive to possible emancipation." See "Einleitung zur Neuausgabe," p. 37.

29. Ibid., pp. 31–45, esp. 37–39.

30. One of the School's chief publications is Theodor W. Adorno's *Negative Dialektik* (Frankfurt–Main: Suhrkamp, 1966).

31. Nikolaus Lobkowicz, "Interesse und Objektivität," *Philosophische Rundschau*, 16 (1969), 249–273, esp. 252, 252, 256–258, 266, 269, 272.

32. Erich Hahn, "Die theoretischen Grundlagen der Soziologie von Jürgen Habermas," in Johannes H. von Heiseler et al., *Die "Frankfurter Schule" im Lichte des Marxismus* (Frankfurt–Main: Verlag Marxistische Blätter, 1970), pp. 70–89, esp. pp. 73, 76, 81–82. Hahn does not seem to notice that, in stressing the "materialistic-monistic" conception of the forces and relations of production as parts of "one and the same process of material activity," he lends support to Habermas' thesis regarding the Marxist tendency to reduce social interaction to instrumental control (amenable to scientific explanation). At another point Hahn expresses himself more cautiously, but also more ambiguously (p. 76): "Historical materialism does not view history as a mere 'extension' of man's natural genesis, but on the basis of this genesis seeks to grasp it in its own peculiar quality, from the perspective of its own motivating forces and unique laws which unfold in the transition to the stage of social production."

33. Ibid., pp. 83–84, 89.

34. Jürgen Ritsert and Claus Rolshausen, *Der Konservativismus der kritischen Theorie* (Frankfurt–Main: Europäische Verlagsanstalt, 1971), pp. 9–10, 20–21, 24–26, 39, 52–57, 88–89, 94.

35. See, e.g., Wilhelm Raymund Beyer, *Die Sünden der Frankfurter Schule; Ein Beitrag zur Kritik der "Kritischen Theorie"* (Frankfurt–Main: Verlag Marxistische Blätter, 1971); also Göran Therborn, "The Frankfurt School," *New Left Review*, No. 63 (1970), pp. 65–96.

36. Maurice Merleau-Ponty, "Hegel's Existentialism," in *Sense and Non-Sense*, trans. Hubert L. and Patricia A. Dreyfus (Evanston, Ill.: Northwestern University Press, 1964), p. 65; Hanns Sachs, *Freud* (New York: Imago, 1945), p. 145.

11. Toward a Critical Reconstruction of Ethics and Politics

1. As J. Robert Oppenheimer observed at one point: "What are we to think of such a civilization, which has not been able to talk about the prospect of killing almost everybody, except in prudential and game-theoretic terms?" Quoted by John W. Chapman, "The Moral Foundations of Political Obligation," in *Political and Legal Obligation*, ed. J. Roland Pennock and Chapman (New York: Atherton Press, 1970), p. 142.

2. Richard B. Brandt, *Value and Obligation: Systematic Readings in Ethics* (New York: Harcourt, Brace and World, 1961), p. 7. For a discussion of "interest-group" liberalism compare Theodore J. Lowi, *The End of Liberalism* (New York: W. W. Norton, 1969).

3. For a general introduction to the school and its major representatives see Martin Jay, *The Dialectical Imagination: An Intellectual History of the Frankfurt School and the Institute of Social Research* (Boston: Little, Brown & Co., 1973), and his "The Frankfurt School and the Genesis of Critical Theory," in *The Unknown Dimension: European Marxism since Lenin*, ed. Dick Howard and Karl E. Klare (New York: Basic Books, 1972), pp. 225–248; also Frankfurt Institute for Social Research, *Aspects of Sociology* (Boston: Beacon Press, 1972).

4. See Felix E. Oppenheim, *Moral Principles in Political Philosophy* (New York: Random House, 1968), esp. pp. 20–52. Brandt distinguishes mainly between "naturalism," "supernaturalism" (divine commandments), "nonnaturalism" (intuitionism), and "noncognitivism"; *Value and Obligation*, pp. 252–254. Apart from segregating cognitivism from noncognitivism, Paul W. Taylor differentiates within the cognitivist camp between "nonnaturalism" or "objectivism" (intuitionism) and "naturalism," subdividing the latter category into "subjectivist" and "instrumentalist" orientations; see *The Moral Judgment: Readings in Contemporary Meta-Ethics* (Englewood Cliffs, N.J.: Prentice-Hall, 1963), pp. 116–118.

5. The distinction between theoretical, practical, and technical reasoning dates back to Aristotle. For representative contemporary studies cf., for example, Alan R. White, ed., *The Philosophy of Action* (London: Oxford University Press, 1968); Richard J. Bernstein, *Praxis and Action: Contemporary Philosophies of Human Activity* (Philadelphia: University of Pennsylvania Press, 1971); Robert Binkley et al., eds., *Agent, Action, and Reason* (Toronto: University of Toronto Press, 1971); William D. Hudson, ed., *New Studies in Practical Philosophy* (New York: Macmillan, 1972); Manfred Riedel, ed., *Rehabilitierung der praktischen Philosophie*, 2 vols. (Freiburg: Rombach Verlag, 1972–73).

6. Ludwig Wittgenstein, *Tractatus Logico-Philosophicus* (Frankfurt–Main: Suhrkamp, 1969), p. 112 (No. 6.42). In a letter of 1919 Wittgenstein commented on the book as follows: ". . . the book's point is a moral one. I once meant to include in the preface a sentence . . .indicating that the book con-

sists of two parts: the one presented here and another comprising all those things which I have not written down. And it is this second part which counts. For, in my book ethics is delimited as it were from the inside; and I am convinced that, strictly speaking, it can only be delimited in this manner. In short: I believe that what many today gab about, I have pinpointed in my study by remaining silent." Wittgenstein, *Briefe an Ludwig von Ficker,* ed. Georg H. von Wright and Walter Methlagl (Salzburg: Otto Müller Verlag, 1969), p. 35.

7. An almost purely emotive theory was presented by Alfred J. Ayer in his *Language, Truth and Logic* (New York: Dover Publications, 1936); an imperative doctrine, but with emotive ingredients and a subtle distinction between noncognitive and cognitive-factual functions of moral statements, was articulated by Charles L. Stevenson in *Ethics and Language* (New Haven, Conn.: Yale University Press, 1944). For versions of cognitive naturalism, especially the "subjectivist" variety, cf. Ralph B. Perry, *General Theory of Value* (New York: Longmans, Green & Co., 1926) and Edward A. Westermarck, *Ethical Relativity* (New York: Humanities Press, 1932).

8. *Philosophical Investigations* (Oxford: Basil Blackwell, 1953), p. 242. Cf. also Hanna F. Pitkin, *Wittgenstein and Justice* (Berkeley: University of California Press, 1972).

9. See Stephen E. Toulmin, *An Examination of the Place of Reason in Ethics* (Cambridge, England: At the University Press, 1950), pp. 9–64, 150, 153, 193; Kurt Baier, *The Moral Point of View, A Rational Basis of Ethics* (Ithaca, N.Y.: Cornell University Press, 1958), pp. 5–46, 309. For similar studies of the time, cf. Paul Edwards, *The Logic of Moral Discourse* (Glencoe, Ill.: Free Press, 1955); Bernard Mayo, *Ethics and the Moral Life* (London: Macmillan, 1958); and Brand Blanchard, *Reason and Goodness* (New York: Macmillan, 1961). In several articles, Kai Nielsen has tried to defend the chiefly descriptive and nonnormative character of Toulmin's inquiry (although acknowledging the need of a prior "commitment" to moral reasoning); for example, "Good Reasons in Ethics: An Examination of the Toulmin-Hare Controversy," *Theoria,* 24 (pt. I, 1958), 9–28. On the other hand, Baier in recent years has sharpened his arguments in favor of a prescriptive position; for example, "Obligation: Political and Moral," in *Political and Legal Obligation,* ed. Pennock and Chapman, pp. 116–141.

10. As Chapman comments: "It now seems safe to say, safer than it would have been a decade ago, that linguistic empiricism casts real doubt on the postulates of logical positivism. For what began with Wittgenstein as a critique of metaphysical thinking has turned into a phenomenology of moral experience, into a new metaethic. Moral psychology, the very conception of which defies positivist distinctions, has reappeared as linguistic analysis." In Pennock and Chapman, eds., p. 162.

11. See Searle, *Speech Acts: An Essay in the Philosophy of Language* (Cambridge, England: At the University Press, 1969), pp. 175–198; Winch, *Moral Integrity* (London: Oxford University Press, 1968) and his "Nature and Convention," *Proceedings of the Aristotelian Society,* 60 (1959–1960), 220–255; Warnock, *Contemporary Moral Philosophy* (London: Macmillan, 1967), p. 66; Beardsmore, *Moral Reasoning* (New York: Schocken Books, Inc., 1969). For a critical review of descriptivist arguments, including the issue of the linkage of needs and moral beliefs, see William D. Hudson,

Modern Moral Philosophy (Garden City, N.Y.: Doubleday, Anchor Books, 1970), pp. 249–329.

12. See MacIntyre, *A Short History of Ethics* (New York: Macmillan, 1966), p. 268; Gellner, *Words and Things: A Critical Account of Linguistic Philosophy and a Study in Ideology* (London: Gollancz, 1959). For a sociopolitical critique, cf. also Rollo Handy, "Doubts About Ordinary Language in Ethics," *Inquiry*, 3 (Winter 1960), 270–277.

13. See *Freedom and Reason* (Oxford: Oxford University Press, 1963), pp. 4–5, and *The Language of Morals* (Oxford, England: At the Clarendon Press, 1952). For a general review, cf. Hudson, *Modern Moral Philosophy*, pp. 155–248.

14. Popper, *The Logic of Scientific Discovery* (London: Hutchinson, 1959), pp. 34–39; Albert, *Trakat über kritische Vernunft* (Tübingen: Mohr, 1969), pp. 73–79; and his "Ethik und Metaethik," in *Werturteilsstreit,* ed. Albert and Ernst Topitsch (Darmstadt: Wissenschaftliche Buchgesellschaft, 1971), pp. 472–516. Another defender of the same approach proposes the term "meta-metaethics" to designate the level on which the plurality of metaethical theories is discussed; see Hans Lenk, "Kann die sprachanalytische Moralphilosophie neutral sein?" ibid., 533–552. For a critique of metaethical neutrality cf. also Alan Gewirth, "Metaethics and Normative Ethics," *Mind,* 69 (April 1960), 187–205, and William T. Blackstone, "Are Metaethical Theories Normatively Neutral?" *Australasian Journal of Philosophy,* 39 (May 1961), 65–74.

15. Commenting on the dispute between empiricists and prescriptive rationalists, Lorenzen notes: "As the title of my lectures is: 'Normative Logic and Ethics,' you will guess that I shall argue for the rationalist side. But you may be assured that this style of 'arguing' will not consist in 'deducing.' To argue in the way I propose, we shall have to look first for a common basis from which we can agree to begin. As such a basis I propose the use of elementary sentences." *Normative Logic and Ethics* (Mannheim: Bibliographisches Institut, 1969), p. 13.

16. As he notes: "It is usual to contrast the mere subjectivity of opinion with the 'objectivity' of truth, but, as we have seen in all our investigations into theoretical philosophy, the truth of sentences always has to be a human accomplishment—an achievement of persons." Ibid., pp. 82.

17. Ibid., pp. 83–85, 87–89. Concerning genetic reconstruction and its relationship with hermeneutics, he comments (pp. 88–89): "This movement should not be a circle, but—as in the case of the famous 'hermeneutic circle', too— should be a spiral. As no other term seems to be at hand I would like to call this spiral movement for constructing normatively genetic accounts the 'dialectical' spiral." Cf. also Lorenzen's "Szientismus versus Dialektik," in *Hermeneutik und Dialektik,* ed Rüdiger Bubner et al. (Tübingen: Mohr, 1970), 1: 57–72. The implications of his approach have recently been further explored in Oswald Schwemmer, *Philosophie der Praxis* (Frankfurt–Main: Suhrkamp, 1971).

18. In Oppenheim's words: "Proponents of natural law often do not seem to realize that they have espoused the metaethical theory of cognitivism and hence, do not see the necessity of even raising this question, let alone of answering it." *Moral Principles,* p. 50. Removed from critical scrutiny philosophy tends to become an idiosyncratic pastime and ethics an esoteric pur-

suit—a result deplored by Baier in these terms: "An esoteric code, a set of precepts known only to the initiated and perhaps jealously concealed from outsiders, can at best be a religion, not a morality. . . . 'Esoteric morality' is a contradiction in terms." *Moral Point of View*, p. 196.

19. Despite his interpretive talent, Leo Strauss sometimes encouraged such an outlook—an aspect acknowledged even by some sympathetic readers. Thus, commenting on one of Strauss's studies, Gerhart Niemeyer observes that "the book does not convey a full philosophical understanding of what Machiavelli has done. Rather, Strauss from the very first substitutes moral judgment for philosophical analysis." See "Humanism, Positivism, Immorality," *The Political Science Reviewer*, 1 (Fall 1971), 293. A religious version of natural law is defended, for example, by Emil Brunner in *Justice and the Social Order*, trans. Mary Hottinger (New York: Harper & Brothers, 1945).

20. For the concern of Catholic natural-law theorists with empirical science see, for example, Johannes Messner, *Social Ethics: Natural Law in the Western World*, rev. ed. (St. Louis: B. Herder Book Co., 1965) and Theodor Steinbüchel, *Die philosophischen Grundlagen der katholischen Sittenlehre*, 4th ed. (Düsseldorf: Patmos Verlag, 1951). For the recovery of the Aristotelian legacy compare especially the pioneering study by Joachim Ritter, "Zur Grundlegung der praktischen Philosophie bei Aristoteles," *Archiv für Rechts- und Sozialphilosophie*, 46 (May 1960), 179–199.

21. In the Anglo-American context, intuitionism is usually linked with the names of Richard Price, Sir W. David Ross, Alfred E. Ewing, George E. Moore, and C. D. Broad. See Brandt, *Value and Obligation*, p. 358; and for a general critique, William D. Hudson, *Ethical Intuitionism* (New York: St. Martin's Press, 1967).

22. See Scheler, *Der Formalismus in der Ethik und die materiale Wertethik* (1916), 4th ed. (Bern: Francke Verlag, 1954); Hartmann, *Ethik* (Berlin & Leipzig: de Gruyter, 1926); and for a critical assessment, Ernst Topitsch, "Kritik der phänomenologischen Wertlehre," in *Werturteilsstreit*, ed. Albert and Topitsch, pp. 16–32. See also Alois Roth, *Edmund Husserls ethische Untersuchungen* (Phaenomenologica 7; The Hague: Martinus Nijhoff, 1960).

23. For the importance of "bracketing" for purposes of intersubjective validation see, for example, Wilhelm E. Mühlmann, " 'Wertfreiheit' and phänomenologische Reduktion im Hinblick auf die Soziologie," in *Werturteilsstreit*, ed. Albert and Topitsch, pp. 189–199. On Heidegger, cf. Reinhart Maurer, "Von Heidegger zur praktischen Philosophie," in *Rehabilitierung*, ed. Riedel, 1: 415–454.

24. For traces of such a position see, for example, Hans-Georg Gadamer, "Hermeneutik als praktische Philosophie," in *Rehabilitierung*, ed. Riedel, 1: 325–344; also Otto Pöggeler, "Die ethisch-politische Dimension der hermeneutischen Philosophie," in *Probleme der Ethik, zur Diskussion gestellt*, ed. Gerd-Günther Grau (Freiburg–Munich: K. Alber, 1972), pp. 45–82. For an attempt to base ethics on the notion of the "life-world," as initiated by Husserl and developed by Alfred Schutz, see Gibson Winter, *Elements for a Social Ethics* (New York: Macmillan, 1966); a broader and philosophically more independent effort to delineate a phenomenological ethics can be found in Paul Ricoeur, *Fallible Man* (Chicago: Henry Regnery, 1965) and *The Symbolism of Evil* (New York: Harper & Row, 1967).

25. See Sartre, *Existentialism and Humanism*, trans. Philip Mairet (Lon-

don: Methuen, 1948). For the relationship between existentialism and ethics see, for example, Frederick A. Olafson, *Principles and Persons, An Ethical Interpretation of Existentialism* (Baltimore: The Johns Hopkins Press, 1967), and Helmut Fahrenbach, *Existenzphilosophie und Ethik* (Frankfurt–Main: Klostermann, 1970); also Joseph J. Kockelmans, *Contemporary European Ethics* (Garden City, N.Y.: Doubleday, Anchor Books, 1972).

26. See Leon D. Trotsky, "Their Morals and Ours" (1938), in *The Basic Writings of Trotsky*, ed. Irving Howe (New York: Random House, 1963), pp. 370–399; also Hans Jörg Sandkühler, "Kant, neukantianischer Sozialismus, Revisionismus," in *Marxismus und Ethik*, ed. Rafael de la Vega and Sandkühler (Frankfurt–Main: Suhrkamp, 1970). For recent developments in Soviet thought see Richard T. de George, *Soviet Ethics and Morality* (Ann Arbor: University of Michigan Press, 1969).

27. See, for example, Leszek Kolakowski, "Ethik ohne Kodex," in his *Traktat über die Sterblichkeit der Vernunft* (Munich: Piper, 1967), pp. 89–122; Gajo Petrović, ed., *Revolutionäre Praxis* (Freiburg: Rombach, 1969); Mihailo Marković, *Dialektik der Praxis* (Frankfurt–Main: Suhrkamp, 1968); Svetozar Stojanović, *Kritik und Zukunft des Sozialismus* (Munich: Hanser Verlag, 1970); Roger Garaudy, *Marxism in the Twentieth Century* (New York: Scribner's, 1970); Leo Kofler, *Perspektiven des revolutionären Humanismus* (Hamburg: Rowohlt, 1968); Robert Havemann, *Dialektik ohne Dogma?* (Hamburg: Rowohlt, 1964). See also Eugene Kamenka, *Marxism and Ethics* (London: Macmillan, 1969), and Karel Kosík et al., *Moral und Gesellschaft* (Frankfurt–Main: Suhrkamp, 1968).

28. See Habermas, *Strukturwandel der Öffentlichkeit* (Berlin: Luchterhand, 1962), esp. paragraph 19; *Theorie und Praxis, Sozialphilosophische Studien* (Neuwied–Berlin: Luchterhand, 1963), esp. pp. 231–257; "Toward a Theory of Communicative Competence" in *Recent Sociology No. 2: Patterns of Communicative Behavior*, ed. Hans P. Dreitzel (New York: Macmillan, 1970), pp. 115–130; "Vorbereitende Bemerkungen zu einer Theorie der kommunikativen Kompetenz" in Habermas and Niklas Luhmann, *Theorie der Gesellschaft oder Sozialtechnologie—Was leistet die Systemforschung?* (Frankfurt–Main: Suhrkamp, 1971), pp. 101–141; *Legitimationsprobleme im Spätkapitalismus* (Frankfurt–Main: Suhrkamp, 1973), esp. pp. 131–196. Cf. also Theodore Kisiel, "Ideology Critique and Phenomenology," *Philosophy Today*, 14 (Fall 1970), 151–160; and Thomas A. McCarthy, "A Theory of Communicative Competence," *Philosophy of the Social Sciences*, 3 (June 1973), 135–156.

29. See Apel, *Charles S. Peirce: Schriften*, 2 vols. (Frankfurt–Main: Suhrkamp, 1967 and 1970). Cf. also his "From Kant to Peirce: The Semiotical Transformation of Transcendental Logic," in *Proceedings of the Third International Kant Congress*, ed. Lewis W. Beck (Dordrecht: Reidel, 1972), pp. 90–104; "Die Kommunikationsgemeinschaft als transzendentale Voraussetzung der Sozialwissenschaften," *Neue Hefte für Philosophie*, Nos. 2–3 (1972), pp. 1–40; "Szientismus oder transzendentale Hermeneutik," in *Hermeneutik und Dialektik*, ed. Rüdiger Bubner et al., 1: 105–144; "Szientifik, Hermeneutik, Ideologiekritik," *Wiener Jahrbuch für Philosophie*, 1 (1968), 15–45; "Wittgenstein und Heidegger," *Philosophisches Jahrbuch*, 75 (March 1967), 56–94; "Die Entfaltung der 'sprachanalytischen' Philosophie und das Problem der 'Geisteswissenschaften'," ibid., 72 (September 1965), 239–289, trans. under the title "Analytic Philosophy of Language and the 'Geisteswis-

senschaften'," *Foundations of Language,* suppl. series 4 (Dordrecht: Reidel, 1967); "Reflexion und materielle Praxis: Zur erkenntnisanthropologischen Begründung der Dialektik zwischen Hegel und Marx," *Hegel-Studien,* suppl. 1 (1962), pp. 151–166.

30. See "Das Apriori der Kommunikationsgemeinschaft und die Grundlagen der Ethik," in Apel, *Transformation der Philosophie,* 2 vols. (Frankfurt–Main: Suhrkamp, 1973), 2: 358–435.

31. Ibid., pp. 385–390. While juxtaposing linguistic and hermeneutical empiricism, Apel sees an advantage in historical understanding over the analysis of language games (ibid., p. 390 n. 41); "The advantage of Heidegger's school of hermeneutics over the perspective of the late Wittgenstein seems to me to reside in the superiority of historical thinking over abstract model-building; the latent affinity between the two schools, however, consists in the circumstance that neither is able to articulate a normative standard and thus a criterion of ethically relevant progress."

32. Ibid., p. 392.

33. Ibid., 399–401. Apel at this point goes somewhat beyond Habermas, by arguing not merely that logical and linguistic faculties need to be supplemented by "communicative competence," but that such competence is a precondition for the understanding and explication of the mentioned faculties. For his comments on Habermas, see esp. p. 402 n. 61.

34. Ibid., pp. 413–415. For the comments on Lorenzen, see pp. 420–422.

35. See, for example, Donald Van De Veer, "Oppenheim's Defense of Noncognitivism," with comments by Oppenheim and rejoinder, *American Political Science Review,* 65 (December 1971), 1,105–1,118. In 1968, Oppenheim observed that, despite continuing controversies, "noncognitivism is the assumption underlying most modern writings dealing with empirical political research. It is also the dominant view among political theorists at the present time." *Moral Principles,* p. 166. Cf., however, Duncan McRae, Jr., "Scientific Communication, Ethical Argument, and Public Policy," *American Political Science Review,* 65 (March 1971), 38–50; also Alan Gewirth, "The Normative Structure of Action," *Review of Metaphysics,* 25 (December 1971), 238–261.

36. See his "Moral Foundations," pp. 165–173. Regarding Rawls, Chapman refers primarily to his "Distributive Justice" in *Philosophy, Politics and Society,* ed. Peter Laslett and W. G. Runciman, 3rd Series (Oxford: Basil Blackwell, 1967), pp. 58–82; see also his *A Theory of Justice* (Cambridge, Mass.: Harvard University Press, 1972), and Michael Lessnoff, "John Rawls' Theory of Justice," *Political Studies,* 19 (March 1971), 63–80.

37. See Rawls, "Legal Obligation and the Duty of Fair Play," in *Law and Philosophy: A Symposium,* ed. Sidney Hook (New York: New York University Press, 1964), p. 15; Baier, "Obligation: Political and Moral," p. 138. For the relationship between ethics and anthropology (and the social sciences) cf., for example, Hudson, *Modern Moral Philosophy,* pp. 320–329; Fahrenbach, "Ein programmatischer Aufriss der Problemlage und systematischen Ansatzmöglichkeiten praktischer Philosophie," in *Rehabilitierung,* ed. Riedel, 1: 15–56.

38. Maurice Merleau-Ponty, *In Praise of Philosophy,* trans. with preface by John Wild and James M. Edie (Evanston, Ill.: Northwestern University Press, 1963), p. 47; *Adventures of the Dialectic,* trans. Joseph Bien (Evanston, Ill.: Northwestern University Press, 1973), pp. 3–6.

Index